Third Edition

A Guide to
the SQL Standard

A user's guide to
the standard relational language SQL

C. J. Date
with
Hugh Darwen

ADDISON-WESLEY PUBLISHING COMPANY

Reading, Massachusetts • Menlo Park, California • New York
Don Mills, Ontario • Wokingham, England • Amsterdam • Bonn
Sydney • Singapore • Tokyo • Madrid • San Juan • Milan • Paris

It is only fitting to dedicate this book to
the many people responsible, directly or indirectly,
for the rise of SQL to its present preeminent position—
the original SQL language designers at IBM,
the implementers of the IBM prototype System R
and the various IBM products derived from that prototype,
and the ISO and ANSI SQL standards committees.
I hope this book does justice to their efforts.

Library of Congress Cataloging-in-Publication Data

Date, C. J.
    A guide to the SQL Standard : a user's guide / by C. J. Date with
Hugh Darwen.—3rd ed.
        p. cm.
    Includes bibliographical references and index.
    ISBN 0-201-55822-X
    1. Data base management.   2. SQL (Computer program language)
I. Darwen, Hugh,   II. Title.
QA76.9.D3D3695 1993
005.75'6—dc20   92-27389
                                                                      CIP

Many of the designations used by manufacturers and sellers to distinguish their products
are claimed as trademarks. Where those designations appear in this book, and Addison-
Wesley was aware of a trademark claim, the designations have been printed in initial caps
or all caps.

The programs and applications presented in this book have been included for their instruc-
tional value. They have been tested with care, but are not guaranteed for any particular
purpose. The publisher does not offer any warranties or representations, nor does it accept
any liabilities with respect to the programs or applications.

1 2 3 4 5 6 7 8 9 10-HA-95949392

Preface to the Third Edition

The purpose of this book is to describe the relational database language SQL—or, more precisely, to describe the official standard version of that language. SQL has been adopted as an international standard by the International Organization for Standardization (ISO); it has also been adopted as a national standard in many countries, including in particular the United States, where it is both an American National Standards Institute (ANSI) standard and a Federal Information Processing Standard (FIPS) as well. Furthermore, of course, numerous SQL-based products—well over 100 of them at the last count—have been available in the marketplace for several years. There can thus be absolutely no doubt that, from a commercial point of view at least, SQL represents an extremely important feature of the database world—which is of course the principal justification for this book.

Now, it is customary when producing a new edition of a book to reprint the prefaces from earlier editions. In the case of the present book, however, this new edition is to all intents and purposes a totally new book, because it deals with a totally new version of SQL—namely, the version that until now has been referred to, informally, as *SQL2*, but henceforth will probably be referred to, still informally, as "SQL/92" (and we will use this latter name). SQL/92, which ISO, ANSI, and other standards bodies have been working on for several years, represents a *major* set of extensions to the earlier SQL standard. (Just how major they are can be gauged from the fact that the official standard document has grown more than sixfold—from roughly 100 pages to well over 600—to incorporate them.) As a result, the third edition of this book is, as already indicated, quite different from the previous two; it is certainly (and regrettably) much longer than it used to be, and its structure has changed considerably. One consequence of these changes is that the previous prefaces are no longer very relevant, and I have therefore decided to drop them. (Another is that there are in fact so many differences between this edition and the previous two that it is frankly not worth even trying to summarize them.)

The subject of this book, then, is the new SQL standard "SQL/92" (and the unqualified name "SQL" is used throughout the body of the text to refer to this new version). Now, some readers may be aware that I have already discussed the SQL language at considerable length in several other books, including the following in particular:*

- *A Guide to INGRES* (Addison-Wesley, 1987)
- *A Guide to SQL/DS* (Addison-Wesley, 1988)
- *A Guide to SYBASE and SQL Server* (Addison-Wesley, 1992)
- *A Guide to DB2* (Addison-Wesley, 4th edition, 1992)

Thus, I am very conscious that I might be accused of writing the same book over and over again "until I get it right." However, the treatment of SQL in the present book differs from that in those other books in a number of significant ways:

- As already explained, the emphasis is on the official standard ("SQL/92") version of SQL instead of on one of the implemented dialects. The book should thus be relevant to *anyone* interested in the SQL language and SQL implementations—not just those from "the IBM world," which is where SQL originated, but also those with an interest in SQL implementations for, e.g., DEC, Data General, Unisys, ICL, ..., and other environments.

- The emphasis in the standard on the use of SQL for programmed (as opposed to interactive) access to the database has many ramifications and repercussions on the way the book is structured and the way the material is presented. In some ways the discussions are almost the reverse of what they were in those other books; those books concentrated primarily on interactive SQL and discussed programming SQL at the end, almost as an afterthought. The present book, by contrast, necessarily deals almost exclusively with the use of SQL by application programs.

- The treatment is more thorough. All aspects of the language are discussed in detail. In the other books, by contrast, I was not aiming at

---

*Colin White was coauthor on the SQL/DS and DB2 books and David McGoveran was principal author on the SYBASE book.

any such completeness, and it was expedient to simplify and/or ignore certain aspects of the language.

- At the same time, the book is (I hope) more "user-friendly" than the official standard, in that it includes a more tutorial treatment of the material, with plenty of examples. The official standard is not very easy to read—partly because it necessarily reflects the structure of the SQL language itself, which in some ways is very ill-structured (despite the fact that the "S" in SQL stands for "Structured"!), and partly too because it presents the language in a most confusing mixture of bottom-up and top-down styles. In this book, by contrast, the material is organized much more along functional lines; thus, there is (e.g.) a chapter on integrity, a chapter on views, a chapter on security, and so on. For pedagogic reasons, moreover, certain "complex" topics—e.g., missing information, date and time support—are ignored entirely in the first few chapters (except for a few forward pointers), thus allowing the presentation to flow in what I hope is a more natural and understandable manner.

- It follows from the previous two paragraphs that the book is intended as both a work of reference and a tutorial guide; it includes both formal definitions and numerous worked examples. As such, I hope it will prove useful to both *SQL users* (i.e., SQL application programmers) and SQL *implementers* (i.e., DBMS designers and developers). HOWEVER, I MUST MAKE IT AS CLEAR AS I POSSIBLY CAN THAT THE BOOK IS NOT INTENDED TO REPLACE THE OFFICIAL STANDARD DOCUMENT, BUT TO COMPLEMENT IT.

The book as a whole is divided into five major parts, as follows, together with a set of appendixes:

    I. Introduction
   II. Some Preliminaries
 III. Data Definition and Manipulation
 IV. Data Control
  V. Advanced Topics

Each part in turn is divided into a number of chapters:

- Part I (two chapters) sets the scene by explaining in general terms what the standard is all about and presenting an overview of the major concepts and facilities of the SQL language. The reader should study the second (at least) of these two chapters fairly carefully before moving on to the later parts of the book.

- Part II (four chapters) covers a number of fundamental issues, such as how to construct legal identifiers and what the scope of uniqueness of names is, and explains certain common underlying constructs, such as *sessions* and *schemas*. Much of this material is provided primarily for reference, however; it is not necessary, and probably not even a good idea, to read these chapters exhaustively before moving on to later parts of the book.

- Part III (seven chapters) addresses what might be considered the heart of the SQL language—the basic SQL data objects and operators, the rules for defining those objects, the rules for combining those operators to form expressions, and so on. In particular, it describes the SQL data manipulation statements, i.e., the statements for retrieving and updating SQL data.

- Part IV (two chapters) describes SQL's integrity and security support (including in particular its support for primary and foreign keys).

- Part V (seven chapters) discusses a number of more esoteric aspects of the standard, including such topics as missing information, date and time support, temporary tables, and so forth.

In addition, there are six appendixes, including one giving a BNF grammar for the SQL language, another explaining the requirements for compliance with the standard, another giving an overview of some currently proposed future extensions ("SQL3"), and so on.

The book is intended to be reasonably self-contained. The only background assumed of the reader is a general interest in the SQL language. All relevant terms and concepts are defined and explained as they are introduced. *Note*: Most of the examples are based on the familiar suppliers-and-parts database (see Chapter 2). I make no apology for trotting out this old warhorse still one more time; basing the examples on such a familiar database should (I hope) make it easy for the reader to relate to those examples, and should also facilitate comparisons between the standard version of SQL and specific vendor implementations—in particular, the implementations described in the books mentioned above (*A Guide to DB2* and the rest). In some respects, in fact, the book can be seen as a complement to those other books.

A NOTE ON THE TEXT

As mentioned above, the official standard is not particularly easy to read. In places, in fact, it is well-nigh impenetrable. The following extract is perhaps worse than most, but it is not atypical:

"However, because global temporary table contents are distinct within SQL-sessions, and created local temporary tables are distinct within <module>s within SQL-sessions, the effective *<schema name> of the schema in which the global temporary table or the created local temporary table is instantiated is an implementation-dependent <schema name> that may be thought of as having been effectively derived from the <schema name> of the schema in which the global temporary table or created local temporary table is defined and the implementation-dependent SQL-session identifier associated with the SQL-session."*

This sentence is taken from a section of the standard entitled—and intended to explain the SQL concept of—"Tables."

Of course, it is precisely because the standard is so hard to understand that a book such as this one can serve a useful purpose. But complexity alone is not the end of the story. The sentence quoted above is not merely hard to understand, it is actually *wrong* (tables are not instantiated in schemas, table *descriptors* are). Which brings us to the next point: The standard contains all too many errors, both errors of omission and errors of commission. As a consequence, the task of reading and understanding it is made much more difficult than it might have been. So too is the task of describing and explaining it!—at least when the topic under discussion is one that suffers from one or more of the aforesaid errors. The best that can be done in such cases is to make it quite clear that the topic in question is indeed one that the standard does not define in a fully satisfactory manner, and of course to try to explain too what the errors in the standard seem to be. In addition, Appendix D provides a consolidated and annotated list of such topics, to serve as a basis for further discussion and investigation.

There is another point to be made on the subject of the text, as follows. I am somewhat embarrassed at the inordinate number of footnotes to be found in this book. I am only too well aware that too many footnotes can quickly become annoying, and can indeed seriously impede readability. But the fact is that any description of SQL is almost forced into a heavy use of footnotes if it wants to be primarily tutorial in nature. The reason is that SQL involves so many inconsistencies, exceptions, and special cases that treating everything "in line"—i.e., at the same level of description—makes it very difficult to see the forest for the trees (indeed, this is another reason why the standard itself is so difficult to understand). Thus, there are numerous places in this book where the major idea is described "in line" in the main body of the text, and exceptions and the like (which must at least be mentioned, for reasons of accuracy and completeness) are relegated to a footnote.

ACKNOWLEDGMENTS

Although I have dropped the prefaces from the first two editions, it does not seem appropriate to drop the acknowledgments to the various friends and colleagues who helped with those editions—so here goes. First, I am delighted to acknowledge my debt to the following people, who helped with numerous technical and procedural questions and reviewed various drafts of the manuscripts of those editions: Lynn Francis, Randell Flint, Carol Joyce, Geoff Sharman, and Phil Shaw. Phil in particular (who has been the IBM representative to the ANSI SQL committee, and also one of the US representatives to the ISO SQL committee, ever since those committees were first formed) reviewed both editions very carefully and made a number of helpful comments and suggestions. I would also like to acknowledge the many attendees at seminars and live presentations (too numerous to mention individually) who offered constructive comments on each of those editions.

Turning now to this new edition specifically, I would like to thank my coauthor Hugh Darwen for his invaluable contribution. Hugh is one of the UK representatives to the ISO SQL committee, and as such was able to obtain answers to the numerous technical questions that arose during my study of the official standard documents. In addition, he reviewed the entire manuscript, and indeed also wrote the first drafts of some of the chapters (although I hasten to add that I am responsible for the final version of the text, and must therefore assume responsibility for any remaining errors it may contain). *Note*: The text does include a number of comments and personal opinions, generally introduced with a phrase such as "in this writer's opinion." Hugh has asked me to make it clear that he agrees with all such explicitly stated opinions; in other words, "this writer" should be taken to mean both of us!

I am also indebted to the other reviewers of this edition, namely Tony Gordon, David McGoveran, Phil Shaw (once again), and Mike Sykes, for their careful and constructive comments on the manuscript.

Third, I am deeply indebted to my long-suffering family, especially my wife Lindy, for her support throughout this project and so many others.

Last, I am (as always) grateful to my editor, Elydia Davis, and to the staff at Addison-Wesley for their assistance and their continually high standards of professionalism. It has been (as always) a pleasure to work with them.

Healdsburg, California   C. J. Date
1992

Hugh Darwen adds:

My role in the production of this book has been primarily that of advisor and technical reviewer, tasks made utterly nontrivial by Chris Date's meticulous questioning and his insistence on a complete understanding of everything. To answer his (hundreds of) questions, I, in turn, have leaned heavily on my fellow British members of the ISO Database Languages committee, Ed Dee, Mike Sykes, and Tony Gordon. I am especially grateful to Jim Melton, the editor of the SQL2 and SQL3 international standards, for similar assistance while he was in the throes of preparing the final SQL2 draft for publication. I am grateful to all members of this committee for an enjoyable and sometimes exhilarating collaboration under the excellent chairmanship of our *rapporteur*, Len Gallagher.

To participate in international standardization can be to distance oneself somewhat from one's employer's immediate business. My involvement was at my own initiative, and I am deeply grateful to Stuart Colvin, who was my manager in 1988, for the initial support, encouragement, and longterm vision, which have happily been continued by his several successors and superiors at the Warwick Software Development Laboratory of IBM.

Shrewley Common, England   Hugh Darwen
1992

Contents

PART II   SOME PRELIMINARIES

PART III   DATA DEFINITION AND MANIPULATION

PART IV   DATA CONTROL

PART V   ADVANCED TOPICS

APPENDIXES

INTRODUCTION

This introductory part of the book consists of two chapters, one giving some pertinent background information and the other a brief overview of the major facilities of the SQL standard. Readers are recommended to read at least the second of these two chapters fairly carefully before studying the later portions of the book.

PART

I

INTRODUCTION

1

Why SQL Is Important

1.1 BACKGROUND

The name "SQL"—the official pronunciation is "ess-cue-ell," although many people pronounce it "sequel"—was originally an abbreviation for "Structured Query Language." The SQL language consists of a set of facilities for defining, accessing, and otherwise managing relational databases. In order to understand why SQL has become so widespread and so generally important, it is helpful to have an appreciation of some of the major developments in database technology over the last 20 years or so. We therefore begin by summarizing those developments.

1. In 1970, E. F. Codd, at that time a member of the IBM Research Laboratory in San Jose, California, published a by now classic paper, "A Relational Model of Data for Large Shared Data Banks" (*Communications of the ACM,* Vol. 13, No. 6, June 1970), in which he laid down a set of abstract principles for database management: the so-called *relational model*. The entire field of relational database technology has its origins in that paper. Codd's ideas led directly to a great deal of experimentation and research in universities, industrial research laboratories, and similar establishments, and that activity in turn led to the numerous relational products now available in the marketplace. The many advantages of the relational approach are too well known to need

repeating here; see, e.g., Chapter 1 ("Why Relational?") in C. J. Date, *Relational Database Writings 1985–1989* (Addison-Wesley, 1990), for more discussion.

2. One particular aspect of the research just referred to was the design and prototype implementation of a variety of relational languages. A relational language is a language that realizes, in some concrete syntactic form, some or all of the features of the abstract relational model. Several such languages were created in the early and mid 1970s. One such language in particular was the "Structured English Query Language" (SEQUEL), defined by Donald Chamberlin and others at the IBM San Jose Research Laboratory (1974), and first implemented in an IBM prototype called SEQUEL-XRM (1974–75).

3. Partly as a result of experience with SEQUEL-XRM, a revised version of SEQUEL called SEQUEL/2 was defined in 1976–77. (The name was subsequently changed to SQL for legal reasons.) Work began on another, more ambitious, IBM prototype called System R. System R, an implementation of a large subset of the SEQUEL/2 (or SQL) language, became operational in 1977 and was subsequently installed in a number of user sites, both internal IBM sites and also (under a set of joint study agreements) selected IBM customer sites. *Note:* A number of further changes were made to the SQL language during the lifetime of the System R project, partly in response to user suggestions; for instance, an EXISTS function was added to test whether some specified data existed in the database.

4. Thanks in large part to the success of System R, it became generally apparent in the late 1970s that sooner or later IBM would develop one or more commercial products based on the System R technology—specifically, products that implemented the SQL language. As a result, other vendors did not wait for IBM but began to construct their own SQL-based products. (In fact, at least one such product, namely ORACLE from Relational Software Inc.—subsequently renamed Oracle Corporation—was actually introduced to the market before IBM's own products.) Then, in 1981, IBM did announce an SQL product,* namely SQL/DS, for the VSE environment. IBM then followed that announcement with one for a VM version of SQL/DS (1982), and another for an MVS product called DB2 that was broadly compatible with SQL/DS (1983).

---

*Note that we are assuming the "ess-cue-ell" pronunciation here. We will favor this pronunciation in this book, even though it is not to everyone's taste, in order to be consistent with the official standard.

5. Over the next several years, numerous other vendors also announced SQL-based products. Those announcements included both entirely new products such as DG/SQL (Data General Corporation, 1984) and SYBASE (Sybase Inc., 1986), and SQL interfaces to established products such as INGRES (Relational Technology Inc., 1981, 1985) and the IDM (Britton-Lee Inc., 1982, 1985).* There are now (1992) well over 100 products in the marketplace that support some dialect of SQL, running on machines that range all the way from quite small micros to the largest mainframes. *SQL has become the de facto standard in the relational database world.*

6. Furthermore, of course, SQL is now an *official* standard also. In 1982, the American National Standards Institute (ANSI) chartered its Database Committee (X3H2) to develop a proposal for a standard relational language. The X3H2 proposal, which was finally ratified by ANSI in 1986, consisted essentially of the IBM dialect of SQL, "warts and all" (except that a few—in this writer's opinion, far too few—minor IBM idiosyncrasies were removed). And in 1987, the ANSI standard was also accepted as an international standard by the International Organization for Standardization (ISO). *Note:* That original standard version of SQL is often referred to, informally, as "SQL/86."

The foregoing is not the end of the story, of course. First, the original SQL standard was extended in 1989 to include an *Integrity Enhancement Feature,* IEF; by analogy with "SQL/86," that extended version is frequently referred to (again informally) as "SQL/89." In addition, a related standard called *Database Language Embedded SQL* was adopted (in the United States, at least), also in 1989. Furthermore, various versions of SQL have been adopted at various subsequent times as

- an X/OPEN standard (for UNIX systems)
- an SAA standard (for IBM systems)
- a Federal Information Processing Standard or FIPS (for US Federal Government systems)

Moreover, a consortium of vendors known as the SQL Access Group has been working to define a set of enhancements to SQL to support interoperability across disparate systems. The first results of that effort were

---

*In the interest of accuracy, we should explain that Relational Technology Inc. later changed its name to Ingres Corporation, and was subsequently acquired by ASK Computer Systems Inc. Similarly, Britton-Lee Inc. changed its name to ShareBase Corporation (and changed the name of its product to ShareBase also), and was subsequently acquired by Teradata Corporation, which later merged with NCR Corporation, which was in turn acquired by AT&T.

demonstrated in July 1991, when the SQL Access Group showed a prototype implementation of such interoperability involving ten different application systems and nine different database management systems. And, finally, the original ISO and ANSI committees have been working for several years to define a revised (and greatly expanded) version of the original standard known informally as "SQL2" (more recently "SQL/92") which became a ratified standard—"International Standard ISO/IEC 9075:1992, *Database Language SQL*"—in late 1992. The principal purpose of this book is to describe this new standard.

Note: As just indicated, we are concerned in this book primarily with the newest ISO version of SQL ("SQL/92"), which from now on will increasingly be the version meant when people refer to "the SQL standard." In this book, therefore, we will take the unqualified name "SQL" (also terms such as "standard SQL," "the standard," "the official standard," etc.) to refer to this new ISO version. When we need to refer to some specific dialect other than the new standard version, we will always use an appropriately qualified name, such as "SQL/86" or "SQL/89" or "SAA SQL" (etc.).

One final point of a historical nature: The original version of SQL was intended for standalone, interactive, "direct" use. However, facilities were added later to allow the invocation of SQL operations from an application program written in a language such as COBOL or PL/I. By contrast, the standard concentrates almost exclusively on these latter (application programming) facilities, presumably on the grounds that standardization is much more significant for portability of programs than it is for interactive interfaces. This emphasis is reflected in the structure of the book, as will be seen.

1.2   IS A STANDARD DESIRABLE?

Before going any further, we should perhaps consider the question of whether an SQL standard is a good thing. On the one hand, the advantages are fairly obvious:*

- *Reduced training costs:* Application developers can move from one environment to another without the need for expensive retraining.

- *Application portability:* Applications—in particular, applications developed by third-party software vendors—can run unchanged in a vari-

---

*We should perhaps stress the point that many of these advantages apply in principle but do *not* necessarily apply in practice. This word of caution is particularly relevant to the "application portability" advantage.

ety of different hardware and software environments. Applications can be developed in one environment (e.g., on a PC) and then run in another (e.g., on a large mainframe).

- *Application longevity:* Standard languages are assured of a reasonably long lifetime. Applications developed using such languages can therefore be assured of a reasonably long lifetime also (other things being equal).

- *Intersystem communication:* Different systems can more easily communicate with one another (in this regard, note the work of the SQL Access Group, mentioned briefly in Section 1.1). In particular, different database management systems might be able to function as equal partners in a single distributed database system if they all support the same standard interface (a consideration that is becoming increasingly important in the commercial world).

- *Customer choice:* If all products support the same interface, customers can concentrate on the problem of choosing the implementation that best meets their own particular needs, without having to get involved in the additional complexity of choosing among different interfaces (possibly widely different interfaces).

On the other hand, there are some significant disadvantages also:

- *A standard can stifle creativity:* Implementers may effectively be prevented from providing "the best" (or a good) solution to some problem because the standard already prescribes some alternative, less satisfactory, solution to that same problem.

- *SQL in particular is very far from ideal as a relational language:* This criticism has been elaborated by the present writers in many places; see, e.g., the books *Relational Database: Selected Writings, Relational Database Writings 1985–1989,* and *Relational Database Writings 1989–1991,* published by Addison-Wesley in 1986, 1990, and 1992, respectively. To quote from the first of these books: ". . . it cannot be denied that SQL in its present form leaves rather a lot to be desired—even that, in some important respects, it fails to realize the full potential of the relational model." The basic problem (in this writer's opinion) is that, although there are well-established principles for the design of formal languages, there is little evidence that SQL was ever designed in accordance with any such principles. As a result, the language is filled with numerous restrictions, ad hoc constructs, and annoying special rules. These factors in turn make the language hard to define, describe, teach, learn, remember, apply, and implement.

- *Standard SQL especially is additionally deficient in a number of respects:* Over and above the deficiencies mentioned under the previous point (i.e., deficiencies that are intrinsic to the original SQL language per se), standard SQL in particular suffers from certain additional deficiencies. Specifically, it fails to include any support at all for several features that are clearly needed in practice (e.g., a truth-valued or Boolean data type), and it leaves as "implementation-defined" or "implementation-dependent"* many aspects that would be much better spelled out as part of the standard (e.g., the column names of the table that results from evaluating certain table expressions). As a result, it seems likely that every realistic implementation of the standard will necessarily include many implementation-specific extensions and variations, and hence that no two "standard" SQL implementations will ever be truly identical.

Despite these drawbacks, however, the fact is that the standard exists, vendors are scrambling to support it, and customers are demanding such support. Hence this book.

---

*The (important) difference between these two concepts is as follows. *Implementation-defined* means that an implementation is free to decide how it will implement the SQL feature in question, but the result of that decision must be documented. *Implementation-dependent* effectively means "undefined"; again, the implementation is free to decide how it will implement the feature in question, and the result of that decision need not even be documented (it might even vary from release to release). Examples of the two cases are the maximum length of a character string (implementation-defined) and the physical representation of data in storage (implementation-dependent).

2

An Overview of SQL

2.1 INTRODUCTION

The aim of this chapter is to present a brief and very informal overview of some of the major facilities of standard SQL, and thereby to pave the way for an understanding of the more formal and thorough treatment of the language in subsequent chapters. The chapter is very loosely based on Chapter 1 ("Relational Database: An Overview") from C. J. Date, *Relational Database: Selected Writings* (Addison-Wesley, 1986). *Note:* One remark that is probably as well to make right at the outset is the following: Space obviously does not permit us to make any detailed comparisons between the facilities of the standard and those of existing SQL products; however, if the reader is familiar with some commercial SQL implementation, he or she may be in for a few surprises.

The primary function of the SQL language is to support the definition, manipulation, and control of data in relational databases. A *relational database* is simply a database that is perceived by the user as a collection of tables, where a *table* is *an unordered collection of rows* ("relation" is just a mathematical term for such a table—speaking *very* loosely!). An example, the suppliers-and-parts database, is shown in Fig. 2.1. Tables S, P, and SP in that figure represent, respectively, suppliers, parts, and shipments of parts by suppliers. Note that each table can be thought of as a *file,* with the rows representing records and the columns fields. However, the SQL standard never uses the terms "file," "record," or "field"; it always uses "table," "row," and "column" instead, and in this book we will do like-wise.*

S

SNO	SNAME	STATUS	CITY
S1	Smith	20	London
S2	Jones	10	Paris
S3	Blake	30	Paris
S4	Clark	20	London
S5	Adams	30	Athens

SP

SNO	PNO	QTY
S1	P1	300
S1	P2	200
S1	P3	400
S1	P4	200
S1	P5	100
S1	P6	100
S2	P1	300
S2	P2	400
S3	P2	200
S4	P2	200
S4	P4	300
S4	P5	400

P

PNO	PNAME	COLOR	WEIGHT	CITY
P1	Nut	Red	12	London
P2	Bolt	Green	17	Paris
P3	Screw	Blue	17	Rome
P4	Screw	Red	14	London
P5	Cam	Blue	12	Paris
P6	Cog	Red	19	London

Fig. 2.1 The suppliers-and-parts database (sample values)

Now, SQL statements in general, and SQL "data manipulation" statements in particular (i.e., SQL statements that perform data retrieval or up-dating functions), can be invoked either interactively ("directly") or from within an application program. Fig. 2.2 illustrates both cases; it shows a data retrieval operation—SELECT in SQL—being used both (a) interactively and (b) from within a PL/I program. In general, interactive invocation means that the statement in question is executed from a workstation and (in the case of retrieval) the result is displayed at that workstation; invocation from within an application program means that the statement is executed as part of the process of executing that program and (in the case of retrieval) the result is fetched into an input area within that program ("SC" in Fig. 2.2(b)). *Note:* The figure illustrates one of the two standard syntactic styles—"embedded SQL"—for invoking SQL from an application program. See Chapter 6 for further discussion of this point.

---

*In fact, the standard never uses the term "relation" either. What is more, it does not even use the term "database"!—at least, not in any formal sense. Instead, it talks about "SQL-data," which is "any data described by schemas [i.e., SQL-schemas—see Section 2.8] that is under the control of an SQL-implementation in an SQL-environment."

(a) *Direct invocation*:

```
SELECT  S.CITY            Result:     CITY
FROM    S
WHERE   S.SNO = 'S4'                  London
```

(b) *Invocation from an application program (PL/I)*:

```
EXEC SQL SELECT S.CITY INTO :SC    Result:   SC
         FROM   S
         WHERE  S.SNO = 'S4' ;                London
```

Fig. 2.2 SQL retrieval example

One further introductory remark: The reader will have noticed that we used qualified column names (S.CITY, S.SNO) in Fig. 2.2. SQL in fact allows qualifiers to be omitted in many contexts (including, in particular, the SELECT and WHERE clauses), provided no ambiguity can result from such omission. Thus, for example, the two SELECT clauses of Fig. 2.2 could have been abbreviated to just "SELECT CITY" in each case. However, it is not wrong to include the qualifiers as we have done. In this book, for reasons of clarity and explicitness, we will generally use qualified column names, even when they are not strictly necessary—except, of course, in contexts where they are expressly prohibited. An example of a context in which qualified column names are prohibited is the left-hand side of a SET clause assignment in an UPDATE statement (see Section 2.3).

2.2 DATA DEFINITION

Fig. 2.1, the suppliers-and-parts database, of course represents that database as it appears at some specific time. Fig. 2.3, by contrast, shows (in outline) how the database would be *defined*. We explain that definition (in outline) as follows:

- The three CREATE TABLE statements define three empty tables with the specified names and specified named columns (with specified data types). Note that column names must be unique within their containing tables.

- Within table S, column SNO is defined as the *primary key*—meaning that, at any given time, no two rows of the table will have the same SNO value. Similarly for column PNO in table P and the combination of columns (SNO,PNO) in table SP. *Note:* Primary key columns are

```
CREATE TABLE S   ( SNO     CHAR(5),
                   SNAME   CHAR(20),
                   STATUS  DECIMAL(3),
                   CITY    CHAR(15),
                   PRIMARY KEY ( SNO ) )

CREATE TABLE P   ( PNO     CHAR(6),
                   PNAME   CHAR(20),
                   COLOR   CHAR(6),
                   WEIGHT  DECIMAL(3),
                   CITY    CHAR(15),
                   PRIMARY KEY ( PNO ) )

CREATE TABLE SP  ( SNO     CHAR(5),
                   PNO     CHAR(6),
                   QTY     DECIMAL(5),
                   PRIMARY KEY ( SNO, PNO ),
                   FOREIGN KEY ( SNO ) REFERENCES S,
                   FOREIGN KEY ( PNO ) REFERENCES P )
```

Fig. 2.3 Data definition example

indicated by double underlining in Fig. 2.1. We will make use of this convention in figures throughout this book.*

- Within table SP, columns SNO and PNO are defined as *foreign* keys, referencing tables S and P respectively. What this means, loosely speaking, is that every value appearing in column SP.SNO must also appear in column S.SNO (the primary key) of table S, and likewise every value appearing in column SP.PNO must also appear in column P.PNO (the primary key) of table P. The intuitive (and correct) interpretation of these constraints is that a shipment cannot exist unless the corresponding supplier and part exist also.

Data can subsequently be entered into the tables via the SQL INSERT statement, discussed in the next section. *Note:* We will be using this database as the basis for most of our examples throughout this book, so it is worth taking a little time to familiarize yourself with it now.

There are two kinds of tables that can be defined in SQL, *base tables* and *viewed tables* (usually referred to simply as *views*). The tables of Fig. 2.3 are all base tables.† A base table is a "real" table—i.e., a table that "really exists" (or, at least, can be thought of as "really existing"); there

---

*The reader should not infer from our convention that the primary key of any given table is always known to SQL. On the contrary, it is known if and only if the table is a "base" table (see later in this section) *and* the user has explicitly chosen to provide a PRIMARY KEY specification for that table.

†Note, therefore, that CREATE TABLE creates a base table specifically. There is a separate CREATE VIEW statement for creating views (see Section 2.5).

might even be physical stored records, and possibly physical access paths such as indexes, in one or more stored files, that directly support that table in physical storage. By contrast, a view is a "virtual" table—i.e., a table that does not "really exist" in the foregoing sense, but looks to the user as if it did. Views are defined, in a manner to be explained in Section 2.5, in terms of one or more underlying base tables.

Note: The foregoing paragraph should *not* be construed as meaning that a base table is a *physically stored* table—i.e., a collection of physically adjacent, physically stored records, each one consisting of a direct copy of a row of the base table. In fact, a base table need have no direct stored counterpart at all! Base tables are best thought of as an *abstraction* of some collection of stored data—an abstraction in which numerous storage-level details (such as physical data location, physical ordering, physical data encodings, physical access paths, etc.) are concealed. Thus, there may be any number of differences between a base table and its stored representation. The point is, however, that users can always *think* of base tables as "really existing," while not having to concern themselves with how the data is physically represented in storage. Views on the other hand do not "really exist" in this sense; views are merely a different way of looking at the data in the base tables.

2.3 DATA MANIPULATION

There are four basic SQL data manipulation operations—SELECT, INSERT, UPDATE, and DELETE. We have already given an example of SELECT (two versions) in Fig. 2.2. Fig. 2.4 gives examples of the other three operations, the so-called update operations. *Note:* The term "update" unfortunately has two meanings in SQL: It is used generically to refer to the three operations INSERT, UPDATE, and DELETE as a class, and also specifically to refer to the UPDATE operation per se. We will distin-

```
INSERT                              Result:   Specified row
INTO SP ( SNO, PNO, QTY )                     added to table SP
VALUES   ('S5','P1',1000 )

UPDATE S                            Result:   STATUS doubled
SET     STATUS = 2 * S.STATUS                 for suppliers in
WHERE   S.CITY = 'London'                     London (i.e., S1
                                              and S4)

DELETE                              Result:   Rows deleted from
FROM    P                                     table P for parts
WHERE   P.WEIGHT > 15                         P2, P3, and P6
```

Fig. 2.4 Update examples

guish between the two meanings in this book by using lower case when the generic meaning is intended and upper case when the specific meaning is intended.

Note that the UPDATE and DELETE operations of Fig. 2.4 operate on multiple rows each, not just on a single row. The same is true in general for INSERT operations (although the INSERT of Fig. 2.4 is actually single-row), and also for SELECT operations. In the case of SELECT, however, standard SQL does not permit a multiple-row SELECT operation to be executed as a separate statement in its own right;* instead, it is necessary to define a *cursor* having that SELECT operation as its "scope," and then to access the rows in that scope one at a time by means of that cursor. For tutorial reasons, however, we defer discussion of cursors to Section 2.4, and assume for the time being that a multiple-row SELECT can indeed be executed as a statement in its own right. Note that single-row SELECTs *can* be executed in this way, as illustrated in Fig. 2.2.

The SELECT operation has the general form "SELECT-FROM-WHERE," as illustrated in Fig. 2.5. (*Note:* The symbol < > in that figure stands for "not equals.") Observe that the result of the SELECT is another table (one that is derived from an existing table, not one that is stored in the database). Note too that:

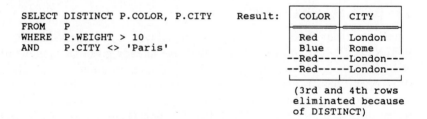

Fig. 2.5   The basic "SELECT-FROM-WHERE"

- If the WHERE clause is omitted, all rows of the FROM table are returned.

- If the DISTINCT option is omitted, the result may contain duplicate rows (in the example, four rows will be returned if DISTINCT is omitted, two if it is included).

---

*Except in "direct" (i.e., interactive) SQL. We are (as usual) tacitly assuming an application programming context.

Join

One of the most crucially important features of relational systems is their support for the relational *join* operator. It is this operator that makes it possible (in SQL terms) to SELECT data from two, three, four, . . . or any number of tables, all by means of a single SELECT operation. An example is given in Fig. 2.6 (the query is "For each part supplied, retrieve part number and names of all cities in which there is located a supplier who supplies the part"). The term "join" arises from the fact that (in the example) tables SP and S are conceptually being *joined* on their common SNO column. Note that the references to columns S.SNO and SP.SNO in the WHERE clause *must* be qualified in this example, to avoid ambiguity.

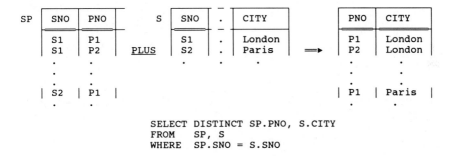

```
SELECT DISTINCT SP.PNO, S.CITY
FROM    SP, S
WHERE   SP.SNO = S.SNO
```

Fig. 2.6 Example involving join

Aggregate Functions

SQL provides a set of special builtin *aggregate functions:* COUNT, SUM, AVG, MAX, MIN, and COUNT(*) (the "*" refers to an entire row of the table concerned). Examples are given in Fig. 2.7. The last example also illustrates the GROUP BY clause, which is used to divide a table (conceptually) into groups so that a function such as SUM can be applied to each individual group. Note, incidentally, that the first three examples are all single-row SELECTs. Note too the use of the AS clause (in all four examples) to specify a name for the column resulting from the use of the aggregate function, which otherwise would be given an implementation-dependent name (refer back to Chapter 1 if you need to refresh your memory regarding the meaning of the term "implementation-dependent").

```
Number of suppliers:

    SELECT  COUNT(*) AS N1
    FROM    S
```

Result:

N1
5

```
Number of suppliers supplying parts:

    SELECT  COUNT ( DISTINCT SP.SNO ) AS N2
    FROM    SP
```

Result:

N2
4

```
Total quantity of part P2:

    SELECT  SUM ( SP.QTY ) AS TOT1
    FROM    SP
    WHERE   SP.PNO = 'P2'
```

Result:

TOT1
1000

```
Part number and total quantity
for each part supplied:

    SELECT  SP.PNO, SUM ( SP.QTY ) AS TOT2
    FROM    SP
    GROUP   BY SP.PNO
```

Result:

PNO	TOT2
P1	600
P2	1000
P3	400
P4	500
P5	500
P6	100

Fig. 2.7   SQL aggregate function examples

2.4 CURSOR OPERATIONS

As mentioned in Section 2.3, a multiple-row SELECT operation cannot be executed as a statement in its own right in standard SQL. The reason for this state of affairs is that the standard is primarily concerned with the use of SQL in conjunction with programming languages such as PL/I and COBOL, and such languages are generally not well equipped to deal with collections of multiple rows as single operands. What is needed, therefore, is a mechanism for stepping through such a collection and picking off the rows one by one; and *cursors* provide such a mechanism. A cursor is an SQL object that is associated (via an appropriate declaration) with a specific SELECT operation. To access the rows corresponding to that SELECT, the user must:

1. OPEN the cursor, which (conceptually) causes the SELECT to be executed, and hence identifies the corresponding collection of rows;

2. Use FETCH repeatedly on the opened cursor, which (on each execution) steps that cursor to the next row in the collection and retrieves that row; and finally

3. CLOSE the cursor when all required rows have been processed.

Special forms of UPDATE and DELETE are also provided for updating or deleting the row on which the cursor is currently positioned. An example is given (in outline—many important details are omitted) in Fig. 2.8. *Note:* The example is written in PL/I. The standard does support other languages as well, of course, but the rules for using SQL with those other languages are essentially the same as those for PL/I (see Chapter 6 for further discussion). For definiteness, therefore, we adopt PL/I as the basis for all of our programming examples, here and throughout the remainder of the book.

```
EXEC SQL DECLARE C1 CURSOR FOR
        SELECT SP.SNO, SP.QTY
        FROM    SP
        WHERE   SP.PNO = 'P2' ;

DECLARE X CHAR(5) ;
DECLARE Y FIXED DECIMAL(5) ;
DECLARE Z FIXED DECIMAL(3) ;

EXEC SQL OPEN C1 ;
DO for all rows accessible via cursor C1 ;
   EXEC SQL FETCH C1 INTO :X, :Y ;
   process X and Y ;
   EXEC SQL UPDATE SP
            SET     QTY = QTY + :Z
            WHERE   CURRENT OF C1 ;
END ;
EXEC SQL CLOSE C1 ;
```

Fig. 2.8 Example of the use of a cursor

Note: As mentioned in Section 2.1, the SQL standard provides two different ways of invoking SQL operations from an application program. Fig. 2.8 illustrates the method more commonly used, namely that of embedding SQL statements directly into the program source text ("embedded SQL"). Embedded SQL statements must be prefixed with EXEC SQL, for purposes of recognition. They can include references to host language variables; such references must be prefixed with a colon (":"), again for purposes of recognition. For more details, see Chapter 6.

2.5 VIEWS

Recall from Section 2.2 that a view (or "viewed table") is a *virtual* table—
i.e., a table that "does not really exist" but looks to the user as if it did.
Views are not directly supported by their own data, separate from the data
in the base tables; instead, they are simply defined to be different ways of
looking at the data in those base tables. Thus, their *definition* in terms of
other tables—base tables and/or other views—is specified as part of the
database definition. Fig. 2.9 shows the definition of a view called LS
("London suppliers").

```
CREATE VIEW LS ( SNO, SNAME, STATUS )
    AS SELECT S.SNO, S.SNAME, S.STATUS
        FROM    S
        WHERE   S.CITY = 'London'
```

Fig. 2.9 CREATE VIEW (example)

The view LS acts as a kind of window, through which the user can see
the SNO, SNAME, and STATUS values (only) of rows in base table S for
which the CITY value is London (only). The SELECT defining this view is
not executed when the view is created but is merely "remembered" by the
system in some way (actually by saving it in the appropriate *schema*—see
Section 2.8). But to the user it now appears as if a table called LS really
does exist in the database. Fig. 2.10 shows an example of a retrieval against
that table.

```
SELECT  LS.SNO                      Result:    SNO
FROM    LS                                     ─────
WHERE   LS.STATUS < 50                         S1
                                               S4
```

Fig. 2.10 Retrieval against a view (example)

Operations against a view are effectively handled by replacing *references* to the view by the expression that *defines* the view (i.e., by the
SELECT operation that was remembered by the system). The system thus
logically "merges" the SELECT of Fig. 2.9 with the SELECT of Fig. 2.10
to give the following modified SELECT:

```
SELECT  LS.SNO
FROM    ( SELECT  S.SNO, S.SNAME, S.STATUS
          FROM    S
          WHERE   S.CITY = 'London' ) AS LS
WHERE   LS.STATUS < 50
```

And this modified SELECT in turn is readily seen to be equivalent to the simpler version shown in Fig. 2.11.

```
SELECT  S.SNO                          Result:    SNO
FROM    S                                        ─────
WHERE   S.CITY = 'London'                          S1
AND     S.STATUS < 50                              S4
```

Fig. 2.11 Equivalent SELECT against the base table

In other words, the original SELECT on the view is effectively converted into an equivalent SELECT on the underlying base table. That equivalent SELECT is then executed in the normal way.

Update operations are handled in a similar fashion; however, update operations on views are subject to a number of restrictions, the details of which are beyond the scope of this chapter. Simplifying matters considerably, standard SQL allows a view to be updated only if it represents a simple row-and-column subset of a single underlying base table (for example, it cannot be a join). See Chapter 13 for further discussion.

Two more examples of views (both nonupdatable) are shown in Fig. 2.12.

```
CREATE VIEW PQ ( PNO, SUMQTY )
    AS SELECT SP.PNO, SUM ( SP.QTY )
       FROM    SP
       GROUP   BY SP.PNO

CREATE VIEW CITY_PAIRS ( SCITY, PCITY )
    AS SELECT DISTINCT S.CITY, P.CITY
       FROM    S, SP, P
       WHERE   S.SNO = SP.SNO
       AND     SP.PNO = P.PNO
```

Fig. 2.12 Additional view examples

2.6 SECURITY AND INTEGRITY

As mentioned in Section 2.1, SQL provides facilities for data control as well as for data definition and data manipulation. Those control facilities include (among other things) certain *security* and *integrity* features, which we briefly discuss in the present section.

Security

There are two principal aspects to security in SQL, the view mechanism and the GRANT operation. First, views. Views can be used to hide sensitive data from unauthorized users. Some examples of views that might be used in this way are shown in Fig. 2.13: The first reveals information only for red parts; the second reveals information only for parts that are supplied by the current user of the view; the third conceals supplier status information; and the fourth gives average shipment quantity per part, but no individual quantities. *Note:* "SELECT *" is shorthand for a SELECT that names all columns of the table—i.e., a SELECT that accesses the entire row (for all rows satisfying the WHERE clause).

```
CREATE VIEW RED_PARTS AS
      SELECT * FROM P WHERE P.COLOR = 'Red'

CREATE VIEW MY_PARTS AS
      SELECT * FROM P WHERE P.PNO IN
                  ( SELECT SP.PNO FROM SP
                    WHERE  SP.SNO = CURRENT_USER )

CREATE VIEW STATUS_HIDDEN AS
      SELECT S.SNO, S.SNAME, S.CITY FROM S

CREATE VIEW AVG_QTYS ( PNO, AVGQTY ) AS
      SELECT SP.PNO, AVG ( SP.QTY ) FROM SP GROUP BY SP.PNO
```

Fig. 2.13 Using views to hide data (examples)

Second, the GRANT operation. To execute any SQL statement at all, the user must hold the appropriate *privilege* for the combination of operation and operand(s) concerned (otherwise the statement will be rejected). The possible privileges include SELECT, INSERT, UPDATE, and DELETE (representing in each case the privilege to perform the indicated operation on the table in question), plus certain others that are beyond the scope of this introductory chapter. INSERT and UPDATE privileges can be further restricted to just specific columns. Privileges are assigned as follows:

- A user who creates a table (base table or view) is automatically granted all applicable privileges on that table, "with the grant option."

- Any user holding a privilege "with the grant option" can in turn grant that privilege to another user, and moreover can optionally pass the grant option on to that other user also (so that that user in turn can go on to grant the privilege to a third party, and so on).

- Granting privileges is performed by means of the GRANT operation, some examples of which are shown in Fig. 2.14. Note that the last example refers to a view (table LS), not a base table; the user receiving the privilege in that example is allowed to perform SELECTs on view LS, but *not* necessarily on the underlying base table S.

```
GRANT INSERT, UPDATE, DELETE ON SP TO JOE

GRANT SELECT ON SP TO ALICE WITH GRANT OPTION

GRANT UPDATE ( STATUS ) ON S TO JUDY

GRANT DELETE ON SP TO BONNIE, CLYDE

GRANT SELECT ON LS TO FRED
```

Fig. 2.14   GRANT examples

Note: In the interest of accuracy, we should mention that the standard does not in fact talk in terms of "users" at all, but rather in terms of what it calls *authorization identifiers*. In Fig. 2.14, for example, JOE, ALICE, JUDY, BONNIE, CLYDE, and FRED are really all authorization identifiers. See Chapters 4 and 15 for further discussion.

Integrity

The term "integrity" refers to the correctness of the data in the database. Standard SQL allows certain *integrity constraints* to be defined by a variety of means—e.g., via appropriate specifications within the CREATE TABLE statement. Any attempted update that would violate any defined constraint is rejected, and the database remains unchanged. Available constraints include the following:

- *UNIQUE:* Can be specified for any column or combination of columns within a specified base table. Any attempt to introduce a row having the same value in the specified column or column combination as some existing row will be rejected.

- *PRIMARY KEY:* A special case of UNIQUE, already discussed briefly in Section 2.2.

- *FOREIGN KEY:* Already discussed briefly in Section 2.2.

- *CHECK:* Can be specified for any column or combination of columns in any base table or combination of base tables. Any attempt to update the database in a way that would cause the specified CHECK to fail will be rejected.

The foregoing is not intended to be an exhaustive list. See Chapter 14 for a comprehensive discussion.

Two further integrity features should also be mentioned here, data type checking and "the check option." First, SQL will reject any attempt to violate data type specifications—e.g., an attempt to insert a character string value into a column defined as DECIMAL. Second, SQL also supports the clause WITH CHECK OPTION on CREATE VIEW. For details of the check option, the reader is referred to Chapter 13.

2.7 RECOVERY AND CONCURRENCY

Standard SQL includes support for the transaction concept. A tutorial on transaction management and the associated concepts of recovery and concurrency can be found in many places; see, e.g., C. J. Date, *An Introduction to Database Systems: Volume I* (5th edition, Addison-Wesley, 1990). We defer detailed discussion of the relevant SQL features to Chapter 5; what follows is only the briefest of sketches.

- A transaction (more precisely, an "SQL-transaction") is a sequence of operations that is guaranteed to be atomic for recovery purposes. Every transaction terminates by executing either a COMMIT operation (normal termination) or a ROLLBACK operation (abnormal termination).*

- Database updates made by a given transaction *T1* are not made visible to any distinct transaction *T2* until and unless *T1* successfully executes COMMIT.† Successful execution of COMMIT causes all updates made by the transaction to be made visible to other transactions; such updates are said to be *committed,* and are guaranteed never to be canceled. If the transaction executes ROLLBACK instead, all updates made by the transaction are canceled (*rolled back*).

---

*Or some equivalent to COMMIT or ROLLBACK. Exactly how a given transaction terminates depends on the environment in which the transaction executes (see Chapter 5).

†Unless transaction *T2* executes at READ UNCOMMITTED isolation level. See Chapter 5.

- By default, the interleaved execution of a set of concurrent transactions is required to be *serializable,* in the sense that it must produce the same result as executing those same transactions one at a time in some (un-specified) serial order. Note, however, that the standard explicitly provides options that permit certain violations of serializability; see the discussion of *isolation level* in Chapter 5.

2.8 SCHEMAS AND CATALOGS

Note: The standard uses both "schemata" and "schemas" as the plural of "schema." We prefer the latter form.

All SQL operations in the standard are performed within the context of an *SQL-environment* ("environment" for short), which includes among other things an arbitrary number of *catalogs,* grouped into *clusters.* Each catalog in turn contains an arbitrary number of *SQL-schemas.* None of these concepts is explained very well in the standard, but the intent seems to be somewhat as follows:

- An *SQL-environment* represents the combination of (a) a particular instance of a particular SQL database management system (DBMS) that is (b) executing at a particular computer site,* together with (c) the collection of all databases accessible to that DBMS instance at that site, together with (d) the collection of all users and programs at that site that are able to use that DBMS instance to access those databases. For example, a single copy of IBM's DB2 DBMS, executing on a single MVS system, together with the set of all DB2 databases under the con-trol of that copy of DB2 and the set of all users and programs on that MVS system that can use that copy of DB2 to access those DB2 data-bases, might constitute such an "environment." *Note:* Since the term "database" is not formally defined within the standard, we are within our rights in assuming that a single environment might contain multiple databases, not necessarily just one.

    SQL operations are not allowed to span environments.

- Each *catalog* within a given environment consists of a set of *schemas* (more correctly, *SQL-schemas*) that in turn contain entries that de-

---

*The standard does *not* say that an SQL-environment is limited to a single site; in fact, it strongly suggests that the opposite might be the case, because it explicitly requires the "SQL-client" to establish an "SQL-connection" to an "SQL-server" (with the implication that the SQL-client and SQL-server might be at different sites) before any database processing can be done. However, it certainly does not preclude the single-site case either, and we will stay with the single-site interpretation for now. See Section 2.9 and Appendix D for further discussion.

scribe what we might reasonably (but not officially!) regard as a *database*. That is, each catalog effectively describes a certain collection of base tables, views, and so on, that somehow—in some implementation-dependent way—constitute a logically related collection of data within the given environment.

- Catalogs are grouped in an implementation-defined way into *clusters*. The intent seems to be that a given cluster should consist of the set of all catalogs that describe any objects that are accessible to a given user. Each SQL-session (see Section 2.9) has exactly one associated cluster, which defines the totality of SQL-data available to that SQL-session. *Note:* It is implementation-defined whether the same catalog can appear in distinct clusters.

  We stated above that SQL operations are not allowed to span environments. More specifically, in fact, they are not allowed to span clusters *within* an environment.

- Each *schema* within a given catalog contains entries that describe some individual user's portion of the complete "database" as described by that catalog; or, to put it another way, each catalog is effectively partitioned into schemas, one for each user who has created objects that are described by that catalog. (This explanation is slightly oversimplified: A given user can be responsible for any number of schemas, not necessarily just one, within a given catalog.)

  Exactly what schemas in general look like is not defined, but every catalog is required to contain one particular schema called the *Information Schema,* whose contents *are* precisely defined. More specifically, the Information Schema consists of a set of SQL tables whose contents effectively echo (in a precisely defined way) all of the definitions from all of the other schemas in all of the catalogs in the cluster that contains the catalog in question. See Chapter 21.

SQL objects such as base tables, views, integrity constraints, etc., are always created within the context of some particular schema (within some catalog within the environment), and are considered to "belong to" or "be owned by" the schema in question.* Note, however, that SQL operations are allowed to span schemas, and even catalogs (and hence, perhaps, "databases"); for example, it is possible to join tables that are described by distinct schemas or distinct catalogs. The only requirement is that all of those schemas and catalogs be part of the same cluster.

---

*More precisely, they are considered to belong to the unique authorization identifier—i.e., user, loosely speaking—that is associated with that schema (see Chapter 4).

The schema name is used as the high-level qualifier for names of objects that belong to the schema (schema names must be unique within their containing catalog). Likewise, schemas always belong to some catalog, and the catalog name is used as the high-level qualifier for names of schemas in the catalog in question (catalog names must be unique within the environment). Note, however, that in practice these high-level qualifiers will frequently be omitted; the standard includes an elaborate system of *defaults,* by which appropriate catalog and schema names are assumed if nothing is specified explicitly (see Chapters 3–6 for details).

2.9   SESSIONS AND CONNECTIONS

The standard also introduces the term "SQL-agent." An SQL-agent can be thought of as the execution of an application program, which we assume for the sake of discussion to include one or more SQL operations. The SQL-agent starts execution under the control of an SQL-environment component called the *SQL-client* (and remains "bound" to that SQL-client— in an implementation-defined way—throughout its execution). In order to perform any database operations, the SQL-agent must first cause the SQL-client to establish an *SQL-connection* to some *SQL-server* (another component of the overall SQL-environment). The SQL-server, in turn, is the component that will actually carry out the database operations requested by the SQL-agent. *Note:* In practice the SQL-client and SQL-server might be— and frequently will be—at one and the same site, but they need not be; the intent is to provide a basis for true remote database access, in which an SQL-agent at one site might genuinely be able to execute SQL operations on data at some distinct site, possibly a site that is geographically remote.

Establishing the necessary SQL-connection between client and server is performed by means of the CONNECT statement, which also has the effect of initiating an *SQL-session* over the SQL-connection. Once the SQL-connection has been established and the SQL-session initiated, the SQL-agent can carry out any number of *SQL-transactions* (see Section 2.7), until such time as it executes a DISCONNECT statement, which breaks the SQL-connection and terminates the SQL-session.

> *Aside:* Matters are a little more complex than the foregoing paragraph suggests. In fact, a given SQL-agent can initiate *multiple* SQL-connections and SQL-sessions, one after another; each such initiation puts the immediately preceding connection and session into a dormant state, but it is always possible to switch back to (i.e., reawaken) a dormant connection and session by means of another statement, SET CONNECTION. Furthermore, switching between connections and ses-

sions can even be done while a transaction is running, implying that a single transaction can span multiple connections and sessions. See Chapter 5 and Appendix D for further discussion. *End of aside.*

We should mention that (as with the business of using catalog and schema names as high-level qualifiers) explicit CONNECT and DISCONNECT operations will frequently be omitted in practice; again the standard includes an elaborate system of defaults, by which default connections and sessions are established and terminated at appropriate times if nothing is specified explicitly. See Chapter 5 for further discussion.

PART II

SOME PRELIMINARIES

This part of the book might be thought of as the "necessary evils" part. Its purpose is to spell out the rules for a number of fundamental issues (such as how to construct legal identifiers and what the scope of uniqueness of names is), and to define and explain certain common underlying constructs (such as sessions and schemas). *CAVEAT:* Much of this material is provided primarily for reference; it is NOT necessary to read these chapters exhaustively before moving on to later parts of the book—*in fact, it is probably better not even to try, owing to the excessive complexity of much of the subject matter.* However, later parts of the book will necessarily refer back to these chapters from time to time.

3

Basic Language Elements

3.1 SQL LANGUAGE CHARACTERS

The most primitive language elements of all are the individual characters
that constitute the *SQL language character set*. The characters of that character set—i.e., the *SQL language characters*—are used to construct higher-
level (nonprimitive) elements of the language. The SQL language character
set consists of the upper case letters A–Z, the lower case letters a–z, the
digits 0–9, and a set of *SQL special characters*; the SQL special characters,
in turn, are as follows:*

    " % & ' ( ) * + , - . / : ; < = > ? _ |

together with a space character. *Note:* For the remainder of this chapter,
the term "character" will be taken to mean an SQL language character
specifically, barring explicit statements to the contrary.

> *Aside:* A given SQL-implementation can support any number of dis-
> tinct character sets; however, it *must* support a character set called
> SQL_TEXT that includes all of the SQL language characters (and pos-
> sibly other characters as well). The whole subject of character sets is

---

*For the reader's information, the only use of the ampersand ("&") is in SQL embedded in
MUMPS.

quite complex, and for this reason we defer detailed discussion of that topic to Chapter 19. We warn the reader, however, that our discussion of identifiers in Section 3.4 below is therefore not quite complete. See Section 19.8. *End of aside.*

3.2 TOKENS AND SEPARATORS

Tokens and separators represent lexical units in the language. We discuss *tokens* first. A token is either a *delimiter* or a *nondelimiter*; the difference is that a delimiter *may* (but need not) be followed by a separator, whereas a nondelimiter *must* be followed by either a separator or a delimiter.

- A *delimiter* is any of the following: (a) a character string literal (see Chapter 7 for a discussion of literals); (b) a date, time, timestamp, or interval string (see Chapter 17); (c) a "delimited identifier" (see Section 3.4 below); (d) an SQL special character; or (e) one of the following symbols*—

  `<>    >=    <=    ||    ..    [    ]`

- A *nondelimiter* is any of the following: (a) a literal of type unsigned numeric, national character string, or bit string (including hexadecimal string); (b) a "regular identifier" (see Section 3.4 below); or (c) a key word (see Section 3.3 below).

Turning now to separators: A *separator* is any combination of spaces and/or newline markers and/or comments. (As already explained, delimiter tokens may optionally be followed by a separator, and nondelimiter tokens must be followed by either a separator or a delimiter.) *Spaces* are self-explanatory. A *newline marker* is an implementation-defined end-of-line indicator. A *comment* consists of two consecutive minus signs ("--"), followed by any sequence of zero or more characters (not necessarily SQL language characters), terminating with a newline marker. *Note:* The syntax notation introduced in Section 3.6 (later) simply ignores separators, for the most part.

No token is allowed to include any separators, except possibly for:

- Character string literals (including national character string literals)—see Chapters 7 and 19

- Bit string literals (including hexadecimal string literals)—see Chapter 7

---

*For the reader's information, the only use of the double period ("..") is in SQL embedded in Ada or Pascal, and the only use of brackets ("[" and "]") is in SQL embedded in Pascal or C.

- Timestamp strings and "day-time intervals" (a special case of interval strings)—see Chapter 17
- Delimited identifiers—see Section 3.4 below

In the foregoing cases certain embedded separators are both allowed and significant, as will be seen.

3.3   KEY WORDS

A *key word* is a word that has some prescribed meaning within the SQL language itself. Some key words are reserved (i.e., cannot be used as a regular identifier), others are not. Here first is a list of those that are reserved:

```
ABSOLUTE  ACTION  ADD  ALL  ALLOCATE  ALTER  AND  ANY  ARE  AS
ASC  ASSERTION  AT  AUTHORIZATION  AVG

BEGIN  BETWEEN  BIT  BIT_LENGTH  BOTH  BY

CASCADE  CASCADED  CASE  CAST  CATALOG  CHAR  CHARACTER
CHAR_LENGTH  CHARACTER_LENGTH  CHECK  CLOSE  COALESCE  COLLATE
COLLATION  COLUMN  COMMIT  CONNECT  CONNECTION  CONSTRAINT
CONSTRAINTS  CONTINUE  CONVERT  CORRESPONDING  COUNT  CREATE
CROSS  CURRENT  CURRENT_DATE  CURRENT_TIME  CURRENT_TIMESTAMP
CURRENT_USER  CURSOR

DATE  DAY  DEALLOCATE  DEC  DECIMAL  DECLARE  DEFAULT
DEFERRABLE  DEFERRED  DELETE  DESC  DESCRIBE  DESCRIPTOR
DIAGNOSTICS  DISCONNECT  DISTINCT  DOMAIN  DOUBLE  DROP

ELSE  END  END-EXEC  ESCAPE  EXCEPT  EXCEPTION  EXEC  EXECUTE
EXISTS  EXTERNAL  EXTRACT

FALSE  FETCH  FIRST  FLOAT  FOR  FOREIGN  FOUND  FROM  FULL

GET  GLOBAL  GO  GOTO  GRANT  GROUP

HAVING  HOUR

IDENTITY  IMMEDIATE  IN  INDICATOR  INITIALLY  INNER  INPUT
INSENSITIVE  INSERT  INT  INTEGER  INTERSECT  INTERVAL  INTO
IS  ISOLATION

JOIN

KEY

LANGUAGE  LAST  LEADING  LEFT  LEVEL  LIKE  LOCAL  LOWER

MATCH  MAX  MIN  MINUTE  MODULE  MONTH

NAMES  NATIONAL  NATURAL  NCHAR  NEXT  NO  NOT  NULL  NULLIF
NUMERIC

OCTET_LENGTH  OF  ON  ONLY  OPEN  OPTION  OR  ORDER  OUTER
OUTPUT  OVERLAPS
```

PARTIAL   POSITION   PRECISION   PREPARE   PRESERVE   PRIMARY   PRIOR
PRIVILEGES   PROCEDURE   PUBLIC

READ   REAL   REFERENCES   RELATIVE   RESTRICT   REVOKE   RIGHT
ROLLBACK   ROWS

SCHEMA   SCROLL   SECOND   SECTION   SELECT   SESSION   SESSION_USER
SET   SIZE   SMALLINT   SOME   SQL   SQLCODE   SQLERROR   SQLSTATE
SUBSTRING   SUM   SYSTEM_USER

TABLE   TEMPORARY   THEN   TIME   TIMESTAMP   TIMEZONE_HOUR
TIMEZONE_MINUTE   TO   TRAILING   TRANSACTION   TRANSLATE
TRANSLATION   TRIM   TRUE

UNION   UNIQUE   UNKNOWN   UPDATE   UPPER   USAGE   USER   USING

VALUE   VALUES   VARCHAR   VARYING   VIEW

WHEN   WHENEVER   WHERE   WITH   WORK   WRITE

YEAR

ZONE

And here is a list of those that are not reserved:*

ADA

C   CATALOG_NAME   CHARACTER_SET_CATALOG   CHARACTER_SET_NAME
CHARACTER_SET_SCHEMA   CLASS_ORIGIN   COBOL   COLLATION_CATALOG
COLLATION_NAME   COLLATION_SCHEMA   COLUMN_NAME   COMMAND_FUNCTION
COMMITTED   CONDITION_NUMBER   CONNECTION_NAME   CONSTRAINT_CATALOG
CONSTRAINT_NAME   CONSTRAINT_SCHEMA   CURSOR_NAME

DATA   DATETIME_INTERVAL_CODE   DATETIME_INTERVAL_PRECISION
DYNAMIC_FUNCTION

FORTRAN

LENGTH

MESSAGE_LENGTH   MESSAGE_OCTET_LENGTH   MORE   MUMPS

NAME   NULLABLE   NUMBER

PAD   PASCAL   PLI

REPEATABLE   RETURNED_LENGTH   RETURNED_OCTET_LENGTH
RETURNED_SQLSTATE   ROW_COUNT

SCALE   SCHEMA_NAME   SERIALIZABLE   SERVER_NAME   SPACE
SUBCLASS_ORIGIN

TABLE_NAME   TYPE

UNCOMMITTED   UNNAMED

---

*The rule by which it is determined within the standard that one key word needs to be reserved while another need not be is not clear to this writer. In practice, it is probably wise to treat all key words as reserved.

Within key words, upper case and lower case letters are treated as interchangeable; thus, e.g., "WHERE" and "where" represent the same key word. In this book we will adhere to the convention by which key words are always given in all upper case (note that this same convention is used in the standard itself).

3.4 IDENTIFIERS AND NAMES

An *identifier* is either a regular identifier or a delimited identifier.

- A *regular* identifier is a string of not more than 128 characters, of which the first must be a letter (upper or lower case); the rest can be any combination of upper or lower case letters, digits, and the underscore character ("_"). No reserved key word can be used as a regular identifier.*

- A *delimited* identifier is any string of not more than 128 characters (not necessarily SQL language characters) enclosed in quotation marks; for example, SELECT is not a valid regular identifier, because it is identical to a reserved key word, but "SELECT" is a valid delimited identifier. Within such a string, the quotation mark character itself is represented by a pair of immediately adjacent quotation marks (such a quotation-mark pair counting, of course, as a single character with respect to the 128-character limit).

For the sake of simplicity, all identifiers used in examples in this book will be regular identifiers, and the unqualified term *identifier* will be taken to mean a regular identifier specifically, barring any explicit statement to the contrary. Furthermore, we will never include any lower case letters in any of our identifiers.

The following are all identifiers in the foregoing sense:

- authorization identifiers
- catalog names
- range variable names
  (or "correlation names"—see Chapter 11)
- module names
- procedure names

---

*The standard provides options by which the letters and digits in a regular identifier can be different from the letters and digits (A–Z, a–z, 0–9) of the SQL language character set. We ignore this possibility throughout this book, except in Chapter 19. Refer to Section 19.8 for further explanation.

- parameter names
  (except that a colon prefix is required—see Chapter 6)
- cursor names
- statement names

The following have names that consist of an identifier in the foregoing sense, preceded by a qualifier that is a catalog name (separated from the identifier by a period):

- schemas

The following have names that consist of an identifier in the foregoing sense, preceded by a qualifier that is a schema name (separated from the identifier by a period):

- domains
- base tables
- views
- constraints
- character sets
- collations
- translations
- conversions

> *Aside:* Collations, translations, and conversions have to do with the general topic of character sets and are discussed, along with character sets per se, in Chapter 19. Note that in the case of conversions the (implicit or explicit) schema name *must* be INFORMATION_ SCHEMA (i.e., conversions are always considered to belong to the Information Schema—see Chapter 21). Note finally that the standard also talks about *character repertoire* names and *form-of-use* names (again, see Chapter 19), but both of these are ultimately defined to be character set names, and so we exclude them from the foregoing list. *End of aside.*

The following have names that consist of an identifier in the foregoing sense, preceded by the key word MODULE (separated from the identifier by a period):

- declared local temporary tables
  (referred to as "Type 1" temporary tables in Chapter 18)

The following have names that consist of an identifier in the foregoing sense, preceded by a qualifier that is a base table name or view name (separated from the identifier by a period):

- columns within base tables and views

Notes:

1. All columns within named tables (i.e., base tables and views) are required by the standard to be named; those names are specified (possibly implicitly, in the case of views) as part of the base table or view definition. The standard also includes a set of rules defining names of columns within *un*named tables (i.e., tables that result from evaluating some table expression), but those column names are sometimes system-generated (and implementation-dependent) and concealed from the user. Refer to Chapter 11 (Section 11.7) for further explanation.

2. As mentioned in Chapter 2, the standard provides a set of default rules by which high-level components can often be omitted from qualified names and suitable defaults assumed. Thus, e.g., the catalog name component might be omitted from a schema name, in which case an appropriate catalog name will be assumed by default. If a high-level qualifier is omitted from a given name, the period that would have separated that qualifier from the rest of the name is omitted too. The default rules are spelled out in detail at appropriate points in the chapters that follow (primarily Chapters 4, 6, and 11).

3.5 UNIQUENESS OF NAMES

In this section we summarize the rules regarding uniqueness of names. First, the following must be unique within the SQL-environment:

- authorization identifiers
  (note that the identifier PUBLIC is not allowed as an authorization identifier)
- catalog names
- module names

The following must be unique within their containing catalog:

- schema names
  (note that no schema can have an unqualified name of DEFINITION_ SCHEMA, and every catalog must include exactly one schema with the unqualified name INFORMATION_SCHEMA)

The following must be unique within the applicable schema:

- domain names
- table names
  ("table" here includes both base tables and views, i.e., a base table and a view cannot have the same unqualified name)
- constraint names
- character set names
- collation names
- translation names
- conversion names
  (as explained above, the applicable schema in this case is always the Information Schema)

The following must be unique within their containing module:

- procedure names
- cursor names
- statement names
- declared local temporary table names

The following must be unique within their containing procedure:

- parameter names

The following must be unique within their containing table (base table or view):

- column names within base tables and views

Finally, range variable names are unique within a certain scope as defined in Chapter 11 (Section 11.3).

Notes:

1. When we say that names of a certain type must be unique within a certain scope, we mean they must be unique with respect to all names *of that type* within that scope. Thus, when we say, for example, that domain names and constraint names must be unique within their containing schema, we mean that no two domains within a given schema can have the same name, and likewise for constraints. However, a domain and a constraint within a given schema can have the same name if desired.

2. All columns within named tables (i.e., base tables and views) are re-
    quired by the standard to have names that are unique within their con-
    taining table. In certain circumstances, however, columns within *un-
    named tables*—i.e., tables that result from evaluating some table
    expression—are (very unfortunately, in this writer's opinion) allowed
    to have nonunique names. In this book we will generally assume that
    all columns have names that are unique within their containing table,
    barring some explicit statement to the contrary. Refer to Chapter 11
    (Section 11.7) for further explanation.

3. Certain objects, namely *SQL-servers, SQL-sessions, SQL-connections,
    SQL-transactions,* and *SQL-agents* (see Chapters 4 and 5), are omitted
    from the lists given in this section because, although those objects most
    certainly do have names, those names are not necessarily identifiers
    (qualified or unqualified) as defined above.

4. Finally, certain objects that are used in connection with the dynamic
    SQL feature (see Chapter 20) are also omitted from the lists given
    above because, although those objects do have names that are indeed
    identifiers as defined above, those identifiers are *generated* by the user
    at run time. The objects in question are *SQL descriptor areas,* certain
    cursors, and certain *statements.* Furthermore, those user-generated
    names* can be defined to have either LOCAL or GLOBAL scope;
    LOCAL means the scope is the containing *module,* GLOBAL means it
    is the current *SQL-session.* The reader is referred to Chapter 20 for
    more details.

3.6 NOTATION

The syntax of SQL language elements is specified in this book by means of
a variant of the well-known BNF notation. The variant in question is defined as follows:

-   Special characters and material in upper case must be written exactly
    as shown. Material in lower case represents a syntactic category that
    appears on the left hand side of another production rule,[†] and hence
    must (eventually) be replaced by specific values chosen by the user.

-   Vertical bars "|" are used to separate alternatives.

---

*Which are represented in an implementation-defined character set, incidentally (see Chapter
19).

[†]In this book, however, some of the production rules at the lowest level of detail, such as the
rules that define the construction of an identifier, are not shown in explicit BNF style but are
instead explained in ordinary prose.

- Square brackets "[" and "]" are used to indicate that the material enclosed in those brackets is optional; i.e., it consists of a set of one or more items (separated by vertical bars) from which at most one is to be chosen.

- Braces "{" and "}" are used to indicate that the material enclosed in those braces consists of a set of several items (separated by vertical bars) from which exactly one is to be chosen.

By way of example, we show a possible set of production rules for the syntactic category "unsigned numeric literal" (see Chapter 7 for a full description of literals):

```
unsigned-numeric-literal
    ::=    unsigned-exact-numeric-literal
        |  unsigned-approximate-numeric-literal

unsigned-exact-numeric-literal
    ::=    unsigned-integer [ . [ unsigned-integer ] ]
        |  . unsigned-integer

unsigned-approximate-numeric-literal
    ::=    unsigned-exact-numeric-literal  E  signed-integer

signed-integer
    ::=    [ + | - ] unsigned-integer
```

The category "unsigned integer" is not further defined here; i.e., it is a *terminal category* with respect to this simple example. (Note, incidentally, that although the production rules shown in this example include numerous embedded spaces for readability reasons, "unsigned numeric literals" are tokens—see Section 3.2—and in fact must *not* include any such spaces.)

Here is another example to illustrate the use of braces (this rule shows the syntax of the *fold* function, which is used to replace upper case letters by their lower case equivalents or vice versa):

```
fold-function-reference
    ::=    { LOWER | UPPER } ( character-string-expression )
```

So far our BNF notation is essentially the same as that used in the SQL standard documentation.* However, we introduce two further simplifying conventions of our own, as follows. First, we define a *syntactic unit* to be either (a) a syntactic category (i.e., something that appears on the left hand

---

*Except that the standard distinguishes syntactic categories by enclosing them in angle brackets, whereas we use hyphenated word strings. For example, we use *unsigned-integer* where the standard uses < *unsigned integer* >. In less formal contexts, we drop the hyphens and enclose the term in quotation marks—for example, "unsigned integer" (see the discussion above). If there is no risk of confusion we might even drop the quotation marks as well.

side of some BNF production rule), or (b) whatever is contained between a pair of matching square brackets or a pair of matching braces. Then:

- If "xyz" is a syntactic unit, then "xyz-list" is a syntactic unit consisting of a sequence of one or more "xyz"s in which each pair of adjacent "xyz"s is separated by at least one separator (i.e., a space, comment, or newline marker).

- If "xyz" is a syntactic unit, then "xyz-commalist" is a syntactic unit consisting of a sequence of one or more "xyz"s in which each pair of adjacent "xyz"s is separated by a comma.

These two rules have the net effect of reducing the overall length and number of production rules required. Here is an example to illustrate their use (a simplified variant of the first few production rules for the CREATE SCHEMA statement, which is discussed in detail in Chapter 4 and later chapters):

```
schema-definition
    ::=    CREATE SCHEMA [ schema ] [ AUTHORIZATION user ]
              [ schema-element-list ]

schema-element
    ::=    base-table-definition
         | view-definition

base-table-definition
    ::=    CREATE TABLE base-table
              ( base-table-element-commalist )

base-table-element
    ::=    column-definition
         | base-table-constraint-definition
```

And so on.

One further point regarding notation: In our BNF we follow the convention that if *xyz* is an SQL object type (e.g., "schema"), then in syntax rules the syntactic category *xyz* stands for the *name* of an object of that type. For example, in the syntax rule already discussed—

```
schema-definition
    ::=    CREATE SCHEMA [ schema ] [ AUTHORIZATION user ]
              [ schema-element-list ]
```

—the syntactic category "schema" stands for a schema name.

Note: We often deliberately use names for syntactic categories that are different from those in the SQL standard. Our primary reason for doing this is that the SQL standard nomenclature is often not particularly apt. As one example, the standard actually uses "qualified identifier" to mean, quite specifically, an *un*qualified identifier. . . . As a second example, the standard uses "table definition" to refer to what we called a "base table definition" above. This usage obscures the important fact that a *view* is also a defined table, and hence that "table definition" ought to include "view definition" as a special case. To pursue this latter point a moment longer: In fact, SQL is generally ambivalent as to the meaning of the term "table"; sometimes it takes it to mean either a base table or a view, sometimes it takes it to mean a base table explicitly. In this book we will use "table" to mean *any* kind of table (base table, view, or more generally the result of evaluating any arbitrary table expression); we will use "base table" explicitly when a base table is what we mean.

4

Catalogs and Schemas

4.1 THE SQL-ENVIRONMENT

As explained in Chapter 2, the SQL standard starts with the concept of an *SQL-environment*, which is effectively an abstraction of the notion of an operational DBMS installation. More precisely, an SQL-environment is defined to consist of the following components:

- An *SQL-implementation*
- Any number of *authorization identifiers* ("authIDs")
- Any number of *modules*
- Any number of *catalogs*
- SQL-data as described by the *SQL-schemas* in the catalogs
- Optionally, other implementation-defined components

  We briefly elaborate on these concepts as follows.

- First, the *SQL-implementation* is effectively just the DBMS itself (i.e., the DBMS *instance*). It must support (a) standard SQL operations to at least Entry level (see Appendix B) and (b) at least one "binding style" (i.e., direct SQL, embedded SQL, or "module"—see Chapter 6).

- Second, an *authorization identifier* (authID for short) can be thought of, informally, as the name by which some user is known to the system;

indeed, we will often use the term "user" in this book instead of "authorization identifier" or "authID." Please note, however, that the standard does not really know anything about "users" as such, it only knows about authIDs.

- Third, a *module* consists essentially of a set of SQL statements that may be executed by a given "compilation unit" (i.e., application program, loosely speaking). Note that regardless of binding style, SQL statements are *always* considered to be contained within some module, at least conceptually.*

- *Catalogs* and *SQL-schemas* (schemas for short) are discussed in more detail in Sections 4.2 and 4.3 below.

We remind the reader that SQL operations are not allowed to span SQL-environments, although they *are* allowed to span schemas, and even catalogs (but not clusters of catalogs), within the same SQL-environment.

4.2 CATALOGS

A catalog is a named collection of schemas within an SQL-environment. For example, a given SQL-environment might include two catalogs called TEST_CAT and PRODUCTION_CAT, describing test and production versions of "the same" database; moving an application over from test to production might then be a simple matter of recompilation (provided the application in question did not explicitly mention either catalog by name, of course). Or different catalogs might correspond to databases at different sites, if the SQL-environment involved some kind of distributed processing.

The standard does not provide any explicit mechanism for creating and dropping (i.e., destroying) catalogs; instead, catalogs are created and dropped in some implementation-defined manner.

As explained in Chapter 3, the catalog name serves as the high-level qualifier for the qualified names of schemas that are contained within the catalog in question. If some schema reference omits the catalog name, a *default* catalog name is assumed, as follows:†

- If the schema reference appears within the SCHEMA clause (or is implied by the AUTHORIZATION clause) of a module definition—see

---

*Except for (a) the nonexecutable statements WHENEVER and BEGIN and END DECLARE SECTION, which appear in embedded SQL only, and (b) certain "standalone" CREATE SCHEMA statements. For a discussion of the second of these two possibilities—it is not clear that it actually *is* a possibility, but if it is it is much the more important of the two—see the subsection "Standalone CREATE SCHEMA Statements" at the end of this chapter.

†We ignore the case here of unqualified references in dynamic SQL. See Chapter 20, Section 20.6.

the subsection "Module Definition" in Chapter 6, Section 6.2—then an implementation-defined catalog name is assumed.

- If the schema reference appears as the schema name (or is implied by the AUTHORIZATION clause) of a CREATE SCHEMA statement, then the catalog name associated with the containing module is assumed.*

- If the schema reference appears in a CREATE SCHEMA statement (other than as described in the previous paragraph), then the catalog name for the schema currently being defined is assumed.

- Otherwise, the catalog name associated with the module that contains the schema reference is assumed (again, see the subsection "Module Definition" in Chapter 6, Section 6.2).

Note: When we talk about a "schema reference," the reader should understand that the commonest occurrence of such a construct is most likely to be as an implicit or explicit qualifier in a reference to some other object, such as a base table.

4.3 SCHEMAS

A schema (more correctly, an *SQL-schema*) is a named collection of "descriptors" within a catalog. To quote the standard, a *descriptor* is "a coded description of an SQL object [that includes] all of the information about the object that a conforming SQL-implementation requires." Each schema contains descriptors for the following types of objects (in general):

- domains
- base tables
- views
- constraints
- privileges
- character sets
- collations
- translations

   Aside: The astute reader might observe a couple of discrepancies between the foregoing list and the list of objects that were stated in Chap-

---

*Note that there always is such a containing module, unless the CREATE SCHEMA is "standalone," in which case an implementation-defined catalog name is assumed. See the subsection "Standalone CREATE SCHEMA Statements" at the end of this chapter.

ter 3 to have names that were "unique within schema." First, *privileges* are described in schemas but do not have names (see Chapter 15). Second, *conversions* have names but are not described in schemas (see Chapter 19). *End of aside.*

Schemas are created and dropped (i.e., destroyed) by means of the CREATE SCHEMA and DROP SCHEMA statements, which we now describe. First, CREATE SCHEMA. The syntax is:

```
CREATE SCHEMA [ schema ] [ AUTHORIZATION user ]
              [ DEFAULT CHARACTER SET character-set ]
              [ schema-element-list ]
```

At least one of "schema" and "AUTHORIZATION user" must appear (see below). We defer explanation of the optional DEFAULT CHARACTER SET clause to Chapter 19. The possible "schema elements" are as follows:

- domain definitions
- base table definitions
- view definitions
- grant statements
- constraint definitions
- character set definitions
- collation definitions
- translation definitions

Each of these items is explained in detail later in this book.

To return to the "schema" and "AUTHORIZATION user" specifications: As already mentioned, at least one and possibly both of these specifications will appear; their purpose is to provide a name for the new schema and to identify the schema's owner, respectively. The effect of omitting one or other of these specifications is as follows:

- If the "schema" specification is omitted, then the "user" value from "AUTHORIZATION user" is taken as the schema name.*
- If "AUTHORIZATION user" is omitted, then the authID of the containing module is taken as the schema owner†—or, if that module does not have an explicit authID, then the SQL-session authID is taken in-

---

*I.e., as the *unqualified* schema name. The corresponding catalog name is decided as explained in Section 4.2 above.

†We are assuming here that the CREATE SCHEMA is not "standalone." See the subsection "Standalone CREATE SCHEMA Statements" at the end of this section.

stead (see the subsection "Module Definition" in Chapter 6, Section 6.2).

We turn now to DROP SCHEMA. The syntax is:

```
DROP SCHEMA schema { RESTRICT | CASCADE }
```

If RESTRICT is specified, the operation will fail unless the specified schema is empty (i.e., contains no descriptors); if CASCADE is specified, the operation will succeed, and will cascade to drop not only the specified schema per se, but also all objects contained in that schema and all objects described by that schema. Assuming the operation is successful, therefore, the effect is to destroy the specified schema (i.e., delete it from the relevant catalog), along with all objects—if any—that it contains and/or describes.

As explained in Chapter 3, schema names (including the implicit or explicit catalog-name component) serve as the high-level qualifier for the qualified names of objects that are associated with the schema in question. If a reference to such an object omits the schema name, a *default* schema name is assumed, as follows:*

- If the reference appears within a CREATE SCHEMA statement, then the schema name for the schema currently being defined is assumed.

- Otherwise, the schema name associated with the module that contains the reference is assumed (note that such a module does always exist— see the subsection "Module Definition" in Chapter 6, Section 6.2).

Standalone CREATE SCHEMA Statements

The standard refers repeatedly to the idea that, regardless of binding style, all SQL statements—at least, all executable SQL statements—are always contained within some module, with the sole possible exception of CREATE SCHEMA statements, which might be "standalone." The reason for the exception is compatibility with SQL/86 and SQL/89, where CREATE SCHEMA statements *had* to be standalone; in fact, the only "official" way of performing data definition operations of any kind in SQL/86 and SQL/89 was in the context of such a standalone CREATE SCHEMA statement (although most vendors went beyond the standard in this respect and allowed data definition operations to be performed from within application programs).

It is now generally agreed that forcing CREATE SCHEMA statements to be standalone was a mistake in SQL/86 and SQL/89. For reasons of

---

*Again we ignore the case of unqualified references in dynamic SQL. See Chapter 20, Section 20.6.

compatibility, however (and also because some vendors did in fact implement some kind of standalone schema processor), the new standard does still permit CREATE SCHEMA statements to stand alone.* But it is not intended that such should be the normal method of operation. In subsequent chapters, therefore, we will generally assume that, indeed, there always is a containing module; here we simply summarize those features of the standard that seem to rely on the possibility that CREATE SCHEMA statements might somehow be "standalone."

- If the standalone CREATE SCHEMA does not include an AUTHORIZATION clause, then the owner of the new schema is taken to be the SQL-session authID instead of the module authID (see Chapter 5, Section 5.3).

- Identifiers and character string literals appearing within a standalone CREATE SCHEMA are assumed by default to be using *either* the SQL language character set (see Chapter 3) *or* the default character set of the schema (see Chapter 19).

---

*It would be more accurate to say that it does not explicitly prohibit such a possibility. Certainly it is not clear from the standard how CREATE SCHEMA (or any other statement, come to that) can possibly *not* be contained within a module.

5

Connections, Sessions, and Transactions

5.1 SQL-AGENTS

As explained in Chapter 2, an *SQL-agent* can be thought of as the execution of an application program (the standard defines it as "an implementation-dependent entity that causes the execution of SQL-statements"). In order for an SQL-agent to be able to issue SQL requests, that SQL-agent must first execute an (explicit or implicit) CONNECT statement. A successful CONNECT establishes an *SQL-connection* between (a) the *SQL-client* (that component of the SQL-environment under the control of which the SQL-agent starts execution) and (b) a *SQL-server* (another component of the SQL-environment that is capable of performing SQL database operations). All subsequent SQL requests from the SQL-agent (except for CONNECT, DISCONNECT, SET CONNECTION, and GET DIAGNOSTICS requests) will be executed by the SQL-server to which the SQL-client is currently connected.

Establishing an SQL-connection also initiates an *SQL-session* over that SQL-connection. The SQL-agent can then execute any number of *SQL-transactions* (but only one at a time; i.e., each SQL-transaction must be executed in its entirety before the next can begin).

Note that the SQL-agent can establish any number of SQL-connections, and thus initiate any number of SQL-sessions; it is not necessary to terminate the current SQL-connection before starting up a new one. However, starting up a new one makes the previous one *dormant* (only one SQL-connection can actually be *current* at any given time). Likewise, only one SQL-session can be current at any time, namely the SQL-session that is associated with the current SQL-connection; SQL-sessions that are associated with dormant SQL-connections are themselves considered to be dormant also. The SET CONNECTION statement allows the SQL-agent to make a dormant SQL-connection (and SQL-session) current again—thereby, of course, making the previously current SQL-connection (and SQL-session) dormant.

When the SQL-agent is finished with a given SQL-connection and SQL-session, it must execute a DISCONNECT statement (again, either explicitly or implicitly), which has the effect of breaking the specified SQL-connection and terminating the corresponding SQL-session.

We now proceed to elaborate on the concepts *SQL-connection, SQL-session,* and *SQL-transaction.*

5.2 SQL-CONNECTIONS

CONNECT

SQL-connections can be established either explicitly or implicitly. The explicit case is handled by means of an explicit CONNECT statement; the implicit case occurs if an SQL-agent invokes a procedure (see Chapter 6) when no SQL-session is currently active, in which case the system automatically issues an implicit CONNECT on the SQL-agent's behalf (except as noted at the end of this subsection). Here is the syntax of CONNECT:

```
CONNECT TO { DEFAULT | string1 [ AS string2 ] [ USER string3 ] }
```

Each of *string1, string2,* and *string3* is a literal, parameter, or host variable, of type character string in each case. *Note:* The phrase "parameter or host variable" appears many times in the standard, and many times in the present book. In all cases, the significance is as follows: If the context is the module language (see Section 6.2), then a parameter is required; if the context is embedded SQL (see Section 6.3), then a host variable is required.

- *Case 1* (DEFAULT): An SQL-connection is established to a "default SQL-server." A "default SQL-connection" is established and a "default SQL-session" is initiated. None of these "default" concepts is further defined in the standard.

■   *Case 2* (otherwise): An SQL-connection is established to the SQL-server identified (in an implementation-defined way) by the value of *string1*. The value of *string2,* if specified, becomes the name of the new SQL-connection; if *string2* is omitted, it defaults to the value of *string1*. The value of *string3,* if specified, defines an authorization identifier for the new SQL-session; if *string3* is omitted, it defaults to an implementation-defined value.

In both cases:

1. The new SQL-connection and SQL-session become current and the previous ones (if any) become dormant.
2. It is an error if the SQL-agent already has an SQL-connection with the same name (or if DEFAULT is specified and the SQL-agent already has a default SQL-connection).
3. It is an error if the SQL-agent currently has an active SQL-transaction and the SQL-implementation does not support SQL-transactions that span multiple SQL-servers.*

As mentioned above, if an SQL-agent invokes a procedure and no SQL-session is currently active, the system will automatically issue an implicit CONNECT TO DEFAULT on the SQL-agent's behalf[†]—*unless* the SQL-agent has previously executed any explicit CONNECT, SET CONNECTION, or DISCONNECT statements. If the latter is the case, an attempt to invoke a procedure when no SQL-session is currently active is treated as an error. The general intent is that a given SQL-agent *either* use explicit CONNECTs, DISCONNECTs, etc., *or* perform all such operations implicitly; mixing the two approaches is not allowed, with the minor exception that any number of implicit CONNECTs (etc.) can be performed before the first explicit one.

SET CONNECTION

SET CONNECTION is used to switch to a dormant SQL-connection and SQL-session (making them current and the previously current ones dormant). The syntax is:

---

*And hence span multiple *SQL-sessions* also. Such a possibility does not accord well with the usual intuitive interpretation of the terms "transaction" and "session," but it seems to be what the standard is saying.

[†]Or an implicit SET CONNECTION DEFAULT, if the SQL-agent has an associated default SQL-connection. This possibility is intended to cater for the situation in which a communication failure occurs and the current connection is the implicit default connection; to recover from such a failure, the system will try an implicit SET CONNECTION DEFAULT.

```
SET CONNECTION { DEFAULT | string }
```

String here is a literal, parameter, or host variable, of type character string, whose value is an SQL-connection name.

- *Case 1* (DEFAULT): The default SQL-connection and default SQL-session are made current.

- *Case 2* (otherwise): The SQL-connection whose name is given by the value of *string* and the corresponding SQL-session are made current.

In both cases:

1. The *context information* for the revived SQL-connection and SQL-session is restored to the state it was in when that SQL-connection and SQL-session became dormant. *Note:* "Context information" includes such things as the current authorization identifier, the current position for all open cursors, the current transaction isolation level, the current diagnostics area size, and so forth. For further details, the reader is referred to the standard.

2. It is an error if the SQL-agent currently has an active SQL-transaction and the SQL-implementation does not support SQL-transactions that span multiple SQL-servers.

Note that it is not an error if the specified SQL-connection is in fact the current SQL-connection, i.e., is in fact not dormant.

DISCONNECT

According to the standard, SQL-connections (and the corresponding SQL-sessions) are terminated either explicitly, by means of an explicit DISCONNECT statement, or implicitly "following the last call to a procedure within the last active module, or by the last execution of a direct SQL statement through the direct invocation of SQL." We concentrate here on the explicit case. Here is the syntax of DISCONNECT:

```
DISCONNECT { DEFAULT | CURRENT | ALL | string }
```

Once again, *string* here is a literal, parameter, or host variable, of type character string, whose value is an SQL-connection name.

- *Case 1* (DEFAULT): The default SQL-connection is terminated. It is an error if that SQL-connection is neither current nor dormant.

- *Case 2* (CURRENT): The current SQL-connection is terminated. It is an error if there is no current SQL-connection.

- *Case 3* (ALL): The current SQL-connection (if any) and all dormant SQL-connections (if any) are terminated.
- *Case 4* (otherwise): The SQL-connection whose name is given by the value of *string* is terminated. It is an error if the specified SQL-connection is neither current nor dormant.

In all cases, it is an error if any of the SQL-connections to be terminated is involved in an SQL-transaction that is still active.*

5.3 SQL-SESSIONS

Each SQL-session has an implementation-dependent name that is unique with respect to the set of currently active SQL-sessions; this name is used (conceptually) in the definition of certain "temporary schemas" that are used to hold descriptors for certain "temporary tables" (see Chapter 18). Each SQL-session also has a number of associated default values for use in certain contexts (assuming in every case, of course, that the user does not provide an appropriate override value). The default values in question are as follows:

- a default authorization identifier
- a default catalog name
- a default schema name
- a default time zone
- a default character set name

Each of these items is set to an implementation-defined "default value" when the SQL-session is initiated,[†] but can subsequently be changed by means of a SET SESSION AUTHORIZATION statement, SET CATALOG statement, SET SCHEMA statement, SET TIME ZONE statement, or SET NAMES statement, as appropriate. SET CATALOG, SET SCHEMA, and SET NAMES have to do with the dynamic SQL feature (also with direct SQL) and are discussed in Chapter 20; SET TIME ZONE has to do with SQL's date and time support and is discussed in Chapter

---

*Remember that we are concerned here with *explicit* DISCONNECT. If instead an SQL-connection is terminated *implicitly,* and an SQL-transaction was active on that SQL-connection, then (a) if an unrecoverable error has occurred in that SQL-transaction, the system automatically executes a ROLLBACK; (b) otherwise, it automatically executes *either* a ROLLBACK *or* a COMMIT (it is implementation-dependent which).

[†]Except that the default authorization identifier can also be set explicitly by means of the USER option on the CONNECT statement. See Section 5.2.

17; SET SESSION AUTHORIZATION is discussed immediately following. The syntax is:

```
SET SESSION AUTHORIZATION { string | user-function }
```

Here *string* is a literal, parameter, or host variable (of type character string in each case), whose value is an authorization identifier, and "user function" is any of the following:

```
USER
CURRENT_USER
SESSION_USER
SYSTEM_USER
```

USER, CURRENT_USER, SESSION_USER, and SYSTEM_USER are all niladic builtin functions* that return an authorization identifier. For further explanation, refer to Chapters 7 and 15.

It is an error to attempt to SET SESSION AUTHORIZATION if the SQL-agent currently has an active SQL-transaction.

5.4 SQL-TRANSACTIONS

An *SQL-transaction* is a *logical unit of work*; i.e., it is a sequence of SQL operations—both data manipulation and data definition operations, in general[†]—that is guaranteed to be atomic for the purposes of recovery. *Note:* Individual SQL operations are *always* atomic, in the sense that they either execute in their entirety or they leave the database unchanged—they cannot fail in the middle and leave the database in an inconsistent state.

An SQL-transaction is initiated when the relevant SQL-agent executes a "transaction-initiating" SQL statement (see below) and the SQL-agent does not already have an SQL-transaction in progress. (Note, therefore, that SQL-transactions cannot be nested. Note too that transaction initiation is always implicit—there is no explicit "BEGIN TRANSACTION" statement.) Each SQL-transaction terminates either with a COMMIT statement ("termination with commit") or with a ROLLBACK statement ("termination with rollback").

Changes made by a given SQL-transaction $T1$ do not become visible to any distinct transaction $T2$ until and unless transaction $T1$ terminates with commit. Termination with commit causes all changes made by the transac-

---

*The term "niladic builtin function" (meaning a builtin function that takes no arguments) is not used in the standard, but there does not seem to be any term that *is* used for the concept either, at least not consistently. In this book we will stay with our term.

[†]Whether data manipulation and data definition operations can in fact be mixed together in the same SQL-transaction is implementation-defined.

tion to become visible to other transactions; such changes are said to be committed, and are guaranteed never to be canceled. Termination with rollback causes all changes made by the transaction to be canceled; such changes will never become visible to other transactions at all.

Note: The foregoing paragraph assumes that all transactions execute at isolation level READ COMMITTED, REPEATABLE READ, or SERIALIZABLE. Special considerations apply to transactions executing at READ UNCOMMITTED isolation level (see the subsection "Concurrency" at the end of this section).

Transaction-Initiating Statements

The following SQL statements are *not* transaction-initiating:

```
CONNECT
SET CONNECTION
DISCONNECT
SET SESSION AUTHORIZATION
SET CATALOG
SET SCHEMA
SET NAMES
SET TIME ZONE
GET DIAGNOSTICS
SET TRANSACTION
SET CONSTRAINTS
COMMIT
ROLLBACK
DECLARE CURSOR
DECLARE LOCAL TEMPORARY TABLE
BEGIN DECLARE SECTION
END DECLARE SECTION
WHENEVER
```

(Futhermore, SET SESSION AUTHORIZATION and SET TRANSACTION can be executed only if no transaction is in progress. It is implementation-defined whether the same is true of CONNECT and SET CONNECTION.) All other SQL statements are transaction-initiating, except possibly for the EXECUTE and EXECUTE IMMEDIATE statements (see Chapter 20), which are transaction-initiating if and only if their target—i.e., the SQL statement to be executed by the EXECUTE or EXECUTE IMMEDIATE in question—is transaction-initiating in turn. Refer to Chapter 6 for a complete list of SQL statements.

COMMIT and ROLLBACK

As indicated above, an SQL-transaction terminates by executing either a COMMIT operation (normal or successful termination) or a ROLLBACK operation (abnormal or unsuccessful termination). Here first are the specifics of COMMIT. The syntax is:

```
COMMIT [ WORK ]
```

An implicit CLOSE is executed for every open cursor (see Chapter 10). An implicit SET CONSTRAINTS ALL IMMEDIATE is executed (see Chapter 14). An implicit DELETE FROM *T* is executed for every temporary table *T* for which ON COMMIT DELETE was specified (see Chapter 18). All changes made by this SQL-transaction since its initiation are committed (i.e., made permanent). The SQL-transaction is terminated successfully* ("termination with commit").

The optional specification WORK is a pure noiseword and can be omitted without affecting the semantics of the operation.

And here are the specifics of ROLLBACK. The syntax is:

```
ROLLBACK [ WORK ]
```

An implicit CLOSE is executed for every open cursor (see Chapter 10). All changes made by this SQL-transaction since its initiation are canceled (i.e., undone). The SQL-transaction is terminated unsuccessfully ("termination with rollback"). Again, the optional specification WORK is a pure noiseword and can be omitted without affecting the semantics of the operation.

Note: The standard explicitly permits an implementation to use non-SQL statements (i.e., statements other than COMMIT and ROLLBACK) to terminate transactions, in order to allow an SQL DBMS to act as just one "resource manager" within some larger context—e.g., to allow an SQL-transaction to perform (nonSQL) operations on some nonSQL database. No matter what statements are used to terminate a transaction, however, successful termination must cause the actions defined for COMMIT to be performed, and unsuccessful termination must cause the actions defined for ROLLBACK to be performed.

SET TRANSACTION

The SET TRANSACTION statement is used to define certain characteristics of the next SQL-transaction to be initiated. (Note that SET TRANSACTION can be executed only when no SQL-transaction is in progress, and is not itself transaction-initiating.) The characteristics in question are the *access mode,* the *diagnostics area size,* and the *isolation level.* The syntax is:

```
SET TRANSACTION option-list
```

---

*Assuming the COMMIT itself succeeds. If instead it fails (which it might do if, e.g., the implicit SET CONSTRAINTS ALL IMMEDIATE fails), the SQL-transaction fails also and is terminated with rollback.

where "option list" contains at most one access mode option, at most one diagnostics area size option, and at most one isolation level option.

The *access mode* option is either READ ONLY or READ WRITE. If neither is specified, READ WRITE is assumed, unless READ UNCOMMITTED isolation level is specified, in which case READ ONLY is assumed. If READ WRITE is specified, the isolation level must not be READ UNCOMMITTED. READ ONLY prohibits updates, of course, except to temporary tables (see Chapter 18); the standard does not say whether it also prohibits "SQL schema statements" (which imply updates to *schemas*).

The *diagnostics area size* option takes the form DIAGNOSTICS SIZE *n*, where *n* is a literal, parameter, or host variable of "exact numeric" type. The value of *n* (which must be greater than zero) specifies the number of "conditions" that can be held at any given time in the "diagnostics area" (see Chapter 22). If the diagnostics area size option is omitted, an implementation-defined value (at least 1) is assumed for *n*.

The *isolation level* option takes the form ISOLATION LEVEL *isolation,* where *isolation* is READ UNCOMMITTED, READ COMMITTED, REPEATABLE READ, or SERIALIZABLE. The default is SERIALIZABLE; if any of the other three is specified, the implementation is free to assign some greater level, where "greater" is defined in terms of the ordering SERIALIZABLE > REPEATABLE READ > READ COMMITTED > READ UNCOMMITTED. For further explanation, see the subsection on "Concurrency" below.

SET CONSTRAINTS

The SET CONSTRAINTS statement is used to define the "constraint mode" (IMMEDIATE or DEFERRED) for certain integrity constraints with respect to either the next SQL-transaction to be initiated (if there is no SQL-transaction currently in progress) or the current SQL-transaction (otherwise). We defer detailed discussion of this statement to Chapter 14.*

Concurrency

If all transactions execute at isolation level SERIALIZABLE (the default), then the interleaved execution of any set of concurrent transactions is guaranteed to be *serializable,* in the sense that it will produce the same effect as

---

*Except to note that the standard explicitly permits the implementation (optionally) to support transactions that span multiple sessions, and states that for such transactions the effects of SET CONSTRAINTS are limited to the current session. But this refinement leads to a number of further unanswered questions. See Appendix D.

some (unspecified) serial execution of those same transactions. However, if any transaction executes at a lesser isolation level, then serializability can be violated in a variety of different ways. More precisely, the standard defines three specific ways in which serializability might be violated: "dirty read," "nonrepeatable read," and "phantoms" (with the implication that these are the *only* permitted violations). We explain each of the three in turn.

- *Dirty read:* Suppose transaction *T1* performs an update on some row, transaction *T2* then retrieves that row, and transaction *T1* then terminates with rollback. Transaction *T2* has then seen a row that no longer exists, and in a sense never did exist (because transaction *T1* effectively never ran).

- *Nonrepeatable read:* Suppose transaction *T1* retrieves a row, transaction *T2* then updates that row, and transaction *T1* then retrieves the "same" row again. Transaction *T1* has now retrieved the "same" row twice but seen two different values for it.

- *Phantoms:* Suppose transaction *T1* retrieves the set of all rows that satisfy some condition (e.g., all supplier rows satisfying the condition that the supplier city is Paris). Suppose that transaction *T2* then inserts a new row satisfying that same condition. If transaction *T1* now repeats its retrieval request, it will see a row that did not previously exist—a "phantom."

More discussion of the foregoing possibilities can be found in C. J. Date, *An Introduction to Database Systems: Volume I* (5th edition, Addison-Wesley, 1990). None of them could occur in a serial execution, of course (and, to repeat, none of them can occur if all transactions execute at isolation level SERIALIZABLE).

The various isolation levels are defined in terms of which of the foregoing violations of serializability they permit. They are summarized in the table below (in which a "Y" means the indicated violation can occur, an "N" means it cannot).

isolation level	dirty read	nonrepeatable read	phantom
READ UNCOMMITTED	Y	Y	Y
READ COMMITTED	N	Y	Y
REPEATABLE READ	N	N	Y
SERIALIZABLE	N	N	N

Note 1: The standard states that "regardless of . . . isolation level, [the various serializability violations] shall not occur during the implied

reading of schema definitions performed on behalf of executing [a given SQL statement] . . . .'' The implications of this requirement are left for the reader to meditate on.

Note 2: A system that supports any isolation level other than SERIALIZABLE (which is, of course, the only totally *safe* level) would normally provide some explicit concurrency control facilities—e.g., explicit LOCK statements—in order to allow users to write their applications in such a way as to guarantee safety in the absence of such a guarantee from the system itself. For example, IBM's DB2 product currently supports two isolation levels that correspond to the standard levels READ COMMITTED and SERIALIZABLE, respectively. But it also provides an explicit LOCK TABLE statement, which allows users operating at the READ COMMITTED level to acquire explicit locks, over and above the ones that DB2 will acquire automatically to enforce that level. The standard, however, includes no such explicit concurrency control mechanisms.

6

Modules, Embedded SQL, and Direct SQL

6.1 BINDING STYLES

As mentioned in Chapter 4, the SQL standard requires an SQL-implementation to support at least one of three possible "binding styles," namely *direct SQL, embedded SQL,* or *module.* The term "binding style" is not defined very precisely in the standard, but it basically refers to the possible context(s) in which SQL statements can be used, or in other words to the various kinds of SQL interface that an implementation might be expected to support. The purpose of this chapter is to explain these concepts in detail.

6.2 THE MODULE LANGUAGE

We start with modules, since the module binding style is in a sense the most fundamental of the three.* The module concept originated with the ANSI committee—i.e., ANSI/X3H2—that defined the very first of the various SQL standards, viz. the one that subsequently became known as "SQL/

---

*This is true so far as the standard is concerned. In practice, however, embedded SQL is usually much more important, both from the user's perspective and from the implementer's.

86.'' Recall that the emphasis in every one of the SQL standards is on the *application programming* aspects of the SQL language. In attempting to define SQL/86, therefore, the ANSI/X3H2 committee was faced with a significant (though nontechnical) problem, namely as follows: ANSI-standard versions of languages such as COBOL and PL/I were already defined, and ANSI committees (e.g., ANSI/X3J4, in the case of COBOL) already existed to protect those standard definitions. Extending each of those standard languages separately to include the required SQL function would have involved a considerable amount of work—work, moreover, that generally would have had little to do with database technology per se—and would have delayed the appearance of an SQL standard by many years. Consequently, the committee proposed the so-called *module language* approach.

The module language is basically just a small language for expressing SQL operations in pure SQL syntactic form. The general idea is that each *compilation unit* (for instance, each PL/I "external procedure") has one or more associated *modules,* each consisting essentially of a set of *procedures*; and a procedure in turn consists essentially of a set of *parameter definitions* and a single *SQL statement* formulated in terms of those parameters. For example:

```
PROCEDURE DELETE_PART
        ( SQLSTATE,
          :PNO_PARAM CHAR(6) ) ;
    DELETE FROM P WHERE P.PNO = :PNO_PARAM ;
```

Note the SQLSTATE parameter, which is used to pass a status code back to the program that invokes the procedure.* A SQLSTATE value of 00000 means that the SQL statement executed successfully and no errors occurred; a value of 02000 means that no rows were found to satisfy the request; other values are discussed in Chapter 22.

The procedure shown above might be invoked from a PL/I program as follows:

```
DCL RETCODE CHAR(5) ;
DCL PNO_ARG CHAR(6) ;
DCL DELETE_PART ENTRY ( CHAR(5), CHAR(6) ) ;
.......
PNO_ARG = 'P2' ;              /* for example             */
CALL DELETE_PART ( RETCODE, PNO_ARG ) ;
IF RETCODE = '00000'
THEN ... ;                    /* delete operation succeeded  */
ELSE ... ;                    /* some exception occurred     */
```

Note (for readers who may be unfamiliar with PL/I): "DCL" is just a standard PL/I abbreviation for DECLARE; an "ENTRY" declaration is just a definition of an external "entry point" or procedure.

---

*SQLSTATE and SQLCODE (see later in this section) are the only exceptions to the general rule that parameter names must have a colon prefix.

The module language thus provides the ability for programs written in host languages such as PL/I, COBOL, etc., to execute SQL operations without requiring any change to the syntax or semantics of those languages. All that is required is:

1. The ability on the part of the host language to invoke procedures that are written in a different language and are separately compiled; together with

2. A correspondence (defined in the standard) between host and module language data types for argument-passing purposes.

In other words, the relationship between the host language and standard SQL is analogous to—actually identical to—that between two host languages: The host language program calls a separately compiled program (i.e., external procedure) that happens to be written in SQL, instead of in the host language under consideration or in some other host language.

As indicated above, each compilation unit can be associated with any number of modules during its execution. (One module per compilation unit is probably the normal case, however, and we will generally assume this case in our discussions.) How the association between compilation units and modules is established is implementation-defined; so too are the mechanisms by which modules are created and dropped. It is also implementation-defined as to whether one compilation unit can pass control to another at execution time.

Note carefully that, at least from a conceptual point of view, there is *always* a module at execution time, even if the binding style is "embedded SQL" or "direct" (see Sections 6.3 and 6.4 below). To repeat from Chapter 4, therefore, a module can be thought of essentially as a set of SQL statements available for execution by a given compilation unit, and SQL statements are *always*—conceptually, at least —executed within the context of some module;* even statements that are "prepared and executed dynamically" are considered to belong to a module, as we shall see in Chapter 20.

Here then is a definition of the module language.

Module Definition

```
module-definition
    ::=   MODULE [ module ] [ NAMES ARE character-set ]
          LANGUAGE { ADA | C | COBOL | FORTRAN | MUMPS
                                              | PASCAL | PLI }
          [ SCHEMA schema ] [ AUTHORIZATION user ]
          [ temporary-table-definition-list ]
          module-element-list
```

_____

*Except possibly for certain CREATE SCHEMA statements, as explained in Chapter 4.

Syntax notes:

1. If "module" is omitted, the module is unnamed. Note that no two modules within the same SQL-environment can have the same name, but any number can be unnamed.

2. We defer explanation of the optional NAMES clause to Chapter 19.

3. The LANGUAGE clause specifies the host language from which procedures within the module will be invoked.

4. At least one of "SCHEMA schema" and "AUTHORIZATION user" must appear (see below).

5. We defer explanation of the optional list of temporary table definitions to Chapter 18.

6. The possible "module elements" are as follows:

   - cursor definitions

   - dynamic cursor definitions

   - procedures

   Cursor definitions (dynamic or otherwise) are explained in detail later in this book; procedures are discussed below.

The purpose of the "SCHEMA schema" and "AUTHORIZATION user" specifications is as follows:

- First, the SCHEMA specification provides a default schema name for use in object references within the module that do not include any schema name explicitly.* If the SCHEMA specification is omitted, then the "user" value from "AUTHORIZATION user" is used as the schema name[†] (note that "AUTHORIZATION user" must be specified if "SCHEMA schema" is omitted). Observe, therefore, that every module *always* has an associated schema. *Note:* If "SCHEMA schema" is specified but defines only an unqualified schema name, an implementation-defined catalog name is assumed by default.

- Second, the AUTHORIZATION specification effectively identifies the module's *owner* (though the standard does not actually talk in terms of modules being "owned"). The specified user, or rather authorization identifier, must hold all necessary privileges for all SQL operations to

---

*Apart from object references within a CREATE SCHEMA statement, for which the schema name for the schema currently being defined is taken as the default. Also, we are ignoring dynamic SQL (see Chapter 20, Section 20.6).

[†]I.e., as the *unqualified* schema name. The corresponding catalog name is implementation-defined.

be executed within the module. If the AUTHORIZATION specification is omitted, then the module does not have an explicit owner; instead, a "user" value is assumed *at run time* that is equal to the authID for the SQL-session. In other words, it is the SQL-session authID that has to hold all the necessary privileges in this case. See Chapter 5, Section 5.3, for a discussion of SQL-sessions.

Procedure Definition

```
procedure-definition
    ::=   PROCEDURE procedure
          ( parameter-definition-commalist ) ;
            SQL-statement ;

parameter-definition
    ::=   parameter data-type
        | SQLCODE
        | SQLSTATE
```

Syntax notes:

1. The procedure name must be unique within its containing module.

2. The parentheses surrounding the commalist of parameter definitions may be omitted. However, if they are, the commas must be omitted too, thereby converting the "commalist" into a "list".*

3. The list or commalist of parameter definitions must include SQLCODE, SQLSTATE, or both. Both of these are used to return status information; the difference between them is that most SQL-CODE values are implementation-defined, whereas many SQLSTATE values are defined within the standard.† In fact, the *only* SQLCODE values that are defined within the standard are as follows: A value of 0 means that the SQL statement executed successfully and no errors occurred; a value of +100 means that no rows were found to satisfy the request; and a negative value means that some error occurred.

Parameters

Each parameter definition (other than the SQLCODE and SQLSTATE definitions) consists of a parameter name—including a colon prefix—and a data type specification (see Chapter 7). Parameters are used to represent:

---

*This alternative "list" format is supported only for compatibility with SQL/89, and constitutes a "deprecated feature"—meaning that it is a feature of the standard that is retained only for compatibility reasons and is likely to be dropped in some future version. See Appendix C.
†In fact, SQLCODE too is now a "deprecated feature" and is likely to be dropped at some future time.

1. "Targets" (i.e., host program variables into which scalar values are to be retrieved). In this capacity, a parameter (other than SQLCODE and SQLSTATE) can be used, e.g., as the operand of an INTO clause in a FETCH or SELECT statement. *Note:* SQLSTATE and SQLCODE are "target" parameters by definition, but they cannot be used as the operand of an INTO clause.

2. Scalar values that are passed from the host program (representing, e.g., a value that is to be used within a WHERE clause to control a database search).

Parameter Data Types

The purpose of specifying the data type for a parameter is to inform the implementation of the data type it can expect for the corresponding argument from the host language. The range of data types that can be specified therefore depends on the range of data types supported by the host language in question; not all SQL data types can be specified for all host languages. For details, the reader is referred to the official standard document.

SQL Statements

SQL statements fall into a number of different categories, as follows:

- SQL schema statements
- SQL data statements
- SQL transaction statements
- SQL connection statements
- SQL session statements
- SQL diagnostics statements
- SQL exception declaration
- SQL dynamic statements

Note: For the purposes of this classification, BEGIN and END DECLARE SECTION are not regarded as SQL statements at all, and they cannot appear within procedures. DECLARE CURSOR, DECLARE LOCAL TEMPORARY TABLE, and WHENEVER are regarded as SQL statements, but they still cannot appear within procedures. In fact, BEGIN and END DECLARE SECTION and WHENEVER can appear only in embedded SQL (see Section 6.3).

The following are *SQL schema statements*:

```
CREATE SCHEMA, DROP SCHEMA
CREATE DOMAIN, ALTER DOMAIN, DROP DOMAIN
CREATE TABLE, ALTER TABLE, DROP TABLE
CREATE VIEW, DROP VIEW
CREATE CHARACTER SET, DROP CHARACTER SET
CREATE COLLATION, DROP COLLATION
CREATE TRANSLATION, DROP TRANSLATION
CREATE ASSERTION, DROP ASSERTION
GRANT, REVOKE
```

The following are *SQL data statements,* also referred to in this book
as *data manipulation* statements:*

```
DECLARE CURSOR
DECLARE LOCAL TEMPORARY TABLE
OPEN, CLOSE
FETCH, "positioned" UPDATE, "positioned" DELETE
SELECT, INSERT, "searched" UPDATE, "searched" DELETE
```

The following are *SQL transaction statements*:

```
SET TRANSACTION
SET CONSTRAINTS
COMMIT, ROLLBACK
```

The following are *SQL connection statements*:

```
CONNECT, DISCONNECT
SET CONNECTION
```

The following are *SQL session statements*:

```
SET SESSION AUTHORIZATION
SET CATALOG
SET SCHEMA
SET TIME ZONE
SET NAMES
```

The following is the only *SQL diagnostics statement*:

```
GET DIAGNOSTICS
```

The following is the only *SQL exception declaration*:

```
WHENEVER
```

We defer discussion of the *SQL dynamic statements* to Chapter 20.

An Example

We close this section with another example of the use of the module language. The purpose of the example is to illustrate the point that, as men-

---

*Most of the SQL dynamic statements (see Chapter 20) are also regarded as SQL data state-
ments.

tioned above, parameters also serve as the mechanism by which values can be returned to the invoking program (more correctly, to the invoking SQL-agent). Of course, this point has already been illustrated for the special case of the SQLSTATE parameter by the DELETE example discussed near the beginning of this section.

Procedure:

```
PROCEDURE GET_WEIGHT
           ( SQLSTATE,
             :PNO_PARAM    CHAR(6),
             :WEIGHT_PARAM DECIMAL(3) ) ;
    SELECT P.WEIGHT
    INTO   :WEIGHT_PARAM
    FROM   P
    WHERE  P.PNO = :PNO_PARAM ;
```

Possible invocation from PL/I:

```
DCL RETCODE    CHAR(5) ;
DCL PNO_ARG    CHAR(6) ;
DCL WEIGHT_ARG DECIMAL(3) ;
DCL GET_WEIGHT ENTRY ( CHAR(5), CHAR(6), DECIMAL(3) ) ;
  .......
PNO_ARG = 'P2' ;                 /* for example             */
CALL GET_WEIGHT ( RETCODE, PNO_ARG, WEIGHT_ARG ) ;
IF RETCODE = '00000'
THEN ... ;                       /* WEIGHT_ARG = retrieved value */
ELSE ... ;                       /* some exception occurred      */
```

6.3   EMBEDDED SQL

The ANSI/X3H2 committee did not necessarily intend (or even primarily intend) that users actually code direct calls to the module language as discussed in Section 6.2 above. Instead, the normal method of operation is to embed SQL statements directly into the text of the host language program, as illustrated by Figs. 2.2(b) and 2.8 in Chapter 2. An embedded SQL example corresponding to the direct call example near the beginning of the previous section might appear as shown below. *Note:* The example is incomplete; the SQLSTATE and PNO declarations need to be nested within an "embedded SQL declare section," delimited by the statements "EXEC SQL BEGIN DECLARE SECTION;" and "EXEC SQL END DECLARE SECTION;" (see later). We remind the reader that (like parameters in the module language) host language variables within embedded SQL statements must be prefixed with a colon (":").

```
DCL SQLSTATE CHAR(5) ;
DCL PNO CHAR(6) ;
  .......
PNO = 'P2' ;                     /* for example              */
EXEC SQL DELETE FROM P WHERE P.PNO = :PNO ;
IF SQLSTATE = '00000'
THEN ... ;                       /* delete operation succeeded */
ELSE ... ;                       /* some exception occurred    */
```

Note that no explicit definition of the procedure DELETE_PART is now needed.

However, "embedded SQL" is not a *fundamental* part of the SQL standard as such. Instead, the embedded SQL code shown above is defined to be a mere syntactic shorthand for the module language version (including the explicit procedure definition and the explicit call) shown in the previous section. The standard defines a set of rules by which a conceptual module is derived from a given program that contains embedded SQL statements. We omit the details here, since they are essentially straightforward (though tedious), except to remark that the "SCHEMA schema" specification in that derived module is implementation-dependent, and there is no "AUTHORIZATION user" specification.

Here is another example—an embedded SQL version of the SELECT example from the end of the previous section, but now including the necessary BEGIN and END DECLARE SECTION statements:

```
EXEC SQL BEGIN DECLARE SECTION ;

    DCL SQLSTATE CHAR(5) ;
    DCL PNO      CHAR(6) ;
    DCL WEIGHT   FIXED DECIMAL(3) ;

EXEC SQL END DECLARE SECTION ;

PNO = 'P2' ;                    /* for example               */
EXEC SQL SELECT P.WEIGHT
         INTO   :WEIGHT
         FROM   P
         WHERE  P.PNO = :PNO ;
IF SQLSTATE = '00000'
THEN ... ;                      /* WEIGHT = retrieved value  */
ELSE ... ;                      /* some exception occurred   */
```

Points arising:

1. Embedded SQL statements are prefixed by EXEC SQL* (so that they can easily be distinguished from statements of the host language), and are terminated as follows:

Ada	— semicolon
C	— semicolon
COBOL	— END-EXEC
FORTRAN	— absence of continuation character (i.e., no explicit terminator)
MUMPS	— right parenthesis
Pascal	— semicolon
PL/I	— semicolon

---

*Except in MUMPS, which uses the prefix "&SQL(" (ampersand–SQL–left parenthesis) instead.

2. An executable SQL statement can appear wherever an executable host statement can appear. Note that we say "executable" SQL statement: Certain SQL statements are *not* executable—for example, DECLARE CURSOR is not, nor is WHENEVER (see paragraph 8 below), and nor are BEGIN and END DECLARE SECTION.

3. SQL statements (from now on we will usually drop the "embedded") can include references to host variables. As already mentioned, such references must be prefixed with a colon to distinguish them from SQL column names. They must not be qualified or subscripted, and must identify scalars, not arrays or structures. They can appear in SQL statements in the same positions that parameters can appear in the module language (see Section 6.2).

4. All host variables that will be referenced in SQL statements must be defined within an *embedded SQL declare section,* which is delimited by the BEGIN and END DECLARE SECTION statements. Such host variable definitions are deliberately limited to certain simple forms (e.g., arrays and structures are not permitted); the reader is referred to the standard document for details. A given program can include any number of embedded SQL declare sections. A host variable must not appear in an embedded SQL statement before it is defined.

5. Every embedded SQL program must include either a host variable called SQLCODE (or SQLCOD in FORTRAN), or a host variable called SQLSTATE (or SQLSTA in FORTRAN), or both. After any SQL statement has been executed, a status indicator is returned to the program in SQLCODE or SQLSTATE or both. See Chapter 22 for further discussion of SQLCODE and SQLSTATE.

6. Host variables must have a data type appropriate to the purposes to which they are put. In particular, a host variable that is to be used as a target must have a data type that is compatible with that of the expression that provides the value to be assigned to that target; likewise, a host variable that is to be used as a source must have a data type that is compatible with that of the SQL column to which values of that source are to be assigned. Similar remarks apply to a host variable that is to be used in a comparison, or indeed in any kind of scalar expression. For details of what it means for data types to be compatible in the foregoing sense, the reader is referred to the official standard document.

7. Host variables and SQL columns can have the same name.

8. Every SQL statement should in principle be followed by a test of the

returned SQLCODE or SQLSTATE value. The WHENEVER statement is provided to simplify this process. The WHENEVER statement
has the syntax:

```
EXEC SQL WHENEVER  condition  action  terminator
```

where "terminator" is as explained in paragraph 1 above, "condition"
is either SQLERROR or NOT FOUND, and "action" is either
CONTINUE or a GO TO statement.* WHENEVER is not an executable statement; rather, it is a directive to the SQL language processor.
"WHENEVER condition GO TO label" causes that processor to insert
an "IF condition GO TO label" statement after each executable SQL
statement it encounters; "WHENEVER condition CONTINUE"
causes it not to insert any such statements, the implication being that
the programmer will insert such statements by hand. The two "conditions" are defined as follows:

```
NOT FOUND    means    no data was found
                      (SQLCODE = +100; SQLSTATE = 02000)
SQLERROR     means    an error occurred
                      (SQLCODE < 0; see Chapter 22 for SQLSTATE)
```

Each WHENEVER statement the SQL processor encounters on its se-
quential scan through the program text (for a particular condition)
overrides the previous one it found (for that condition).

6.4 DIRECT SQL

The term "direct SQL" refers to the direct execution of SQL statements
from an interactive terminal, with results being returned to that terminal.
To quote the standard: "The method of invoking direct SQL statements,
the method of raising conditions that result from the execution of direct
SQL statements, the method of accessing the diagnostics information that
results from the execution of direct SQL statements, and the method of
returning results . . . are all implementation-defined" (slightly para-
phrased). Furthermore, there is supposed to be an implicit implementation-
defined module to which the direct SQL statements are considered to belong (though in fact the standard never seems to come out and state as
much explicitly—see Appendix D). Many other aspects of direct SQL are
also implementation-defined. In view of all of this lack of specificity, it
seems best in this book to ignore direct SQL entirely from this point forward.

---

*"GO TO" can be spelled as shown here, as two words, or as one word without the space
("GOTO").

PART III

DATA DEFINITION AND MANIPULATION

This part of the book addresses what might be considered the heart of the SQL language—the basic SQL data objects and operators, the rules for defining those objects, the rules for combining those operators to form expressions, and so on. In particular, it describes the SQL statements for retrieving data from, and updating data in, SQL databases. *Note*: It is convenient to continue in the harmless pretense that there is such a thing as an "SQL database."

7

Scalar Objects, Operators, and Expressions

7.1 INTRODUCTION

In this chapter we describe the scalar (i.e., elementary) objects and operators supported by SQL. The basic data object is the *individual scalar value*; for example, the object appearing at the intersection of a given row and a given column of a given table is a scalar value. Each such value is of some particular scalar *data type*. For each such data type, there is an associated format for writing *literals* of that type. Scalar data types and literals are discussed in Sections 7.2 and 7.3, respectively.

Scalar objects can be operated upon by means of certain *scalar operators*. For example, two numeric values can be added together by means of the scalar arithmetic operator " + ", and can be tested for equality by means of the scalar comparison operator " = ". In addition, SQL provides

- Certain *scalar functions* (e.g., the POSITION and SUBSTRING functions), which can also be regarded as scalar operators, and
- Certain *aggregate functions* (e.g., the SUM and AVG functions), which have the effect of reducing some "aggregate," or collection of scalar

values, to a single scalar value. *Note:* "Aggregate" and "aggregate function" are not standard terms.

Scalar objects and operators and functions can be combined in various ways to form *scalar expressions*. The operators and scalar functions available for each data type, and the corresponding scalar expressions, are discussed in Section 7.4. Section 7.5 then discusses the various aggregate functions. Finally, Section 7.6 considers the general operations of *assignment* and *comparison*.

Note: In addition to the data types discussed in Section 7.2 immediately following, SQL also supports a variety of *date and time* data types. We defer all discussion of these data types to Chapter 17. Also, the SQL support for character strings includes a large number of options and complications that we prefer not to get into at this comparatively early point in the book; we therefore defer detailed discussion of this topic also, to Chapter 19. Third, no description of scalar data in SQL would be complete without a detailed explanation of *nulls,* which are SQL's way of representing the fact that some piece of data is missing for some reason. The fact is, however, that nulls give rise to an inordinate amount of undesirable and unnecessary complexity. *WE THEREFORE CHOOSE TO DEFER ALL DISCUSSION OF NULLS AND RELATED MATTERS TO CHAPTER 16* (except for the occasional unavoidable brief mention). The reader is warned, however, that many of our discussions prior to that point will need to be revisited and extended when that chapter is reached.

7.2 DATA TYPES

SQL supports the following scalar data types:

CHARACTER (n)	Fixed length string of exactly n characters ($n > 0$)
CHARACTER VARYING (n)	Varying length string of up to n characters ($n > 0$)
BIT (n)	Fixed length string of exactly n bits ($n > 0$)
BIT VARYING (n)	Varying length string of up to n bits ($n > 0$)
NUMERIC (p,q)	Decimal number, p digits and sign, with assumed decimal point q digits from the right ($0 \le q \le p$, $p > 0$)
DECIMAL (p,q)	Decimal number, m digits and sign, with assumed decimal point q digits from the right ($0 \le q \le p \le m, p > 0$—see below for an explanation of m)
INTEGER	Signed integer, decimal or binary (see below)

SMALLINT   Signed integer, decimal or binary (see below)

FLOAT (p)   Floating point number N say, represented by a binary fraction f of m binary digits precision ($-1 < f < +1, 0 < p \leq m$—see below for an explanation of m) and a binary integer exponent e, such that $N = f * (10 ** e)$

Note: The symbol "**" here stands for exponentiation. Note, however, that SQL does not in fact support any such operator (see Section 7.4).

Notes:

1. The string length specifications (n), the precision specifications (p, m), and the scale specifications (q) must all be unsigned decimal integers.

2. The following abbreviations and alternative spellings are permitted:

   - CHARACTER is an abbreviation for CHARACTER(1)
   - CHAR is an abbreviation for CHARACTER
   - VARCHAR is an abbreviation for CHARACTER VARYING (or CHAR VARYING)
   - INT is an abbreviation for INTEGER
   - NUMERIC(p) is an abbreviation for NUMERIC(p,0)
   - NUMERIC is an abbreviation for NUMERIC(p), where p is implementation-defined
   - DEC is an abbreviation for DECIMAL
   - DECIMAL (p) is an abbreviation for DECIMAL(p,0)
   - DECIMAL is an abbreviation for DECIMAL(p), where p is implementation-defined
   - FLOAT is an abbreviation for FLOAT(p), where p is implementation-defined
   - REAL is an alternative spelling for FLOAT(s), where s is implementation-defined
   - DOUBLE PRECISION is an alternative spelling for FLOAT(d), where d is implementation-defined

3. The following items are all implementation-defined:

   - The maximum value of n, the declared length of a character string (fixed or varying length)
   - The maximum value of n, the declared length of a bit string (fixed or varying length)

- Whether INTEGER and SMALLINT are decimal or binary (though they must be the same)

- The actual precision for INTEGER and SMALLINT (though the latter must not exceed the former)

- The maximum value of p, the declared precision for NUMERIC and DECIMAL

- The default precision for NUMERIC and DECIMAL if there is no declared precision

- The actual precision m for DECIMAL (though the actual precision m must not be less than the declared or implied precision p)

- The maximum value of p, the declared precision for FLOAT

- The default precision for FLOAT if there is no declared precision

- The actual precision m for FLOAT (though the actual precision m must be greater than or equal to the declared or implied precision p)

- The actual precisions s and d for REAL and DOUBLE PRECISION (though d must be greater than s)

4. Data types CHARACTER and CHARACTER VARYING are known collectively as character string data types. Data types BIT and BIT VARYING are known collectively as bit string data types. Data types character string and bit string are known collectively as string data types.

5. Data types NUMERIC, DECIMAL, INTEGER, and SMALLINT are known collectively as exact numeric data types. Data type FLOAT, together with the "alternative spelling" data types REAL and DOUBLE PRECISION, are known collectively as approximate numeric data types. Data types exact numeric and approximate numeric are known collectively as numeric data types.

6. (With acknowledgments to Phil Shaw.) It is probably worth pointing out explicitly the distinction between NUMERIC and DECIMAL. NUMERIC(p,q) means that the precision must be *exactly* p digits; DECIMAL(p,q) means that it must be *at least* p digits, with the actual precision being implementation-defined. Thus, e.g., the implementation might store both NUMERIC and DECIMAL values as packed decimal. NUMERIC(2,1) and DECIMAL(2,1) items would then both be stored as two-byte packed decimal values. Since two-byte packed decimal fields can hold three digits plus a sign, the DECIMAL items would be allowed to have values in the range -99.9 to $+99.9$; the NUMERIC items, by contrast, would be constrained to values in the range -9.9 to $+9.9$. In other words, the range of NUMERIC values

is strictly defined, for maximum portability, whereas the range of DECIMAL values adjusts to the implementation, for maximum exploitation of the implementation's capability.

Domains

Domains represent an absolutely fundamental ingredient in the theoretical relational model (see Chapter 1, Section 1.1). This is not the place to go into details; suffice it to say that the SQL standard unfortunately includes only a *very weak* form of support for the domain concept. Within the standard, in fact, almost the only purpose of domains is to serve as a means of factoring out column data type specifications. In the case of suppliers-and-parts, for example, we might define a domain called CITIES, as follows:

```
CREATE DOMAIN CITIES CHAR(15)
```

Now, instead of defining columns S.CITY and P.CITY explicitly as CHAR(15), we could define each to be "based on" the CITIES domain:

```
CREATE TABLE S  ( ... , CITY CITIES, ... )

CREATE TABLE P  ( ... , CITY CITIES, ... )
```

The CITIES definition thus effectively serves as a shorthand.

Note: Domains in SQL do provide slightly more functionality than the foregoing rather trivial example might suggest. See Chapter 8 for further discussion.

7.3 LITERALS

The various kinds of literal value supported in SQL are as follows:

character string	Written as a sequence of characters enclosed in single quotes (as usual, the single quote character itself is represented within a character string literal by two immediately adjacent single quotes)

E.g.:   `'123 Main St.'`   `'Pig'`   `'honey don''t'`

bit string	Written *either* as a sequence of 0s and 1s enclosed in single quotes and preceded by the letter B *or* as a sequence of hexadecimal digits enclosed in single quotes and preceded by the letter X

E.g.:   `B'11000001'`   `B'0101'`   `B'0'`
        `X'C1'`   `X'5'`   `X'fed'`

Note: The hexadecimal digits are 0, 1, 2, 3, 4, 5, 6, 7, 8, 9, A (or a), B (or b), C (or c), D (or d), E (or e), and F (or f). They represent the bit strings 0000 through 1111 in the usual way. Thus, the 1st and 4th of the examples above represent the same value, as do the 2nd and 5th.

exact
numeric
Written as a signed or unsigned decimal number, possibly with a decimal point

E.g.: `4  7.  -95.7  +364.05  0.007  .6333`

approximate
numeric
Written as an exact numeric literal, followed by the letter E, followed by a signed or signed decimal integer

E.g.: `4E3  -95.7E46  +364E-5  0.7E1  -.15E-15`

Note: The expression xEy represents the value $x * (10 ** y)$.

Points arising:

1. The terms "signed numeric literal," "unsigned numeric literal," and "hexadecimal literal" are also sometimes used. Each has the obvious meaning.

2. The standard also includes an extended format for writing string literals when the literal in question spans multiple text lines. In this extended format, the literal value is divided up into segments, each with its own opening and closing single quote, and adjacent segments are separated by any *separator* that includes a newline marker. (Recall from Chapter 3 that, in general, a separator in SQL is any combination of spaces and/or newline markers and/or comments.) Here is an example of such a literal (of type X):

```
X'ab'      -- Segment 1
  'cd'      -- Segment 2
  'ef'      -- Segment 3
```

Data Types of Literals

Literal data types are as indicated below:

character
string
CHARACTER (n), where n is the actual length specified (in characters)

bit string
BIT (n), where n is the actual length specified (in bits)

exact
numeric
NUMERIC (p,q), where p and q are the actual precision and scale specified

approximate   FLOAT (p), where p is the actual precision specified
numeric

7.4   SCALAR OPERATORS AND FUNCTIONS

SQL provides a number of builtin scalar operators and functions that can
be used in the construction of scalar expressions. We summarize those oper-
ators and functions below (in alphabetic order), for purposes of reference.
Note: For a discussion,of the builtin *aggregate* functions, see Section 7.5.
For a discussion of the functions having to do with dates and times, see
Chapter 17. For a discussion of additional functions—TRANSLATE,
CONVERT, and COLLATE—having to do with character strings, see
Chapter 19.

- Arithmetic operators

  The usual arithmetic operators " + ", " − ", "*", and "/" are supported, all with the usual meanings.

- BIT_LENGTH

  Returns the length of a string in bits. The string in question is specified
  by means of an arbitrary string expression.

- CASE

  See the subsection "CASE Operations" below, immediately following
  this list of functions.

- CAST

  Converts a specified scalar value to a specified scalar data type. The
  syntax is:

  ```
  CAST ( scalar-expression AS { data-type | domain } )
  ```

  The value of the specified scalar expression is converted either to "data
  type" (if "data type" is specified explicitly), or to the data type underlying "domain" (otherwise).* *Note:* Not all pairs of data types are mutually convertible; for example, conversions between numbers and bit
  strings are not supported. The reader is referred to the official standard
  document for details of precisely which data types can be converted to
  which.

---

*It is an error if "domain" is specified and the converted value fails to satisfy some integrity
constraint associated with "domain" (see Chapters 8 and 14).

- CHARACTER_LENGTH or CHAR_LENGTH

  Returns the length of a string in characters or "octets" (see OCTET_LENGTH below). The string in question is specified by means of an arbitrary string expression; the result is the length in characters if the string is of type character, in "octets" otherwise.

- Concatenation

  The concatenation operator "||" can be used to concatenate two character strings or two bit strings. It is written as an infix operation; e.g., the expression INITIALS || LASTNAME can be used to concatenate the values of INITIALS and LASTNAME (in that order). The arguments can be any character string or bit string expressions, so long as they are both of the same type (and, in the case of character string expressions, the same character set—see Chapter 19).

- CURRENT_USER

  Returns a character string representing the current authorization ID. Refer to Chapter 15 for further explanation.

- LOWER and UPPER

  Return a character string that is identical to a specified character string, except that all upper case letters are replaced by their lower case equivalents (for LOWER), or vice versa (for UPPER). The string argument can be any character string expression. *Note:* LOWER and UPPER are referred to generically as *fold* functions.

- OCTET_LENGTH

  Returns the length of a string in "octets." The string in question is specified by means of an arbitrary string expression; the result is the bit length of the string divided by 8 (ignoring any remainder from the division).

- POSITION

  Returns the position within a specified character string (*string2*) of another specified character string (*string1*). Each of *string1* and *string2* is specified as an arbitrary character string expression. More precisely, the expression POSITION (*string2* IN *string1*) is defined to return a value as follows:

1. If the CHARACTER_LENGTH of *string2* is zero,* the result is one

2. Otherwise, if *string2* occurs as a substring within *string1,* the result is one greater than the number of characters in *string1* that precede the first such occurrence

3. Otherwise, the result is zero

Note that POSITION does not apply to bit strings.

- SESSION_USER

Returns a character string representing the SQL-session authorization ID. Refer to Chapter 15 for further explanation.

- SUBSTRING

Extracts a substring of a string. For example, the expression SUBSTRING (S.SNAME FROM 1 FOR 3) extracts the first three characters of the specified supplier name. In general, the string argument can be any character or bit string expression, and the FROM and FOR arguments can be any numeric expressions (of type exact numeric with a scale of zero). If the key word FOR and its associated argument are omitted, the effect is to extract the entire right hand portion of the given string, starting at the specified FROM position.

- SYSTEM_USER

Returns a character string representing the ID of the operating system user who invoked the module containing the SYSTEM_USER reference.

- TRIM

Returns a character string that is identical to a specified character string, except that leading and/or trailing pad characters are removed. More precisely, the expression TRIM (*ltb pad* FROM *string*), where *string* is an arbitrary character string expression, *ltb* is LEADING, TRAILING, or BOTH, and *pad* is a character string expression that evaluates to a single character, removes leading and/or trailing (as specified) *pad* characters from *string*. If *ltb* is omitted, BOTH is assumed. If *pad* is omitted, the pad character is assumed to be a space.

---

*Note that a character string can have a length of zero even though zero is not valid as a value for *n* in the data type declaration CHARACTER(*n*). Similarly for bit strings.

If *ltb* and *pad* are both omitted, the key word FROM must be omitted too.

Note: One of the principal uses of TRIM is in connection with varying length character strings. Suppose column *C* of base table *T* is of data type CHARACTER VARYING(100), say. In a host language such as COBOL that does not support such a data type, any host variable, *H* say, corresponding to column *C* will have to be defined to be (in effect) "CHARACTER FIXED(100)." Now suppose that *H* has the value "Smith" followed by 95 blanks. Then the statement

```
INSERT
INTO T ( ..., C, ... )
VALUES ( ..., :H, ... )
```

will set *C* to the value "Smith" followed by 95 blanks. By contrast, the statement

```
INSERT
INTO T ( ..., C, ... )
VALUES ( ..., TRIM (:H), ... )
```

will set *C* to just "Smith" (with no trailing blanks).

- USER

  Same as CURRENT_USER.

CASE Operations

A CASE operation returns one of a specified set of values, depending on some condition. The general format is as follows:

```
CASE
    when-clause-list
    ELSE scalar-expression
END
```

where a "when clause" takes the form

```
WHEN conditional-expression THEN scalar-expression
```

The when-clauses are processed in sequence as written. As soon as one is found for which the conditional expression evaluates to *true,* the value of the corresponding scalar expression is taken as the overall result, and the process stops. If none of the conditional expressions evaluates to *true,* the value of the scalar expression in the ELSE clause is taken as the overall result. Here is an example:

```
CASE
   WHEN S.STATUS <  5 THEN 'Last resort'
   WHEN S.STATUS < 10 THEN 'Dubious'
   WHEN S.STATUS < 15 THEN 'Not too good'
   WHEN S.STATUS < 20 THEN 'Mediocre'
   WHEN S.STATUS < 25 THEN 'Acceptable'
   ELSE                    'Fine'
END
```

A second CASE format also exists. It effectively serves as a shorthand for a particular version of the first format. The syntax is:

```
CASE scalar-expression-1
   type-2-when-clause-list
   ELSE scalar-expression-4
END
```

where a "type 2 when clause" takes the form

```
WHEN scalar-expression-2 THEN scalar-expression-3
```

This CASE operation is defined to be equivalent to a CASE operation of the first format in which each when-clause includes a conditional expression of the form "scalar-expression-1 = scalar-expression-2." For example, the CASE operation

```
CASE P.COLOR
   WHEN 'Red'    THEN 1
   WHEN 'Yellow' THEN 2
   WHEN 'Blue'   THEN 3
   WHEN 'Green'  THEN 4
   ELSE          0
END
```

is equivalent to the CASE operation

```
CASE
   WHEN P.COLOR = 'Red'    THEN 1
   WHEN P.COLOR = 'Yellow' THEN 2
   WHEN P.COLOR = 'Blue'   THEN 3
   WHEN P.COLOR = 'Green'  THEN 4
   ELSE                    0
END
```

Note: There are a couple of other variants of the basic CASE operation, NULLIF and COALESCE, both having to do with *nulls*. As already indicated, we defer all detailed discussion of everything to do with nulls to Chapter 16.

Scalar Expressions

As mentioned at the beginning of this section, the scalar operators and functions can be used (in conjunction with scalar operands and arguments) to construct scalar expressions. A scalar expression is an expression that evaluates to a scalar value.* Generally speaking, such expressions can appear wherever a *literal* of the appropriate type is permitted (e.g., as operands in SELECT, WHERE, and HAVING clauses—see Chapters 9–12). However, there are one or two exceptions to this general rule; such exceptions are noted at appropriate points in the book.

There are basically five types of scalar expression, characterized according to the data type of the value they represent: numeric, character string, bit string, date/time, and interval expressions. Here we consider the first three types only; as already explained, all details of dates and times (including intervals) are deferred to Chapter 17. First, *numeric* expressions. The syntax is:

```
numeric-expression
    ::=   numeric-term
        | numeric-expression { + | - } numeric-term

numeric-term
    ::=   numeric-factor
        | numeric-term { * | / } numeric-factor

numeric-factor
    ::=   [ + | - ] numeric-primary
```

And a "numeric primary" is any of the following: (a) a possibly qualified column name; (b) a parameter, host variable, or unsigned numeric literal; (c) a reference to a scalar function (possibly CASE or CAST) or aggregate function; (d) a table expression enclosed in parentheses; or (e) a scalar expression enclosed in parentheses. In each case, of course, the "numeric primary" must yield a value of data type numeric. In case (d), moreover, the table expression must evaluate to a table containing exactly one column and exactly one row, and the value is taken to be, precisely, the single scalar value contained within that table.[†]

Note: The syntax rules imply that (e.g.) "X − −3" is a valid numeric expression, involving two immediately adjacent minus signs. Note, however, that the " − −3" will not be interpreted (as the user might expect) as

---

*For details regarding the data type, precision, etc., of the result of a scalar expression, the reader is referred to the official standard document. Note, however, that CAST can be used to *force* the result to be of a prescribed data type, precision, etc. (within certain limits).

[†]It is an error if the table contains more than one row. If instead it contains no rows at all, the value of the scalar expression is taken to be null (see Chapter 16).

"+3"; instead, the "−−" will be taken as marking the beginning of a comment.

Here are some examples of numeric expressions:

```
STATUS

WEIGHT * 454

SALARY + COMMISSION + BONUS

( QTY + 1500 ) / 75.2

( CHAR_LENGTH ( SNAME ) - 1 ) * 2

50 - ( AVG ( QTY ) / 100 )

( SELECT S.STATUS FROM S WHERE S.SNO = 'S3' )
```

We turn now to *character string* expressions—syntax:

```
character-string-expression
    ::=   character-string-concatenation
        | character-string-primary

character-string-concatenation
    ::=   character-string-expression || character-string-primary
```

Note: The symbol "| |" here represents the concatenation operator—it should not be confused with the vertical bar "|" that is used to separate alternatives in the grammar.

And a "character string primary" is syntactically identical to a "numeric primary"—but, of course, it must yield a value of data type character string instead of numeric. Here are some examples of character string expressions:

```
PNAME

INITIALS || LASTNAME

MIN ( COLOR )

USER

SUBSTRING ( S.SNAME FROM 1 FOR 3 )

( CASE WHEN P.WEIGHT < 50
  THEN 'Light' ELSE 'Heavy' END ) || ' ' || 'part'
```

Finally, a *bit string* expression is syntactically similar to a character string expression, but of course the "bit string primary" operands must yield values of type bit string, not character string.

7.5 AGGREGATE FUNCTIONS

Standard SQL provides a set of five builtin aggregate functions: COUNT, SUM, AVG, MAX, and MIN.* Apart from the special case of COUNT(*)—see later—each of these functions operates on a certain "aggregate," namely the collection of scalar values in one column of some table (frequently a *derived* table, i.e., a table constructed in some way from the given base tables), and produces a single scalar value defined as follows as its result:

```
COUNT     number of scalars in the column

SUM       sum of the scalars in the column

AVG       average of the scalars in the column

MAX       largest scalar in the column

MIN       smallest scalar in the column
```

As indicated in Section 7.4, an aggregate function reference is a special case of a scalar "primary," and so can be used within scalar expressions. The syntax is as follows:

```
aggregate-function-reference
    ::=   COUNT(*)
        | { AVG | MAX | MIN | SUM | COUNT }
                ( [ ALL | DISTINCT ] scalar-expression )
```

Points arising:

1. For SUM and AVG the argument must be of type numeric.

2. Except for the special case of COUNT(*), the argument may optionally be preceded by the key word DISTINCT, to indicate that redundant duplicate values are to be eliminated before the function is applied. The alternative to DISTINCT is ALL; ALL is assumed if nothing is specified. We remark that DISTINCT is legal but meaningless for MAX and MIN.

3. The special function COUNT(*)—DISTINCT not allowed—is provided to count all rows in a table without any duplicate elimination.

---

*EXISTS and UNIQUE (see Chapter 12) can also be considered as aggregate functions of a kind; however, they differ from the functions discussed in the present section in that (a) their argument is specified in a different syntactic style (actually a more logical style), and (b) they return a truth value, not, e.g., a number or a character string, and truth values are not an SQL data type.

4. The argument cannot involve any aggregate function references or table expressions, at any level of nesting. Thus, for example, an expression such as

```
SELECT AVG ( SUM ( QTY ) ) AS AQ          -- *** ILLEGAL *** ! ! !
FROM    ...
```

is *** *ILLEGAL* ***. (By contrast, the more complex expression

```
SELECT AVG ( X ) AS AQ
FROM    ( SELECT SUM ( QTY ) AS X ... )
 ...
```

is legal!) Refer to Chapter 11 for a full discussion of such expressions.

5. If the aggregate function reference appears within a table expression that is in turn nested within another table expression, and the argument to the aggregate function reference includes a column reference whose implicit or explicit range variable qualifier has that "outer" expression as its scope, then that column reference must be the only column reference within that argument. Furthermore, the aggregate function reference in question must appear within either a SELECT clause or a HAVING clause, and the table expression nesting must be "immediate" (i.e., no other table expression can intervene between the two table expressions in question). *Note:* We mention this rule for completeness. It is very difficult to explain it in intuitive terms, especially since it seems to be logically unnecessary (at the very least, it is more restrictive than it needs to be).

6. Any nulls in the argument are always eliminated before the aggregate function is applied, regardless of whether DISTINCT is specified, *except* for the case of COUNT(*), where nulls are handled just like nonnull values.

7. If the argument happens to be an empty set, COUNT returns a value of zero; the others all return null.

8. For details regarding the data type (etc.) of the result of an aggregate function reference, the reader is referred to the official standard document.

We give a number of examples of the use of aggregate functions. Each of the following examples could form the basis of a single-row SELECT statement (see Chapter 9) or could be nested within some more complex expression, such as a table expression (see Chapter 11). *Note:* If an aggregate function reference appears within a SELECT clause and the select-expression does not include a GROUP BY clause, then the SELECT clause must not include any reference to a column of the applicable table *unless* that reference is the argument (or part of the argument) to an aggregate function reference. For example, the following is *** *ILLEGAL* *** :

```
SELECT SP.PNO, AVG ( SP.QTY ) AS AQ      -- *** ILLEGAL *** !!!
FROM    SP
```

Refer to Chapter 11 for further discussion.

Example 1:   Get the total number of suppliers.

```
SELECT COUNT(*) AS N1
FROM    S
```

Result: A table consisting of a single column (called N1) and a single row, containing the single value 5.

Example 2:   Get the total number of suppliers currently supplying parts.

```
SELECT COUNT ( DISTINCT SP.SNO ) AS N2
FROM    SP
```

Result: A table consisting of a single column (called N2) and a single row, containing the single value 4.

Example 3:   Get the number of shipments for part P2.

```
SELECT COUNT(*) AS N3
FROM    SP
WHERE   SP.PNO = 'P2'
```

Result: A table consisting of a single column (called N3) and a single row, containing the single value 4.

Example 4:   Get the total quantity of part P2 supplied.

```
SELECT SUM ( SP.QTY ) AS TOT1
FROM    SP
WHERE   SP.PNO = 'P2'
```

Result: A table consisting of a single column (called TOT1) and a single row, containing the single value 1000.

Example 5:   Get supplier numbers for suppliers with status value less than the current maximum status value in the S table.

```
SELECT S.SNO
FROM    S
WHERE   S.STATUS <
      ( SELECT MAX ( S.STATUS )
        FROM    S )
```

Result: A table consisting of a single column (called SNO) containing the values S1, S2, and S4. Note that we have not bothered to introduce a column name for the single column of the (single-row!) intermediate result table produced by the nested select expression. The reason is that we have no need to refer to that column by name anywhere. By contrast, we always ensure in our examples that the *final* result table does have a proper name for every column.

Example 6:   Get supplier numbers for suppliers whose status is greater than or equal to the average for their particular city.

```
SELECT  SX.SNO
FROM    S SX
WHERE   SX.STATUS >=
      ( SELECT AVG ( SY.STATUS )
        FROM    S SY
        WHERE   SY.CITY = SX.CITY )
```

Result: A table consisting of a single column (called SNO) containing the values S1, S3, S4, and S5.

7.6 ASSIGNMENTS AND COMPARISONS

Assignments

Assignment operations are performed when values are retrieved from the database (e.g., via SELECT) or stored into the database (e.g., via UPDATE). In general, an assignment involves assigning the value of some scalar expression (the *source*) to some scalar object (the *target*). The data type of the source and the data type of the target must be *compatible*. Compatibility is defined as follows:

1. All numbers are compatible with one another.
2. All character strings are compatible with one another.*
3. All bit strings are compatible with one another.
4. There are no other instances of compatibility (other than those having to do with dates and times—see Chapter 17).

Assignments are performed as follows:

1. For a character string assignment:
    - For retrieval operations, if the target is fixed length, the source string is conceptually truncated on the right or padded on the right with space characters (as necessary) to make it the same length as the target before the assignment is performed. For store operations the

---

*A slight oversimplification. See Chapter 19 for further discussion.

same rules apply, except that it is an error if truncation is required and it would cause any nonspace characters to be lost.

- If the target is varying length, its current actual length is set to the lesser of its declared maximum length and the length of the source, and the assignment is then performed as in the fixed length case.

2. Bit string assignments are performed in a like manner, except that (a) any necessary padding is with 0-bits instead of space characters, and (b) for store operations truncation is not allowed.

3. It is not possible to assign to a substring of a given string.

4. For a numeric assignment, the source is converted to the data type of the target (including precision, and scale if applicable) before the assignment is performed.

5. Note that targets of assignments in INSERT and UPDATE operations (i.e., target columns) must be designated by *unqualified* column names. See Chapter 3 for a discussion of qualified and unqualified names.

Comparisons

Comparisons are performed under many circumstances—for example, when SQL is eliminating duplicate values (see the discussion of DISTINCT in Chapter 11 and elsewhere). A comparison is also one kind of *conditional expression* (though not the only kind); conditional expressions are used in, e.g., CASE operations (see above), in WHERE and HAVING clauses (see Chapter 11), and elsewhere. *Note:* Conditional expressions can be regarded as a special kind of scalar expression, but a scalar expression that evaluates to a truth value instead of to one of the SQL-supported data types.

The *basic* form* of a comparison is

```
comparand  operator  comparand
```

where:

- The two comparands must be *compatible* (as that term is defined under "Assignments" above). In other words, the comparands must be scalar expressions of the same type—i.e., both numeric or both character string or . . . (etc.). The data types of the two expressions are *not* required to be absolutely identical.

- The operator must be one of the following: =, <, < =, >, > =, or < > ("not equals").

---

*But we stress the point that there are many other forms, over and above this "basic" form.

Comparisons are evaluated as follows:

1. Numbers compare algebraically (negative values are considered to be smaller than positive values, regardless of their absolute magnitude).

2. Character strings are compared character by character from left to right. The individual pairwise comparisons are performed in accordance with the appropriate collating sequence (see Chapter 19). If every pairwise comparison yields "equal," the character strings are equal; otherwise, the first pairwise comparison that does not yield "equal" determines the overall result. *Note:* If two character strings of different lengths are to be compared, the shorter is conceptually padded at the right with spaces to make it the same length as the longer before the comparison is done.*

3. Bit strings are compared bit by bit from left to right. The individual pairwise comparisons are performed in accordance with the convention that a 0-bit is less than a 1-bit. If every pairwise comparison yields "equal," the bit strings are equal; otherwise, the first pairwise comparison that does not yield "equal" determines the overall result. *Note:* A bit string *b1* that is shorter than some other bit string *b2,* but "compares equal" to that leading substring of *b2* that is the same length as *b1,* is always considered to be less than *b2* even if all remaining bits of *b2* are 0-bits. For example, if *b1* and *b2* have the values "101" (length 3) and "1010" (length 4), then *b1* < *b2.*

Here are some examples of comparisons:

```
SP.SNO = 'S1'

WEIGHT * 454 > 1000

SUBSTRING ( P.CITY FROM 1 FOR 1 ) = 'L'

SUM ( QTY ) > 500
```

---

*This explanation assumes that PAD SPACE applies to the collating sequence in question. If instead NO PAD applies, a character string *c1* that is shorter than some other character string *c2,* but "compares equal" to that leading substring of *c2* that is the same length as *c1,* is considered to be less than *c2* even if all remaining characters of *c2* are spaces. For example, if *c1* and *c2* have the values "xyz" (length 3) and "xyz*" (length 4, with the "*" representing a space), respectively, then *c1* < *c2* under NO PAD. See Chapter 19 for further discussion.

8

Data Definition: Domains and Base Tables

8.1 INTRODUCTION

Domains and base tables are *defined* by means of the statements CREATE DOMAIN and CREATE TABLE, respectively. These statements can be executed as independent operations in their own right, or they can be executed as "schema elements" within a CREATE SCHEMA statement (see Chapter 4). Also, existing domains and existing base tables can be *altered* by means of the statements ALTER DOMAIN and ALTER TABLE, and can be *dropped* by means of the statements DROP DOMAIN and DROP TABLE; unlike their CREATE counterparts, however, these ALTER and DROP operations must be executed as independent statements, they cannot appear as "schema elements" within a CREATE SCHEMA statement. Despite this latter fact, however, note carefully that (as explained in Chapter 4) every domain and every base table does belong to some schema, even if the corresponding CREATE statement is executed "independently," and creating a new domain or base table ("independently" or otherwise), or altering or dropping an existing domain or base table (necessarily "independently"), thus has the effect—among other things—of updating the relevant schema in the appropriate manner.

Note: The reader will observe from the foregoing paragraph that the term "TABLE" in the CREATE, ALTER, and DROP TABLE statements refers to a base table specifically. This fact is a trifle unfortunate, since base tables are only one special case (albeit an important special case) of tables in general. Now, we cannot change the syntax of SQL, but (as mentioned at the end of Chapter 3) we will be careful in this book, in our prose explanations, always to say "base table" when we mean a base table specifically, and to reserve the term "table," unqualified, to mean any kind of table (base table or view or intermediate query result or final query result or . . .).

We now proceed to discuss the foregoing ideas in detail. *Note:* In what follows, we choose to discuss domains before base tables, because domains are actually much more fundamental in a theoretical sense—even though, as mentioned in the previous chapter, the SQL support for the domain concept is very weak, and indeed does not even have to be used.

8.2 DOMAINS

CREATE DOMAIN

As suggested in Chapter 7, a domain definition in SQL is essentially nothing more than a kind of factored-out column definition that can be shared by any number of actual columns in any number of actual base tables. Domains are defined using CREATE DOMAIN—syntax:

```
domain-definition
    ::=   CREATE DOMAIN domain [ AS ] data-type
                        [ default-definition ]
                        [ domain-constraint-definition-list ]
```

Here "domain" is the name for the new domain,* "data type" is the underlying data type for that domain, and the optional "default definition" and "domain constraint definition list" specify a default value and a set of integrity constraints that will apply to every column[†] defined on the domain. Default values are discussed in more detail below; constraints (of all kinds) are discussed in Chapter 14. *Note:* The optional "AS" is a pure noiseword and can be omitted without affecting the semantics of the operation.

The optional "default definition" takes the form

```
DEFAULT { literal | niladic-function | NULL }
```

---

*If the name is qualified by a schema name and the CREATE DOMAIN appears within the context of a CREATE SCHEMA statement, then that schema name must identify the schema that would have been assumed by default anyway, viz. the schema being created (see Section 4.3).

[†]Well, not quite *every* column; if a column has its own explicit default definition, then that definition takes precedence over the one specified at the domain level.

where "niladic function" is a reference to any of the following:

```
USER
CURRENT_USER
SESSION_USER
SYSTEM_USER
CURRENT_DATE
CURRENT_TIME
CURRENT_TIMESTAMP
```

(see Chapter 7 for an explanation of the first four of these and Chapter 17 for the rest). Here is an example:

```
CREATE DOMAIN CITIES CHAR(15) DEFAULT '???'

CREATE TABLE S ( ... , CITY CITIES, ... )
```

Now, if the user inserts a row into table S and does not provide a value for the CITY column within that row, then the value "???" will be placed in that position by default. Thus, the general purpose of a default definition is to specify a value to be placed in some column—a "default value," or simply "default"—if the user does not provide a value on INSERT. "DEFAULT literal" means that the specified literal is the default; "DEFAULT niladic-function" means that the value of the specified niladic builtin function is the default (see Chapter 7); and "DEFAULT NULL" means that null is the default (see Chapter 16).

If CREATE DOMAIN does not specify an explicit default, the domain in question initially has no default value. However, one can be added later by means of ALTER DOMAIN (see below). ALTER DOMAIN can also be used to remove the default value from a domain that does have one (again, see below).

For further discussion of defaults, see Section 8.3.

ALTER DOMAIN

Just as a new domain can be created at any time via CREATE DOMAIN, so an existing domain can be *altered* at any time in a variety of ways via ALTER DOMAIN—syntax:

```
domain-alteration
    ::=   ALTER DOMAIN domain domain-alteration-action

domain-alteration-action
    ::=   domain-default-alteration-action
        | domain-constraint-alteration-action

domain-default-alteration-action
    ::=   SET default-definition
        | DROP DEFAULT
```

As the syntax suggests, ALTER DOMAIN allows a new default definition to be attached ("SET") to an existing domain (replacing the previous one, if any) or an existing default definition to be removed. In the first case, the new default automatically applies to all columns defined on the domain, except for columns that have their own explicit default (see Section 8.3 below). In the second case, the existing default definition is copied down to all columns defined on the domain (except for columns that have their own explicit default) before it is removed from the domain.

```
domain-constraint-alteration-action
    ::=   ADD domain-constraint-definition
        | DROP CONSTRAINT constraint
```

ALTER DOMAIN also allows a new integrity constraint to be attached to an existing domain or an existing integrity constraint to be removed. Again, we defer all detailed discussion of integrity constraints to Chapter 14.

DROP DOMAIN

Finally, an existing domain can be dropped by means of DROP DOMAIN—syntax:

```
DROP DOMAIN domain { RESTRICT | CASCADE }
```

If RESTRICT is specified and "domain" is referenced in any column definition or (within a CAST operation) in any view definition (see Chapter 13) or integrity constraint (see Chapter 14), the DROP DOMAIN will fail; otherwise it will succeed, and the specified domain will be dropped (i.e., its descriptor will be removed from the relevant schema). If CASCADE is specified, any referencing view definitions and integrity constraints will be dropped also; referencing columns will not be dropped, but will effectively be "altered," as follows:

- Instead of being defined on the now dropped domain, they will now be considered to be defined directly on the underlying data type of that domain instead.

- If they previously had no explicit default, they will now be considered to have the explicit default (if any) defined for the now dropped domain.*

- They will also effectively inherit any integrity constraints that were previously associated with the now dropped domain.

---

*Likewise, if they previously had no explicit collation, they will now be considered to have the collation (if any) defined for the now dropped domain. See Chapter 19 for a discussion of collations.

8.3 BASE TABLES

As indicated in Section 8.1, a base table is an important special case of the more general concept "table." Let us therefore begin by making that general concept more precise. Here then is a definition: A *table* in a relational system consists of a row of *column headings,* together with zero or more rows of *data values* (different numbers of data rows at different times, in general). For a given table:

- The column heading row specifies one or more columns (giving, among other things, a data type for each).

- Each data row contains exactly one scalar value for each of the columns specified in the column heading row. Furthermore, all the values in a given column are of the same data type, namely the data type specified in the column heading row for that column.

The number of data rows in a given table is called the *cardinality* of that table. The number of columns is called the *degree.* (However, neither of these terms is much used in SQL contexts.) *Note:* The unqualified term "row" invariably refers to a data row, not to the row of column headings, and we will follow this convention in the present book from this point forward.

Several points arise in connection with the foregoing definition.

1. First, note that in the relational model no table is ever permitted to contain any duplicate rows. That is, the body of every table is guaranteed to be a true mathematical *set* of rows (sets in mathematics do not contain duplicate elements). In SQL, however, this discipline is (very unfortunately, in this writer's opinion) not enforced,* and tables are indeed permitted to contain duplicate rows. In this book, however, we will never permit duplicate rows in any of our tables, and users are strongly recommended to follow this same discipline in practice.

2. Note that there is no mention in the definition of *row ordering.* Strictly speaking, the rows of a relational table are considered to be unordered. It is possible, as we shall see in Chapter 10, to *impose* an order on those rows when they are accessed through a cursor, but such an ordering should be regarded as nothing more than a convenience for the user—it is not intrinsic to the notion of a table per se.

---

*As a matter of fact, the situation is even worse than this sentence suggests—it is not merely that the discipline is not enforced, but rather that SQL actually includes certain options (such as the ALL option on UNION) that are specifically designed to *generate* tables with duplicate rows.

3. In contrast to the previous point, the columns of a table *are* considered to be ordered, left to right.* For example, in the suppliers table S (see Fig. 2.1 in Chapter 2), column SNO is the first column, column SNAME is the second column, and so on.

To turn now to base tables specifically: A base table is an *autonomous, named* table. By "autonomous," we mean that the table exists in its own right—unlike (e.g.) a view, which does not exist in its own right but is derived from one or more base tables (it is merely an alternative way of looking at those base tables). By "named," we mean that the table is explicitly given a name via an appropriate CREATE statement—unlike (e.g.) a table that is merely constructed as the result of evaluating some table expression, which does not have any explicit name of its own and has only ephemeral existence.

CREATE TABLE

Base tables are defined by means of the CREATE TABLE statement. The syntax is as follows:[†]

```
base-table-definition
    ::=   CREATE TABLE base-table
              ( base-table-element-commalist )
```

Here "base table" is the name for the new (and initially empty) base table,[‡] and each "base table element" is either a column definition or a base table constraint definition).[§] Column definitions are discussed below; constraints (of all kinds) are discussed in Chapter 14. Refer to Fig. 2.3 in Chapter 2 for some examples of CREATE TABLE.

---

*At least, they are considered to be so ordered in SQL, although such ordering is properly not part of the relational model. The fact is, however, there are very few situations in which column ordering is important in practice; in the interest of simplicity, therefore, we will tend to ignore such ordering in this book, except where it cannot be avoided.

[†]Ignoring temporary tables. We remind the reader that (as mentioned in Chapter 3 and elsewhere) we are deferring everything to do with temporary tables to Chapter 18.

[‡]If the name is qualified by a schema name and the CREATE TABLE appears within the context of a CREATE SCHEMA statement, then that schema name must identify the schema that would have been assumed by default anyway, viz. the schema being created (see Section 4.3).

[§]Note that the syntax permits column definitions and base table constraint definitions to be arbitrarily interspersed. In this book we will adopt the convention that the column definitions always come first.

The syntax of "column definition" is as follows:

```
column-definition
    ::=    column { data-type | domain }
                  [ default-definition ]
                  [ column-constraint-definition-list ]
```

Here "column" is the unqualified name for the column in question, "data type" or "domain" specifies the corresponding data type (see Section 8.2 above), and the optional "default definition" is discussed immediately below. (Once again, all discussion of constraints is deferred to Chapter 14.)
The syntax of "default definition" is as follows:

```
DEFAULT { literal | niladic-function | NULL }
```

(exactly like a default definition in CREATE or ALTER DOMAIN). The effect is to specify an explicit default for the column in question. In general, therefore, the default value for a given column is determined as follows:

- If the column has an explicit DEFAULT clause, then the value specified in that clause is the default.
- Otherwise, if the column is defined on a domain and that domain has an explicit DEFAULT clause, then the value specified in that clause is the default.
- Otherwise, the default is null.

Note that if the default for a given column is explicitly or implicitly defined to be null, but that column is also defined to be NOT NULL (see Chapter 16), then that column effectively has no default at all—implying that a value *must* be provided for the column on INSERT. Informally, we will refer to such a column as one that "has no default." *Note:* In SQL/89 (but not in the new standard), specifying both DEFAULT NULL explicitly and NOT NULL for the same column was illegal.

Observe, incidentally, that omitting the default definition for a given column and specifying DEFAULT NULL explicitly for that column are *not* equivalent (because the former permits the column to inherit a domain-level default, while the latter does not).

ALTER TABLE

Just as an existing domain can be altered via ALTER DOMAIN, so an existing base table can be altered (in a variety of ways) via ALTER TABLE:

```
base-table-alteration
    ::=    ALTER TABLE base-table base-table-alteration-action

base-table-alteration-action
    ::=    column-alteration-action
         | base-table-constraint-alteration-action

column-alteration-action
    ::=    ADD [ COLUMN ] column-definition
         | ALTER [ COLUMN ] column
                  { SET default-definition | DROP DEFAULT }
         | DROP [ COLUMN ] column { RESTRICT | CASCADE }
```

As the syntax suggests, ALTER TABLE with a "column alteration action" allows a new column to be added to, or an existing column to be altered in, or an existing column to be removed from, an existing base table. Here is an example of ADD COLUMN:*

```
ALTER TABLE S ADD COLUMN DISCOUNT SMALLINT DEFAULT -1
```

This statement adds a DISCOUNT column to the S table. All existing S rows are extended from four columns to five; the value of the new fifth column is −1 in every case. *Note:* If (a) the new column had been defined on a domain instead of having its own data type specification, and (b) that domain had a default definition, and (c) the new column did *not* have its own default definition, then the value of the new column in existing rows would of course be set to the default defined for the domain.

The foregoing example is sufficient to explain ADD COLUMN. ALTER COLUMN allows a new default definition to be attached ("SET") to an existing base table column (replacing the previous default definition, if any) or an existing default definition to be removed.[†] DROP COLUMN allows an existing base table column to be removed; note, however, that the operation will fail (a) if it attempts to remove the only column from a single-column base table, or (b) if RESTRICT is specified and the column in question is referenced in any view definition (see Chapter 13) or integrity constraint[‡] (see Chapter 14). If CASCADE is specified instead of RESTRICT, the DROP COLUMN will cascade to drop not only the specified column, but also all such view definitions and integrity constraints.

---

*The optional key word COLUMN in ADD COLUMN is a pure noiseword and can be omitted without affecting the semantics of the operation. The same is true for ALTER COLUMN and DROP COLUMN.

[†]Note that these are the *only* "column alterations" supported. In particular, note that ALTER COLUMN does not support any kind of change to the data type of an existing column.

[‡]Excluding base table integrity constraints on the base table in question that reference the column in question and no others.

```
base-table-constraint-alteration-action
    ::=   ADD base-table-constraint-definition
          | DROP CONSTRAINT constraint { RESTRICT | CASCADE }
```

ALTER TABLE also allows a new integrity constraint to be attached to an existing base table or an existing integrity constraint to be removed. Once again, we defer all detailed discussion of constraints to Chapter 14.

DROP TABLE

Finally, an existing base table can be dropped by means of DROP TABLE—syntax:

```
DROP TABLE base-table { RESTRICT | CASCADE }
```

If RESTRICT is specified and "base table" is referenced in any view definition (see Chapter 13) or integrity constraint (see Chapter 14), the DROP TABLE will fail; otherwise it will succeed, and the specified base table will be dropped. If CASCADE is specified, any referencing view definitions and integrity constraints will be dropped also.

9

Data Manipulation:
Noncursor Operations

9.1 INTRODUCTION

As explained briefly in Chapter 2, the SQL data manipulation operations
can be divided into two broad classes, those that involve cursors and those
that do not. In this chapter we restrict our attention to those that do not;
cursor operations will be discussed in Chapter 10. Thus, the operations we
will be discussing in the present chapter are as follows:

```
SELECT (single-row)
INSERT
UPDATE (searched)
DELETE (searched)
```

Note: For tutorial reasons, we assume throughout this chapter that all
named tables—at least, all those that are to be updated, i.e., those that are
the target of an INSERT, UPDATE, or DELETE operation—are base tables. The special considerations that apply to views are deferred to Chapter
13. We also ignore the possibility of errors (for the most part); in particular,
we ignore the possibility that any integrity violations might occur (i.e., we
assume that no attempt is made to introduce a row that violates a primary
or foreign key constraint, or to enter a value into a column that is of the
wrong data type, etc., etc.).

9.2 SINGLE-ROW SELECT

As explained in Chapter 2, the noncursor SELECT operation in standard SQL is *not* the fully general (set-level) SELECT operation that readers might already be familiar with; instead, it is what is usually called a *single-row SELECT,* i.e., a SELECT that retrieves *at most one row.* For example:

```
SELECT P.WEIGHT, P.COLOR
INTO   :WEIGHT_PARAM, :COLOR_PARAM
FROM   P
WHERE  P.PNO = 'P4'
```

It is an error if the result table, i.e., the table to be retrieved, contains more than one row (which is not possible in the example, because PNO is the primary key for table P). Here are some more examples (valid examples, that is—meaning examples that do retrieve at most one row in each case):

```
SELECT S.SNO, S.SNAME, S.STATUS, S.CITY
INTO   :SNO_PARAM, :SNAME_PARAM, :STATUS_PARAM, :CITY_PARAM
FROM   S
WHERE  S.SNO = 'S7'

SELECT AVG ( SP.QTY )
INTO   :AVG_QTY_PARAM
FROM   SP

SELECT MAX ( SP.QTY ) - MIN ( SP.QTY )
INTO   :ARITH_PARAM
FROM   SP
WHERE  SP.PNO = 'P4'
```

The general syntax is:*

```
  SELECT [ ALL | DISTINCT ] select-item-commalist
  INTO   target-commalist
  FROM   table-reference-commalist
[ WHERE  conditional-expression ]
[ GROUP  BY column-commalist ]
[ HAVING conditional-expression ]
```

Explanation:

1. If neither ALL nor DISTINCT is specified, ALL is assumed.

2. Each "select item" is a scalar expression, typically (but not necessarily) involving one or more columns of table *T1*—see paragraph 4 below). *Note:* It is possible to assign names to the columns that result from evaluating the select-items. It is also possible to use certain shorthands (involving the use of asterisks) for specifying certain commalists of

---

*Observe that a single-row SELECT is limited to being what we will refer to in Chapter 11 as a "select expression," instead of the more general "table expression." The reason for this slight lack of orthogonality is very likely nothing more than historical accident. *Note:* The concept of orthogonality is amplified in Appendix C.

select-items. We omit the details here; see Section 11.6 in Chapter 11 for further discussion.

3. Each "target" is a parameter or host variable. There must be exactly one target for each select-item; the target identified by the *i*th entry in the target-commalist corresponds to the *i*th select-item.

4. We make no attempt at this juncture to explain the FROM, WHERE, GROUP BY, and HAVING clauses in any detail (those explanations are deferred to Chapter 11). However, note that, no matter which of those clauses are specified and which omitted, the conceptual result of evaluating them is always a table, which we will refer to as table *T1* (even though the conceptual result is in fact unnamed). *Note:* Table *T1* might be a "grouped" table (see Chapter 11), but if it is it must contain at most one group. We can then reinterpret *T1* as referring to that single group (if indeed there is such a group), or to an empty table otherwise.

5. Let *T2* be the table that is derived from *T1* by evaluating the specified select-items against *T1*.

6. Let *T3* be the table that is derived from *T2* by eliminating redundant duplicate rows from *T2* if DISTINCT is specified, or a table that is identical to *T2* otherwise.

7. If table *T3* contains exactly one row, that row is retrieved; if it contains no rows, a "not found" exception occurs; if it contains more than one row, an error occurs.

9.3 INSERT

The INSERT statement is used to insert new rows into a named table. Two examples are given below: The first inserts a single row, the second inserts multiple rows. For the second example we have assumed that we have another named table, TEMP, with columns SNO and CITY (where the data types of columns TEMP.SNO and TEMP.CITY are compatible with the data types of columns S.SNO and S.CITY, respectively).

```
INSERT
INTO    S ( SNO, CITY, SNAME )
VALUES ( :SNO_PARAM, DEFAULT, :SNAME_PARAM )

INSERT
INTO    TEMP ( SNO, CITY )
        SELECT S.SNO, S.CITY
        FROM   S
        WHERE  S.STATUS > :STATUS_PARAM
```

The general syntax is:

```
INSERT INTO table [ ( column-commalist ) ] source
```

where "table" identifies the target table, the optional "column commalist" identifies some or all of the columns of that table (by their *unqualified* column names), and "source" is explained below. Omitting the parenthesized commalist of column names is equivalent to specifying all of the columns of the target table, in their left-to-right order within that table.

The "source" in an INSERT statement is either a *table expression* (i.e., an expression that evaluates to a table of zero or more rows), or an expression of the form

```
DEFAULT VALUES
```

The parenthesized commalist of column names must be omitted if DEFAULT VALUES is specified.

Explanation:

1. If an INSERT statement contains an explicit commalist of column names that omits one or more columns of the target table *T*, then any row inserted into *T* by that statement will contain the appropriate default (possibly null) in each such omitted column. It is an error if a column is omitted and that column has no default (see Chapter 8).

2. If a source of DEFAULT VALUES is specified, a single row is inserted into the target table *T* that contains the appropriate default (possibly null) in every column. It is an error if any column has no default (again, see Chapter 8).

3. The full syntax of table expressions is quite complex, and for that reason we defer the details to Chapter 11. However, we give an outline explanation of two particular cases here—basically the only two cases that were supported in SQL/89 (see paragraphs 4 and 5 below).

4. *Case 1:* The table expression takes the form

   ```
   VALUES ( insert-atom-commalist )
   ```

   where each "insert atom" is either a scalar expression or one of the self-explanatory key words DEFAULT or NULL. The effect is to insert a single row into the target table. The *i*th "insert atom" is inserted into the column identified by the *i*th entry in the (explicit or implicit) commalist of column names in the INTO clause.

5. *Case 2:* The table expression takes the form

   ```
   SELECT ... FROM ... [ WHERE ... ]  [ etc. ]
   ```

The effect is to insert multiple rows (in general) into the target table. The table expression is evaluated to yield an intermediate result table *R*. Each row of *R* in turn is then treated as if the scalar values in that row were specified as the "insert atoms" in the single-row version of the INSERT statement discussed in paragraph 4.

9.4 SEARCHED UPDATE

The searched UPDATE statement is used to update rows in a named table without using a cursor. The update is multiple-row, in general; i.e., the statement updates zero, one, two, . . . , or any number of rows in a single operation. Here is an example (a variation on an example from Chapter 2):

```
UPDATE S
SET     STATUS = 2 * S.STATUS
WHERE   S.CITY = :CITY_PARAM
```

The general syntax is:

```
UPDATE table
SET       assignment-commalist
[ WHERE   conditional-expression ]
```

where "table" identifies the target table (*T,* say), "assignments" are discussed below, and "conditional expression" identifies the rows of *T* that are to be updated. (Conditional expressions are discussed in detail in Chapter 12.) Omitting the WHERE clause means that the UPDATE is to be applied to all rows of *T.*

Each assignment has the form

```
column = update-atom
```

where "column" is the *un*qualified name of a column of table *T,* and "update atom" (like "insert atom"—see Section 9.3) is either a scalar expression or one of the self-explanatory key words DEFAULT or NULL. The rows of *T* that satisfy the conditional expression in the WHERE clause (or all rows of *T,* if the WHERE clause is omitted) are updated in accordance with the assignments in the SET clause. *Note:* For each row to be updated, any reference within an "update atom" to a column of table *T* denotes the value of that column (in that target row) before any of the assignments have been performed. The example at the beginning of this section provides an illustration of this point.

We close this section with another, more complex, example. The example is somewhat contrived, but is intended as an illustration of the fact that one possible form of scalar expression is a "subquery" that extracts a data value from elsewhere in the database:

```
UPDATE P
SET    CITY = ( SELECT  S.CITY
                FROM    S
                WHERE   S.SNO = 'S5' )
WHERE  P.COLOR = 'Red'
```

The effect of this UPDATE is to set the city for each red part to be equal to the city for supplier S5.

9.5 SEARCHED DELETE

The searched DELETE statement is used to delete rows in a named table without using a cursor. The delete is multiple-row, in general; i.e., the statement deletes zero, one, two, . . . , or any number of rows in a single operation. Here is an example (again a variation on an example from Chapter 2):

```
DELETE
FROM   P
WHERE  P.WEIGHT > :WEIGHT_PARAM
```

The general syntax is:

```
  DELETE
  FROM    table
[ WHERE   conditional-expression ]
```

where "table" identifies the target table (T, say) and "conditional expression" identifies the rows of T that are to be deleted. (Once again, conditional expressions are discussed in detail in Chapter 12.) Omitting the WHERE clause means that the DELETE is to be applied to all rows of T.

10

Data Manipulation:
Cursor Operations

10.1 INTRODUCTION

The basic concept of cursor-based access was explained in Chapter 2, Section 2.4; refer back to that section if you need to refresh your memory regarding the general idea. In this chapter we consider the cursor operations in some detail. The operations in question are as follows:

```
OPEN
FETCH
UPDATE (positioned) -- i.e., UPDATE ... CURRENT
DELETE (positioned) -- i.e., DELETE ... CURRENT
CLOSE
```

Section 10.2 explains exactly what a cursor is and what is involved in defining a cursor. Section 10.3 then discusses the five cursor operations in detail. Finally, Sections 10.4 and 10.5 present a comprehensive example that ties together many of the ideas introduced in the earlier sections (Section 10.4 gives a module language version of the example, Section 10.5 gives an embedded SQL equivalent). *Note:* As in the previous chapter, we assume for simplicity that all named tables—at least all those to be updated, i.e., those that are the target of an UPDATE or DELETE CURRENT operation—are base tables; the special considerations that apply to views are deferred to Chapter 13. We also (for the most part) ignore the possibility of errors.

10.2 CURSORS

A cursor consists essentially of a kind of *pointer* that can be used to run through an ordered collection of rows, pointing to each of the rows in that collection in turn and thus providing addressability to those rows one at a time. If cursor *C* is pointing to row *R,* it is said to be *positioned on* row *R.* Row *R* can then be updated or deleted via the "positioned" form of the UPDATE and DELETE operations (UPDATE/DELETE . . . WHERE CURRENT OF *C*).*

Each cursor has an associated *table expression,*† specified as part of the statement that defines the cursor. The expression can be *parameterized* by means of parameters (in the module language) or host variables (in embedded SQL). For example:

```
DECLARE X CURSOR
    FOR SELECT SP.SNO, SP.QTY
        FROM    SP
        WHERE   SP.PNO = :PNO_PARAM
        ORDER   BY SNO
```

This statement defines a cursor called X, with associated table expression "SELECT . . . :PNO_PARAM" (where :PNO_PARAM is a parameter). That table expression is not evaluated at this time; DECLARE CURSOR is a purely declarative operation. The expression *is* (effectively) evaluated when cursor X is opened (see Section 10.3). The collection of rows resulting from the evaluation of that expression then becomes associated with the cursor, and remains so until the cursor is closed again (again, see Section 10.3). Furthermore, the cursor also specifies an *ordering* for that collection of rows, thanks to the ORDER BY clause in the cursor definition.

Note: If the expression is parameterized (as it is in the example above), the values of the corresponding arguments are conceptually fixed at OPEN time—i.e., changing the values of those arguments after the cursor has been opened (and while it remains open) has no effect on the collection of rows accessible via the cursor. An analogous remark applies to the niladic functions CURRENT_USER, CURRENT_DATE, etc.

---

*In other words, for a positioned UPDATE or DELETE, the cursor must be in the "on state"; i.e., it must be positioned on some row. (This remark of course assumes that updates are permitted through the cursor in the first place; see the subsection "Cursor Definition" later in this section.)

†The standard calls it a *query* expression, and ascribes a different (more restricted) meaning to the term "table expression."

While it is open, therefore, a cursor designates a certain collection of rows and a certain ordering for that collection. It also designates a certain *position* with respect to that ordering. The possible positions are as follows:

- *on* some specific row ("on" state)
- *before* some specific row ("before" state)
- *after* the last row ("after last" state)

OPEN positions the cursor before the first row. FETCH NEXT positions the cursor on the next row or (if there is no next row) after the last row (see Section 10.3 for a discussion of other FETCH formats). If the cursor is on or before some row and that row is deleted via the cursor (i.e., by means of an appropriate DELETE CURRENT operation), the cursor is positioned before the next row or (if there is no next row) after the last row.* Note that the cursor can be "before the first row" or "after the last row" even in the special case where the collection of rows is empty.

All cursors are in the closed state at SQL-transaction initiation and are forced into the closed state (if open) at SQL-transaction termination. While the SQL-transaction is executing, however, the same cursor can be opened and closed any number of times. And if the cursor definition is parameterized, then those parameters can have different values on different openings, implying that the same cursor can be associated with different collections of rows on different openings.

Cursor Definition

For definiteness, we assume until further notice that we are working with the module language rather than embedded SQL. Recall from Chapter 6 that cursor definitions are one type of "module element" (*procedures* are the other; cursor definitions and procedures can be arbitrarily interspersed within the module, except that each cursor definition must physically precede all procedures that use that cursor). The syntax for a cursor definition is:

```
DECLARE cursor [ INSENSITIVE ] [ SCROLL ] CURSOR
        FOR cursor-specification
```

And a "cursor specification" looks like this:

---

*INSERT, UPDATE, or DELETE operations that either use some distinct cursor or do not use a cursor at all would seem to have similar potential for changing cursor state and positioning. However, all the standard has to say on such matters is the following: "[If INSENSITIVE is not specified,] whether the effect of [such updates] will be visible through [the cursor] is implementation-dependent."

```
    table-expression
[ ORDER BY order-item-commalist ]
[ FOR { READ ONLY | UPDATE [ OF column-commalist ] } ]
```

Explanation:

1. Let *T* be the table that results from evaluating the table expression when the cursor is opened. If INSENSITIVE is specified, OPEN will effectively cause a *separate copy* of *T* to be created, and the cursor will access that copy; thus, updates that affect *T* that are made through other cursors, or made without cursors at all, will not be visible through this opening of this cursor. UPDATE and DELETE CURRENT operations will not be allowed on a cursor for which INSENSITIVE is specified.

   If INSENSITIVE is not specified, then in general OPEN may or may not cause a separate copy of *T* to be created. Whether updates that affect *T* that are made through other cursors, or are made without cursors at all, will be visible through this opening of this cursor is implementation-dependent.

   Note that OPEN will definitely *not* create a separate copy of *T* if "the cursor is updatable"—see paragraph 3 below.*

2. SCROLL means that all forms of FETCH (see Section 10.3) are legal against this cursor. If SCROLL is not specified, only FETCH NEXT is legal. Note that UPDATE and DELETE CURRENT operations *are* allowed on a cursor for which SCROLL is specified, in general.

3. We defer a detailed explanation of "table expression" to Chapter 11. However, the general purpose of that expression (in the context under discussion) is to define the collection of rows that will be accessible via the cursor when the cursor is opened. That collection of rows will be updatable via the cursor (i.e., UPDATE and DELETE CURRENT operations will be allowed, or "the cursor will be updatable," to use an inaccurate but common expression) if and only if (a) the table expression would define an updatable view if it appeared in the context of a view definition (see Chapter 13) *and* (b) the cursor definition does not specify INSENSITIVE or FOR READ ONLY.

4. When the cursor is opened (and not before), the table expression is evaluated to yield a table of, in general, multiple rows. The purpose of

---

*Conceptually, the result of evaluating *any* table expression is *always* a brand new, unnamed table. For instance, evaluating the expression "SELECT * FROM P" conceptually yields a brand new, unnamed table that just happens to be isomorphic to table P. However, in certain simple cases—specifically, those cases in which "the cursor is updatable"—the result of evaluating the table expression is considered for cursor definition purposes actually to *be* that named table, instead of the "brand new, unnamed" table.

the ORDER BY clause is to specify an ordering for those rows (as seen through the cursor). Further details are given in the subsection "The ORDER BY Clause" below.

5. The specification FOR READ ONLY means that UPDATE and DELETE CURRENT operations will not be requested (and will not be allowed) on this cursor. The specification FOR UPDATE—with or without "OF column-commalist"—is permitted only if "the cursor is updatable" (see paragraph 3 above). If "OF column-commalist" is specified, every column name in the commalist must be the *unqualified* name of a column of table *T* (the table that results from the evaluation of the table expression); omitting "OF column-commalist" is equivalent to specifying all of the columns of table *T.* The meaning of the FOR UPDATE clause is that columns identified in that clause (and no others) may be the target of an assignment within an UPDATE CURRENT operation against this cursor.*

If neither FOR READ ONLY nor FOR UPDATE is specified, then:

- If *T* is not updatable or if INSENSITIVE, SCROLL, or ORDER BY is specified, FOR READ ONLY is assumed

- Otherwise FOR UPDATE (without "OF column-commalist") is assumed

The ORDER BY Clause

As indicated above, the ORDER BY clause specifies a commalist of "order items." Each "order item" takes the form:

```
{ column | unsigned-integer } [ ASC | DESC ]
```

The left-to-right sequence of order-items in the ORDER BY clause corresponds to major-to-minor ordering in accordance with familiar convention. Usually each order-item consists of a simple column name (*un*qualified, observe), identifying a column of the result table *T,* with an optional specification of ASC or DESC; ASC (default) means ascending order and DESC means descending order. Alternatively, an order-item can consist of an unsigned decimal integer, as in the following example:

```
DECLARE Y CURSOR
    FOR SELECT SP.PNO, AVG ( SP.QTY )
        FROM    SP
        GROUP   BY SP.PNO
        ORDER   BY 2
```

---

*Note that a column that is mentioned in the ORDER BY clause cannot be the target of such an assignment even if it is also mentioned in the FOR UPDATE clause.

The integer refers to the ordinal (left-to-right) position of the column within the result table *T*. This feature makes it possible to define an ordering for a collection of rows on the basis of a column that does not have a proper, user-known column name of its own. In the example, the "2" refers to the column of averages.

Note, however, that it is never necessary to use the foregoing "integer" trick, because it is always possible to introduce a proper, user-known column name for a column that would not otherwise have one. For example:

```
DECLARE Y CURSOR
    FOR SELECT SP.PNO, AVG ( SP.QTY ) AS AQ
        FROM    SP
        GROUP   BY SP.PNO
        ORDER   BY AQ
```

(Refer to Chapter 11, Section 11.6, for further discussion of the AS clause.) For this reason, integer order-items are regarded as a "deprecated feature" of the standard, and are likely to be dropped at some future time.

Note that (as already indicated) each order-item must identify a column of the *result table*. Thus, for example, the following is *** *ILLEGAL* *** :

```
DECLARE Z CURSOR
    FOR SELECT S.SNO
        FROM    S
        ORDER   BY CITY          -- This is *** ILLEGAL *** !!!
```

Finally, if no ORDER BY clause is specified, the rows of the result table *T* (as seen through the cursor) will have an implementation-dependent ordering. Likewise, if an ORDER BY clause is specified that does not define a total ordering for table *T*, then the relative order of rows (as seen through the cursor) that have the same value for the order-item(s) will again be implementation-dependent. For example:

```
DECLARE W CURSOR
    FOR SELECT SP.SNO, SP.PNO, SP.QTY
        FROM    SP
        ORDER   BY SNO
```

In this example, the relative order of SP rows with the same PNO value (as seen through cursor W) will be implementation-dependent.

10.3 CURSOR-BASED MANIPULATION STATEMENTS

OPEN

For each cursor definition in a given module, there must be exactly one procedure in that module whose function it is to open the cursor in question. The OPEN statement takes the form

```
OPEN cursor
```

where "cursor" identifies a cursor (*C,* say). Cursor *C* must currently be in the closed state. The table expression in the definition of *C* is evaluated, using current values for any parameters referenced in that table expression, to yield a certain collection of rows as explained in Section 10.2. An ordering for that collection is defined as described above, and cursor *C* is placed in the open state and positioned before the first row (in accordance with that ordering) of that collection. *Note:* We will refer to the collection of rows, together with the corresponding ordering, as the *ordered table* associated with cursor *C.*

Here is an example of a procedure that opens the cursor X defined near the beginning of Section 10.2:

```
PROCEDURE OPENX
  ( SQLSTATE,
    :PNO_PARAM CHAR(6) ) ;
    OPEN X ;
```

Note that any parameter mentioned in the definition of a given cursor must be defined in the procedure that opens that cursor.

FETCH

The FETCH statement takes the form

```
FETCH [ [ row-selector ] FROM ] cursor INTO target-commalist
```

where "cursor" identifies a cursor (*C,* say), "target-commalist" is a commalist of parameters (in the module language) or host variables (in embedded SQL), and "row selector" is any of the following:

```
NEXT
PRIOR
FIRST
LAST
ABSOLUTE n
RELATIVE n
```

Here:

- NEXT is the only legal "row selector" unless "cursor" is defined to be of type SCROLL

- FROM is basically just a noiseword* (though it is required if "row selector" is specified explicitly)

---

*Not a very *good* noiseword at that, since the retrieval is not "from the cursor," it is from the row the cursor is positioned on.

- NEXT is assumed if "row selector" is omitted
- The specification *n* in the ABSOLUTE and RELATIVE cases must be a literal, parameter, or host variable of data type exact numeric with a scale of zero
- The meanings of NEXT, PRIOR, FIRST, and LAST are self-explanatory
- "ABSOLUTE *n*" refers to the *n*th row in the ordered table *T* that is associated with cursor *C* (a negative value of *n* means counting backwards from the end of *T*)
- "RELATIVE *n*" refers to the *n*th row in *T,* counting relative to the row on which cursor *C* is currently positioned (again, a negative value of *n* means counting backwards)

The target commalist must contain exactly one target for each column of table *T*; the *i*th target in that commalist corresponds to the *i*th column of *T*.

Cursor *C* must currently be open. Assuming that "row selector" does identify a row of the ordered table *T*—i.e., there is a NEXT row or PRIOR row or FIRST row or LAST row, as applicable, in the case of NEXT/ PRIOR/FIRST/LAST, or the value of *n* identifies a row between the first and last row (inclusive), in the case of ABSOLUTE *n* or RELATIVE *n**— then cursor *C* is positioned on that row, values are retrieved from that row, and assignments are made to targets in accordance with the specifications in the INTO clause. If "row selector" does not identify a row of the ordered table *T*—i.e., there is no NEXT row or PRIOR row or FIRST row or LAST row, as applicable, in the case of NEXT/PRIOR/FIRST/LAST, or the value of *n* is out of range, in the case of ABSOLUTE *n* or RELATIVE *n*—then no data is retrieved, and cursor *C* is positioned "after the last row" or "before the first row," depending on whether "row selector" was attempting to go forward or backward from cursor *C*'s previous position. Note that (as mentioned previously) cursor *C* can be "after the last row" or "before the first row" even if *T* is empty.

Here is an example of FETCH, again using the cursor X defined near the beginning of Section 10.2:

```
FETCH NEXT FROM X INTO :SNO_PARAM, :QTY_PARAM
```

---

*A value of zero for *n* means the current row for RELATIVE but is out of range for ABSOLUTE.

Positioned UPDATE

The positioned UPDATE statement takes the form

```
UPDATE table
SET     assignment-commalist
WHERE   CURRENT OF cursor
```

where "table" identifies the target table (*T,* say), "cursor" identifies a cursor (*C,* say), and the SET clause is exactly as for searched UPDATE (see Section 9.4). Cursor *C* must currently be open, must be "updatable," and must be positioned on a row of table *T.* That row of *T* is updated in accordance with the assignments in the SET clause. Each column to be updated must have been mentioned in an (explicit or implicit) FOR UPDATE clause in the definition of cursor *C.*

Example:

```
UPDATE SP
SET     QTY = SP.QTY + :INCR_PARAM
WHERE   CURRENT OF X
```

Note that a positioned UPDATE must not update any column that was mentioned (either directly or indirectly) in an ORDER BY clause for the relevant cursor.

Positioned DELETE

The positioned DELETE statement takes the form

```
DELETE
FROM    table
WHERE   CURRENT OF cursor
```

where "table" identifies the target table (*T,* say) and "cursor" identifies a cursor (*C,* say). Cursor *C* must currently be open, must be "updatable," and must be positioned on a row of table *T.* That row is deleted from *T.*

Example:

```
DELETE
FROM    SP
WHERE   CURRENT OF X
```

Cursor X will now be positioned before the row immediately following the row just deleted, or after the last row if no such immediately following row exists.

CLOSE

The CLOSE statement takes the form

```
CLOSE cursor
```

where "cursor" identifies a cursor (*C*, say). Cursor *C* (which must currently be open) is placed in the closed state.
Example:

```
CLOSE X
```


10.4   A COMPREHENSIVE EXAMPLE (MODULE VERSION)

We conclude with a somewhat contrived, but comprehensive, example that shows how many of the ideas introduced in this chapter (and earlier chapters) fit together. The host program (which is written in PL/I) accepts four input values—a part number (GIVENPNO), a city name (GIVENCIT), a status increment (GIVENINC), and a status level (GIVENLVL). The program scans all suppliers of the part identified by GIVENPNO. For each such supplier, if the supplier city is GIVENCIT, then the status is increased by GIVENINC; otherwise, if the status is less than GIVENLVL, the supplier is deleted, together with all shipments for that supplier. In all cases supplier information is displayed to the user ("PUT SKIP LIST"), with an indication of how that particular supplier was handled by the program.

Note: Observe that we choose to delete shipment rows *before* we delete the corresponding supplier row. The reason is, of course, that if we attempted to delete the supplier first, and the supplier in question in fact did have some corresponding shipments, the DELETE might fail, because of the foreign key constraint from shipments to suppliers (see Chapter 14). We remark that careful concurrency control needs to be applied here in order to prevent some concurrent SQL-transaction from (e.g.) inserting another shipment for the current supplier between our two DELETEs. Unfortunately, the standard does not include any explicit concurrency control facilities (explicit locking, etc.). On the other hand, if all SQL-transactions execute at isolation level 3 (see Chapter 5, Section 5.4), then the system will guarantee that violations of serializability such as the one just mentioned cannot occur.

Here then is the host program:

```
PLIEX: PROC OPTIONS (MAIN) ;

        /* program input */

        DCL GIVENPNO       CHAR(6) ;
        DCL GIVENCIT       CHAR(15) ;
```

```
DCL GIVENINC       FIXED DECIMAL(3) ;
DCL GIVENLVL       FIXED DECIMAL(3) ;

/* targets for "FETCH SUPPLIER" */

DCL SNO            CHAR(5) ;
DCL SNAME          CHAR(20) ;
DCL STATUS         FIXED DECIMAL(3) ;
DCL CITY           CHAR(15) ;

/* housekeeping variables */

DCL DISP           CHAR(7) ;
DCL MORE_SUPPLIERS BIT(1) ;

/* SQL return code variable */

DCL RETCODE        CHAR(5) ;

/* SQL entry point declarations, in alphabetical order */

DCL CLOSE_PROC     ENTRY ( CHAR(5) ) ;
DCL COMMIT_PROC    ENTRY ( CHAR(5) ) ;
DCL DELETE_S_PROC  ENTRY ( CHAR(5) ) ;
DCL DELETE_SP_PROC ENTRY ( CHAR(5), CHAR(5) ) ;
DCL FETCH_PROC     ENTRY ( CHAR(5), CHAR(5),
                                    CHAR(20),
                                    FIXED DECIMAL(3),
                                    CHAR(15) ) ;
DCL OPEN_PROC      ENTRY ( CHAR(5), CHAR(6) ) ;
DCL ROLLBACK_PROC  ENTRY ( CHAR(5) ) ;
DCL UPDATE_PROC    ENTRY ( CHAR(5), FIXED DECIMAL(3) ) ;

/* database exception handler */

ON CONDITION ( DBEXCEPTION )
BEGIN ;
   PUT SKIP LIST ( RETCODE ) ;
   CALL ROLLBACK_PROC ( RETCODE ) ;
   PUT SKIP LIST ( RETCODE ) ;
   GO TO QUIT ;
END ;

/* main program logic */

GET LIST ( GIVENPNO, GIVENCIT, GIVENINC, GIVENLVL ) ;
CALL OPEN_PROC ( RETCODE, GIVENPNO ) ;
IF ¬ ( RETCODE = '00000' )
THEN SIGNAL CONDITION ( DBEXCEPTION ) ;
MORE_SUPPLIERS = '1'B ;
DO WHILE ( MORE_SUPPLIERS ) ;
   CALL FETCH_PROC ( RETCODE, SNO, SNAME, STATUS, CITY ) ;
   SELECT ;              /* a PL/I SELECT, not a SQL SELECT */
      WHEN ( RETCODE = '02000' )
         MORE_SUPPLIERS = '0'B ;
      WHEN ¬ ( RETCODE = '02000' | RETCODE = '00000' )
         SIGNAL CONDITION ( DBEXCEPTION ) ;
      WHEN ( RETCODE = '00000' )
         DO ;
            DISP = '       ' ;
            IF CITY = GIVENCIT
            THEN
               DO ;
```

```
                              CALL UPDATE_PROC
                                  ( RETCODE, SNO, GIVENINC ) ;
                              IF ¬ ( RETCODE = '00000' )
                              THEN SIGNAL CONDITION ( DBEXCEPTION ) ;
                              DISP = 'UPDATED' ;
                         END ;
                    ELSE
                    IF STATUS < GIVENLVL
                    THEN
                         DO ;
                              CALL DELETE_SP_PROC ( RETCODE, SNO ) ;
                              IF ¬ ( RETCODE = '00000'
                                   | RETCODE = '02000' )
                              THEN SIGNAL CONDITION ( DBEXCEPTION ) ;
                              CALL DELETE_S_PROC ( RETCODE, SNO ) ;
                              IF ¬ ( RETCODE = '00000' )
                              THEN SIGNAL CONDITION ( DBEXCEPTION ) ;
                              DISP = 'DELETED' ;
                         END ;
                    PUT SKIP LIST
                              ( SNO, SNAME, STATUS, CITY, DISP ) ;
                  END ;    /* WHEN ( RETCODE = '00000' ) ... */
          END ;    /* PL/I SELECT */
     END ;    /* DO WHILE */
     CALL CLOSE_PROC ( RETCODE ) ;
     IF ¬ ( RETCODE = '00000' )
     THEN SIGNAL CONDITION ( DBEXCEPTION ) ;
     CALL COMMIT_PROC ( RETCODE ) ;
     IF ¬ ( RETCODE = '00000' )
     THEN SIGNAL CONDITION ( DBEXCEPTION ) ;
QUIT: RETURN ;
     END ;    /* PLIEX */
```

And here is the corresponding module:

```
MODULE SQLEXMOD
        LANGUAGE PLI
        SCHEMA CJD_CATALOG.CJD_SCHEMA
        AUTHORIZATION CJD

        DECLARE Z CURSOR FOR
           SELECT S.SNO, S.SNAME, S.STATUS, S.CITY
           FROM   S
           WHERE  S.SNO IN
                  ( SELECT SP.SNO
                    FROM   SP
                    WHERE  SP.PNO = :PNO )      -- PNO is a parameter
           FOR UPDATE OF STATUS

PROCEDURE CLOSE_PROC
     ( SQLSTATE ) ;
        CLOSE Z ;

PROCEDURE COMMIT_PROC
     ( SQLSTATE ) ;
        COMMIT ;

PROCEDURE DELETE_S_PROC
     ( SQLSTATE ) ;
        DELETE FROM S WHERE CURRENT OF Z ;
```

```
PROCEDURE DELETE_SP_PROC
     ( SQLSTATE,
       :SNO CHAR(5) ) ;
       DELETE FROM SP WHERE SP.SNO = :SNO ;

PROCEDURE FETCH_PROC
     ( SQLSTATE,
       :SNO     CHAR(5),
       :SNAME   CHAR(20),
       :STATUS  DECIMAL(3),
       :CITY    CHAR(20) ) ;
       FETCH NEXT FROM Z INTO :SNO, :SNAME, :STATUS, :CITY ;

PROCEDURE OPEN_PROC
     ( SQLSTATE,
       :PNO CHAR(6) ) ;
       OPEN Z ;

PROCEDURE ROLLBACK_PROC
     ( SQLSTATE ) ;
       ROLLBACK ;

PROCEDURE UPDATE_PROC
     ( SQLSTATE,
       :GIVENINC DECIMAL(3) ) ;
       UPDATE S
       SET     STATUS = S.STATUS + :GIVENINC
       WHERE   CURRENT OF Z ;
```

10.5 A COMPREHENSIVE EXAMPLE (EMBEDDED SQL VERSION)

A host language program with embedded SQL statements—an "embedded SQL host program"—consists of an otherwise standard host program plus a set of embedded SQL declare sections, a set of embedded cursor definitions, a set of embedded exception declarations, and a set of embedded SQL statements. We show below an embedded SQL version of the example from the previous section. Refer back to Chapter 6, Section 6.3, if you need to refresh your memory regarding the specifics of embedded SQL.

```
SQLEX: PROC OPTIONS (MAIN) ;

     EXEC SQL BEGIN DECLARE SECTION ;

        /* program input */

        DCL GIVENPNO     CHAR(6) ;
        DCL GIVENCIT     CHAR(15) ;
        DCL GIVENINC     FIXED DECIMAL(3) ;
        DCL GIVENLVL     FIXED DECIMAL(3) ;

        /* targets for "FETCH SUPPLIER" */

        DCL SNO          CHAR(5) ;
        DCL SNAME        CHAR(20) ;
        DCL STATUS       FIXED DECIMAL(3) ;
        DCL CITY         CHAR(15) ;
```

```
    /* SQL return code variable */

    DCL SQLSTATE          CHAR(5) ;

EXEC SQL END DECLARE SECTION ;

/* housekeeping variables */

DCL DISP              CHAR(7) ;
DCL MORE_SUPPLIERS BIT(1) ;

/* exception declarations */

EXEC SQL WHENEVER NOT FOUND CONTINUE ;
EXEC SQL WHENEVER SQLERROR  CONTINUE ;

/* database exception handler */

ON CONDITION ( DBEXCEPTION )
BEGIN ;
   PUT SKIP LIST ( SQLSTATE ) ;
   EXEC SQL ROLLBACK ;
   PUT SKIP LIST ( SQLSTATE ) ;
   GO TO QUIT ;
END ;

/* cursor definition */

EXEC SQL DECLARE Z CURSOR FOR
   SELECT S.SNO, S.SNAME, S.STATUS, S.CITY
   FROM   S
   WHERE  S.SNO IN
        ( SELECT SP.SNO
          FROM   SP
          WHERE  SP.PNO = :GIVENPNO ) ;

GET LIST ( GIVENPNO, GIVENCIT, GIVENINC, GIVENLVL ) ;
EXEC SQL OPEN Z ;
IF ¬ ( SQLSTATE = '00000' )
THEN SIGNAL CONDITION ( DBEXCEPTION ) ;
MORE_SUPPLIERS = '1'B ;
DO WHILE ( MORE_SUPPLIERS ) ;
   EXEC SQL FETCH Z INTO :SNO, :SNAME, :STATUS, :CITY ;
   SELECT ;             /* a PL/I SELECT, not a SQL SELECT */
      WHEN ( SQLSTATE  = '02000' )
         MORE_SUPPLIERS = '0'B ;
      WHEN ¬ ( SQLSTATE = '02000' | SQLSTATE = '00000' )
         SIGNAL CONDITION ( DBEXCEPTION ) ;
      WHEN ( SQLSTATE = '00000' )
         DO ;
            DISP = '       ' ;
            IF CITY = GIVENCIT
            THEN
               DO ;
                  EXEC SQL UPDATE S
                           SET    STATUS =
                                  S.STATUS + :GIVENINC
                           WHERE  CURRENT OF Z ;
                  IF ¬ ( SQLSTATE = '00000' )
                  THEN SIGNAL CONDITION ( DBEXCEPTION ) ;
                  DISP = 'UPDATED' ;
               END ;
            ELSE
```

```
              IF STATUS < GIVENLVL
              THEN
                  DO ;
                      EXEC SQL DELETE
                              FROM    SP
                              WHERE   SP.SNO = :SNO ;
                      IF ¬ ( SQLSTATE = '00000'
                           | SQLSTATE = '02000' )
                      THEN SIGNAL CONDITION ( DBEXCEPTION ) ;
                      EXEC SQL DELETE
                              FROM    S
                              WHERE   CURRENT OF Z ;
                      IF ¬ ( SQLSTATE = '00000' )
                      THEN SIGNAL CONDITION ( DBEXCEPTION ) ;
                      DISP = 'DELETED' ;
                  END ;
              PUT SKIP LIST
                  ( SNO, SNAME, STATUS, CITY, DISP ) ;
          END ;    /* WHEN ( SQLSTATE = '00000' ) ... */
      END ;    /* PL/I SELECT */
  END ;    /* DO WHILE */
  EXEC SQL CLOSE Z ;
  IF ¬ ( SQLSTATE = '00000' )
  THEN SIGNAL CONDITION ( DBEXCEPTION ) ;
  EXEC SQL COMMIT ;
  IF ¬ ( SQLSTATE = '00000' )
  THEN SIGNAL CONDITION ( DBEXCEPTION ) ;
QUIT: RETURN ;
  END ;    /* SQLEX */
```

11

Table Expressions

11.1 INTRODUCTION

In this chapter we explain the crucially important construct "table expression," which appears in numerous contexts throughout the SQL language; in many ways, in fact, it can be regarded as being at the top of the syntax tree. *Note:* As mentioned in Chapter 10, the standard refers to this construct as a *query* expression, and ascribes a different meaning to the term "table expression." We prefer our term, because the whole point is, precisely, that the expression does evaluate to a *table* (actually an *unnamed* table). By contrast, what the standard calls a "table expression" is merely a special case (it corresponds to what we refer to as a "select expression" below, minus the SELECT clause itself).

We begin by giving the full BNF definition of "table expression," for purposes of subsequent reference. We then go on to explain that definition piecemeal in the sections that follow.

```
table-expression
    ::=   join-table-expression
        | nonjoin-table-expression
```

```
join-table-expression
    ::=    table-reference [ NATURAL ] [ join-type ] JOIN
                  table-reference [ ON conditional-expression
                                  | USING ( column-commalist ) ]
         | table-reference CROSS JOIN table-reference
         | ( join-table-expression )

table-reference
    ::=    table [ [ AS ] range-variable
                      [ ( column-commalist ) ] ]
         | ( table-expression ) [ AS ] range-variable
                              [ ( column-commalist ) ]
         | join-table-expression

join-type
    ::=    INNER
         | LEFT [ OUTER ]
         | RIGHT [ OUTER ]
         | FULL [ OUTER ]
         | UNION

nonjoin-table-expression
    ::=    nonjoin-table-term
         | table-expression { UNION | EXCEPT } [ ALL ]
              [ CORRESPONDING [ BY ( column-commalist ) ] ]
                    table-term

nonjoin-table-term
    ::=    nonjoin-table-primary
         | table-term INTERSECT [ ALL ]
              [ CORRESPONDING [ BY ( column-commalist ) ] ]
                    table-primary

table-term
    ::=    nonjoin-table-term
         | join-table-expression

table-primary
    ::=    nonjoin-table-primary
         | join-table-expression

nonjoin-table-primary
    ::=    TABLE table
         | table-constructor
         | select-expression
         | ( nonjoin-table-expression )

table-constructor
    ::=    VALUES row-constructor-commalist

row-constructor
    ::=    ( atom-commalist ) | ( table-expression )

select-expression
    ::=    SELECT [ ALL | DISTINCT ] select-item-commalist
              FROM table-reference-commalist
                 [ WHERE conditional-expression ]
                    [ GROUP BY column-commalist ]
                       [ HAVING conditional-expression ]

select-item
    ::=    scalar-expression [ [ AS ] column ]
         | [ range-variable . ] *
```

11.2 JOIN EXPRESSIONS

First, table expressions in general are divided into join and nonjoin table expressions:*

```
table-expression
    ::=    join-table-expression
       |  nonjoin-table-expression
```

In this section we consider the first of these two cases only. Broadly speaking, a join table expression ("join expression" for short) represents an explicit join of some kind between two tables, each of which is represented by a "table reference" (see Section 11.3, later). More precisely, a join expression is either (a) a "cross join" or (b) a join involving an explicit or implicit "join type" (or it might consist of a join expression in parentheses; however, the parentheses are included purely for syntactic reasons and have no effect on the semantics of the expression):

```
join-table-expression
    ::=    table-reference CROSS JOIN table-reference
       |  table-reference [ NATURAL ] [ join-type ] JOIN
               table-reference [ ON conditional-expression
                              |  USING ( column-commalist ) ]
       |  ( join-table-expression )
```

Cross Join

"Cross join" is just another term for Cartesian product. That is, the expression *A* CROSS JOIN *B* evaluates to a table consisting of all possible rows *ab* such that *ab* is the concatenation of a row *a* from *A* and a row *b* from *B*.† It follows that the join expression *A* CROSS JOIN *B* is semantically identical to the select-expression

```
SELECT *
FROM   A, B
```

(see Section 11.6 for an explanation of select-expressions).

Other Joins

The syntax for other join expressions (to repeat) is:

---

*Do not be misled by this terminology: A nonjoin table expression might still represent a join, as we saw in Chapter 2. The point is simply that join table expressions directly involve the explicit key word JOIN, and nonjoin table expressions do not.

†This definition requires a certain amount of care and refinement if either *A* or *B* includes any duplicate rows. See Appendix D.

```
table-reference [ NATURAL ] [ join-type ] JOIN table-reference
      [ ON conditional-expression | USING ( column-commalist ) ]
```

"Join type" in turn is any of the following:

```
INNER
LEFT [ OUTER ]
RIGHT [ OUTER ]
FULL [ OUTER ]
UNION
```

Syntax rules:

- NATURAL and UNION cannot both be specified
- If either NATURAL or UNION is specified, neither an ON clause nor a USING clause can be specified
- If neither NATURAL nor UNION is specified, then either an ON clause or a USING clause must be specified
- If "join type" is omitted, INNER is assumed by default

Note: The optional OUTER on LEFT, RIGHT, and FULL is a mere noiseword and has no effect on the overall meaning of the expression.

LEFT, RIGHT, FULL (with or without the noiseword OUTER), and UNION all have to do with nulls; we therefore defer discussion of them to Chapter 16. So we are left with the following cases to consider:

1. `table-reference JOIN table-reference ON conditional-expression`

2. `table-reference JOIN table-reference USING ( column-commalist )`

3. `table-reference NATURAL JOIN table-reference`

In each case, let *A* and *B* be the tables resulting from evaluation of the two table references. Then *Case 1* ("*A* JOIN *B* ON *C*," where *C* is a conditional expression) is defined to be semantically identical to the following select-expression:

```
SELECT *
FROM    A, B
WHERE   C
```

(again, see Section 11.6 for an explanation of select-expressions; conditional expressions are discussed in Chapter 12).

In *Case 2,* let the commalist of columns in the USING clause be *C1,* *C2, . . . , Cn.* Each of *C1, C2, . . . , Cn* must be *un*qualified and must identify both a column of *A* and a column of *B.* Then the join expression is defined to be semantically identical to a Case 1 expression in which the ON clause is of the form—

```
ON A.C1 = B.C1 AND A.C2 = B.C2 AND ... AND A.Cn = B.Cn
```

—except that (a) each of the common columns *C1, C2, . . . , Cn* appears only once, not twice, in the final result, and (b) the result column ordering is different—the common columns appear first (i.e., at the left), then the other columns of *A,* then the other columns of *B.*

Finally, a *Case 3* expression is defined to be semantically identical to a Case 2 expression in which the commalist of columns specifies *all* of the columns that are common to *A* and *B. Note:* It is possible that there are no common columns at all, in which case *A* NATURAL JOIN *B* degenerates to *A* CROSS JOIN *B.*

Here are some examples (all based as usual on the suppliers-and-parts database):

```
S JOIN SP ON S.SNO = SP.SNO

S JOIN SP USING ( SNO )

S NATURAL JOIN SP
```

These three expressions are all equivalent, except that the first produces a table with two identical SNO columns and the second and third produce a table with just one such column.

11.3 TABLE REFERENCES

A table reference is a reference to some table, either named (i.e., a base table or a view) or unnamed. Table references in SQL serve two general purposes: They specify the operands in FROM clauses in select-expressions (see Section 11.6), and they specify the operands in explicit joins (i.e., join expressions—see Section 11.2 above). Syntactically, a table reference consists of *either* a join expression (already discussed in Section 11.2) *or* one of the following: (a) a table name, or (b) a table expression in parentheses. In case (a), the table reference can optionally also include an AS clause, whose purpose is to introduce a *range variable* that ranges over the table in question, and optionally to introduce a set of column names for the columns of that table as well; in case (b), it *must* include such an AS clause. Thus, the overall syntax is:

```
table-reference
    ::=    table [ [ AS ] range-variable
                     [ ( column-commalist ) ] ]
         | ( table-expression ) [ AS ] range-variable
                     [ ( column-commalist ) ]
         | join-table-expression
```

Here is a simple example:

```
S AS SX
```

Here SX is a range variable that ranges over the suppliers table S. *Note:* The AS is a mere noiseword and can be omitted without changing the meaning, thus:

```
S SX
```

In order to explain the range variable concept, we consider the following example: "Get all pairs of supplier numbers such that the two suppliers concerned are located in the same city." One possible SQL formulation for this query is as follows:*

```
SELECT  FIRST.SNO AS XX, SECOND.SNO AS YY
FROM    S AS FIRST, S AS SECOND
WHERE   FIRST.CITY = SECOND.CITY
```

This expression involves a join of table S with itself over matching cities, as we now explain. Suppose for a moment that we had two separate copies of table S, the "first" copy and the "second" copy. Then the logic of the query is as follows: We need to examine all possible pairs of supplier rows, one from the first copy of S and one from the second, and to retrieve the two supplier numbers from such a pair of rows if and only if the two CITY values are equal. We therefore need to be able to reference two supplier rows at the same time. In order to distinguish between the two references, we introduce the two "range variables" FIRST and SECOND, each of which "ranges over" table S (for the duration of the evaluation of the containing table expression). At any particular time, FIRST represents some row from the "first" copy of table S, and SECOND represents some row from the "second" copy. The result of the query is found by examining all possible pairs of FIRST/SECOND values and checking the WHERE condition in every case:

XX	YY
S1	S1
S1	S4
S2	S2
S2	S3
S3	S2
S3	S3
S4	S1
S4	S4
S5	S5

---

*The SELECT-FROM-WHERE in this example is multiple-row and so cannot be executed as a separate statement in its own right (other than in "direct" SQL). Instead, we must use that SELECT-FROM-WHERE as the basis for defining a *cursor* (as described in Chapter 10), and then use that cursor to retrieve the desired data. For simplicity, however, it is convenient to assume that multiple-row SELECTs *can* be executed in their own right, and for tutorial reasons we will make that assumption throughout the remainder of this chapter, and indeed throughout many of the chapters that follow also.

Notice the introduced names XX and YY for the result columns (see Section 11.6 below for further discussion of such introduced names). *Note:* We can tidy up the result by extending the WHERE clause as follows:

```
SELECT FIRST.SNO AS XX, SECOND.SNO AS YY
FROM   S AS FIRST, S AS SECOND
WHERE  FIRST.CITY = SECOND.CITY
AND    FIRST.SNO < SECOND.SNO
```

The effect of the condition FIRST.SNO < SECOND.SNO is twofold: (a) It eliminates pairs of supplier numbers of the form (x,x); (b) it guarantees that the pairs (x,y) and (y,x) will not both appear. Result:

XX	YY
S1	S4
S2	S3

This is the first example we have seen in this book in which the explicit use of range variables has been necessary. However, it is never wrong to introduce such variables, even when they are not explicitly required, and sometimes they can help to make the expression clearer. They can also save writing, if table names are on the lengthy side.

In general, then, a range variable is a variable that ranges over some specified table—i.e., a variable whose permitted values are rows of that table. In other words, if range variable R ranges over table T, then, at any given time, the expression "R" represents some row r of T. For example, consider the query "Get supplier numbers for suppliers in Paris with status > 20." A "natural" formulation of this query in SQL would be:

```
SELECT S.SNO
FROM   S
WHERE  S.CITY = 'Paris'
AND    S.STATUS > 20
```

However, it could equally well be expressed as follows:

```
SELECT SX.SNO
FROM   S AS SX
WHERE  SX.CITY = 'Paris'
AND    SX.STATUS > 20
```

The range variable here is SX, and it ranges over table S.

As a matter of fact, SQL *always* requires select expressions (and join expressions) to be formulated in terms of range variables. If no such variables are specified explicitly, then SQL assumes the existence of *implicit* range variables with the same name(s) as the corresponding table(s). For example, the expression

```
SELECT T.C
FROM   T
  .....
```

(where *T* is a table name) is treated by SQL as if it had been written as follows:

```
SELECT T.C
FROM   T AS T
.....
```

—in other words, "*T*" itself is an implicit range variable name, representing a range variable called *T* that ranges over the table called *T*.*

Note: The standard does not use the term "range variable." Instead, it refers to names such as SX in the example above as "correlation names," and does not say what kind of object is denoted by such names. "Range variable" is the orthodox term, however, and in this book we will stick with it.

The table corresponding to a given range variable is not necessarily a named table (i.e., base table or view). For example, consider the following:

```
SELECT JX.SNO, JX.CITY, JX.PNO
FROM   ( S NATURAL JOIN SP ) AS JX
```

In this example, the range variable JX ranges over an unnamed table—to be specific, a table that is the natural join of tables S and SP over supplier numbers.

Here is another example of a table reference involving an AS clause, to illustrate the introduction of column names for the result (the result, that is, of evaluating the table expression nested within the table reference):

```
SELECT JSNO, JCITY, JPNO
FROM   ( S NATURAL JOIN SP )
       AS JX ( JSNO, JSNAME, JSTATUS, JCITY, JPNO, JQTY )
```

Again the expression S NATURAL JOIN SP evaluates to a table that is the natural join of tables S and SP over supplier numbers (and JX is a range variable that ranges over that table). The columns of that table are then given names (in left-to-right order) JSNO, JSNAME, JSTATUS, JCITY, JPNO, and JQTY. Note that the column-commalist, if specified, must include a name (*un*qualified) for every column in the relevant table, and must not include any duplicates.

To repeat a remark from the beginning of this section, table references in SQL serve two purposes: They specify the operands in FROM clauses (within select-expressions), and they specify the operands in explicit joins

---

*There is actually a tiny difference between "SELECT *T.C* FROM *T*" and "SELECT *T.C* FROM *T* AS *T*," as follows. In the first case, references elsewhere in the overall table expression—e.g., in a WHERE clause—to column *T.C* can optionally be qualified by a schema name. In the second case, such references *must* be of the form "*T.C*" only. See the final paragraph of the present section.

(i.e., join expressions). Now, as we saw above, every table reference serves to introduce a range variable, at least implicitly. The *scope* of that range variable—i.e., the set of contexts in which it can be referenced, and the scope within which its name must be unique—is defined as follows.*

- If the table reference represents a FROM-clause operand, then the scope is the select-expression that immediately contains that FROM clause (i.e., the SELECT clause, the FROM clause itself, the WHERE clause if any, the GROUP BY clause if any, and the HAVING clause if any, that go to make up that select-expression)—*excluding* any select-expression or join expression that is nested anywhere within the original select-expression in which another range variable is introduced with the same name.

- If the table reference represents a JOIN operand, then the scope is the join expression that immediately contains that JOIN—*excluding* any select-expression or join expression that is nested anywhere within the original join expression in which another range variable is introduced with the same name. See Appendix D for an extended discussion of this JOIN operand case.

  Note: The foregoing paragraph does not quite tell the whole story. If the join expression containing the table reference represents a FROM-clause operand, then the scope extends out to include the select-expression that immediately contains that FROM clause as well. Thus, e.g., the following is legal:

```
SELECT SP.PNO
FROM   S NATURAL JOIN SP
```

The intent seems to be that the scope in such a case should be just as if the join expression were replaced by the two join operands separated by a comma. In the example, therefore, the scope of the range variables S and SP is exactly as it would be in the expression

```
SELECT ...
FROM   S, SP
```

One very counterintuitive consequence of this unorthodox scoping rule is illustrated by the following example: The result of the expression

```
SELECT SP.*
FROM   S NATURAL JOIN SP
```

---

*It might help to observe that the rules are somewhat analogous to the rules regarding the scope of names in a block-structured language such as Algol 60 or Pascal.

will include columns PNO and QTY but *not* column SNO, because—believe it or not—there is no column "SP.SNO" in the result of the join expression.* Instead, there is a column called SNO that is the result of a kind of "coalescing" of columns S.SNO and SP.SNO.

If a reference appears in, e.g., a WHERE or GROUP BY clause to an unqualified column name, that reference must be within the scope of a range variable whose associated table includes a column with the specified name, and that range variable is then taken as the implicit qualifier.[†]

Note finally that if an explicit range variable is introduced for a given table, then for naming purposes it effectively replaces that table throughout its scope. Thus, for example, the following is *** *ILLEGAL* ***:

```
SELECT  S.SNO                       -- This is *** ILLEGAL *** !!!
FROM    S AS SX
WHERE   S.CITY = 'Paris'            -- This is *** ILLEGAL *** !!!
AND     S.STATUS > 20              -- This is *** ILLEGAL *** !!!
```

(all of the "S." qualifiers should be replaced by "SX.").

11.4 UNIONS, DIFFERENCES, AND INTERSECTIONS

The SQL UNION, EXCEPT, and INTERSECT operations are based on the well-known *union, difference,* and *intersection* operations of set theory. The two tables that represent the direct operands of the union, difference, or intersection must be of the same degree (i.e., they must have the same number of columns), and corresponding columns must be of compatible data types (refer to Chapter 7, Section 7.5, for a definition of data type compatibility). For details regarding the data types (precision, scale, etc.) of columns of the result, the reader is referred to the official standard document.

UNION and EXCEPT appear in "nonjoin table expressions" and INTERSECT appears in "nonjoin table terms." Here is a summary of the syntax:

Indeed, replacing "SP." by "SP.SNO" in the example will give rise to a syntax error.

[†]If there is more than one such range variable, then the "nearest"—i.e., the one with the most local scope—is taken as the qualifier. If the "nearest" is not uniquely determined it is an error, except for the case where (a) there are exactly two such "nearest," (b) they represent the two operands of a NATURAL JOIN or JOIN . . . USING expression, and (c) the column reference is a reference to a common column of those operands. Note in this latter case that no possible explicit qualifier exists—i.e., the column reference *must* be unqualified. Again, the reader is referred to the official standard for further discussion.

```
nonjoin-table-expression
    ::=   nonjoin-table-term
        | table-expression { UNION | EXCEPT } [ ALL ]
                   [ CORRESPONDING [ BY ( column-commalist ) ] ]
                       table-term

nonjoin-table-term
    ::=   nonjoin-table-primary
        | table-term INTERSECT [ ALL ]
                   [ CORRESPONDING [ BY ( column-commalist ) ] ]
                       table-primary
```

A "table term" is either a join expression (explained in Section 11.2 above) or a "nonjoin table term" (explained in the present section); a "table primary" is either a join expression (again, see Section 11.2 above) or a "nonjoin table primary," which is explained in Section 11.5. Of necessity, we assume for the purposes of the present section that the construct "nonjoin table primary" is understood (it might, for example, be a select-expression, of the form SELECT-FROM-WHERE), and concentrate on "nonjoin table expressions" and "nonjoin table terms."

INTERSECT

To fix our ideas, let us focus first on the "nonjoin table term"

```
table-term INTERSECT [ ALL ]
    [ CORRESPONDING [ BY ( column-commalist ) ] ] table-primary
```

Let us agree to refer to such an expression (for the moment) as an *intersection*. Let *A* and *B* be the tables resulting from evaluation of the table-term and table-primary, respectively. Then the various possible intersections we have to consider are as follows*—

```
1. A INTERSECT CORRESPONDING BY ( column-commalist ) B
```

```
2. A INTERSECT CORRESPONDING B
```

```
3. A INTERSECT B
```

—plus three further cases that are identical to the ones above except that they additionally specify the option ALL.

In *Case 1,* let the commalist of columns in the BY clause be *C1, C2,* . . . , *Cn*. Each of *C1, C2,* . . . , *Cn* must be *un*qualified and must identify

---

*Conceptually, that is. The three cases as shown are not intended to reflect valid SQL syntax. Specifically, the operands to INTERSECT *cannot* be specified as simple table names, contrary to what the "intersections" shown suggest. A similar remark applies to UNION and EXCEPT (see later).

both a column of *A* and a column of *B*. This case is defined to be semantically identical to an expression of the form

```
( SELECT C1, C2, ..., Cn FROM A )
   INTERSECT
( SELECT C1, C2, ..., Cn FROM B )
```

In other words: Let *AC* be a table that is derived from *A* by dropping all columns not mentioned in the BY clause, and let *BC* be a table that is derived from *B* analogously. Then the result of the intersection is a table of *n* columns; a given row *r* appears in that result if and only if *r* appears in *AC and* in *BC*. The result does not contain any duplicate rows.

Here is an example of Case 1:

```
( SELECT * FROM P )
      INTERSECT CORRESPONDING BY ( PNO )
         ( S NATURAL JOIN SP )
```

The result is a table of part numbers, containing just those part numbers that are common to (a) the parts table P and (b) the natural join of the suppliers and shipments tables (S and SP) over supplier numbers.

A *Case 2* intersection is defined to be semantically identical to a Case 1 intersection in which the commalist of columns specifies *all* of the columns that are common to *A* and *B*.* Here is an example:

```
( SELECT * FROM P )
      INTERSECT CORRESPONDING
         ( S NATURAL JOIN SP )
```

The columns that are common to the two operands here are PNO and CITY. Thus, the result is a table of part-number/city-name pairs, containing just those pairs that appear in both (a) the parts table P and (b) the natural join of the suppliers and shipments tables over supplier numbers.

Finally, a *Case 3* intersection is performed, not by matching columns with the same name as in Cases 1 and 2, but by matching columns with the same *ordinal position*. That is, the *i*th column of *A* is matched with the *i*th column of *B* (for all *i* in the range 1 to *n,* where *n* is the degree—recall that *A* and *B* must have the same degree). The result will also have degree *n*; a given row will appear in that result if and only if it appears in both *A* and *B*. Once again, the result will not contain any duplicate rows.

The ALL versions of the three cases are analogous, except that the result can include duplicate rows. More precisely, suppose a given row *r* appears exactly *m* times in the first operand and exactly *n* times in the sec-

---

*It is an error if the set of common column names is empty (contrast the situation with NATURAL JOIN).

ond ($m \geq 0$, $n \geq 0$). Then row r will appear exactly p times in the result, where p is the lesser of m and n.*

UNION

Now we turn our attention to "nonjoin table expressions" of the form

```
table-expression UNION [ ALL ]
    [ CORRESPONDING [ BY ( column-commalist ) ] ] table-term
```

Let us agree to refer to such an expression (for the moment) as a *union*. Let A and B be the tables resulting from evaluation of the table-expression and table-term, respectively. Then the various possible cases to consider are exactly analogous to the intersection cases discussed above; in other words, the cases are conceptually[†] as follows—

```
1. A UNION CORRESPONDING BY ( column-commalist ) B

2. A UNION CORRESPONDING B

3. A UNION B
```

—plus three further cases that are identical to the ones above except that they additionally specify the option ALL. They are (of course) defined analogously to the intersection cases, except that, for UNION, a given row appears in the result if and only if it appears in *at least one* of the two operands. By default, the result does not contain any duplicate rows. If ALL is specified, however, then suppose again that a given row r appears exactly m times in the first operand and exactly n times in the second ($m \geq 0$, $n \geq 0$). Then row r will appear exactly p times in the result, where $p = m + n$.

EXCEPT

Finally, EXCEPT. The various possible cases (which we will refer to as *differences*) are again analogous to the intersection cases[‡]—

---

*Note the difference between INTERSECT and SELECT with regard to duplicate elimination: With SELECT, the user can specify ALL or DISTINCT, and ALL is the default; with INTERSECT, the user can specify only ALL explicitly (omitting the specification is like specifying "DISTINCT"), and "DISTINCT" (by omission) is the default. A similar remark applies to UNION and EXCEPT (see later). We remind the reader that, in our opinion, duplicate rows in tables are *always* ill-advised.

†The three unions shown are not intended to reflect valid SQL syntax.

‡Once again the syntax is not meant to be accurate.

```
1. A EXCEPT CORRESPONDING BY ( column-commalist ) B

2. A EXCEPT CORRESPONDING B

3. A EXCEPT B
```

—plus three further cases that are identical to the ones above except that they additionally specify the option ALL. Again the three cases are defined analogously to the intersection cases, except that, for EXCEPT, a given row appears in the result if and only if it appears in the first operand *and not in* the second. By default, again, the result does not contain any duplicate rows. If ALL is specified, however, then suppose once again that a given row r appears exactly m times in the first operand and exactly n times in the second ($m \geq 0$, $n \geq 0$). Then row r will appear exactly p times in the result, where p is the greater of $m - n$ and zero.

11.5 TABLE PRIMARIES

As indicated in the previous section, a "table primary" is used to specify the second operand of an intersection. To repeat from that section, a "table primary" is either a join expression (see Section 11.2) or a "nonjoin table primary." A "nonjoin table primary," in turn, is one of the following: (a) a nonjoin table expression enclosed in parentheses (see Section 11.4 once again); (b) a select-expression (explained in Section 11.6, later); (c) a "table constructor"; or (d) an expression of the form "TABLE table." These last two cases (c) and (d) are discussed in the present section.

First, the expression "TABLE table" is defined to be semantically identical to the select-expression

```
( SELECT * FROM table )
```

(see Section 11.6). Here is an example:

```
TABLE SP
```

Second, a "table constructor" takes the form

```
VALUES row-constructor-commalist
```

In other words, a table constructor consists of the key word VALUES followed by a commalist of row constructors. Each such row constructor specifies one row, and the table constructor then evaluates to a table that is the "UNION ALL" of those rows. For example, the table constructor

```
VALUES ( 'S1', 'Smith', 20, 'London' ),
       ( 'S2', 'Jones', 10, 'Paris'  ),
       ( 'S3', 'Blake', 30, 'Paris'  ),
       ( 'S4', 'Clark', 20, 'London' ),
       ( 'S5', 'Adams', 30, 'Athens' )
```

evaluates to a table that is identical to the body of the suppliers table S as given in Fig. 2.1.

A row constructor in turn takes one of the following two forms:

```
( atom-commalist ) | ( table-expression )
```

In other words, a row constructor consists of either a commalist of "atoms" or a table expression, enclosed in parentheses in both cases, where:

- An "atom" is identical to an "insert atom" or "update atom" as defined in Chapter 9; in other words, it is a scalar expression or one of the key words DEFAULT or NULL.* The value of the row constructor is then the row formed by the specified "atom" values. *Note:* If the commalist involves just one atom, the surrounding parentheses can be omitted.

- The parenthesized table expression must evaluate to a table containing exactly one row, in which case the value of the row constructor is taken to be, precisely, that single row. (It is an error if the table contains more than one row. If instead it contains no rows at all, the value of the row constructor is taken to be a row of all nulls.)

Here are some examples of row constructors. Note that the second of these examples would be valid only in the context of an INSERT statement.

```
( 'S1', 'Smith', 20, 'London' )
( 'S1', 'Smith', DEFAULT, 'London' )
( 'S1' )
'S1'
( SELECT S.STATUS, S.CITY FROM S WHERE S.SNO = 'S4' )
```

11.6 SELECT EXPRESSIONS

A select-expression can be thought of, loosely, as a table expression that does not involve any UNIONs, EXCEPTs, or INTERSECTs ("loosely," because, of course, such operators might be involved in expressions that are *nested inside* the select-expression). The syntax is:

---

*Note, however, that DEFAULT and NULL are permitted if and only if the row constructor is being used to specify a row (possibly one row in a collection of rows) that is to serve as the source for an INSERT operation.

```
select-expression
   ::=   SELECT [ ALL | DISTINCT ] select-item-commalist
         FROM table-reference-commalist
         [ WHERE conditional-expression ]
            [ GROUP BY column-commalist ]
               [ HAVING conditional-expression ]
```

We explain the various clauses of a select-expression one by one in the subsections that follow.

The SELECT Clause

The SELECT clause takes the form

```
SELECT [ ALL | DISTINCT ] select-item-commalist
```

(see below for a detailed discussion of select-items). *Note:* The following explanation is partly a repeat of material already presented in Chapter 9 (Section 9.2).

1. If neither ALL nor DISTINCT is specified, ALL is assumed.

2. We assume for the sake of this explanation that the FROM, WHERE, GROUP BY, and HAVING clauses have already been evaluated. No matter which of those clauses are specified and which omitted, the conceptual result of evaluating them is always a table,* which we will refer to as table *T1* (even though the conceptual result is in fact unnamed).

3. Let *T2* be the table that is derived from *T1* by evaluating the specified select-items against *T1* (see below).

4. Let *T3* be the table that is derived from *T2* by eliminating redundant duplicate rows from *T2* if DISTINCT is specified, or a table that is identical to *T2* otherwise.

5. Table *T3* is the final result.

We turn now to an explanation of select-items. There are two cases to consider, of which the second is really just shorthand for a commalist of select-items of the first form; thus, the first case is really the more fundamental one.

Case 1: The select-item takes the form

```
scalar-expression [ [ AS ] column ]
```

■   The scalar expression will typically (but not necessarily) involve one or more columns of table *T1* (see paragraph 2 above). For each row of

---

*Possibly a "grouped" table. See the subsections on the GROUP BY and HAVING clauses later in this section.

T1, the scalar expression is evaluated, to yield a scalar result. The commalist of such results (corresponding to evaluation of all select-items in the SELECT clause against a single row of *T1*) constitutes a single row of table *T2* (see paragraph 3 above). If the select-item includes an AS clause, the *un*qualified column name "column" from that clause is assigned as the name of the corresponding column of table *T2*.* *Note:* As usual, the optional key word AS is just noise and can be omitted without affecting the meaning.

- If a select-item includes an aggregate function reference *and* the select-expression does not include a GROUP BY clause (see below), then no select-item in the SELECT clause can include any reference to a column of table *T1* unless that column reference is the argument (or part of the argument) to an aggregate function reference. Thus, for example, the following is *** *ILLEGAL* ***—

```
SELECT SP.PNO, AVG ( SP.QTY )    -- This is *** ILLEGAL *** !!!
FROM   SP
```

—because (a) there is no GROUP BY clause *and* (b) the SELECT clause includes an aggregate function reference *and* (c) the SELECT clause also includes a reference to a column of "table *T1*" (i.e., table SP, in the example) that is not contained within such an aggregate function reference.

Case 2: The select-item takes the form

```
[ range-variable . ] *
```

- If the qualifier is omitted (i.e., the select-item is just an unqualified asterisk), then this select-item must be the *only* select-item in the SELECT clause. This form is shorthand for a commalist of all of the columns of table *T1,* in left-to-right order.[†]

- If the qualifier is included (i.e., the select-item consists of an asterisk qualified by a range variable name *R,* thus: "*R.**"), then the select-item represents a commalist of all of the columns of the table associated with range variable *R,* in left-to-right order. (Recall that a table name can and often will be used as an implicit range variable. Thus, the select-item will frequently be of the form "*T.**" rather than "*R.**".)

---

*Because it is, specifically, the name of a column of table *T2,* not table *T1,* any name introduced by such an AS clause cannot be used in the WHERE, GROUP BY, and HAVING clauses (if any) directly involved in the construction of that table *T1.* It can, however, be referenced in an associated ORDER BY clause in a cursor definition, and also in an "outer" table expression that contains the select-expression under discussion nested within it.

[†]Except in the context of EXISTS. See Chapter 12.

- If an "asterisk-style" select-item, qualified or unqualified, appears within a view definition or integrity constraint (see Chapters 13 and 14, respectively), it will be expanded out at the time that view or constraint is created. Thus (e.g.) adding a new column to the corresponding table at some later time will not affect that view or constraint.

The FROM Clause

The FROM clause takes the form

```
FROM table-reference-commalist
```

Let the table references in the commalist evaluate to tables $A, B, \ldots, C,$ respectively. Then the result of evaluating the FROM clause is a table that is equal to the Cartesian product of $A, B, \ldots, C.$ *Note:* The Cartesian product of a single table T is defined to be equal to $T.$ In other words, it is (of course) legal for the FROM clause to contain just a single table reference.

The WHERE Clause

The WHERE clause takes the form

```
WHERE conditional-expression
```

Let T be the result of evaluating the immediately preceding FROM clause. Then the result of the WHERE clause is a table that is derived from T by eliminating all rows for which the conditional expression does not evaluate to *true.* If the WHERE clause is omitted, the result is simply $T.$

The GROUP BY Clause

The GROUP BY clause takes the form

```
GROUP BY column-commalist
```

It is probably best to introduce this clause by means of an example. Consider the following query: "For each part supplied, get the part number and the total shipment quantity for that part." A possible SQL formulation is as follows:

```
SELECT PNO, SUM ( SP.QTY ) AS PQTY
FROM    SP
GROUP   BY SP.PNO
```

Given the sample data of Fig. 2.1, the result is:

PNO	PQTY
P1	600
P2	1000
P3	400
P4	500
P5	500
P6	100

This result is obtained by (conceptually) rearranging table SP into *groups of rows,* one group for each distinct part number, and then extracting the corresponding part number and average part quantity from each such group.

More generally, let T be the result of evaluating the immediately preceding FROM clause and WHERE clause (if any). Each "column" mentioned in the GROUP BY clause must be the (optionally qualified) name of a column of T. The result of the GROUP BY clause is a "grouped table"—i.e., a set of groups of rows, derived from T by conceptually rearranging it into the minimum number of groups such that within any one group all rows have the same value for the combination of columns identified by the GROUP BY clause. Note carefully, therefore, that the result is thus *not* a proper table. However, a GROUP BY clause never appears without a corresponding SELECT clause whose effect is to derive a proper table from that improper intermediate result, so not much harm is done by this temporary deviation from the pure tabular framework.

If a select-expression includes a GROUP BY clause, then there are restrictions on the form that the SELECT clause can take. To be specific, each select-item in the SELECT clause (including any that are implied by an asterisk shorthand) must be *single-valued per group.* Thus, such select-items must not include any reference to any column of table T that is not mentioned in the GROUP BY clause itself—*unless* that reference is the argument, or part of the argument, to one of the aggregate functions COUNT, SUM, AVG, MAX, or MIN, whose effect is to reduce some collection of multiple scalar values from a group to a single such value.

The HAVING Clause

The HAVING clause takes the form

```
HAVING conditional-expression
```

Let G be the grouped table resulting from the evaluation of the immediately preceding FROM clause, WHERE clause (if any), and GROUP BY clause (if any). If there is no GROUP BY clause, then *G* is taken to be the result of evaluating the FROM and WHERE clauses, considered as a grouped table that contains a single group;* in other words, there is an implicit GROUP BY clause in this case that specifies *no grouping columns at all.*[†] The result of the HAVING clause is a grouped table that is derived from *G* by eliminating all groups for which the conditional expression does not evaluate to *true*.

Note 1: If the HAVING clause is omitted but the GROUP BY clause is included, the result is simply *G*. If the HAVING and GROUP BY clauses are both omitted, the result is simply the "proper"—i.e., nongrouped— table *T* resulting from the FROM and WHERE clauses.

Note 2: Scalar expressions in a HAVING clause must be single-valued per group (like scalar expressions in the SELECT clause if there is a GROUP BY clause, as discussed above).

Note 3: It is worth mentioning that the HAVING clause is totally redundant—i.e., for every select expression that involves such a clause, there is a semantically identical select expression that does not.

Examples

Here are some examples of select-expressions. Most are presented without additional discussion.

Example 1: Get part numbers for all parts supplied.

```
SELECT DISTINCT SP.PNO
FROM   SP
```

Example 2: Get supplier numbers for suppliers in Paris with status > 20.

```
SELECT S.SNO
FROM   S
WHERE  S.CITY = 'Paris'
AND    S.STATUS > 20
```

Example 3: Get all supplier-number/part-number combinations such that the supplier and part in question are located in the same city.

```
SELECT S.SNO, P.PNO
FROM   S, P
WHERE  S.CITY = P.CITY
```

---

*This is what the standard says, though logically it should say *at most one* group (there will be no group at all if the FROM and WHERE clauses yield an empty table).

[†]Despite the fact that such a GROUP BY clause is syntactically invalid! Note too the implication that if a select-expression includes a HAVING clause and no GROUP BY clause, the SELECT clause cannot include any references to columns of *T* (where *T* is the result of evaluating the FROM and WHERE clauses) except inside aggregate function references.

Example 4: Get all supplier-number/part-number combinations such that the supplier city follows the part city in alphabetical order.

```
SELECT  S.SNO, P.PNO
FROM    S, P
WHERE   S.CITY > P.CITY
```

Example 5: Get all supplier-number/part-number combinations such that the supplier and part in question are located in the same city, but omitting suppliers with status 20.

```
SELECT  S.SNO, P.PNO
FROM    S, P
WHERE   S.CITY = P.CITY
AND     S.STATUS <> 20
```

Example 6: Get all pairs of city names such that a supplier located in the first city supplies a part stored in the second city.

```
SELECT  DISTINCT S.CITY AS SCITY, P.CITY AS PCITY
FROM    S, SP, P
WHERE   S.SNO = SP.SNO
AND     SP.PNO = P.PNO
```

Example 7: Get all pairs of supplier numbers such that the two suppliers concerned are located in the same city.

```
SELECT  FIRST.SNO AS XX, SECOND.SNO AS YY
FROM    S FIRST, S SECOND
WHERE   FIRST.CITY = SECOND.CITY
```

This example was discussed in detail in Section 11.3 above.

Example 8: For each part supplied, get the part number, maximum quantity, and minimum quantity supplied of that part, excluding shipments by supplier S1.

```
SELECT  SP.PNO, MAX ( SP.QTY ) AS XXX, MIN ( SP.QTY ) AS YYY
FROM    SP
WHERE   SP.SNO <> 'S1'
GROUP   BY SP.PNO
```

Result:

PNO	XXX	YYY
P1	300	300
P2	400	200
P4	300	300
P5	400	400

Example 9: Get part numbers for all parts supplied by more than one supplier.

```
SELECT SP.PNO
FROM   SP
GROUP  BY SP.PNO
HAVING COUNT(*) > 1
```

Example 10:   For all red and blue parts such that the total quantity supplied is greater than 350 (excluding from the total all shipments for which
the quantity is less than or equal to 200), get the part number, the weight
in grams, the color, and the maximum quantity supplied of that part. We
assume for the sake of the example that weights are given in table P in
pounds.

```
SELECT P.PNO,
       'Weight in grams =' AS TEXT1,
       P.WEIGHT * 454 AS GMWT,
       P.COLOR,
       'Max quantity =' AS TEXT2,
       MAX ( SP.QTY ) AS MQY
FROM   P, SP
WHERE  P.PNO = SP.PNO
AND    ( P.COLOR = 'Red' OR P.COLOR = 'Blue')
AND    SP.QTY > 200
GROUP  BY P.PNO, P.WEIGHT, P.COLOR
HAVING SUM ( SP.QTY ) > 350
```

Explanation: We explain this example in some detail in order to provide
a kind of summary of some of the material discussed earlier in this section.
First note that, as explained above, the clauses of a select-expression are
conceptually executed in the order suggested by that in which they are written—with the sole exception of the SELECT clause itself, which is executed
last. In the example, therefore, we can imagine the result being constructed
as follows:

1. *FROM:* The FROM clause is evaluated to yield a new table that is the
   Cartesian product of tables P and SP.

2. *WHERE:* The result of Step 1 is reduced by the elimination of all rows
   that do not satisfy the WHERE clause. In the example, rows not satisfying the conditional expression

   ```
   P.PNO = SP.PNO AND
   ( P.COLOR = 'Red' OR P.COLOR = 'Blue') AND
   SP.QTY > 200
   ```

   are eliminated.

3. *GROUP BY:* The result of Step 2 is grouped by values of the column(s)
   named in the GROUP BY clause. In the example, those columns are
   P.PNO, P.WEIGHT, and P.COLOR.

4. *HAVING:* Groups not satisfying the condition

   ```
   SUM ( SP.QTY ) > 350
   ```

are eliminated from the result of Step 3.

5. *SELECT:* Each group in the result of Step 4 generates a single result row, as follows. First, the part number, weight, color, and maximum quantity are extracted from the group. Second, the weight is converted to grams. Third, the two literal strings "Weight in grams =" and "Max quantity =" are inserted at the appropriate points in the row. Note, incidentally, that—as the phrase "appropriate points in the row" suggests—we are relying here on the fact that columns of tables have a left-to-right ordering in SQL. The literal strings would not make much sense if they did not appear at those "appropriate points."

The final result looks like this:

PNO	TEXT1	GMWT	COLOR	TEXT2	MQY
P1	Weight in grams =	5448	Red	Max quantity =	300
P5	Weight in grams =	5448	Blue	Max quantity =	400
P3	Weight in grams =	7718	Blue	Max quantity =	400

Note: To return to the GROUP BY clause for a moment: In theory P.PNO alone would be sufficient as the grouping column in this example, since P.WEIGHT and P.COLOR are themselves single-valued per part number. However, SQL is not aware of this latter fact, and will raise an error condition if P.WEIGHT and P.COLOR are omitted from the GROUP BY clause, because they *are* mentioned in the SELECT clause.

Example 11: Define a *versatile supplier,* VS say, to be a supplier who (a) supplies at least one part and (b) supplies at least as many different parts as the average for suppliers in the same city as VS. For each versatile supplier, get the supplier number, name, status, and city, together with the number of different parts supplied and the average number of different parts supplied by suppliers in the same city.

```
SELECT SNO, SNAME, STATUS, CITY, PCT, APCT
FROM    S
        NATURAL JOIN
      ( SELECT SNO, COUNT(*) AS PCT
        FROM    SP
        GROUP  BY SNO ) AS XXX
        NATURAL JOIN
      ( SELECT CITY, AVG ( PCT ) AS APCT
        FROM    S
                NATURAL JOIN
              ( SELECT SNO, COUNT(*) AS PCT
                FROM    SP
                GROUP  BY SNO ) AS YYY
        GROUP  BY CITY ) AS ZZZ
WHERE   PCT > APCT
```

The meaning of this expression is not immediately apparent! The purpose of the example is to show a select expression involving a reasonably complex degree of nesting; in practice, however, such complex expressions are probably best built up a step at a time from smaller subexpressions. We leave it as an exercise for the reader to determine how the single-expression formulation shown above might have been arrived at. *Note:* The three AS clauses are required by SQL's syntax rules, even though the range variables introduced by those clauses (XXX, YYY, and ZZZ) are never explicitly referenced.

11.7   DERIVED TABLE COLUMN NAMES

A *derived table* is the table that results from the evaluation of a table expression. In Sections 11.1–11.6 above, we have explained how such tables are conceptually constructed. One question we have not addressed, however (at least, not properly), is that of how the columns of such tables are *named*. In this section we consider this question in detail.

1. First, of course, every column of a base table or view has a *declared* name. Such column names are unique within their containing table.

2. Second, if "xyz" is a table expression of any kind, then "(xyz)" is a table expression with identical semantics. In particular, therefore, the column names of the result of evaluating the table expression "(xyz)" are identical to those of the result of evaluating the table expression "xyz".

3. *Join expressions:* CROSS JOIN and "JOIN . . . ON" are both defined in terms of select-expressions. "JOIN . . . USING" is defined in terms of "JOIN . . . ON." NATURAL JOIN is defined in terms of "JOIN . . . USING." Thus, all of these cases ultimately reduce to the select-expression case (see paragraph 9 below).

4. *Table references:* We ignore the "join expression" case, since it has already been covered in the previous paragraph. A table reference that includes an AS clause with a commalist of column names evaluates to a table with column names as specified in that AS clause. A table reference that either includes an AS clause without a commalist of column names, or does not include an AS clause at all, evaluates to a table that inherits column names in the obvious way from the "table" or "table expression" component of that table reference.

5. *INTERSECT:* An intersection that specifies a BY clause with a commalist of column names evaluates to a table with column names as specified in that BY clause. An intersection that specifies a CORRESPONDING clause without a BY clause is defined to be shorthand for a special case of an intersection that does have a BY clause.

And an intersection that matches columns on their ordinal position evaluates to a table in which column names are determined as follows:

(a) If the *i*th column of both operand tables is called *C*, then the *i*th column of the result is also called *C*;

(b) Otherwise, the *i*th column of the result has a name that is unique within its containing table but is otherwise implementation-dependent.

6. *UNION and EXCEPT:* The INTERSECT rules apply to UNION and EXCEPT also, mutatis mutandis.

7. *TABLE:* A table expression of the form "TABLE table" evaluates to a table that inherits column names in the obvious way from its "table" argument.

8. *Table constructors:* The result of evaluating a "table constructor" is a table in which each column has a name that is unique within its containing table but is otherwise implementation-dependent.

9. *Select expressions:* As explained in Section 11.6, the value of a select-expression is determined by evaluating the FROM, WHERE, GROUP BY, HAVING, and SELECT clauses, in that order.

-   *FROM:* The result of evaluating the FROM clause is a table, *T1* say, that is equal to the Cartesian product of the tables identified by the table references in that FROM clause. Each column of *T1* inherits its name from the corresponding column of the applicable operand table. Note that the column names of *T1* are thus not necessarily unique within *T1*.*

-   *WHERE:* The result of evaluating the WHERE clause, table *T2* say, inherits its column names from table *T1*.

-   *GROUP BY:* As explained in Section 11.6, evaluating the GROUP BY clause yields an "improper" (grouped) table, *G1* say, so it is a little difficult to say precisely what the column names of that table are. Perhaps the best way to think of the situation is to regard *each group* as having the same column names as table *T2*. Furthermore, those column names can be partitioned into two disjoint subsets, namely those that refer to "grouping columns" (i.e., those mentioned in the GROUP BY clause) and those that do not. Names from

---

*There are fundamentally only two ways in which a table can be produced that does have nonunique column names, and this is the more important of the two (the other is illustrated by the example "SELECT *C, C* FROM *T*"). Nonunique column names are best avoided; indeed, certain SQL operations—NATURAL JOIN is a case in point—*require* column names to be unique, and raise an error if this requirement is violated. See the official standard document for further details.

the first subset can appear in the corresponding SELECT clause directly; names from the second subset can appear in that clause only in the context of an aggregate function reference.

- *HAVING:* The result of evaluating the HAVING clause, table *G2* say, inherits its column names from table *G1*.

- *SELECT:* After any necessary expansion of "asterisk-style" select-items, the SELECT clause effectively specifies a commalist of scalar expressions, each optionally accompanied by an AS clause. The result of evaluating that clause is a table, *T* say, that is derived from table *G2* by evaluating those scalar expressions as explained in Section 11.6. Table *T* contains one column for each such scalar expression, with a column name defined as follows:

(a) If the scalar expression has an accompanying AS clause, then the column name is the name specified in that clause;

(b) Otherwise, if the scalar expression consists simply of a (possibly qualified) column name, then the column name is the unqualified version of that name;

(c) Otherwise, the column has a name that is unique within its containing table but is otherwise implementation-dependent.

Note that, as a consequence of the foregoing rules, *every* table in the SQL standard does have names for *every* column (an improvement over SQL/89, incidentally). It is, however, unfortunately still the case (as it was in SQL/89) that column names are not necessarily unique within their containing table (though they are so in the case of *named* tables, i.e., base tables and views). It is also the case that some column names in derived tables are implementation-dependent, not specified within the standard. Finally, it is also the case that those implementation-dependent column names are not made visible to the user;* that is, they cannot be referenced in, e.g., a SELECT or WHERE clause.

---

*Except via DESCRIBE OUTPUT (see Chapter 20).

12

Conditional Expressions

12.1 INTRODUCTION

In this chapter we explain another vitally important SQL concept, viz. conditional expressions, which (like table expressions, the subject of the previous chapter) appear in numerous contexts throughout the SQL language. In particular, of course, conditional expressions are used in WHERE, ON, and HAVING clauses to qualify or disqualify rows or groups for subsequent processing. *Note:* Once again, we are departing here from official standard terminology; the standard refers to conditional expressions as "search conditions," and does not use the term "conditional expression" at all.

As in the previous chapter, we begin by giving the full BNF definition for the construct under consideration, for purposes of subsequent reference. We then go on to explain that definition piecemeal in the sections that follow. We remind the reader, however, that we are still ignoring everything (or almost everything) to do with nulls; conditional expressions, perhaps more than most other parts of the language, require significantly extended treatment when the implications (and complications) of nulls are taken into account, and certain conditional expression formats—not shown below—are provided purely to deal with certain aspects of "the nulls problem."

```
conditional-expression
   ::=    conditional-term
      |  conditional-expression OR conditional-term

conditional-term
   ::=    conditional-factor
      |  conditional-term AND conditional-factor

conditional-factor
   ::=    [ NOT ] conditional-test

conditional-test
   ::=    conditional-primary [ IS [ NOT ] { TRUE | FALSE } ]

conditional-primary
   ::=    simple-condition | ( conditional-expression )

simple-condition
   ::=    comparison-condition
      |   between-condition
      |   like-condition
      |   in-condition
      |   match-condition
      |   all-or-any-condition
      |   exists-condition
      |   unique-condition

comparison-condition
   ::=    row-constructor comparison-operator row-constructor

comparison-operator
   ::=    = | < | <= | > | >= | <>

between-condition
   ::=    row-constructor [ NOT ] BETWEEN row-constructor
                                  AND row-constructor

like-condition
   ::=    character-string-expression [ NOT ] LIKE pattern
                                          [ ESCAPE escape ]

in-condition
   ::=    row-constructor [ NOT ] IN ( table-expression )
      |  scalar-expression [ NOT ] IN
                          ( scalar-expression-commalist )

match-condition
   ::=    row-constructor MATCH [ UNIQUE ] ( table-expression )

all-or-any-condition
   ::=    row-constructor
              comparison-operator { ALL | ANY | SOME }
                                  ( table-expression )

exists-condition
   ::=    EXISTS ( table-expression )

unique-condition
   ::=    UNIQUE ( table-expression )
```

For completeness, we should mention that there are two further "simple conditions," one (IS [NOT] NULL) having to do with nulls and the

other (OVERLAPS) with dates and times. These two conditions are described in Chapters 16 and 17, respectively. In addition, the "match condition" has certain options, not shown above, that once again have to do with nulls; those options also are described in Chapter 16.

12.2 GENERAL REMARKS

In general, a conditional expression is an expression that evaluates to one of the truth values *true* or *false*. As the syntax shows, such an expression is basically a collection of "conditional primaries," combined together using the logical operators AND, OR, and NOT, and parentheses to enforce a desired order of evaluation. Each such "conditional primary" in turn (a) is either a "simple condition" or a conditional expression enclosed in parentheses, and (b) is optionally followed by one of the following:

```
IS TRUE
IS NOT TRUE
IS FALSE
IS NOT FALSE
```

We explain these four expressions by means of the following truth table. Let *p* be a conditional primary. Then the meanings of the four expressions are as indicated:*

p	true	false
p IS TRUE	true	false
p IS NOT TRUE	false	true
p IS FALSE	false	true
p IS NOT FALSE	true	false

A "simple condition" is any of the following:

- a comparison-condition
- a between-condition
- a like-condition
- an in-condition
- a match-condition
- an all-or-any-condition
- an exists-condition
- a unique-condition

---

*The expressions were introduced primarily in an attempt to help with certain problems that arise over nulls. They are (rather obviously) of somewhat limited usefulness in the context of the present chapter. See Chapter 16 for further discussion.

One further general remark: As will be seen, many of the foregoing "simple conditions" involve one or more *row constructors* (see, e.g., the discussion of comparison conditions in Section 12.3 immediately following). It is worth pointing out that, in practice, such a "row constructor" will more often than not consist of the special case that is simply a *scalar expression,* without surrounding parentheses. Many of our examples will illustrate this special case.

12.3 COMPARISON CONDITIONS

The syntax of a comparison condition ("comparison" for short) is as follows:

```
row-constructor comparison-operator row-constructor
```

Here:

- The comparison operator must be one of the following: =, <, < =, >, > =, or < > ("not equals").
- A "row constructor" is exactly as defined in Chapter 11. In other words, it is either a commalist of "atoms" or a table expression, enclosed in parentheses in each case—except that (as always for row constructors) in the first case the parentheses can be omitted if the commalist involves just one atom, and in the second case the table expression must evaluate to a table containing at most one row.* See Section 11.5 for further discussion.

Let the two row constructors evaluate to rows *Left* and *Right,* respectively. *Left* and *Right* must be of the same degree (i.e., they must contain the same number, n say, of scalar values each). Let i range from 1 to $n,$ and let the ith components of *Left* and *Right* be Li and $Ri,$ respectively. The data type of Li must be compatible with the data type of Ri (see Chapter 7 for a definition of data type compatibility). Then the result of the comparison condition is defined as follows:

- "*Left* = *Right*" is *true* if and only if for all $i,$ "$Li = Ri$" is *true*
- "*Left* < > *Right*" is *true* if and only if there exists some j such that "$Lj < > Rj$" is *true*
- "*Left* < *Right*" is *true* if and only if there exists some j such that "$Lj < Rj$" is *true* and for all $i < j,$ "$Li = Ri$" is *true*

---

*We remind the reader that if it evaluates to a table that contains no rows, it is effectively converted to a table that contains exactly one row, every component of which is null.

- "*Left > Right*" is *true* if and only if there exists some *j* such that "*Lj > Rj*" is *true* and for all *i* < *j*, "*Li* = *Ri*" is *true*
- "*Left < = Right*" is *true* if and only if "*Left < Right*" is *true* or "*Left = Right*" is *true*
- "*Left > = Right*" is *true* if and only if "*Left > Right*" is *true* or "*Left = Right*" is *true*

Finally, of course, "*Left $ Right*" (where "$" stands for any of =, < >, <, < =, >, > =) is *false* if and only if it is not *true*.*

Here is a fairly nontrivial example of the use of a comparison within a query ("Get supplier numbers for suppliers who are located in the same city as supplier S1"):

```
SELECT S.SNO
FROM    S
WHERE   S.CITY = ( SELECT S.CITY
                   FROM    S
                   WHERE   S.SNO = 'S1' )
```

And here is an example of a comparison involving rows of degree greater than one:

```
( SELECT S.STATUS, S.CITY
  FROM    S
  WHERE   S.SNO = 'S1' )    =    ( 20, 'London' )
```

In terms of the sample data of Fig. 2.1, this expression evaluates to *true*.

12.4 BETWEEN AND LIKE CONDITIONS

BETWEEN Conditions

Between-conditions are really nothing more than shorthands. The syntax is

```
row-constructor [ NOT ] BETWEEN
                        row-constructor AND row-constructor
```

The semantics are as follows. First, the between-condition

```
y BETWEEN x AND z
```

is defined to be semantically equivalent to

```
x <= y AND y <= z
```

---

*Perhaps we should point out that this apparently trite observation will cease to be valid when nulls are taken into account. See Chapter 16.

(note that the range includes the two extreme values x and z). Second, the between-condition

```
y NOT BETWEEN x AND z
```

is defined to be semantically equivalent to

```
NOT ( y BETWEEN x AND z )
```

Here is an example of the use of a between-condition:

```
SELECT  P.PNO
FROM    P
WHERE   P.WEIGHT BETWEEN 16 AND 19
```

LIKE Conditions

Like-conditions are intended for simple pattern matching—i.e., for testing a given character string to see whether it conforms to some prescribed pattern. The syntax is:

```
character-string-expression [ NOT ] LIKE pattern
                            [ ESCAPE escape ]
```

Here "pattern" is represented by an arbitrary character string expression, and "escape" (if specified) is represented by a character string expression that evaluates to a character string of length one (in other words, to a single character). Here is an example:

```
SELECT  P.PNO, P.PNAME
FROM    P
WHERE   P.PNAME LIKE 'C%'
```

("Get part numbers and names for parts whose names begin with the letter C"). The result is:

PNO	PNAME
P5	Cam
P6	Cog

In general, provided no ESCAPE clause is specified, characters within "pattern" are interpreted as follows:

- The underscore character (_) stands for *any single character.*
- The percent character (%) stands for *any sequence of n characters* (where n may be zero).
- All other characters stand for themselves.

In the example, therefore, the query returns rows from table P for which the PNAME value begins with an upper case C and has any sequence of zero or more characters following that C.

Here are some more examples:

`ADDRESS LIKE '%Berkeley%'`	— will evaluate to *true* if ADDRESS contains the string "Berkeley" anywhere inside it
`SNO LIKE 'S__'`	— will evaluate to *true* if SNO is exactly 3 characters long and the first is "S"
`PNAME LIKE '%c___'`	— will evaluate to *true* if PNAME is 4 characters long or more and the last but three is "c"
`STRING LIKE '\_%'` `ESCAPE '\'`	— will evaluate to *true* if STRING begins with an underscore character (see below)

In this last example, the backslash character " \ " has been specified as the escape character, which means that the special interpretation given to the characters " _ " and "%" can be disabled, if desired, by preceding such characters with a backslash character.

Finally, the like-condition

```
x NOT LIKE y [ ESCAPE z ]
```

is defined to be semantically equivalent to

```
NOT ( x LIKE y [ ESCAPE z ] )
```

12.5 IN AND MATCH CONDITIONS

IN Conditions

In-conditions come in two different formats, of which the second is effectively just shorthand for a special case of the first (it is provided principally for compatibility with SQL/89), and the first is just a different spelling for an all-or-any-condition (see Section 12.6). From a logical standpoint, therefore, in-conditions are totally redundant. However, they do display a certain degree of intuitive attractiveness, so in this section we discuss them in a little more detail than they might otherwise be felt to deserve.

Format 1: The first, more general, format of an in-condition is as follows:

```
row-constructor [ NOT ] IN ( table-expression )
```

This expression is defined to be semantically identical to

```
row-constructor =ANY  ( table-expression )
```

if NOT is not specified, and to

```
row-constructor <>ALL ( table-expression )
```

otherwise (see Section 12.6). However, IN and NOT IN are perhaps easier to understand intuitively than =ANY and <>ALL. Here is an example of IN:

```
SELECT DISTINCT S.SNAME
FROM    S
WHERE   S.SNO IN
      ( SELECT SP.SNO
        FROM    SP
        WHERE   SP.PNO = 'P2' )
```

("Get names of suppliers who supply part P2"). *Explanation:* The system evaluates the inner select-expression first (conceptually, at any rate), to yield the set of supplier numbers {S1,S2,S3,S4}. It then evaluates the outer select expression to obtain the names of suppliers whose supplier numbers are contained within that set.

Here is a more complex example, involving multiple levels of nesting:

```
SELECT DISTINCT S.SNAME
FROM    S
WHERE   S.SNO IN
      ( SELECT SP.SNO
        FROM    SP
        WHERE   SP.PNO IN
              ( SELECT P.PNO
                FROM    P
                WHERE   P.COLOR = 'Red' ) )
```

("Get supplier names for suppliers who supply at least one red part").

We repeat this latter example with all explicit name qualifiers omitted, in order to make another point:

```
SELECT DISTINCT SNAME
FROM    S
WHERE   SNO IN
      ( SELECT SNO
        FROM    SP
        WHERE   PNO IN
              ( SELECT PNO
                FROM    P
                WHERE   COLOR = 'Red' ) )
```

In this formulation, each unqualified column name is *implicitly* qualified by a range variable name defined (explicitly or implicitly) in the nearest applicable FROM clause. (For full details of how implicit qualifiers are determined, see Chapter 11 or refer to the official standard document. Explicit qualification is to be recommended in practice if there is any possible doubt.)

We show another example of IN in order to introduce yet another concept, namely *outer reference*. The query is "Get names of suppliers who supply part P2" (the same as the first example in this section; the following is another possible formulation of that query).

```
SELECT DISTINCT S.SNAME
FROM    S
WHERE   'P2' IN
      ( SELECT SP.PNO
        FROM    SP
        WHERE   SP.SNO = S.SNO )
```

This example differs from the previous ones in that the inner table expression cannot be evaluated once and for all before the outer one is evaluated, because that inner expression depends on a *variable,* namely S.SNO, whose value changes as the system examines different rows of table S. Conceptually, therefore, evaluation proceeds as follows:

1. The system examines some row of table S; let us assume this is the row for S1. The variable S.SNO thus currently has the value S1, so the system evaluates the inner table expression

   ```
   ( SELECT SP.PNO
     FROM    SP
     WHERE   SP.SNO = 'S1' )
   ```

   to obtain the set {P1,P2,P3,P4,P5,P6}. Now it can complete its processing for S1; it will select the SNAME value for S1, namely Smith, if and only if P2 is in this set (which of course it is).

2. Next the system moves on to repeat this kind of processing for another supplier row, and so on, until all rows of table S have been dealt with.

In this example, the reference to "S.SNO" in the inner table expression is an *outer reference*; that is, it is a reference to an (explicit or implicit) range variable that is not defined within the table expression in question, but rather in some "outer" table expression. *Note:* We have introduced this concept in the context of in-conditions, but of course outer references can appear in other contexts also. Examples of such other contexts are given in Sections 12.7 and 12.8 later.

Here is another example involving an outer reference, this time with explicit range variables. The query is "Get supplier numbers for suppliers who supply at least one part supplied by supplier S2."

```
SELECT DISTINCT SPX.SNO
FROM    SP AS SPX
WHERE   SPX.PNO IN
      ( SELECT SPY.PNO
        FROM    SP AS SPY
        WHERE   SPY.SNO = 'S2' )
```

The result is:

SNO
S1
S2
S3
S4

Note: Explicit range variables are not *required* in this example. Here is a formulation of the query without them:

```
SELECT DISTINCT SP.SNO
FROM    SP
WHERE   SP.PNO IN
      ( SELECT SP.PNO
        FROM    SP
        WHERE   SP.SNO = 'S2' )
```

Here, however, references to SP in the inner expression do not mean the same thing as references to SP in the outer expression. The two "SP"'s are really *two different variables*. Introducing explicit range variables SPX and SPY, as in the previous formulation, makes this fact quite clear.

We turn now to the second (and simpler) form of the in-condition. Here is the syntax.

Format 2: The second in-condition format is:

```
scalar-expression [ NOT ] IN ( scalar-expression-commalist )
```

Note that the scalar expression on the left-hand side can be regarded as a special case of a row constructor. And, if "rhs" is the commalist of scalar expressions enclosed in parentheses on the right-hand side, that entire right-hand side is defined to be semantically identical to a parenthesized table expression of the form

```
( VALUES rhs )
```

(observe that this table expression must necessarily evaluate to a table containing a single column). Thus "Format 2" is indeed equivalent to a special case of "Format 1," as stated previously. Here is an example of the use of "Format 2":

```
SELECT  P.PNO
FROM    P
WHERE   P.WEIGHT IN ( 12, 16, 17 )
```

Of course, a "Format 2" in-condition can be defined in a more intuitive fashion, as follows: The in-condition

```
x IN ( a, b, ..., z )
```

is defined to be semantically equivalent to

```
x = a OR x = b OR ... OR x = z
```

The negated form can also be defined more intuitively, thus: The in-condition

```
x NOT IN ( rhs )
```

is defined to be semantically equivalent to

```
NOT ( x IN ( rhs ) )
```

MATCH Conditions

A match-condition takes the form

```
row-constructor MATCH [ UNIQUE ] ( table-expression )
```

Let *r1* be the row that results from evaluating "row constructor" and let *T* be the table that results from evaluating "table expression." Then, if UNIQUE is specified, the match-condition evaluates to *true* if and only if *T* contains *exactly* one row, *r2* say, such that the comparison condition

```
r1 = r2
```

evaluates to *true*. If UNIQUE is not specified, the match-condition evaluates to *true* if and only if *T* contains *at least* one row, *r2* say, such that the comparison condition

```
r1 = r2
```

evaluates to *true*. Note, therefore, that if UNIQUE is not specified, the match-condition is equivalent to the following in-condition*

```
row-constructor IN ( table-expression )
```

Here is an example of the use of MATCH:

---

*This equivalence is valid only in the absence of nulls.

```
SELECT SP.*
FROM   SP
WHERE  NOT ( SP.SNO MATCH UNIQUE ( SELECT S.SNO FROM S ) )
```

("Get shipments that do not have exactly one matching supplier in the suppliers table"). Such a query might be useful in checking the integrity of the database, because, of course, there should not *be* any such shipments.if the database is correct. See Chapter 14 for a detailed discussion of integrity. *Note:* In the example, the UNIQUE is actually redundant (why?).

12.6 ALL-OR-ANY CONDITIONS

An all-or-any condition has the general form

```
row-constructor
    comparison-operator { ALL | ANY | SOME }
                                ( table-expression )
```

where the comparison operator is any of the usual set ($=$, $<$, $<=$, $>$, $>=$, or $<>$), and SOME is just a different spelling for ANY. In general, an all-or-any condition evaluates to *true* if and only if the corresponding comparison condition without the ALL (respectively ANY) evaluates to *true* for all (respectively any) of the rows in the table represented by the table expression. (*Note:* If that table is empty, the ALL conditions return *true,* the ANY conditions return *false.*) Here is an example ("Get part names for parts whose weight is greater than that of every blue part"):

```
SELECT DISTINCT PX.PNAME
FROM   P AS PX
WHERE  PX.WEIGHT >ALL ( SELECT DISTINCT PY.WEIGHT
                        FROM   P AS PY
                        WHERE  PY.COLOR = 'Blue' )
```

The result looks like this:

Explanation: The nested table expression returns the set of weights for blue parts, namely the set {17,12}. The outer SELECT then returns the name of the only part whose weight is greater than every value in this set, namely part P6. In general, of course, the final result might contain any number of part names (including zero).

Note: A word of caution is appropriate here, at least for native English speakers. The fact is, all-or-any conditions are seriously error-prone. A very natural English formulation of the foregoing query would use the word "any" in place of "every," which could easily lead to the (incorrect) use of >ANY instead of >ALL. Analogous criticisms apply to every one of the ANY and ALL operators.

12.7 EXISTS CONDITIONS

Exists-conditions are used to test a specified table—normally a derived table—for the existence of at least one row (i.e., to test whether the table in question is nonempty). The syntax is:

```
EXISTS ( table-expression )
```

The condition evaluates to *false* if the table expression evaluates to an empty table, the value *true* otherwise. Here are some examples.

Example 1: Get supplier names for suppliers who supply at least one part.

```
SELECT DISTINCT S.SNAME
FROM    S
WHERE   EXISTS
      ( SELECT *
        FROM    SP
        WHERE   SP.SNO = S.SNO )
```

The exists-condition here is testing for the existence of a row in table SP that satisfies the condition that its SNO component has a value that is equal to the value represented by the outer reference S.SNO. A couple of points arising:

1. Note that the EXISTS argument is a select-expression in which the SELECT clause is of the form "SELECT *"; in practice, EXISTS arguments are almost always of this form. But note too that the "*" is almost meaningless—it could be replaced by almost anything without affecting the result of evaluating the exists-condition. Partly for this reason, the standard says that in this context the "*" does not stand for "all of the columns of the table" but is effectively replaced by an arbitrary literal (e.g., 42).

2. Note that the EXISTS argument includes an outer reference ("S.SNO"). In practice, EXISTS arguments will very frequently include at least one such outer reference.

Example 2: Get supplier names for suppliers who do not supply at least one part.

```
SELECT DISTINCT S.SNAME
FROM    S
WHERE   NOT EXISTS
      ( SELECT *
        FROM    SP
        WHERE   SP.SNO = S.SNO )
```

Example 3:   Get supplier names for suppliers who supply all parts.

```
SELECT DISTINCT S.SNAME
FROM    S
WHERE   NOT EXISTS
      ( SELECT *
        FROM    P
        WHERE   NOT EXISTS
              ( SELECT *
                FROM    SP
                WHERE   S.SNO = SP.SNO
                AND     SP.PNO = P.PNO ) )
```

This SQL formulation corresponds to the following informal version of the query: "Get supplier names for suppliers such that there does not exist a part that they do not supply."

12.8 UNIQUE CONDITIONS

Unique-conditions are used to test that all rows within some table are distinct (i.e., there are no duplicates). The syntax is:

```
UNIQUE ( table-expression )
```

The condition evaluates to *true* if the table expression evaluates to a table in which the rows are all distinct, the value *false* otherwise. Note in particular, therefore, that the condition will always evaluate to *true* if the argument table contains just one row or is empty (i.e., contains no rows at all). It will also necessarily evaluate to *true* if the argument is of the form "SELECT DISTINCT . . . " (or any of several other forms of table expression that guarantee that there will be no duplicates in the result—for instance, a union without the ALL option).

Here is an example ("Get names of suppliers who supply at least two distinct parts in the same quantity"):

```
SELECT DISTINCT S.SNAME
FROM    S
WHERE   NOT UNIQUE ( SELECT SP.QTY
                     FROM    SP
                     WHERE   SP.SNO = S.SNO )
```

Note: The reader might realize that we are making a virtue of necessity here. We have mentioned the point several times in this book that it is our opinion that tables should *never* be allowed to contain duplicate rows. If that discipline were followed, of course, then UNIQUE would be useless (because it would always evaluate to *true*). We contrived the "realistic" example above in order to illustrate a "realistic" application of a unique-condition, but the reader should not infer from that example that the system *must* permit duplicate rows in order to support queries such as the one discussed. Here, for example, is a formulation of that query that does not involve UNIQUE:

```
SELECT DISTINCT S.SNAME
FROM    S
WHERE   EXISTS ( SELECT * FROM SP SPX WHERE
        EXISTS ( SELECT * FROM SP SPY WHERE
                 SPX.SNO = S.SNO AND
                 SPY.SNO = S.SNO AND
                 SPX.QTY = SPY.QTY AND
                 SPX.PNO <> SPY.PNO ) )
```

12.9 A FINAL REMARK

We close this chapter by reminding the reader yet again that throughout this chapter we have ignored virtually everything to do with nulls. *Every one* of the conditional expression formats we have discussed in the foregoing sections will need to be revisited when we reach Chapter 16.

13

Views

13.1 INTRODUCTION

Throughout our discussion of data manipulation operations in Chapters 9 and 10, we deliberately assumed for simplicity that all named tables were base tables. Now we turn our attention to the special considerations that apply to views (or "viewed tables," to use the official standard term).

Recall from Chapter 2 that a view is a named, virtual table—i.e., a named table that does not exist in its own right, but looks to the user as if it did. In other words, the data that is visible through a given view "really belongs" to some underlying base table (or base tables, plural) rather than to the view per se. Thus, views are not supported by any separately distinguishable underlying data of their own. Instead, all that happens when a view is created is that the *definition* of that view in terms of other named tables (base tables and/or other views) is remembered by the system in some way (actually by storing it in the appropriate *schema*—see Chapter 21). Here is an example:

```
CREATE VIEW GOODSUPPS
    AS  SELECT S.SNO, S.STATUS, S.CITY
        FROM    S
        WHERE   S.STATUS > 15
```

Note the similarity to the definition of a cursor: As with a cursor definition, a view definition includes a table expression that defines a certain

167

"scope"; and as with a cursor definition, that table expression is *not* evaluated at the time of definition,* but is instead merely remembered by the system (under the specified view name). *To the user, however, it is now as if there really were a table in the database with the specified name.* In the example, it is as if there really were a table called GOODSUPPS, with rows and columns as shown in the unshaded portions (only) of Fig. 13.1.

GOODSUPPS	SNO	SNAME	STATUS	CITY
	S1	Smith	20	London
	S2	Jones	10	Paris
	S3	Blake	30	Paris
	S4	Clark	20	London
	S5	Adams	30	Athens

Fig. 13.1   GOODSUPPS as a view of base table S (unshaded portions)

Here is an example making use of GOODSUPPS:

```
SELECT *
FROM    GOODSUPPS
WHERE   GOODSUPPS.CITY <> 'London'
```

The system will translate this select expression, involving the view GOODSUPPS, into an equivalent expression involving the underlying base table instead. The translation is done by "merging" the expression written by the user with the expression that was saved in the schema—in effect, by replacing references to the view *name* by the corresponding view *definition*. In the example, this process will produce an expression along the following lines:

```
SELECT GOODSUPPS.*
FROM    ( SELECT S.SNO, S.STATUS, S.CITY
          FROM    S
          WHERE   S.STATUS > 15 ) AS GOODSUPPS
WHERE   GOODSUPPS.CITY <> 'London'
```

And this expression can now be evaluated in the usual way, since it references only "real" (base) tables, no virtual tables.

The translation process just illustrated (or something very like it, at any rate) applies to update operations also. For example, the UPDATE operation

---

*Unlike a cursor definition, however, a view definition cannot include any references to parameters or host variables.

```
UPDATE  GOODSUPPS
SET     CITY = 'New York'
WHERE   GOODSUPPS.CITY = 'Paris'
```

effectively translates to

```
UPDATE  S
SET     CITY = 'New York'
WHERE   S.STATUS > 15
AND     S.CITY = 'Paris'
```

And, of course, INSERT and DELETE operations are handled in the same general way. For example, the INSERT operation

```
INSERT
INTO    GOODSUPPS ( SNO, STATUS, CITY )
VALUES ( 'S6', 25, 'Madrid' )
```

effectively translates to:

```
INSERT
INTO    S ( SNO, STATUS, CITY )
VALUES ( 'S6', 25, 'Madrid' )
```

(note that SNAME, which is excluded from the GOODSUPPS view, will necessarily be set to the applicable default value in an INSERT via that view). Likewise, the DELETE operation

```
DELETE
FROM    GOODSUPPS
WHERE   GOODSUPPS.CITY = 'New York'
```

effectively translates to:

```
DELETE
FROM    S
WHERE   S.STATUS > 15
AND     S.CITY = 'New York'
```

As we have seen, views are defined by means of the statement CREATE VIEW. There is also a DROP VIEW statement, for dropping an existing view (note, however, that there is no ALTER VIEW statement). Like CREATE DOMAIN and CREATE TABLE, CREATE VIEW can be executed as an independent operation in its own right, or it can be executed as a "schema element" within a CREATE SCHEMA statement (see Chapter 4). DROP VIEW, however, like DROP DOMAIN and DROP TABLE, must be executed as an independent operation—it cannot appear within a CREATE SCHEMA statement. But despite this latter fact, note carefully that (as explained in Chapter 4) every view does belong to some schema, even if the corresponding CREATE statement is executed "independently," and creating a new view ("independently" or otherwise), or dropping an existing view (necessarily "independently"), thus has the effect—among other things—of updating the relevant schema in the appropriate manner.

13.2 DATA DEFINITION OPERATIONS

CREATE VIEW

The general syntax of CREATE VIEW is:

```
view-definition
    ::=   CREATE VIEW view [ ( column-commalist ) ]
              AS table-expression
                    [ WITH [ CASCADED | LOCAL ] CHECK OPTION ]
```

Here "view" is the name of the new view,* the "column commalist" (if specified) lists the unqualified names of the columns of the view, the table expression defines the scope of the view, and the optional WITH CHECK OPTION clause is explained in Section 13.4, later. See the examples below for a discussion of when the commalist of column names can be omitted.

As stated in Section 13.1, the table expression in CREATE VIEW cannot include any parameter or host variable references. It also cannot include any references, either direct or indirect, to the name of the view currently being defined; in other words, no recursion is permitted, either direct or indirect, among view definitions. Furthermore, no column in the result of evaluating the table expression is allowed to have a "coercibility" property of **no collating sequence** (see Chapter 19 for further explanation of this point).

Here then are some examples of CREATE VIEW:

```
1. CREATE VIEW REDPARTS ( PNO, PNAME, WEIGHT, CITY )
        AS SELECT P.PNO, P.PNAME, P.WEIGHT, P.CITY
           FROM   P
           WHERE  P.COLOR = 'Red'
```

The effect of this statement is to create a new view with (unqualified) name REDPARTS, and with four columns called PNO, PNAME, WEIGHT, and CITY, corresponding respectively to the four columns PNO, PNAME, WEIGHT, and CITY of the underlying table P. For the sake of the example, we have specified column names for the newly created view explicitly, even though those exact same names would otherwise be inherited from the underlying table anyway. The general principle is as follows:

- First, every column of the view must *have* a proper, user-known column name that is unique within the view.

- Second, the view will inherit its column names from the underlying

---

*If the name is qualified by a schema name and the CREATE VIEW appears within the context of a CREATE SCHEMA statement, then that schema name must identify the schema that would have been assumed by default anyway, viz. the schema being created (see Section 4.3).

table (where by "underlying table" we mean the table that results from the evaluation of the table expression) *unless* new column names are specified explicitly.

Thus, explicit specification of column names is *required* only if some column of the underlying table has a name that is implementation-dependent (see Section 11.7), and/or two columns of that underlying table have the same name. (Of course, explicit specification is never wrong, even if it is not required.) Note that if explicit specification is used, explicit names must be specified for *all* columns of the view, even if some of those columns have an obvious inherited name.

```
2. CREATE VIEW LREDPARTS
       AS SELECT REDPARTS.PNO, REDPARTS.WEIGHT
          FROM    REDPARTS
          WHERE   REDPARTS.CITY = 'London'
```

It is perfectly possible to define a view in terms of other views, as this example illustrates. The unqualified column names for LREDPARTS are PNO and WEIGHT (inherited from REDPARTS).

```
3. CREATE VIEW CITYPAIRS ( SCITY, PCITY )
       AS SELECT DISTINCT S.CITY, P.CITY
          FROM    S, SP, P
          WHERE   S.SNO = SP.SNO
          AND     SP.PNO = P.PNO
```

The meaning of this view is as follows: A pair of city names (x,y) will appear in the view if and only if a supplier located in city x supplies a part stored in city y. For example, supplier S1 supplies part P1; supplier S1 is located in London and part P1 is stored in London; and so the pair (London,London) appears in the view. Notice that the definition of this view involves a join (actually a "3-way join"), so that this is an example of a view that is derived from multiple underlying base tables. Note also that the names of the two columns of the result of evaluating the table expression are both CITY, and hence that new column names *must* be specified explicitly, as shown.

Note: The following view definition would have produced the same effect:

```
CREATE VIEW CITYPAIRS
    AS SELECT DISTINCT S.CITY AS SCITY, P.CITY AS PCITY
       FROM    S, SP, P
       WHERE   S.SNO = SP.SNO
       AND     SP.PNO = P.PNO
```

In fact, the ability to specify new column names in the CREATE VIEW clause is logically unnecessary; it is provided primarily for compatibility with SQL/89, which did not support the AS clause on select-items.

```
4. CREATE VIEW PQ
       AS SELECT SP.PNO, SUM ( SP.QTY ) AS TOTQTY
          FROM   SP
          GROUP  BY SP.PNO
```

The column names for this view are PNO and TOTQTY. Notice that, although this view is derived from a single underlying base table, it is not just a simple row-and-column subset of that base table—unlike the views REDPARTS and GOODSUPPS shown earlier.* Rather, it is a kind of *statistical summary* of that underlying table.

DROP VIEW

An existing view can be dropped by means of DROP VIEW—syntax:

```
DROP VIEW view { RESTRICT | CASCADE }
```

If RESTRICT is specified and "view" is referenced in any other view definition or in an integrity constraint (see Chapter 14), the DROP VIEW will fail; otherwise it will succeed, and the specified view will be dropped. If CASCADE is specified, any referencing view definitions and integrity constraints will be dropped also.

13.3 DATA MANIPULATION OPERATIONS

We have already explained in outline (in Section 13.1) how retrieval operations on a view are translated into equivalent operations on the underlying base table(s). In the case of retrieval operations that translation process is reasonably straightforward and works perfectly well.[†] In the case of update operations, however, the situation is much more complex, as we will see.

The basic point is that *a given view may or may not be updatable*. We demonstrate this point by means of the two views GOODSUPPS and CITYPAIRS from Sections 13.1 and 13.2, respectively. For convenience we first repeat their definitions:

---

*Note that we do not include the view LREDPARTS in our list of views here that are row-and-column subsets of their underlying base table. In fact, LREDPARTS *is* a row-and-column subset of the base table P, but only because (a) LREDPARTS is a row-and-column subset of its underlying table REDPARTS, and (b) that underlying table in turn is a row-and-column subset of *its* underlying table P.

[†]It is worth mentioning that this statement has not always been true for commercial SQL products in the past; that is, some retrievals on some views have sometimes been known to fail in surprising ways. Nor was it true for earlier versions of the standard (see the previous editions of this book).

```
CREATE VIEW GOODSUPPS
     AS SELECT S.SNO, S.STATUS, S.CITY
        FROM   S
        WHERE  S.STATUS > 15

CREATE VIEW CITYPAIRS
     AS SELECT DISTINCT S.CITY AS SCITY, P.CITY AS PCITY
        FROM   S, SP, P
        WHERE  S.SNO = SP.SNO
        AND    SP.PNO = P.PNO
```

Of these two views, GOODSUPPS is logically updatable, while CITYPAIRS is logically not. It is instructive to examine why this is so. In the case of GOODSUPPS:

- We can INSERT a new row into the view—say the row (S6,40,Rome)— by actually inserting the corresponding row (S6,DEFAULT,40,Rome) into the underlying base table (we assume that column S.SNAME does have a default).

- We can DELETE an existing row from the view—say the row (S1,20,London)—by actually deleting the corresponding row (S1,Smith,20,London) from the underlying base table.

- We can UPDATE an existing value in the view—say the CITY value for supplier S1 (namely London), to change it to Rome—by actually making that change to the corresponding value in the underlying base table.

Now consider the view CITYPAIRS. As explained in Section 13.2, one of the rows in that view is the row (London,London). Suppose it were possible to DELETE that row. What would such a DELETE signify?—i.e., what updates (DELETEs or otherwise) on the underlying data would such a DELETE correspond to? The only possible answer has to be "We don't know"; there is simply no way (in general) that we can go down to the underlying base tables and make an appropriate set of updates there. In fact, such an "appropriate set of updates" does not even exist; there is *no* set of updates that could be applied to the underlying data (in general) that would have precisely the effect of removing the specified row from the view while leaving everything else in the view unchanged. In other words, *the original DELETE is an intrinsically unsupportable operation.* Similar arguments can be made to show that (in general) INSERT and UPDATE operations are also intrinsically not supportable on this view.

Thus we see that some views are inherently updatable, whereas others are inherently not. *Note the word "inherently" here.* It is not just a question of some systems being able to support certain updates while others cannot. *No* system can consistently support updates on a view such as

CITYPAIRS unaided (by "unaided" here, we mean "without help from some human user").

For further discussion of which views are theoretically updatable and which not, the reader is referred to the chapter "Updating Views" in C. J. Date, *Relational Database: Selected Writings* (Addison-Wesley, 1986). Here, however, we are not concerned so much with what is theoretically possible, but rather with what SQL will allow, which is a very different thing. In SQL, a view is updatable if and only if all of the following conditions 1–8 below apply:

1. The table expression that defines the scope of the view is a select expression;* that is, it does not directly contain any of the key words JOIN, UNION, INTERSECT, or EXCEPT.

2. The SELECT clause of that select expression does not directly contain the key word DISTINCT.

3. Every select-item in that SELECT clause (after any necessary expansion of "asterisk-style" select-items) consists of a possibly qualified column name (optionally accompanied by an AS clause), representing a simple reference to a column of the underlying table (see paragraph 5 below).

4. The FROM clause of that select expression contains exactly one table reference.

5. That table reference identifies either a base table or an updatable view. *Note:* From this point forward, we will refer to the table identified by that table reference as *the* (single) underlying table on which the updatable view in question is "immediately" (or "directly") defined.

6. That select expression does not include a WHERE clause that includes a nested table expression that includes a FROM clause that includes a reference to the same table as is referenced in the FROM clause mentioned in paragraph 4 above.

7. That select expression does not include a GROUP BY clause.

8. That select expression does not include a HAVING clause.

Finally, to state the obvious (well, maybe it is not so obvious): The operations INSERT, UPDATE, and DELETE can be applied to a given view only if that view is updatable as defined above. Observe in particular

---

*Or an expression of the form "TABLE table." However, an expression of this form was defined in Chapter 11 to be equivalent to a certain select expression anyway; thus, we can consider the table expression that defines the scope of the view to be a select expression in all cases, without loss of generality.

that UPDATE either *can* or *cannot* be applied to a given view; it is not possible to have some columns updatable and others not within the same view (although some commercial products do support such a capability). Observe too that updatability is "all or nothing," in the sense that *either* all three of INSERT, UPDATE, or DELETE can be applied to a given view *or* none of them can; it is not possible for (e.g.) DELETE to be applicable but INSERT not (although, again, some commercial products do go beyond the standard in this respect).

Note: It has to be said that the list of conditions quoted above is excessively stringent. In fact, *every single one* of those conditions, except (arguably) number 5, is actually stronger than is logically necessary. However, this is not the place to go into details; as stated above, we are concerned in this book not with what is logically possible, but rather with what SQL will allow.

13.4 THE CHECK OPTION

The topic of this section, the check option, also has to do with view updating—indeed, the check option can be specified for a given view only if that view is updatable according to the precepts laid down in the previous section. However, the topic is sufficiently complex that it seems advisable to devote a separate section to it.*

We return to the GOODSUPPS view once again in order to introduce the basic idea. As explained in Section 13.3, that view is updatable. But consider the following UPDATE:

```
UPDATE  GOODSUPPS
SET     STATUS = 10
WHERE   GOODSUPPS.SNO = 'S1'
```

Should this UPDATE be accepted? If it is, it will have the effect of removing supplier S1 from the view, since the S1 row will no longer satisfy the view-defining condition ("S.STATUS > 15"). Likewise, the INSERT operation

```
INSERT
INTO    GOODSUPPS ( SNO, STATUS, CITY )
VALUES ( 'S8', 7, 'Stockholm' )
```

---

*For further discussion of the ideas underlying the material of this section, the reader is referred to the chapter "Without Check Option" in C. J. Date and Hugh Darwen, *Relational Database Writings 1989–1991* (Addison-Wesley, 1992).

(if accepted) will create a new supplier row, but that row will instantly vanish from the view. The check option is designed to deal with such situations. If the clause

```
WITH CHECK OPTION
```

is included in the definition of a view, then all INSERTs and UPDATEs against that view will be checked to ensure that the newly INSERTed or UPDATEd row does indeed satisfy the view-defining condition. If it does not, then the operation will be rejected.

As mentioned above, the check option can be specified only if the view is updatable.

Inheritability

But the foregoing is not the end of the story. There are some complex issues that need to be discussed that arise over the question of *inheritability* (or otherwise) of the check option. For the purposes of the following discussion, we revise the GOODSUPPS example, as follows.

First, we define another view over base table S, as follows:

```
CREATE VIEW AVGSUPPS
    AS   SELECT S.SNO, S.STATUS, S.CITY
         FROM   S
         WHERE  S.STATUS < 25
```

With our usual sample data, view AVGSUPPS ("average suppliers") will include rows for suppliers S1, S2, and S4 (with status 20, 10, and 20, respectively), and no others.

Now we *re*define view GOODSUPPS in terms of AVGSUPPS (instead of directly in terms of base table S):

```
CREATE VIEW GOODSUPPS
    AS   SELECT AVGSUPPS.SNO, AVGSUPPS.STATUS, AVGSUPPS.CITY
         FROM   AVGSUPPS
         WHERE  AVGSUPPS.STATUS > 15
```

This view will include rows for suppliers S1 and S4 only (both with status 20). Fig. 13.2 illustrates the situation at this point.

We now proceed to consider what happens in four possible cases:

1. Neither view has the check option

2. AVGSUPPS has the check option but GOODSUPPS does not

3. GOODSUPPS has the check option but AVGSUPPS does not

4. Both views have the check option

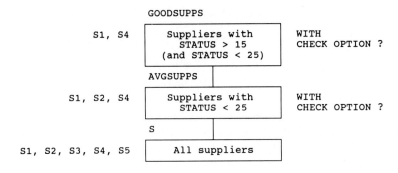

Fig. 13.2   Views GOODSUPPS and AVGSUPPS and base table S

Case 1: Neither view has the check option.

Consider the following UPDATE:

```
UPDATE GOODSUPPS
SET    STATUS = GOODSUPPS.STATUS + 20
```

The astonishing effect of this UPDATE is that *table GOODSUPPS will now be empty!*—suppliers S1 and S4 will each now have status 40, and thus will no longer appear in view AVGSUPPS, and hence a fortiori will no longer appear in view GOODSUPPS. Note very carefully the counterintuitive nature of this result: The user of view GOODSUPPS believes, correctly, that all suppliers visible in that view have STATUS > 15,* and surely has a right to expect that *increasing* those STATUS values—assuming that the UPDATE operation is accepted in the first place—obviously cannot violate that condition and so can have no strange side-effects.

Here is another example. The INSERT operation

```
INSERT
INTO   GOODSUPPS ( SNO, STATUS, CITY )
VALUES ( 'S9', 30, 'Athens' )
```

will create a new supplier row, but that row will instantly disappear from AVGSUPPS and—a fortiori, albeit counterintuitively—from GOODSUPPS also. Thus, INSERTs as well as UPDATEs can "cause rows to disappear." For simplicity, however, we concentrate in the remainder of our discussions on the UPDATE example primarily.

---

*For the sake of the discussion we are assuming, perhaps a little unrealistically, that the user does *not* know that all suppliers visible in GOODSUPPS also have STATUS < 25. After all, this latter fact is not explicitly stated in the GOODSUPPS definition.

Case 2: AVGSUPPS has the check option but GOODSUPPS does not.

The only way to avoid the anomalous behavior described in Case 1 is to have the system check UPDATEs (and INSERTs) on GOODSUPPS against the view-defining condition for AVGSUPPS. If this is done, the UPDATE operation discussed in Case 1 will be rejected, and the counterintuitive result will not occur.

Suppose, therefore, that we specify the check option for AVGSUPPS (but not for GOODSUPPS, since the view-defining condition for GOODSUPPS is not an issue, for the moment). The question now is: Will that AVGSUPPS check option be inherited by GOODSUPPS?—i.e., will it apply to UPDATEs and INSERTs via GOODSUPPS, as well as to updates via AVGSUPPS directly? And the answer to this question depends on whether the check option for AVGSUPPS specifies CASCADED or LOCAL, as follows.

- *CASCADED:* In this case the check option *will* be inherited, unconditionally. That is, if an UPDATE or INSERT on GOODSUPPS would cause a row to disappear from AVGSUPPS, that UPDATE or INSERT will be rejected. Note, however, that from the perspective of the GOODSUPPS user, the original UPDATE certainly *looks* reasonable; there is no way it can violate the GOODSUPPS view-defining condition (STATUS > 15). Yet it fails! Furthermore, the user will receive a diagnostic message from the system to the effect that there has been a check option violation—even though, so far as the user is concerned, there *is* no check option. Thus, it could be argued that "encapsulation" has been violated: The user cannot think in terms of view GOODSUPPS in isolation, but has to have some awareness of the definition of that view in terms of its underlying table (and similarly for that table in turn, if that table in turn is another view, and so on, recursively—assuming, of course, that all of those views have a CASCADED check option in turn).

  Referring back to Fig. 13.2, it is perhaps worth pointing out that the "cascaded" effect is in an *upward,* not a downward, direction.

- *LOCAL:* In this case, the check option will be inherited, but only conditionally. If an UPDATE or INSERT on GOODSUPPS would cause a row to disappear from AVGSUPPS *but not from the (single) underlying table on which AVGSUPPS is defined,* then that UPDATE or INSERT will be rejected. In the case at hand, the single underlying table on which AVGSUPPS is defined is a *base* table, and there is no way that an UPDATE or INSERT can cause a row to disappear from a base table, and so the check option *will* effectively be inherited. But suppose AVGSUPPS were defined in terms of another view V, where V in turn is defined in terms of the underlying base table S. Then whether or not the check option on AVGSUPPS is inherited by GOODSUPPS will depend, in general, on how AVGSUPPS and V are defined, and possibly also on the specific UPDATE or INSERT under consideration.*

Case 3: GOODSUPPS has the check option but AVGSUPPS does not.

Suppose now, contrariwise, that AVGSUPPS does not have the check option, but GOODSUPPS does. What happens to the original UPDATE now? Again, the answer to this question depends on whether the check option (for GOODSUPPS this time) specifies CASCADED or LOCAL.

- *CASCADED:* The UPDATE will be rejected, because it would cause a row to disappear from GOODSUPPS. Note once again, however, that from the perspective of the GOODSUPPS user, the UPDATE certainly looks reasonable; there is no way it can violate the GOODSUPPS view-defining condition. Yet again it fails. Furthermore, the diagnostic message will again say that there has been a check option violation—even though, so far as the user is concerned, there is apparently no way this could happen. Thus, it could be argued again that encapsulation has been violated.

- *LOCAL:* The UPDATE will be accepted, because although it does cause rows to disappear from GOODSUPPS, *those rows also disappear from the (single) underlying table on which GOODSUPPS is defined* (namely, AVGSUPPS). Of course, the UPDATE does still have the counterintuitive effect that table GOODSUPPS will now be empty. That is, specifying the LOCAL check option for GOODSUPPS has made *no difference* to this result.

Case 4: Both views have the check option.

The only safe way—it is tempting to say the only really *comprehensible* way—to proceed seems to be to specify the check option (CASCADED, not LOCAL) for both views. Then UPDATEs and INSERTs on GOODSUPPS will unequivocally be checked against both view-defining conditions. More generally, it is this writer's opinion that views (updatable views, that is) should *never* be without a (CASCADED) check option. And the user needs to understand that, if he or she is operating on a view *V1* that is defined in

---

*Suppose, for example, that AVGSUPPS is defined as "SELECT * FROM V" and V is defined as "SELECT SNO, STATUS, CITY FROM S WHERE STATUS < 25" (i.e., AVGSUPPS and V are actually isomorphic to one another). Then it would not be possible for an UPDATE or INSERT to cause a row to disappear from AVGSUPPS without its disappearing from V as well, and so a LOCAL check option on AVGSUPPS could not possibly be inherited by GOODSUPPS.

terms of a view *V2* that is defined in terms of a view (etc., etc.) . . . that is defined in terms of a view *Vn* that is defined on a base table *B,* then updates against view *V1* are subject to a "check option" that is the *logical AND* of the check options for *V1, V2,* . . . , and *Vn.* It is true that (as mentioned above) this recommendation does lead to a minor "violation of encapsulation," but that violation seems a small price to pay for the improved comprehensibility and predictability (and correctness?) that is achieved.

We close this discussion (and this chapter) with a brief summary of the general syntax and semantics of the check option. To repeat from Section 8.2, the syntax of a view definition is:

```
CREATE VIEW view [ ( column-commalist ) ]
    AS table-expression
            [ WITH [ CASCADED | LOCAL ] CHECK OPTION ]
```

The clause WITH CHECK OPTION (with, optionally, either CASCADED or LOCAL) can be specified only if the view is updatable. If neither CASCADED nor LOCAL is specified, CASCADED is assumed by default.

If the WITH CHECK OPTION clause is omitted, the view does not have a check option of its own, but updates on the view may still be subject to the check options of views on which this view is directly or indirectly defined (see below). Thus, such updates may still give rise to "check option violations," even though the direct target of such updates *has* no check option.

If WITH CASCADED CHECK OPTION is specified, then UPDATEs and INSERTs on this view and on any view directly or indirectly defined on this view are required not to cause any rows to disappear from this view.

If WITH LOCAL CHECK OPTION is specified, then UPDATEs and INSERTs on this view and on any view directly or indirectly defined on this view are required *either* not to cause any rows to disappear from this view *or,* if they do cause rows to disappear, then they must also cause the counterparts of those rows to disappear from the (single) underlying table for this view.

PART IV

DATA CONTROL

This part of the book consists of two chapters, one on integrity and one on security. The integrity chapter discusses the various kinds of *integrity constraints* supported by SQL, with special attention to foreign key ("referential") constraints. The security chapter discusses the various *privileges* that users (more precisely, "authorization IDs") must possess in order to perform SQL operations.

14

Integrity

14.1 INTRODUCTION

The SQL standard provides a variety of methods for defining *integrity constraints* that are to be enforced by the SQL-implementation. An integrity constraint (constraint for short) is basically a conditional expression (see Chapter 12) that is required not to evaluate to *false*. Indeed, some constraints are actually specified in terms of the conditional expression syntax of Chapter 12, as we shall see; others, however, are not, but instead use a special syntax of their own, which can nevertheless be regarded as—in fact, is actually defined to be—just shorthand for an equivalent "conditional expression" formulation. Here is a simple example ("total shipment quantity must be less than 500,000"):

```
CREATE ASSERTION IC35
       CHECK ( ( SELECT SUM ( SP.QTY ) FROM SP ) < 500000 )
```

Note: As the syntax in this example suggests, the standard uses the term "assertion" for certain constraints—specifically, those that we will be referring to in this chapter as *general* constraints. See Section 14.3 below.

When a user attempts to create a new constraint, the system checks that the constraint is not already violated by existing data in the database. If any violation is found, the new constraint cannot be accepted; otherwise, the constraint *is* accepted, and is enforced from that point forward.

All constraints have an appropriate *constraint name*; if the user does not specify such a name explicitly, the system will implicitly provide an implementation-dependent one anyway. In the example above, "IC35" ("integrity constraint number 35") is the constraint name (note that "general" constraints *must* be explicitly named by the user). If a constraint is violated, its name will be made available to the user as part of the relevant diagnostic information (see Chapter 22).

For the purposes of this chapter, we divide integrity constraints into the following broad categories:

1. Domain constraints
2. General constraints
3. Base table constraints
   (including "column constraints")

We explain these categories very briefly as follows:

1. Domain constraints are constraints that are associated with a specific domain, and apply to every column that is defined on that domain.*
2. General constraints are constraints that apply to arbitrary combinations of columns in arbitrary combinations of base tables in the database.
3. Base table constraints are constraints that are associated with a specific base table. "Column constraints" are just syntactic shorthands for certain common base table constraints.

The plan of the chapter is as follows. Following this introductory section, we discuss domain constraints in Section 14.2, general constraints in Section 14.3, and base table constraints (including column constraints) in Section 14.4. Section 14.5 then deals with a very important special case of base table constraints, namely *foreign key* constraints. Finally, Section 14.6 addresses the question of when integrity checking is actually performed (prior to that section, we will simply assume—for the most part, at any rate—that such checking is performed whenever any update operation is executed).

A few final introductory remarks:

1. No integrity constraint is allowed to include any references to parameters or host variables (because, of course, constraints are independent of specific applications).

---

*They also apply to attempts to CAST a specified scalar value to the data type of a specified domain. We do not discuss this case further in this chapter. See Chapter 7, Section 7.4.

2. No integrity constraint is allowed to include any references to any of the niladic functions USER, CURRENT_USER, SESSION_USER, SYSTEM_USER, CURRENT_DATE, CURRENT_TIME, or CURRENT_TIMESTAMP (refer to Chapters 7, 15, and 17 for detailed discussion of these functions). The rationale for this restriction is that such references will return different values on different invocations, in general.

3. No integrity constraint is allowed to include a conditional expression that is "possibly nondeterministic." See Chapter 19, Section 19.7, subsection entitled "Equal but Distinguishable," for further explanation.

4. It is sometimes useful to regard the entire database as being subject to just one giant integrity constraint, which is the conjunction ("logical AND") of all of the individually specified constraints. In particular, note that every base table is required to satisfy, not only all of the general and base table constraints that apply to that table directly, but also all of the domain constraints that apply to columns within that table.

5. For completeness, we remind the reader that there are two additional features of the standard that might—very loosely!—be regarded as integrity features of a kind, namely *data type checking* and the *check option:*

   ▪ First, SQL will reject any attempt to violate data type specifications on INSERT or UPDATE—e.g., an attempt to insert a string value into a column defined as numeric. (In fact, data type specifications can be regarded as a primitive form of domain constraint. Note, however, that data type violations are a syntax error, whereas domain constraint violations in general cannot be detected until run time.)

   ▪ Second, SQL will reject any attempt to perform an INSERT or UPDATE on a view that violates the defining condition for that view (and possibly for views on which that view is defined), so long as an appropriate check option is specified. Refer to Chapter 13 for a detailed discussion of the check option.

14.2 DOMAIN CONSTRAINTS

Domain constraints can be initially specified by means of CREATE DOMAIN, and can be added to or dropped from an existing domain by means of ALTER DOMAIN. Note, however, that dropping a domain does *not* drop any domain constraints that were previously associated with that domain, as we shall see.

CREATE DOMAIN

To repeat from Chapter 8, the syntax of a domain definition is as follows:

```
domain-definition
   ::=   CREATE DOMAIN domain [ AS ] data-type
                       [ default-definition ]
                       [ domain-constraint-definition-list ]
```

A "domain constraint definition" in turn looks like this:

```
[ CONSTRAINT constraint ] CHECK ( conditional-expression )
```

Here the optional specification "CONSTRAINT constraint" defines a name for the new constraint,* and "conditional expression" defines the constraint per se. If the specification "CONSTRAINT constraint" is omitted, the constraint does not have a user-defined name. (Note that the syntax is indeed "CONSTRAINT constraint," whereas in a general constraint—see Section 14.3 or the example in Section 14.1—it is "ASSERTION constraint.") *Note:* No domain constraint is allowed to refer directly to the domain (*D,* say) to which it applies, nor to any other domain if that other domain in turn has a domain constraint that refers directly or indirectly to *D*; in other words, recursive definitions are prohibited.

Here is an example of a domain definition that includes a domain constraint:

```
CREATE DOMAIN CITIES CHAR(15)
       CONSTRAINT ICCITIES
       CHECK ( VALUE IN ( 'Athens', 'Dublin', 'London',
                          'Madrid', 'New York', 'Oslo',
                          'Paris', 'Rome', 'Stockholm' ) )
```

An attempt (via an INSERT or UPDATE operation) to place a scalar value *v* into a column defined on domain *D* is considered to violate a domain constraint for *D* if the conditional expression specified within that constraint evaluates to *false* for *v*. *Note:* The special symbol VALUE can be used in a domain constraint *and nowhere else.* It stands for the actual scalar value in question (*v* in the foregoing discussion). It inherits its data type—CHAR(15) in the example above—from the applicable domain.

It is perhaps worth pointing out that (somewhat surprisingly) NOT NULL is *not* a valid domain constraint. Thus, for example, the following is *** *INVALID* ***:

```
CREATE DOMAIN CITIES CHAR(15) NOT NULL  -- *** ILLEGAL *** !!!
```

---

*If the name is qualified by a schema name and the constraint definition appears within the context of a CREATE SCHEMA statement, then that schema name must identify the schema that would have been assumed by default anyway, viz. the schema being created (see Section 4.3).

The correct way to say that nulls are not allowed for a given domain is as illustrated by the following example:

```
CREATE DOMAIN CITIES CHAR(15)
             CHECK ( VALUE IS NOT NULL )
```

ALTER DOMAIN

Recall from Chapter 8 that ALTER DOMAIN supports "domain constraint alteration actions" of two possible forms:

```
domain-constraint-alteration-action
  ::=   ADD domain-constraint-definition
      | DROP CONSTRAINT constraint
```

ADD permits a new constraint to be attached to an existing domain (the new constraint will be logically ANDed with any existing constraints for the domain in question). DROP permits an existing domain constraint to be removed.

DROP DOMAIN

As explained in Section 8.2, dropping a domain that has any domain constraints will *not* drop those constraints, but will instead effectively convert them into base table constraints and attach them to every base table that includes a column defined on the domain in question.* Note the contrast with ALTER DOMAIN . . . DROP CONSTRAINT; this latter operation really does drop the constraint (for all columns defined on the domain in question).

14.3 GENERAL CONSTRAINTS

CREATE ASSERTION

As mentioned in the introduction to this chapter, we use the term "general constraint" to refer to a constraint of arbitrary complexity, involving an

---

*It would be conceptually clearer to regard this as a two-step process: First, convert each such domain constraint into a *column* constraint (by replacing each occurrence of VALUE by the relevant column name) for every column defined on the domain; second, convert each such column constraint into the equivalent base table constraint and attach it to the relevant base table. Such an explanation would make it clear that if base table *T* includes multiple columns defined on domain *D,* and *D* is dropped, then *T* will acquire multiple base table constraints accordingly. The problem with this explanation is that the first step may fail, in that it may generate syntactically incorrect column constraints. See Appendix D.

arbitrary collection of columns from an arbitrary collection of base tables. Such constraints are created by CREATE ASSERTION—syntax:

```
CREATE ASSERTION constraint CHECK ( conditional-expression )
```

Here "constraint" is the name of the new constraint* (as mentioned above, a general constraint must indeed have a name). Here are some examples:

1. Every supplier has status at least five:

```
CREATE ASSERTION IC13 CHECK
       ( ( SELECT MIN ( S.STATUS ) FROM S ) > 4 )
```

2. Every part has a positive weight:

```
CREATE ASSERTION IC18 CHECK
       ( NOT EXISTS ( SELECT * FROM P
                      WHERE  NOT ( P.WEIGHT > 0 ) ) )
```

Note: Examples 1 and 2 are conceptually very similar ("weight positive" means "weight greater than zero," which is of the same form as "status greater than four"), so either one could alternatively be expressed in the syntactic style of the other.

3. All red parts must be stored in London:

```
CREATE ASSERTION IC99 CHECK
       ( NOT EXISTS ( SELECT * FROM P
                      WHERE  P.COLOR = 'Red'
                      AND    P.CITY <> 'London' ) )
```

"There does not exist a part where the color is red and the city is not London."

4. No shipment has a total weight (part weight times shipment quantity) greater than 20,000:

```
CREATE ASSERTION IC46 CHECK
       ( NOT EXISTS ( SELECT * FROM P, SP
                      WHERE  P.PNO = SP.PNO
                      AND    ( P.WEIGHT * SP.QTY ) > 20000 ) )
```

5. No supplier with status less than 20 can supply any part in a quantity greater than 500:

---

*If the name is qualified by a schema name and the CREATE ASSERTATION appears within the context of a CREATE SCHEMA statement, then that schema name must identify the schema that would have been assumed by default anyway, viz. the schema being created (see Section 4.3).

```
CREATE ASSERTION IC95 CHECK
     ( NOT EXISTS ( SELECT * FROM S
                    WHERE  S.STATUS < 20
                    AND    EXISTS
                         ( SELECT * FROM SP
                           WHERE  SP.SNO = S.SNO
                           AND    SP.QTY > 500 ) ) )
```

Observe that most of the foregoing examples (effectively all, in fact) involve a conditional expression that begins with "NOT EXISTS." This is to be expected, because integrity constraints are usually of the form "Every *x* satisfies *y*," which in turn usually has to be expressed in SQL as "No *x* does not satisfy *y*"; but it does serve to stress the fundamental importance of the EXISTS operator. (It is only fair to point out, however, that EXISTS in general, and NOT EXISTS in particular, hold traps for the unwary in SQL, as will be explained in Chapter 16.) We will return to this question of the form of the conditional expression in Section 14.4 below.

Note: It is probably worth mentioning that expressing constraints as base table constraints instead of as general constraints (which can *always* be done) will often have the effect of eliminating the need for that preliminary "NOT EXISTS." In Section 14.4 below, we will show "base table constraint" equivalents of the five examples given above. We should perhaps point out the converse too—namely, that base table constraints (including "column constraints") can *always* be reformulated as general constraints.* Domain constraints, by contrast, cannot be expressed as general constraints (why not?).

DROP ASSERTION

General constraints—i.e., constraints created by means of CREATE ASSERTION—can be dropped by means of DROP ASSERTION. Syntax:

```
DROP ASSERTION constraint
```

The specified constraint is dropped. Note that, unlike all forms of DROP discussed previously in this book, DROP ASSERTION does not offer a RESTRICT or CASCADE option.

14.4 BASE TABLE AND COLUMN CONSTRAINTS

To repeat from Section 14.1, base table constraints are constraints that are associated with a specific base table. Note carefully, however, that "associ-

---

*Except for the "referential action" portion of foreign key constraints. See Section 14.6.

ated with a specific base table" does not mean that such constraints cannot span multiple base tables (on the contrary, in fact, some base table constraints—foreign key constraints in particular—usually *will* span multiple base tables). Rather, it means simply that the constraint cannot exist if the associated base table does not exist, and in particular that dropping the base table will drop the constraint too. In fact, as suggested in the previous section, base table constraints are essentially just shorthand; there is nothing that can be expressed by means of a base table constraint that cannot alternatively be expressed as a general constraint—*except* for the "referential action" portion of a foreign key constraint (see Section 14.5).

Base table constraints can be initially specified by means of CREATE TABLE, and can be added to or dropped from an existing base table by means of ALTER TABLE. Also, as just mentioned, DROP TABLE automatically drops any base table constraints that were previously associated with the base table in question.

CREATE TABLE

As we saw in Chapter 8, a base table definition takes the form of "CREATE TABLE base-table," followed by a parenthesized commalist of "base table elements," where each "base table element" is either a column definition or a base table constraint definition.* A base table constraint definition in turn is any of the following:

1. a candidate key definition
2. a foreign key definition
3. a "check constraint" definition

Each of these can optionally be preceded by "CONSTRAINT constraint" (exactly as for domain constraints), in order to provide a name for the new constraint. For brevity, we will omit this option from our further discussions of the syntax below.

Candidate key definitions: In the relational model, a *candidate key* is basically just a unique identifier for (the rows of) a table. A given table can have any number of candidate keys,[†] exactly one of which is designated as the *primary* key (at least for base tables), and the rest if any are said to be *alternate* keys.

---

*We remind the reader that the syntax permits column definitions and base table constraint definitions to be arbitrarily interspersed. In this book, however, we adopt the convention that the column definitions always come first.

[†]At least one, because tables in the relational model never contain duplicate rows. SQL, however, unfortunately permits tables with no candidate keys at all.

In SQL, a candidate key definition (supported for base tables only, please note) takes the form

```
{ PRIMARY KEY | UNIQUE } ( column-commalist )
```

where each "column" is the *un*qualified name of a column of the base table in question. The identified column or combination of columns constitutes a candidate key for that table. *Note:* For a given base table, at most one candidate key definition can specify PRIMARY KEY (we would recommend, of course, that *exactly* one should do so). Informally, we will call a candidate key definition that specifies PRIMARY KEY a "primary key definition," and one that specifies UNIQUE an "alternate key definition." (This usage is admittedly a trifle sloppy, because SQL permits a given base table to have UNIQUE constraints without a PRIMARY KEY constraint, and so it is not quite accurate to regard UNIQUE constraints as defining "candidate keys that are not the primary key." As already indicated, however, we would recommend, strongly, that *every* base table have a PRIMARY KEY constraint.)

We can define the semantics of a candidate key definition (a trifle loosely) in terms of a "check constraint," as follows: The database will satisfy the candidate key constraint shown above if and only if it satisfies the "check constraint" (q.v.).

```
CHECK ( UNIQUE ( SELECT column-commalist FROM T ) )
```

where *T* is the base table whose definition contains the candidate key definition in question. *Note:* If the candidate key definition is in fact a *primary* key definition, each component column is additionally assumed to be NOT NULL, even if NOT NULL is not specified explicitly (see Chapter 16). Refer back to Chapter 12 if you need to refresh your memory regarding unique-conditions.

Foreign key definitions: In the relational model, a *foreign key* is a column or combination of columns in one base table *T2* whose values are required to match values of the primary key in some base table *T1* (again, speaking somewhat loosely). For example, in the suppliers-and-parts database, column SP.SNO of table SP is a foreign key matching the primary key S.SNO of table S; every supplier number value appearing in column SP.SNO must also appear in column S.SNO (for otherwise the database would not be consistent). Likewise, column SP.PNO of table SP is a foreign key matching the primary key P.PNO of table P; every part number value appearing in column SP.PNO must also appear in column P.PNO.

In SQL, a foreign key definition takes the form

```
FOREIGN KEY ( column-commalist ) references-definition
```

where each "column" is the unqualified name of a column of the base table in question (the identified column or combination of columns constitutes a foreign key within that table), and "references definition" is explained in Section 14.5. *Note:* The full details of foreign key definitions are quite complex; we therefore defer discussion of those details to Section 14.5. However, we give a couple of examples here—namely, definitions for the two foreign keys in table SP:

```
FOREIGN KEY ( SNO ) REFERENCES S
FOREIGN KEY ( PNO ) REFERENCES P
```

We can define the semantics of a foreign key definition (a trifle loosely once again) in terms of a "check constraint," as follows: The database will satisfy the foreign key constraint

```
FOREIGN KEY fk REFERENCES T ( ck )
```

if and only if it satisfies the "check constraint" (q.v.)

```
CHECK ( fk MATCH ( SELECT ck FROM T ) )
```

Refer back to Chapter 12 if you need to refresh your memory regarding match-conditions.

We remark in passing that, whereas the relational model requires a foreign key to refer, very specifically, to a *primary* key, SQL permits a foreign key to refer to *any candidate key*—i.e., to a primary key or to an alternate key.

Check constraint definitions: A "check constraint definition" takes the form

```
CHECK ( conditional-expression )
```

An attempt to create a row *r* within base table *T* is considered to violate a check constraint for *T* if the conditional expression specified within that constraint evaluates to *false* for *r*—or, to state matters a little less precisely, if the specified conditional expression evaluates to *false* for any row of *T*. *Note:* It is that phrase—*for any row*—that makes the preliminary "NOT EXISTS" found in the typical general constraint unnecessary in the equivalent base table constraint. In other words, where the typical general constraint says something like "NOT EXISTS *x* WHERE NOT *y*," the equivalent base table constraint says simply "*y*".* Here, for instance, are "base

---

*The explicit or implicit conditional expression in *any* constraint is required to conform to certain rules of "well-formedness." Specifically, every variable reference (necessarily representing database data, not host language data) must be *quantified*. In general constraints, the quantifiers are explicit; in base table and domain constraints, certain quantifiers are implicit (this is why these latter constraints are often—arguably—easier to understand). Note that in this context, the aggregate functions SUM, etc., can be regarded as quantifiers of a kind; so too can the UNIQUE of a unique-condition.

table constraint" analogs of the "general constraint" examples from Section 14.3. Each is intended to be part of the CREATE TABLE for the relevant base table (which implies, incidentally, that the table-name qualifiers could optionally be dropped from many of the qualified column names; e.g., "S.STATUS" in Example 1 could be abbreviated to just "STATUS," if desired).

1. Every supplier has status at least five:

```
CONSTRAINT IC13 CHECK ( S.STATUS > 4 )
```

2. Every part has a positive weight:

```
CONSTRAINT IC18 CHECK ( P.WEIGHT > 0 )
```

3. All red parts must be stored in London:

```
CONSTRAINT IC99 CHECK ( P.COLOR <> 'Red' OR
                        P.CITY <> 'London' )
```

"For any given part, either the color is not red or the city is not London."

4. No shipment has a total weight (part weight times shipment quantity) greater than 20,000:

```
CONSTRAINT IC46 CHECK
       ( SP.QTY * ( SELECT P.WEIGHT FROM P
                    WHERE  P.PNO = SP.PNO ) <= 20000 )
```

This constraint must be specified as part of the CREATE TABLE for base table SP.

5. No supplier with status less than 20 can supply any part in a quantity greater than 500:

```
CONSTRAINT IC95 CHECK
       ( SP.QTY <= 500 OR ( SELECT S.STATUS FROM S
                            WHERE  S.SNO = SP.SNO ) >= 20 )
```

This constraint also must be specified as part of the CREATE TABLE for base table SP.

One slightly counterintuitive consequence of the foregoing is worth pointing out explicitly. The base table check constraint CHECK (y) is defined to be equivalent to the general constraint

```
NOT EXISTS ( SELECT * FROM T WHERE NOT ( y ) )
```

where T is the base table to which y is attached. Note, therefore, that the original constraint y will *always* be satisfied if T is empty, no matter what form y might take—even if, e.g., y is of the form "T must contain at least one row"! (or even the form "*T* must contain -5 rows," or the form "$1 = 0$," come to that).

ALTER TABLE

Recall from Chapter 8 that ALTER TABLE supports "base table constraint alteration actions" of two possible forms:

```
base-table-constraint-alteration-action
    ::=    ADD base-table-constraint-definition
         | DROP CONSTRAINT constraint { RESTRICT | CASCADE }
```

ADD permits a new constraint to be attached to an existing base table; DROP permits an existing base table constraint to be removed from an existing base table. RESTRICT and CASCADE have meaning if and only if the constraint is a candidate key definition: An attempt to drop a candidate key definition will fail if any foreign key references that candidate key, unless CASCADE is specified (in which case all such foreign key definitions will be dropped too).

Column Constraints

If a base table constraint applies to a single column within a single base table, it can optionally be specified (in abbreviated syntactic form, in most cases) as part of the definition of the column in question, instead of as a distinct "base table element." That is, a column definition can optionally include any number of "column constraint definitions." A column constraint definition in turn can be any of the following:

1. NOT NULL
2. PRIMARY KEY or UNIQUE
3. a references-definition
4. a "check constraint" definition

Each of these can optionally be preceded by "CONSTRAINT constraint," exactly as for domain and base table constraints. For brevity, we will omit this option from our discussions below; note, however, that if the option *is* specified, it is inherited by the base table constraint that the column constraint is defined to be shorthand for.

NOT NULL: Specifying NOT NULL for a column *C* is defined to be shorthand for specifying the base table constraint

```
CHECK ( C IS NOT NULL )
```

for the base table that contains *C*. See Chapter 16.

PRIMARY KEY and UNIQUE: Specifying **PRIMARY KEY** or UNIQUE for a column *C* is defined to be shorthand for specifying the base table constraint

```
PRIMARY KEY ( C )
```

or

```
UNIQUE ( C )
```

(as appropriate) for the base table that contains *C*.

References definition: Specifying a references-definition, *ref-def* say, for a column *C* is defined to be shorthand for specifying the base table constraint

```
FOREIGN KEY ( C ) ref-def
```

for the base table that contains *C*. Refer to Section 14.5 below for further discussion.

Check constraint: Specifying a check constraint for a column *C* is defined to be shorthand for specifying that very same check constraint as a base table constraint for the base table that contains *C*. Note, however, that *C* must be the only column referenced within that check constraint.*

Column constraints can be specified only within a column definition. Thus, they must be defined when the column per se is defined, either by means of CREATE TABLE or by means of ALTER TABLE. Once defined, however, they logically become *base table* constraints; thus, they can be dropped from an existing base table by means of ALTER TABLE . . . DROP CONSTRAINT (or by DROP TABLE, of course), but there is no way to add a new column constraint to an existing column, nor to remove an existing column constraint from an existing column.

14.5 FOREIGN KEYS

We begin this section with a quick overview of the relevant ideas from the relational model; then we move on to examine the details of the SQL support for those ideas.

1. First, as explained in the previous section, a foreign key in the relational model is basically a column or combination of columns in one base table *T2* whose values are required to match values of the primary

---

*Given that this is so, it might have been nice to use the special symbol VALUE to stand for the column in question (analogous to the use of VALUE in a domain constraint), and then to prohibit *all* explicit column references within the check constraint.

key in some base table *T1*. For example, columns SNO and PNO in the shipments table SP are foreign keys that match the primary keys SNO and PNO of the suppliers table and parts table, respectively—meaning that every value appearing in column SP.SNO must also appear in column S.SNO, and every value appearing in column SP.PNO must also appear in column P.PNO. Note, incidentally, that the converse is *not* a requirement—that is, a primary key value can exist without a matching foreign key value. For example, given the suppliers-and-parts sample data of Fig. 2.1, supplier S5 currently does not supply any parts, and hence the value S5 occurs in column S.SNO but not in column SP.SNO.

2. *Terminology:* A given foreign key value represents a *reference* from the row(s) containing it to the row containing the matching primary key value. For that reason, the problem of ensuring that every foreign key value does in fact match a value of the corresponding primary key is known as the *referential integrity* problem. The base table containing the foreign key is called the *referencing table*; the base table containing the corresponding primary key is called the *referenced table*. The integrity constraint is called a *referential constraint* or *foreign key constraint*.

3. The referenced table *T1* and the referencing table *T2* in our (loose) definition of "foreign key" above do not necessarily have to be distinct. That is, a base table might include a foreign key whose values are required to match values of the primary key of that same base table. An example might be a base table

```
CHILDOF ( CHILD, MOTHER )
```

where each MOTHER is in turn a CHILD of some other MOTHER (etc.). Here CHILD is the primary key and MOTHER is a foreign key matching CHILD (i.e., the MOTHER value in a given row must be equal to the CHILD value in some other row).

4. The foregoing example is actually just a special case of a more general situation, namely the situation in which there is a *referential cycle*—i.e., a cycle of base tables *T1, T2, T3, . . . , Tn,* such that *T1* includes a foreign key matching the primary key of *T2, T2* includes a foreign key matching the primary key of *T3,* and so on, . . . , and *Tn* includes a foreign key matching the primary key of *T1*. We remark that, in order to specify such a cycle, it will be necessary to specify at least one of the foreign keys by means of ALTER TABLE . . . ADD instead of

by means of CREATE TABLE, because a foreign key definition cannot refer to a base table that does not yet exist.*

5. The CHILDOF example also serves to illustrate another point—namely, that foreign key values will sometimes be missing, and perhaps therefore will have to have "nulls allowed." In the case at hand, there will presumably be at least one CHILD whose mother in turn is not represented as a CHILD in any CHILDOF row. Thus, we will be forced in the present section to discuss nulls, albeit briefly! As always, we defer as much of the detail as possible to Chapter 16; the basic point, however, is that we must now modify our earlier definition of "foreign key" slightly, as follows: A foreign key is a column or combination of columns in the referencing table *T2* such that, for each row of *T2,* that column or column combination *either* is null *or* contains a value that matches the value of the primary key in some row of the referenced table *T1.*[†]

Let us now turn to SQL specifically. Remember that a foreign key constraint is a special case of a base table constraint, and so foreign key definitions appear within CREATE TABLE (or ALTER TABLE) statements. The syntax is as follows:

```
FOREIGN KEY ( column-commalist ) references-definition
```

(optionally preceded, like all base table constraint definitions, by "CONSTRAINT constraint"; we omit this option for brevity). The "references definition" in turn takes the form:

```
REFERENCES base-table [ ( column-commalist ) ]
    [ MATCH { FULL | PARTIAL } ]
    [ ON DELETE { NO ACTION | CASCADE | SET DEFAULT | SET NULL } ]
    [ ON UPDATE { NO ACTION | CASCADE | SET DEFAULT | SET NULL } ]
```

---

*Unless all of the CREATE TABLEs involved appear as elements within the same CREATE SCHEMA operation. Since individual SQL statements are supposed to be "atomic," the elements within a single CREATE SCHEMA must be thought of as—somehow—all being executed simultaneously.

[†]This is the definition usually given in discussions of the relational model, and it is the definition adopted in SQL (except that, as already noted in Section 14.4, SQL permits a foreign key to match *any candidate key* of the referenced table, not necessarily the primary key specifically). We should note, however, that considerable controversy exists regarding nulls in general, and nulls in foreign keys in particular. See the chapter entitled "Notes Toward a Reconstituted Definition of the Relational Model," in C. J. Date and Hugh Darwen, *Relational Database Writings 1989–1991* (Addison-Wesley, 1992).

Explanation:

- The "column commalist" in the FOREIGN KEY clause per se identifies the column or combination of columns that constitutes the foreign key. Each column must be identified by its *un*qualified name.

- The "base table" in the references-definition identifies the referenced table.

- The optional "column commalist" in the references-definition must be the same (except possibly for the sequence in which the columns are listed) as the "column commalist" in some candidate key definition for the referenced table (again, each column must be identified by its unqualified name). Omitting that second column commalist is equivalent to specifying a column commalist that is identical to that in the *primary* key definition for the referenced table (the referenced table must possess a defined primary key in this case).

- The optional MATCH clause has to do with nulls. We defer further discussion to Chapter 16.

- Finally, the optional ON DELETE and ON UPDATE clauses (which can appear in either order) are explained in the subsection "Referential Actions" below. Here we simply note that omitting either clause is equivalent to specifying that clause with the NO ACTION option.

Here is an example:

```
CREATE TABLE SP
     ( SNO ... , PNO ... , QTY ... ,
       PRIMARY KEY ( SNO, PNO ),
       FOREIGN KEY ( SNO ) REFERENCES S,
       FOREIGN KEY ( PNO ) REFERENCES P )
```

The first of the two FOREIGN KEY clauses here states that column SP.SNO is a foreign key matching the primary key of base table S (note that base table S must have a defined PRIMARY KEY for this references-definition to be legal). The second FOREIGN KEY clause is analogous.

Points arising:

1. It so happens in the example that each of the two foreign keys is a component of the primary key of the containing base table. However, this is *not* a requirement. In fact, *any column* or column combination (within a single base table) can be a foreign key. For example, column CITY of base table S might be a foreign key, if the database included another base table representing cities.

2. As mentioned in Section 14.4, if a foreign key is single-column (as in both of the examples above), the references-definition can be included

directly in the column definition instead of being made part of a separate FOREIGN KEY clause. For example:

```
CREATE TABLE SP
     ( SNO ... REFERENCES S,
       PNO ... REFERENCES P,
       QTY ... ,
       PRIMARY KEY ( SNO, PNO ) )
```

However, references-definitions that are part of an individual column definition are defined to be merely a shorthand for corresponding base table foreign key definitions, as explained earlier.

3. Observe that (again as mentioned in Section 14.4) the standard permits a foreign key to match *any candidate key* in the referenced table, not necessarily the primary key specifically. In our examples, however, we will follow the discipline that foreign keys always reference primary keys, never alternate keys.

4. A foreign key and its matching candidate key must contain the same number of columns, n say; the ith column of the foreign key corresponds to the ith column of the matching candidate key ($i = 1$ to n), and corresponding columns must have the same data type.

5. Let $T2$ and $T1$ be a referencing table and the corresponding referenced table, respectively, and let $T2.FK$ and $T1.CK$ be the foreign key and matching candidate key in those two tables. Assume for the moment that the foreign key definition includes neither an ON DELETE clause nor an ON UPDATE clause. Then, in order to maintain the referential constraint between $T2.FK$ and $T1.CK$, the system will simply reject* any operation that would violate it. The operations that will be rejected are:

   Case 1: An INSERT on $T2$ or an UPDATE on $T2.FK$ that would introduce a value for $T2.FK$ that does not exist as a value of $T1.CK$

   Case 2: A DELETE on $T1$ or an UPDATE on $T1.CK$ that would leave "dangling references" in $T2$ (i.e., rows in $T2$ that have no counterpart in $T1$)

   If on the other hand the foreign key definition does include either an ON DELETE clause or an ON UPDATE clause, then Case 2 updates

---

*"Simply reject" is not quite accurate for Case 2 updates (q.v.). Instead, what happens—at least conceptually—for Case 2 is that the system actually does the update, and then undoes it again if the referential constraint has been violated. In most situations the net effect is indeed as if the update had simply been rejected in the first place; in certain complex situations, however (discussed briefly in the subsection entitled "Guaranteeing Predictable Behavior" at the end of the present section), the apparently tiny distinction turns out to be significant. See also Appendix E.

will not necessarily be rejected after all. (Case 1 updates will always be rejected out of hand, however, regardless of whether there is an ON DELETE clause or an ON UPDATE clause.) See the subsection "Referential Actions" immediately following.

Referential Actions

The general idea behind "referential actions" is that it may sometimes be possible to maintain referential integrity, not by simply rejecting an update that would violate it, but rather by performing another, compensating update in addition to the one originally requested. For example, instead of simply rejecting an attempt to delete the row for supplier S1 from the suppliers table (on the grounds that there are rows for supplier S1 in the shipments table), it might be better to go ahead and delete that supplier row *and* the matching shipment rows as well. Certainly referential integrity will be maintained that way.

Suppose once again, therefore, that *T2* and *T1* are a referencing table and the corresponding referenced table, respectively, and *T2.FK* and *T1.CK* are the relevant foreign key and matching candidate key. Suppose, moreover, that *T2.FK* has an associated ON DELETE clause and an associated ON UPDATE clause.

- The ON DELETE clause defines the *delete rule* for the referenced table *T1* with respect to this foreign key—that is, it defines what happens if an attempt is made to delete a row from *T1* (the "target row"), and there are some rows in *T2* that match that target row. The possible specifications ("referential actions") are NO ACTION, CASCADE, SET DEFAULT, and SET NULL, with meanings as follows:

    1. *NO ACTION:* Specifying NO ACTION is equivalent to omitting the ON DELETE clause entirely, the effect of which has already been explained.

    2. *CASCADE:* The DELETE "cascades" to delete all matching rows in *T2* also.*

       Note that *T2* might in turn be referenced by a foreign key in some other base table *T3*. If it is, then if any DELETE on *T1* cascades to some row *r2* in *T2*, then the effect is exactly as if an attempt

---

*It might be helpful to point out that the CASCADE option on the ON DELETE clause is somewhat analogous to the CASCADE option on various DROP statements. Likewise, the NO ACTION option on ON DELETE is somewhat—though less—analogous to the RESTRICT option on DROP. The important difference is that the options are specified *dynamically* (at execution time) in the case of DROP, but *statically* (as part of the data definition) in the case of DELETE.

had been made to DELETE that row *r2* directly; i.e., it depends on the delete rule specified for the foreign key from *T3* to *T2*. And so on, recursively, to any number of levels.

3. *SET DEFAULT:* The target row is deleted, and each component of the foreign key is set to the applicable default value in all matching rows in *T2*. Note that in this case a row must already exist in *T1* in which each component of the candidate key *T1.CK* has the appropriate default value (unless the default for some foreign key component is in fact null—see Chapter 16).

4. *SET NULL:* In this case, every component of the foreign key must have "nulls allowed." The target row is deleted and each component of the foreign key is set to null in all matching rows in *T2*.

■ The ON UPDATE clause defines the *update rule* for the referenced candidate key *T1.CK* with respect to this foreign key—that is, it defines what happens if an attempt is made to UPDATE the candidate key *CK* within some row of *T1* (the "target row"), and there are some rows in *T2* that match that target row. The possible specifications ("referential actions") are the same as for the ON DELETE clause—i.e., NO ACTION, CASCADE, SET DEFAULT, and SET NULL—with meanings as follows:

1. *NO ACTION:* Specifying NO ACTION is equivalent to omitting the ON UPDATE clause entirely, the effect of which has already been explained.

2. *CASCADE:* The UPDATE "cascades" to update the foreign key in all matching rows of *T2* also.

3. *SET DEFAULT:* The target row is updated, and components of the foreign key that correspond to updated components of the candidate key are set to the applicable default value in all matching rows in *T2*. Note that in this case, a row must already exist in *T1* in which each component of the candidate key *T1.CK* has the appropriate value (unless the default for some foreign key component is in fact null—see Chapter 16).

4. *SET NULL:* The target row is updated, and components of the foreign key that correspond to updated components of the candidate key are set to null in all matching rows in *T2*. (Those foreign key components must have "nulls allowed.")

Note that *T2.FK* might be a candidate key for *T2* and might in turn be referenced by a foreign key in some other base table *T3*. If it is, then if any UPDATE on *T1.CK* cascades to some row *r2* in *T2*, or sets *T2.FK* to a default value or null in some row *r2* in *T2*, then the effect is exactly as if an attempt had been made to UPDATE that row *r2* directly; i.e., it depends on the update rule specified for the foreign key from *T3* to *T2*. And so on, recursively, to any number of levels.

Here is an example:

```
CREATE TABLE SP
     ( SNO ... , PNO ... , QTY ... ,
       PRIMARY KEY ( SNO, PNO ),
       FOREIGN KEY ( SNO ) REFERENCES S
                           ON DELETE CASCADE
                           ON UPDATE CASCADE,
       FOREIGN KEY ( PNO ) REFERENCES P
                           ON DELETE CASCADE
                           ON UPDATE CASCADE )
```

With this definition for base table SP, an attempt to delete a specific supplier row or part row will cascade to delete all shipment rows for that supplier or part as well; likewise, an attempt to update the primary key value in a specific supplier row or part row will cascade to update the foreign key value in the same way in all shipment rows for that supplier or part as well.

Guaranteeing Predictable Behavior

It is well known that certain combinations of

1. referential structures (i.e., sets of base tables that are interrelated via referential constraints),
2. referential action specifications, and
3. actual data values in the database

can together lead to certain conflict situations and can potentially cause unpredictable behavior on the part of the implementation; see, e.g., Chapters 5 and 6 ("Referential Integrity and Foreign Keys, Parts I and II") in C. J. Date, *Relational Database Writings 1985–1989* (Addison-Wesley, 1990). The details are beyond the scope of this book; suffice it to say that the SQL standard identifies cases involving such potential unpredictability and requires the implementation to treat them as run-time errors—i.e., the attempted update must be rejected and an exception condition raised. Such exceptions can occur on DELETEs and primary key UPDATEs against certain referenced tables. *Note:* The interested reader can find a helpful analysis and explanation of this aspect of the standard in Bruce M. Horowitz, "A Run-Time Execution Model for Referential Integrity Maintenance," in the Proceedings of the 8th International Data Engineering Conference (February 1992). Also, an example of one specific conflict situation is discussed in Appendix E of the present book.

14.6 DEFERRED CONSTRAINT CHECKING

Up to this point we have tacitly been making the assumption that all integrity constraints are effectively checked "immediately," i.e., as the final step in executing any SQL statement—and, if any constraint is found to be violated, the offending SQL statement is canceled, so that its overall effect on the database is nil. Sometimes, however, it is necessary that certain constraints not be checked until some later time, on the grounds that if they are checked "immediately" they will always fail.

- An example is provided by referential cycles. Suppose we have two base tables, *T1* and *T2,* each of which includes a foreign key that references the primary key of the other, and suppose we start with both tables empty. Then, if all foreign key checking is done immediately, there is no way to get started: Any attempt to insert a row into either table will fail, because there is no target row in the other table that it can reference.

The facilities described in this section are intended to address this issue.

- At any given time, with respect to any given SQL-transaction, any given constraint must be in one of two "modes," *immediate* or *deferred*. *Immediate* means the constraint is checked "immediately" (as explained above); *deferred* means it is not.*

- Any given constraint definition can optionally include either or both of the following:

```
INITIALLY { DEFERRED | IMMEDIATE }
```

```
[ NOT ] DEFERRABLE
```

These specifications appear as the final syntactic component of the constraint definition. They can be stated in either order.

  - The specifications INITIALLY DEFERRED and NOT DEFERRABLE are mutually exclusive. If neither INITIALLY DEFERRED nor INITIALLY IMMEDIATE is specified, INITIALLY IMMEDIATE is implied. If INITIALLY IMMEDIATE is specified or implied, then if neither DEFERRABLE nor NOT DEFERRABLE is specified, NOT DEFERRABLE is implied. If

---

*This paragraph is true in general terms, but there are some constraints where deferred checking seems to make no sense. Domain constraints might be a case in point, and a strong argument could be made that NOT NULL and candidate key constraints are also. Indeed, if candidate key *CK* is referenced by some foreign key *FK,* then the standard *requires* the candidate key constraint for *CK* to be NOT DEFERRABLE.

INITIALLY DEFERRED is specified, then (as already explained) NOT DEFERRABLE must not be specified; DEFERRABLE may be specified, but is implied anyway.

- INITIALLY DEFERRED and INITIALLY IMMEDIATE specify the "initial" mode of the constraint—i.e., its mode immediately after it is defined and at the start of every SQL-transaction—as *deferred* or *immediate,* respectively.

- DEFERRABLE and NOT DEFERRABLE specify whether or not this constraint can ever be in *deferred* mode. DEFERRABLE means it can; NOT DEFERRABLE means it cannot.

- The SET CONSTRAINTS statement is used to set the mode for specified constraints with respect to the current SQL-transaction (or the next SQL-transaction to be initiated, if the SQL-agent has no SQL-transaction currently executing).* The syntax is:

```
SET CONSTRAINTS { constraint-commalist | ALL }
                        { DEFERRED | IMMEDIATE }
```

Each "constraint" mentioned by name must be DEFERRABLE; ALL is shorthand for "all DEFERRABLE constraints." If DEFERRED is specified, the mode of all indicated constraints is set to *deferred*. If IMMEDIATE is specified, the mode of all indicated constraints is set to *immediate,* and those constraints are then checked; if any check fails, the SET CONSTRAINTS fails, and the mode of all indicated constraints remains unchanged. (Note that because of the next paragraph, the checks should not fail if the SET CONSTRAINTS statement is executed while the SQL-agent has no current transaction.)

- COMMIT implies SET CONSTRAINTS ALL IMMEDIATE. If some implied integrity check then fails, the COMMIT fails, and the transaction fails also (i.e., is rolled back).

To revert to the example mentioned at the beginning of this section (the referential cycle involving two tables): We could deal with the problem using the foregoing facilities as indicated by the following pseudocode.

---

*As mentioned in Chapter 5, the standard permits transactions to span multiple sessions and (more to the point) multiple servers. For such a transaction, the effects of SET CONSTRAINTS are limited to the current session and current server. See Appendix D for further discussion.

Data definitions:

```
CREATE TABLE T1 ...
       CONSTRAINT T1FK FOREIGN KEY ... REFERENCES T2
                 INITIALLY DEFERRED

CREATE TABLE T2 ...
       CONSTRAINT T2FK FOREIGN KEY ... REFERENCES T1
                 INITIALLY DEFERRED
```

SQL-transaction:

```
INSERT INTO T1 ( ... ) VALUES ( ... )

INSERT INTO T2 ( ... ) VALUES ( ... )

SET CONSTRAINTS T1FK, T2FK IMMEDIATE

IF SQLSTATE = code meaning "SET CONSTRAINTS failed"
THEN ROLLBACK                          -- cancel the INSERTs
```

15

Security

15.1 INTRODUCTION

As explained in Chapter 4, every domain, every base table, every view, and every integrity constraint—also every character set, every collation, and every translation (see Chapter 19)—is described by some *schema*. As also explained in that chapter, every schema in turn has an associated user, the schema *owner,* who can be regarded as the owner not only of the schema per se, but of everything described by that schema also. Now, users can certainly operate on data they do not themselves own; if their operation is to succeed, however, the user that does own the data must first have granted them the appropriate *access privilege* for that operation and that data.*
Access privileges (privileges for short) are thus SQL's mechanism for providing *data security*. Accordingly, the SQL standard specifies a variety of "Access Rules," which define the privileges needed for various combinations of data objects and operations. It also defines two statements, GRANT and REVOKE, that allow users to grant privileges to one another, and subsequently to revoke such privileges. In this chapter, we examine these ideas in some detail.

We remind the reader that, despite our use of the term "user" above

---

*The granting might have been indirect. See the discussion of the grant option in Section 15.5.

(and elsewhere in this book), the standard does not in fact talk in such terms at all, but rather in terms of what it calls *authorization identifiers* (authIDs for short). In this chapter, we will still use the term "user" from time to time for intuitive reasons, but the reader should understand that our use of that term is only informal. Thus, the mapping between authIDs and real users as understood by the external operating system is completely implementation-defined;* in particular, there is no reason why a single authID should not map to an entire *group* of real users, and indeed there are reasons why this might be a good idea in practice.

The plan of the chapter is as follows. Following this brief introduction, Section 15.2 discusses certain important authIDs that need to be understood in order to appreciate the overall SQL security mechanism. Section 15.3 then summarizes the various privileges that are defined within the standard, indicating which privileges are needed for which SQL operations. Section 15.4 describes the GRANT and REVOKE statements. Finally, Section 15.5 discusses "the grant option" and the associated notion of *grant authority*.

15.2 AUTHORIZATION IDENTIFIERS

There are a number of authIDs that need to be understood and clearly distinguished in any discussion of SQL security—the *SQL-session* authID, the *module* authID, the *schema* authID, and the *current* authID. (Remember from Part II of this book that, conceptually speaking, all SQL operations—except possibly for certain CREATE SCHEMA operations—belong to some module, and all SQL operations are executed in some SQL-session.) *Note:* In practice, of course, these various different authIDs might very well all have the same *value,* but conceptually, at least, they are all distinct.

1. The *SQL-session authID* serves as a default authID for use in contexts where no explicit authID is provided to override it (for example, if the AUTHORIZATION clause is omitted in a module definition—see below). It is initially established by means of the USER clause on the CONNECT statement that initiates the SQL-session; if that clause is omitted, the initial SQL-session authID is implementation-defined. However, it can subsequently be changed at any time—any time there is no SQL-transaction running, that is—by means of the statement SET SESSION AUTHORIZATION. See Section 5.3 for a discussion of CONNECT and SET SESSION AUTHORIZATION. *Note:* No particular privileges are required in order to execute either of these two statements; however, the implementation is explicitly permitted to impose

---

*The standard says it is implementation-*dependent,* but this is surely an error in the standard.

implementation-defined restrictions on them, so that, for example, CONNECT can be prohibited from setting the SQL-session authID to anything other than the module authID.

The niladic builtin function SESSION_USER returns the SQL-session authID.

2. The *module authID* for a given module identifies the owner of that module. It is established by means of the AUTHORIZATION clause on the MODULE statement that defines that module (see Section 6.2); if that clause is omitted, the module does not have an owner (or an authID). As we will see in Section 15.3, most SQL data manipulation statements require the owner of the module containing the statement in question to hold the necessary privileges to execute that statement; if the module does not have an owner, then the SQL-session authID is required to hold those privileges instead.

   The standard does not say what privileges if any are needed to create a module, because the whole mechanism for creating modules is implementation-defined anyway. The intent is presumably that some external agency will control that mechanism in an appropriate manner.

3. The *schema authID* for a given schema identifies the owner of that schema (and hence the owner of everything described by that schema also). It is established by means of the AUTHORIZATION clause on the CREATE SCHEMA statement that creates that schema (see Section 4.3); if that clause is omitted, the owner of the schema is taken to be the owner, if any, of the module that contains the CREATE SCHEMA statement, or the SQL-session authID if that module has no owner.*

   The privileges needed to execute a CREATE SCHEMA operation are implementation-defined. The intent is presumably that some external agency will decide who is allowed to create new schemas.

4. The *current authID* identifies the "current" user. It is the authID against which authorization checking is actually done. For example, an attempt to perform a SELECT operation against some base table causes the system to check that the current authID holds the privilege to perform SELECT operations on that base table. Likewise, an attempt to ALTER some base table in some schema causes the system to check that the current authID is the owner of that schema.

   The current authID is taken to be the module authID if there is one, the SQL-session authID otherwise. The niladic builtin function

---

*It is also taken to be the SQL-session authID if the CREATE SCHEMA is "standalone" and does not include an AUTHORIZATION clause.

CURRENT_USER (which can be abbreviated to just USER) returns the current authID.*

Note carefully that, as a consequence of all of the foregoing, if (a) an application uses several modules, say one with owner *A,* one with owner *B,* and one with no owner, and if (b) the session authID is *C,* then authorization checking will be done variously against *A, B,* or *C,* depending on which module is invoked. Thus, e.g., *A*'s module might be able to update tables that *B*'s module cannot (and that authID *C* cannot either).

15.3 PRIVILEGES AND ACCESS RULES

The following list summarizes all of the privileges that are defined within the standard. *Note:* The privileges listed, excluding USAGE, are sometimes referred to collectively as "table privileges." Note specifically that "table privileges" apply to views as well as base tables, in general.

- *USAGE:* Privilege to use a specific domain (or character set, collation, or translation—see Chapter 19).

- *SELECT:* Privilege to access all of the columns of a specific named table, including any columns added to that table later.

- *INSERT(x):* Privilege to INSERT into a specific column *x* of a specific named table.

- *INSERT:* Privilege to INSERT into all columns of a specific named table; implies INSERT(*x*) privilege for all columns *x* of that table, including any columns added to that table later.

- *UPDATE(x):* Privilege to UPDATE a specific column *x* of a specific named table.

- *UPDATE:* Privilege to UPDATE all columns of a specific named table; implies UPDATE(*x*) for all columns *x* of that table, including any columns added to that table later.

- *DELETE:* Privilege to DELETE rows from a specific named table.

- *REFERENCES(x):* Privilege to reference a specific column *x* of a specific named table in integrity constraints.†

---

*We remind the reader that (as explained in Chapter 14) the niladic functions SYSTEM_USER (see Chapter 7), SESSION_USER, and CURRENT_USER (or USER) are not permitted within integrity constraints.

†Note that—despite the name—this privilege is required for *all* integrity constraints, not just referential constraints.

- *REFERENCES:* Privilege to reference all columns of a specific named table in integrity constraints; implies REFERENCES(x) for all columns x of that table, including any columns added to that table later.

We now present a summary of the "Access Rules" for each SQL statement (more accurately, each SQL *construct*) discussed so far in this book.* SQL constructs previously discussed but not included in the following summary are defined in the standard as having "Access Rules: None."

- *CREATE SCHEMA:* Requires implementation-defined privileges.

- *DROP SCHEMA, CREATE/ALTER/DROP DOMAIN, CREATE/ ALTER/DROP TABLE, CREATE/DROP VIEW, CREATE/DROP ASSERTION* (excluding CREATEs executed as "schema elements" within CREATE SCHEMA): The current authID must be the same as the authID of the affected schema.

- *CAST:* The operation CAST (. . . AS domain) requires USAGE on "domain."

- *Column definition:* Defining a column on "domain" requires USAGE on "domain."

- *Table reference:* Requires SELECT on the referenced table (except for table references within integrity constraints, q.v.).

- *Column reference:* Requires SELECT on the base table or view containing the referenced column (except for column references within integrity constraints, q.v.). *Note:* A column reference is just an implicitly or explicitly qualified column name.

- *Integrity constraint:* Requires REFERENCES(x) on every column x referenced, or REFERENCES(x) for at least one column x of table T if T is referenced but no explicit column of T is.

- *INSERT:* Requires INSERT(x) for every column x explicitly mentioned, or INSERT on the target table if no columns are explicitly mentioned.

- *UPDATE:* Requires UPDATE(x) for every target column x.

- *DELETE:* Requires DELETE on the target table.

- *GRANT and REVOKE:* See Section 15.4, later.

---

*The (relevant) constructs not so far discussed are character sets, collations, and translations. To CREATE or DROP such an object, the current authID must be the same as the authID of the affected schema. Any use of such an object requires the USAGE privilege on the object in question.

Certain implications and ramifications of the foregoing are worth spelling out explicitly.

1. First, we should explain that the owner of any object is automatically granted all privileges that make sense for that object (see Section 15.4 below). For example, in the case of a base table, the owner is automatically granted the SELECT, INSERT, UPDATE, DELETE, and REFERENCES privileges on that base table, with "grant authority" in each case (see Section 15.5). The "user" granting all of these privileges is considered to be a hypothetical user with the special—syntactically invalid!—authID of _SYSTEM.

2. Likewise, in the case of a view, the owner is automatically granted the SELECT and REFERENCES privileges on that view. If the view is updatable (see Chapter 13) *and* the owner holds the INSERT privilege and/or the UPDATE privilege and/or the DELETE privilege on the (single) underlying table of the view (again, see Chapter 13), then the owner is automatically granted the INSERT and/or UPDATE and/or DELETE privileges (as applicable) on that view also. Each of these privileges will include "grant authority" if and only if the user already holds the corresponding privilege on the underlying table with grant authority. Again, the authID granting all of these privileges is considered to be _SYSTEM.

3. Note that CREATE VIEW involves a table expression, which in turn involves one or more table references, and so requires the SELECT privilege on every named table (base table or view) identified by those table references, at any level of nesting.

4. In order to define a foreign key, the user needs the REFERENCES privilege on every column of the referenced candidate key. More generally, in order to define *any* integrity constraint, the user needs the REFERENCES privilege on every referenced column of every referenced named table—except in the special case of a constraint that references some named table but does not mention any specific column of that table (an example might be a constraint to the effect that the count of suppliers must be less than 100). In this special case, the user needs only the REFERENCES privilege on *at least one* column of the referenced named table.

5. INSERT by definition always inserts an entire row into the target table. If the user does not have the INSERT privilege for some column of that table, then the user cannot explicitly mention that column in the

INSERT; that column will thus be set to the applicable default value in the new row.

6. Note that the UPDATE statement (e.g.)

```
UPDATE T SET C = 1 ...
```

requires the UPDATE privilege on column *C* of table *T,* whereas the UPDATE statement (e.g.)

```
UPDATE T SET C = T.C + 1 ...
```

requires the SELECT privilege on *T* as well, because of the column reference *T.C.*

15.4 GRANT AND REVOKE

As indicated in the previous section, the owner of an object is automatically granted all privileges that make sense for that object. Furthermore, those privileges are granted "with the grant option." In general, if a privilege is granted "with the grant option," we will say that the recipient of the privilege has *grant authority* (not a standard term) for that privilege, which means that the recipient can in turn grant that same privilege—with or without the grant option—to some further user, and so on.

Granting privileges is done by means of the GRANT statement, which is discussed in detail below. Thus, the owner of an object can use the GRANT statement to grant privileges on that object to other users; furthermore, such a GRANT statement can optionally include the specification WITH GRANT OPTION, and if it does, then the recipient can grant the same privilege to a third party, etc., etc. However, we defer detailed discussion of the grant option to Section 15.5, and concentrate in the present section on the use of GRANT (and REVOKE) without that option.

Note: GRANT (like CREATE DOMAIN, CREATE TABLE, etc.) can be executed as an independent operation in its own right, or it can be executed as a "schema element" within a CREATE SCHEMA statement (see Chapter 4). REVOKE must be executed as an independent operation.

We remark that GRANT and REVOKE can logically be thought of as "CREATE AUTHORIZATION" and "DROP AUTHORIZATION," respectively—except that (a) there is no such thing as an "authorization" within the standard (there are "privilege descriptors" instead), and (b) those "authorizations" (or privilege descriptors) have no names (unlike objects that are created and destroyed by means of CREATE and DROP statements).

GRANT

The general format of GRANT is

```
GRANT privileges ON object TO users [ WITH GRANT OPTION ]
```

where:

- "Privileges" is a commalist of privileges or the phrase ALL PRIVILEGES. *Note:* ALL PRIVILEGES does not literally mean all privileges—it means all privileges on "object" for which the current authID (i.e., the user issuing the GRANT) has grant authority. Also, the privilege "INSERT(x,y)" (where x and y are commalists of column names) is defined to be shorthand for the commalist of privileges "INSERT(x), INSERT(y)" (and similarly for UPDATE and REFERENCES).

- "Object" is one of the following:

```
DOMAIN domain
[ TABLE ] table
CHARACTER SET character-set
COLLATION collation
TRANSLATION translation
```

  Note that the key word "TABLE" is optional in the TABLE case, and furthermore that in this context (unlike most others in SQL), "table" means *any* named table—i.e., it includes views as well as base tables. If "object" specifies anything other than a table, "privileges" must specify USAGE (only). If "object" specifies a table, "privileges" can specify any collection of table privileges; any columns mentioned explicitly (e.g., column x in "INSERT(x)") must be contained within the specified table.

- "Users" is either a commalist of authIDs or the special key word PUBLIC (meaning all authIDs known to the system at any given time).

- WITH GRANT OPTION is discussed in Section 15.5.

The specified privileges on the specified object are granted to each of the specified authIDs. The user issuing the GRANT—i.e., the current authID—must hold all of the specified privileges and must have grant authority for each of them; no user can grant a privilege not held by that user with the grant option.*

---

*This statement is undeniably true. According to the standard, however, it is not actually an error if some of the privileges a user tries to grant are not held by that user with the grant option (or indeed are not held by that user at all); all that happens is that the privileges in question are not granted, and a "completion condition" (see Chapter 22) is raised. An analogous remark applies to REVOKE also.

Note: More precisely, we should say, not that privileges are granted, but rather that privilege *descriptors* are *created*. Each such descriptor indicates that a certain *grantor* authID has granted a certain *grantee* authID the authority to perform a certain *action* on a certain *object*. It is particularly important to keep the distinction between a privilege and a privilege descriptor clear when considering what happens if, e.g., users *A* and *B* both grant the same privilege *P* to another user *C,* and *A* then revokes *P* from *C* (the two GRANTs create two descriptors, and the REVOKE drops one of them; thus *C* still possesses privilege *P*). Most of the time in this chapter, however, it is not necessary for us to be quite so precise.

For some examples of GRANT, refer to Chapter 2 (Section 2.6).

We conclude this discussion of GRANT by repeating the point from Section 15.3 that if user *U* holds the SELECT, INSERT, UPDATE, or REFERENCES privilege (in the last three cases non-column-specific) on base table *T,* and a new column *C* is added to *T,* user *U*'s privileges are automatically extended to include the relevant privilege on the new column *C*.

REVOKE

The general format of REVOKE is

```
REVOKE [ GRANT OPTION FOR ] privileges ON object FROM users
                              { RESTRICT | CASCADE }
```

where "privileges," "object," and "users" are as for GRANT, and the GRANT OPTION FOR and RESTRICT/CASCADE options are discussed in Section 15.5.

The specified privileges on the specified object are revoked from each of the specified authIDs (more precisely, the corresponding privilege descriptors are dropped—refer back to the discussion of GRANT above for an explanation of privilege descriptors). *Note:* The user issuing the REVOKE—i.e., the current authID—must have been the user who granted the privileges in the first place.

Dropping a domain, base table, column, or view* automatically revokes all privileges on the dropped object from all users.

15.5 THE GRANT OPTION

If user *U1* has the authority to grant a privilege *P* to another user *U2,* then user *U1* also has the authority to grant that privilege *P* to user *U2* "with the grant option" (by specifying WITH GRANT OPTION in the GRANT

---

*Or character set, collation, or translation.

statement). Passing the grant option along from *U1* to *U2* in this manner means that *U2* in turn now has grant authority on *P,* and so can grant *P* to some third user *U3*. And therefore, of course, *U2* also has the authority to pass the grant option for *P* along to *U3* as well, etc., etc. For example:

User *U1*:

```
GRANT SELECT ON TABLE S TO U2 WITH GRANT OPTION
```

User *U2*:

```
GRANT SELECT ON TABLE S TO U3 WITH GRANT OPTION
```

User *U3*:

```
GRANT SELECT ON TABLE S TO U4 WITH GRANT OPTION
```

And so on.

What happens if user *U1* now tries to revoke "SELECT ON TABLE S" from user *U2*? Suppose for the moment that the REVOKE succeeds, so that *U2* no longer holds that privilege. The privileges held by users *U3* and *U4* are now said to be "abandoned"—they were derived from the privilege held by *U2,* and that privilege no longer exists.

The possibility of "abandoned privileges" is the principal reason for the RESTRICT/CASCADE option on REVOKE. If CASCADE is specified, the REVOKE succeeds, and cascades down to revoke any privileges that would otherwise be abandoned. If RESTRICT is specified, the REVOKE succeeds only if revoking the privileges identified explicitly in the REVOKE operation *and no others* will not leave any abandoned privileges. In the example, therefore, the REVOKE will fail if RESTRICT is specified, but will succeed (and will revoke *U3*'s privilege and *U4*'s privileges as well) if CASCADE is specified. By contrast, user *U3* could successfully revoke "SELECT ON S" from user *U4* with a mere RESTRICT specification— assuming, of course, that *U4* has not gone on to grant the privilege to some further user *U5,* etc.

It is not only privileges that might become "abandoned," incidentally. For example, a view might become abandoned if its owner loses the SELECT privilege on some table that is used in the definition of that view. Again, REVOKE . . . RESTRICT will fail if it leads to any abandoned objects; REVOKE . . . CASCADE will succeed, and will cause those abandoned objects to be dropped. The reader is referred to the standard document for further details.

Finally, the optional phrase GRANT OPTION FOR in the REVOKE statement means that the issuing user is not trying to revoke the specified privileges per se, but only grant authority for those privileges. In this case, of course, the user issuing the REVOKE—i.e., the current authID—must have executed the original GRANT with the grant option in the first place.

PART **V**

ADVANCED TOPICS

This, the final part of the book, discusses a number of more esoteric aspects of the standard. By and large, it is not necessary to understand all of this material in detail in order to get a broad appreciation of what the standard is all about (with the possible exception of the topic of Chapter 16, Missing Information and Nulls). Needless to say, however, a proper understanding of these topics *is* essential to a full appreciation of the scope of the SQL language.

16

Missing Information
and Nulls

CAVEAT: It is only fair to the reader to explain right at the outset that the topic of this chapter CANNOT be described in a manner that is simultaneously comprehensive and comprehensible. The reason is that both the theoretical ideas on which the relevant SQL features are based and—even more so—those SQL features per se, are themselves not consistent, and indeed are fundamentally at odds in some ways with the way the world behaves. This is not the place to go into details; the interested reader can find extensive discussion of the problem in three books:

- *Relational Database: Selected Writings (1986)*

- *Relational Database Writings 1985–1989 (1990)*

- *Relational Database Writings 1989–1991 (1992)*

(all by the present author(s) and published by Addison-Wesley).

16.1 INTRODUCTION

With the foregoing caveat out of the way, let us get down to some specifics. First of all, SQL represents missing information by means of special markers called *nulls*. For example, we might say, loosely, that the weight of some part, say part P7, is null. What we mean by such a remark is, more precisely, that (a) we know that part P7 exists, and of course (b) it does have a weight, but (c) we do not know what that weight is. In other words, we do not know a genuine weight value that can sensibly be put in the WEIGHT position in the row in table P for that part. Instead, therefore, we *mark* that position as "null," and we interpret that mark to mean, precisely, that we do not know what the real value is.

Informally, we often think of such a position as "containing a null," or of the corresponding value as "being null," and such terms are certainly the ones most often heard in SQL contexts. But the previous paragraph should serve to show that such a manner of speaking *is* only informal, and indeed not very accurate. That is why the expression "null value," which is heard very frequently (and indeed is used throughout the standard), is to be deprecated: The whole point about nulls is precisely that they are not values.

Recall from Chapter 8 that columns in base tables usually have an associated default value, and that default value is often defined, explicitly or implicitly, to be null. Furthermore, columns in base tables always *permit* nulls, unless there is an integrity constraint—probably just NOT NULL— for the column in question that expressly bans them (see Chapter 14). The representation of nulls is implementation-dependent; however, it must be such that the system can distinguish nulls from all possible nonnull values.

Note: As just explained, nulls can appear as "values" in columns in tables; however, they do not have a data type, precisely because they are *not* genuine values. Also, they cannot appear as "values" of host variables or parameters (at least, not directly; see the subsection entitled "Indicator Parameters and Variables" in Section 16.2).

We now proceed to explore the detailed effects of the foregoing ideas on the SQL language. Section 16.2 discusses scalar values and scalar expressions; Section 16.3 describes *three-valued logic* and its implications for conditional expressions; Section 16.4 considers table expressions, and in particular introduces some new table operators called "outer joins"; and Section 16.5 examines the implications for integrity constraints. Finally, Section 16.6 offers some specific recommendations.

16.2   EFFECT OF NULLS ON SCALAR EXPRESSIONS

"Literals"

SQL provides a special construct, NULL, that might be thought of in some respects as a kind of literal representation of null. Note, however, that this construct certainly cannot appear in all contexts in which literals can appear; as the standard puts it, "there is no <literal> for a null value, although the key word NULL is used in some places to indicate that a null value is desired." To be specific, the "literal" NULL can appear in the following contexts *only*:*

1. As a default specification within a column or domain definition—i.e., DEFAULT NULL

2. As an "atom" within a row constructor specifying a "value" to be placed in a column position on INSERT

3. As an "atom" within a SET clause specifying a "value" to be placed in a column position on UPDATE

4. As a CAST source operand—i.e., CAST (NULL AS . . .)

5. As a CASE result—i.e., CASE . . . THEN NULL . . . END, or CASE . . . ELSE NULL END

6. As part of a referential specification—i.e., SET NULL

Number 1 in this list was discussed in Chapter 8, numbers 2 and 3 were discussed in Chapter 9, and number 6 is discussed in Section 16.5 later. The other two are discussed under "Scalar Operators and Functions" below. First, however, there are a couple of specific consequences of the foregoing that are worth pointing out explicitly:

- It is not possible to specify NULL explicitly as a select-item—e.g., "SELECT . . . , NULL, . . ." is illegal.

- It is not possible to specify NULL explicitly as an operand of a scalar expression—e.g., "X + NULL" is illegal.

- It is not possible to specify NULL explicitly as an operand of a conditional expression—e.g., "WHERE X = NULL" is illegal.

Scalar Operators and Functions

Let A and B be scalar values of some numeric data type. First, if A is null, then each of the expressions $+A$ and $-A$ is defined to evaluate to null. Second, if A is null or B is null or both, then each of the expressions

```
A + B     A - B     A * B     A / B
```

---

*SQL also provides an "IS NULL" construct (and its converse, "IS NOT NULL") for use in conditional expressions. Note, however, that these constructs should *not* be regarded as containing the "literal" NULL; instead, they should be seen as distinct constructs in their own right, representing certain truth-valued functions. Indeed, the expressions "x IS NULL" and "x IS NOT NULL" might better have been written ISNULL(x) and NOT (ISNULL(x)), respectively. See Section 16.3.

is also defined to evaluate to null. These definitions are all justified by the intended interpretation of null as "value unknown"; after all, if A is unknown, then obviously (e.g.) $A + 1$ is unknown too.*

Analogous considerations apply to all other data types and all other scalar operations (including scalar functions); that is, if any operand evaluates to null, then the result of the operation or function is defined to evaluate to null also. In particular, the operation CAST (x AS . . .) evaluates to null if x evaluates to null.† The only operation that needs any further attention is the CASE operation, which we now discuss.

First, as indicated above, any THEN clause and/or the ELSE clause within a CASE operation can specify explicitly that the result of that CASE operation (if that clause in fact provides the result) is NULL. In fact, if the ELSE clause is omitted, an ELSE clause of "ELSE NULL" is assumed by default.

Second, two shorthand forms of CASE are provided specifically to deal with certain null-related issues, as follows:

- The expression NULLIF(x,y) is defined to be equivalent to the expression

```
CASE WHEN x = y THEN NULL ELSE x END
```

  In other words, NULLIF(x,y) returns null if its operands are equal, and returns its first operand otherwise.

- The expression COALESCE(x,y) is defined to be equivalent to the expression

```
CASE WHEN x IS NOT NULL THEN x ELSE y END
```

  More generally, COALESCE(x,y, . . . , z) returns null if and only if its operands all evaluate to null; otherwise it returns the value of its first nonnull operand. See Section 16.3 for a discussion of "IS NOT NULL."

Aggregate Functions

To repeat a couple of points already made in Chapter 7: First, the aggregate functions (SUM, AVG, etc.) do *not* behave in accordance with the rules for

---

*Perhaps "justified" should be in quotes here. Note, for example, that according to that "justification" the expression $A - A$, which should clearly yield zero, actually yields null.

†We remark that the expression (e.g.) CAST (NULL AS INTEGER) provides a way of producing a kind of "null literal" of a specific data type. Thus, e.g., the expression "X + NULL" is illegal, as already explained, but the more complex expression "X + CAST (NULL AS INTEGER)" is legal.

scalar operators ("plus," etc.) explained above, but instead simply ignore any nulls in their argument (except for COUNT(*)). Thus, for example, the SUM function cannot be explained as simply an iterated addition. Second, if the argument to such a function happens to evaluate to an empty set, the functions all return null (except for COUNT, which returns zero).

Scalar Expressions

In general, the result of evaluating a scalar expression in which any of the operands evaluates to null can be deduced from the rules described above (in most cases, of course, the result is null in turn). However, there is one aberrant case: If the scalar expression is in fact a table expression enclosed in parentheses, then normally that table expression is required to evaluate to a table containing exactly one column and exactly one row; the value of the scalar expression is then taken to be, precisely, the single scalar value contained within that table. But if the table expression evaluates to a table that contains no rows at all, the value of the scalar expression is—quite incorrectly!—defined to be null.*

Indicator Parameters and Variables

Consider the following example of a procedure in the module language:

```
PROCEDURE GET_WEIGHT
             (¯SQLSTATE,
               :PNO_PARAM     CHAR(6),
               :WEIGHT_PARAM DECIMAL(3) ) ;
    SELECT P.WEIGHT
    INTO   :WEIGHT_PARAM
    FROM   P
    WHERE  P.PNO = :PNO_PARAM ;
```

Suppose there is a possibility that the value of WEIGHT might be null for some part. The SELECT statement shown above will fail if the WEIGHT selected is null: SQLSTATE will be set to 22002, and the target parameter :WEIGHT_PARAM will be left in an implementation-dependent state. In general, if it is possible that a value to be retrieved might be null,

---

*In an exactly analogous fashion, a row constructor is also allowed to consist of a table expression enclosed in parentheses, and that table expression is normally required to evaluate to a table containing exactly one row—in which case the value of the row constructor is taken to be, precisely, that single row. But if instead it evaluates to a table that contains no rows at all, the value of is taken, quite incorrectly, to be a row of all nulls.

the user should specify an *indicator parameter* in addition to the normal target parameter for that value, as we now illustrate:

```
PROCEDURE GET_WEIGHT
              ( SQLSTATE,
                :PNO_PARAM    CHAR(6),
                :WEIGHT_PARAM DECIMAL(3),
                :WEIGHT_INDIC DECIMAL(5) ) ;
    SELECT P.WEIGHT
    INTO   :WEIGHT_PARAM INDICATOR :WEIGHT_INDIC
    FROM   P
    WHERE  P.PNO = :PNO_PARAM ;
```

If the value to be retrieved is null and an indicator parameter has been specified, then that indicator parameter will be set to -1 (minus one); if the value to be retrieved is nonnull, the indicator parameter will be set to zero.* Indicator parameters are specified as shown—i.e., following the corresponding ordinary target parameter, and optionally separated from that ordinary parameter by the key word INDICATOR. They must be of data type "exact numeric" with a scale of zero (the precise data type is implementation-defined).

The foregoing example shows the use of an indicator parameter in conjunction with a target parameter in a single-row SELECT. FETCH is treated analogously, of course. Also, indicator parameters can be used with ordinary parameters (i.e., parameters that are merely used to supply values), as well as with target parameters. For example, the UPDATE statement

```
UPDATE P
SET    WEIGHT = :WEIGHT_PARAM INDICATOR :WEIGHT_INDIC
WHERE  P.CITY = 'London'
```

will set the weight for all London parts to null if the value of WEIGHT_INDIC is negative (any negative value, not necessarily just -1). So also of course will the statement

```
UPDATE P
SET    WEIGHT = NULL
WHERE  P.CITY = 'London'
```

Note: Indicator parameters can also be used in conditional expressions—in particular, in WHERE clauses—but probably should not be. For example, even if the value of :WEIGHT_INDIC is negative, the following statement will *not* retrieve part numbers for parts where the weight is null.

---

*A slight oversimplification. If the value to be retrieved is nonnull and is a character or bit string of length $n1$ (characters or bits, respectively), and if the data type of the target parameter is respectively CHARACTER($n2$) or BIT($n2$), and if $n1 > n2$, then the result is truncated by dropping the rightmost $n1 - n2$ characters or bits, and the indicator parameter is set to $n1$.

Exercise for the reader: What will it do? (You will need at least a basic understanding of the ideas of Section 16.3 in order to answer this question.)

```
SELECT  P.PNO
INTO    :PNO_PARAM
FROM    P
WHERE   P.WEIGHT = :WEIGHT_PARAM INDICATOR :WEIGHT_INDIC
```

The correct way to retrieve part numbers where the weight is null is:

```
SELECT  P.PNO
INTO    :PNO_PARAM
FROM    P
WHERE   P.WEIGHT IS NULL
```

(Again, see Section 16.3.)

We conclude this subsection (and section) by observing that in embedded SQL, indicator *variables* can (and must) be used in a manner precisely analogous to the way indicator *parameters* are used in the module language. For example (PL/I):

```
EXEC SQL SELECT P.WEIGHT
         INTO    :WEIGHT INDICATOR :WEIGHT_INDIC
         FROM    P
         WHERE   P.PNO = :PNO ;
IF WEIGHT_INDIC < 0 THEN ... /* no WEIGHT retrieved */ ;
```

16.3 EFFECT OF NULLS ON CONDITIONAL EXPRESSIONS

Conditional expressions are also affected—dramatically so—by nulls. First let us consider the basic comparison operations introduced in Section 7.5. Let A and B be two scalar values that are compatible for comparison purposes. Then, if A is null or B is null or both, then each of the comparison conditions

```
A = B      A <> B
A < B      A <= B
A > B      A >= B
```

evaluates, not to *true,* nor to *false,* but rather to the *unknown* truth value. The justification for this rule (again) is the intended interpretation of null as "value unknown": If the value of A is unknown, then clearly it is *unknown* whether, e.g., $A = 3$ (despite the fact that, as indicated in Section 16.1, the standard says that null is "distinct from all nonnull values," which might reasonably be taken to imply that "$A = 3$" should yield *false* if A is null).

Note very carefully that, as a particular case of the foregoing, two nulls are not considered to be equal to one another—that is, the comparison condition "null = null" (not intended to be valid SQL syntax) evaluates to *unknown,* not *true* (and not *false*). In particular, note that "$A = A$" evaluates to *unknown,* not *true,* if *A* is null. Likewise, "*A* > *A*" and "*A* < *A*" both evaluate to *unknown,* not *false,* if *A* is null.

The concept of nulls thus leads us into a *three-valued logic* (so called because there are three truth values, namely *true, false,* and *unknown*). The three-valued logic truth tables for AND, OR, and NOT are shown below (t = *true,* f = *false,* u = *unknown*):

AND	t u f		OR	t u f		NOT	
t	t u f		t	t t t		t	f
u	u u f		u	t u u		u	u
f	f f f		f	t u f		f	t

Suppose, for example, that $A = 3$, $B = 4$, and C is null. Then the following logical (i.e., conditional) expressions have the indicated truth values:

```
A > B AND B > C  :  false
A > B OR  B > C  :  unknown
A < B OR  B < C  :  true
NOT ( A = C )    :  unknown
```

In Chapter 11, we stated that when SQL applies a WHERE clause to some table *T,* it eliminates all rows of *T* for which the conditional expression in that WHERE clause does not evaluate to *true.* Now, this is still correct as a statement of fact under three-valued logic, but it needs to be clearly understood that "not evaluating to *true*" means "evaluating either to *false* or to *unknown.*" (Analogous remarks apply to the ON and HAVING clauses, of course.) We will elaborate on this point and related matters in Section 16.4.

We now proceed to investigate the implications of the foregoing ideas for conditional expressions in general.

Comparison Conditions

To repeat from Chapter 12, the syntax of a comparison condition ("comparison" for short) is:

```
row-constructor comparison-operator row-constructor
```

In Section 12.3, we defined what it meant for this expression to evaluate to *true,* and we assumed, tacitly, that the expression evaluated to *false* if and only if it did not evaluate to *true.* Now, however, we have to consider what happens if any component of either of the two row constructors happens to be (or to evaluate to) null.

First we repeat the definition of the *true* cases (refer back to Section 12.3 for an explanation of the notation):

- "*Left = Right*" is *true* if and only if for all *i*, "*Li = Ri*" is *true*
- "*Left <> Right*" is *true* if and only if there exists some *j* such that "*Lj <> Rj*" is *true*
- "*Left < Right*" is *true* if and only if there exists some *j* such that "*Lj < Rj*" is *true* and for all *i < j*, "*Li = Ri*" is *true*
- "*Left > Right*" is *true* if and only if there exists some *j* such that "*Lj > Rj*" is *true* and for all *i < j*, "*Li = Ri*" is *true*
- "*Left <= Right*" is *true* if and only if "*Left <* Right" is *true* or "*Left = Right*" is *true*
- "*Left >= Right*" is *true* if and only if "*Left > Right*" is *true* or "*Left = Right*" is *true*

Now we have to add the following:

- "*Left = Right*" is *false* if and only if "*Left <> Right*" is *true*
- "*Left <> Right*" is *false* if and only if "*Left = Right*" is *true*
- "*Left < Right*" is *false* if and only if "*Left >= Right*" is *true*
- "*Left > Right*" is *false* if and only if "*Left <= Right*" is *true*
- "*Left <= Right*" is *false* if and only if "*Left > Right*" is *true*
- "*Left >= Right*" is *false* if and only if "*Left < Right*" is *true*

Finally, let "$" stand for any of =, <>, <, <=, >, >=. Then:

- "*Left $ Right*" is *unknown* if and only if it is not *true* and not *false*

Here are some examples:

```
( 1, 2, NULL ) = ( 3, NULL, 4 )  :  false
( 1, 2, NULL ) < ( 3, NULL, 4 )  :  true
( 1, 2, NULL ) = ( 1, NULL, 4 )  :  unknown
( 1, 2, NULL ) > ( NULL, 2, 4 )  :  unknown
```

Tests for Null

As mentioned briefly in Section 16.2 above, SQL provides two special comparison operators, IS NULL and IS NOT NULL, to test for the presence or absence of nulls. The syntax is:

```
row-constructor IS [ NOT ] NULL
```

(an additional case of "simple condition"—see Chapter 12). First, the conditional expression "*x* IS NULL," where *x* is a scalar expression (a special case of a row constructor, of course), evaluates to *true* if *x* evaluates to null and to *false* otherwise, and the conditional expression "*x* IS NOT NULL" is defined to be equivalent to the conditional expression "NOT (*x* IS NULL)." For example, suppose again that $A = 3$, $B = 4$, and C is null. Then the following conditional expressions have the indicated truth values:

```
C IS NULL        :   true
A IS NULL        :   false
B IS NOT NULL    :   true
```

(Note that IS NULL and IS NOT NULL never return *unknown*.)

The more general case, in which *x* is not a scalar expression but a general row constructor, with scalar components *r1, r2, . . . , rn* say, is defined as follows:

▪ The expression

```
( r1, r2, ..., rn ) IS NULL
```

is defined to be equivalent to the expression

```
( r1 IS NULL ) AND ( r2 IS NULL ) AND ... AND ( rn IS NULL )
```

▪ The expression

```
( r1, r2, ..., rn ) IS NOT NULL
```

is defined to be equivalent to the expression

```
( r1 IS NOT NULL ) AND ( r2 IS NOT NULL ) AND ...
                   AND ( rn IS NOT NULL )
```

▪ The expression

```
NOT ( r1, r2, ..., rn ) IS NULL
```

is defined to be equivalent to the expression

```
NOT ( ( r1, r2, ..., rn ) IS NULL )
```

▪ The expression

```
NOT ( r1, r2, ..., rn ) IS NOT NULL
```

is defined to be equivalent to the expression

```
NOT ( ( r1, r2, ..., rn ) IS NOT NULL )
```

Observe, therefore, that the expressions

```
x IS NOT NULL
```

and

```
NOT x IS NULL
```

are not equivalent, in general! For example, if *x* has two components, *r1* and *r2,* then the first is equivalent to

```
r1 IS NOT NULL AND r2 IS NOT NULL
```

The second is equivalent to

```
r1 IS NOT NULL OR r2 IS NOT NULL
```

Tests for True, False, Unknown

As we saw in Chapter 12, any "conditional primary" *p* (*p* is either a "simple condition," q.v., or a conditional expression enclosed in parentheses) can optionally be followed by one of the following:

```
IS TRUE
IS NOT TRUE
IS FALSE
IS NOT FALSE
```

Now we have two more tests to add to this list:

```
IS UNKNOWN
IS NOT UNKNOWN
```

We explain the various possibilities by extending the truth table from Section 12.2. Note that (like IS NULL and IS NOT NULL) these tests never return *unknown*.

p	true	false	unknown
p IS TRUE	true	false	false
p IS NOT TRUE	false	true	true
p IS FALSE	false	true	false
p IS NOT FALSE	true	false	true
p IS UNKNOWN	false	false	true
p IS NOT UNKNOWN	true	true	false

Observe, therefore, that the expressions

```
p IS NOT TRUE
```

and

```
NOT p
```

are not equivalent, in general! For example, if *p* is *unknown,* the first expression evaluates to *true,* but the second evaluates to *unknown.**

---

*In other words, the NOT in NOT TRUE is not the "NOT" of three-valued logic. Then again, the NOT of three-valued logic is not the "not" of ordinary English . . .

BETWEEN Conditions

The between-condition

```
y BETWEEN x AND z
```

is still defined (as in Chapter 12) to be semantically equivalent to

```
x <= y AND y <= z
```

but, of course, either of the two component expressions can now evaluate to *unknown,* giving an overall result of either *unknown* or *false* (depending on the value of the other component expression). NOT BETWEEN is revised correspondingly.

LIKE Conditions

The like-condition

```
character-string-expression [ NOT ] LIKE pattern [ ESCAPE escape ]
```

evaluates to *unknown* if any of its operands "character string expression," "pattern," or "escape" evaluates to null (otherwise it evaluates to *true* or *false* as explained in Chapter 12). NOT LIKE is revised accordingly.

IN Conditions

A "Format 1" in-condition is equivalent to an all-or-any condition involving the comparison operator $=$ANY (or $<>$ALL, in the negated case); see the subsection on all-or-any conditions immediately following. The "Format 2" in-condition

```
x IN ( a, b, ..., z )
```

is still defined (as in Chapter 12) to be semantically equivalent to

```
x = a OR x = b OR ... OR x = z
```

but, of course, any of the component expressions can now evaluate to *unknown,* thus possibly giving an overall result of *unknown.* NOT IN is revised correspondingly.

All-or-Any Conditions

Let "$" stand for any of $=$, $<>$, $<$, $<=$, $>$, $>=$. Then the all-or-any condition

```
x  $ALL  ( table-expression )
```

evaluates to *true* if the expression

```
x  $  y
```

evaluates to *true* for every *y* in the result of evaluating the table expression (or if that result is empty); it evaluates to *false* if the expression

```
x  $  y
```

evaluates to *false* for at least one *y* in the result of evaluating that table expression; and it evaluates to *unknown* otherwise. Likewise, the all-or-any condition

```
x  $ANY  ( table-expression )
```

evaluates to *true* if the expression

```
x  $  y
```

evaluates to *true* for at least one *y* in the result of evaluating the table expression; it evaluates to *false* if the expression

```
x  $  y
```

evaluates to *false* for every *y* in the result of evaluating that table expression (or if that result is empty); and it evaluates to *unknown* otherwise.

MATCH Conditions

The syntax of match-conditions includes a "PARTIAL or FULL" option, not shown and not discussed in Chapter 12, that can affect the result if nulls are present:

```
row-constructor MATCH [ UNIQUE ]
                      [ PARTIAL | FULL ] ( table-expression )
```

There are six cases to consider, depending on (a) whether the UNIQUE option is missing or specified and (b) whether the "PARTIAL or FULL" option is missing or specified (and if specified, which it is). We refer to the six cases as indicated by the following table:*

	missing	PARTIAL	FULL
missing	Case 1	Case 2	Case 3
UNIQUE	Case 4	Case 5	Case 6

---

*It is difficult to resist the temptation to point out that this table includes certain row-and-column positions for which information is missing for some reason, and yet we do *not* show "nulls" in those positions. There is probably a moral here.

In all cases, let *r1* be the row that results from evaluating the row constructor and let *T* be the table that results from evaluating the table expression.*

- *Case 1* (no UNIQUE, no PARTIAL or FULL):

  The result is *true* if either (a) any component of *r1* is null, or (b) *T* contains at least one row, *r2* say, such that the comparison condition "*r1 = r2*" evaluates to *true*; otherwise the result is *false*.

- *Case 2* (no UNIQUE, PARTIAL specified):

  The result is *true* if either (a) every component of *r1* is null, or (b) *T* contains at least one row, *r2* say, such that each nonnull component within *r1* is equal to its counterpart in *r2*; otherwise the result is *false*.

- *Case 3* (no UNIQUE, FULL specified):

  The result is *true* if either (a) every component of *r1* is null, or (b) every component of *r1* is nonnull and *T* contains at least one row, *r2* say, such that the comparison condition "*r1 = r2*" evaluates to *true*; otherwise the result is *false*.

- *Case 4* (UNIQUE, no PARTIAL or FULL):

  The result is *true* if either (a) any component of *r1* is null, or (b) *T* contains exactly one row, *r2* say, such that the comparison condition "*r1 = r2*" evaluates to *true*; otherwise the result is *false*.

- *Case 5* (UNIQUE, PARTIAL specified):

  The result is *true* if either (a) every component of *r1* is null, or (b) *T* contains exactly one row, *r2* say, such that each nonnull component within *r1* is equal to its counterpart in *r2*; otherwise the result is *false*.

- *Case 6* (UNIQUE, FULL specified):

  The result is *true* if either (a) every component of *r1* is null, or (b) every component of *r1* is nonnull and *T* contains exactly one row, *r2* say, such that the comparison condition "*r1 = r2*" evaluates to *true*; otherwise the result is *false*.

Note: The standard makes use of the foregoing in its definition of foreign key constraints and referential actions. See Section 16.5.

---

*It is worth pointing out explicitly that PARTIAL and FULL have no effect—and can thus safely be ignored—if either (a) *r1* and *T* are noncomposite (i.e., contain just one scalar value and one column, respectively), or (b) every component of *r1* has "nulls not allowed."

EXISTS Conditions

The definition of EXISTS is not affected by nulls; to repeat from Chapter 12, the expression "EXISTS (table-expression)" is defined to return the value *false* if the table expression evaluates to an empty table, the value *true* otherwise. However, as mentioned in Chapter 14, there are certainly some traps for the unwary in this area. Consider the following example: "Get part names for parts whose weight is greater than that of every blue part." First we show a solution (repeated from Chapter 12) that uses ">ALL":

```
SELECT DISTINCT PX.PNAME
FROM    P AS PX
WHERE   PX.WEIGHT >ALL ( SELECT DISTINCT PY.WEIGHT
                         FROM    P AS PY
                         WHERE   PY.COLOR = 'Blue' )
```

And here is another putative—but actually *** *INCORRECT* ***— solution using EXISTS (or rather, NOT EXISTS):

```
SELECT DISTINCT PX.PNAME
FROM    P AS PX
WHERE   NOT EXISTS
        ( SELECT *
          FROM    P AS PY
          WHERE   PY.COLOR = 'Blue'
          AND     PY.WEIGHT > PX.WEIGHT )
```

("Get part names for parts such that there does not exist a blue part with a greater weight"). On the face of it, this alternative formulation looks as if it should be logically equivalent to the previous one (involving >ALL), and indeed so it is, *unless* both of the following are true:

- There is at least one blue part with a null weight
- There is no blue part with a nonnull weight

What happens if these two conditions both apply? With the ">ALL" formulation, the nested expression evaluates to a single-column table containing nothing but nulls; the ">ALL" condition therefore evaluates to *unknown* for every row in table P (i.e., every possible value of the range variable PX), and so nothing is retrieved. Thus, the final result is an empty set of part names (remember that the WHERE clause eliminates rows for which the condition in that clause evaluates to *false* or to *unknown*).

With the NOT EXISTS formulation, however, the EXISTS argument evaluates to an empty set for every row in table P; the EXISTS condition therefore evaluates to *false* for every part; negating that condition therefore evaluates to *true* for every part; and so the final result includes all of the part names, instead of none of them.

The real problem is that the user intuitively, and quite justifiably, expects EXISTS in SQL to behave like the "existential quantifier" of (three-valued) logic, but it does not. In the case at hand, we would like the EXISTS to return *unknown* for every row in table P (it *is* unknown, after all, whether there exists a blue part with a greater weight, because the weight of every blue part is null). But, as we have seen, the EXISTS actually returns *false*.

Perhaps we should point out that the two formulations of the query *are* equivalent in the absence of nulls.

UNIQUE Conditions

The expression "UNIQUE (table-expression)" is defined to return *false* if the result of evaluating the table expression contains two distinct rows, *r1* and *r2* say, such that the comparison condition "*r1* = *r2*" evaluates to *true*; otherwise it returns *true*. Note carefully, however, that "*r1* = *r2*" does not evaluate to *true* if either *r1* or *r2* includes any null components; e.g., if column *C* of the 5-row table *T* contains the values 1, 2, 3, NULL, and NULL, the expression UNIQUE (SELECT *C* FROM *T*) will return *true*. Thus we see that, just as EXISTS sometimes returns *false* when *unknown* would be more logically correct, so UNIQUE sometimes returns *true* when *unknown* would be more logically correct.

Note: The standard makes use of UNIQUE in its definition of candidate key constraints. See Section 16.5.

16.4   EFFECT OF NULLS ON TABLE EXPRESSIONS

Conditional Expressions Within Select Expressions

We have already mentioned that when SQL applies a WHERE clause to some table *T,* it eliminates all rows of *T* for which the conditional expression in that WHERE clause evaluates to *false* or to *unknown*. Likewise, when SQL applies a HAVING clause to some grouped table *G,* it eliminates all groups of *G* for which the conditional expression in that HAVING clause evaluates to *false* or to *unknown*.

The foregoing remarks apply equally to WHERE and HAVING clauses within "searched UPDATE" and "searched DELETE" statements, of course; in fact, the "table . . . WHERE conditional expression" component of such statements is effectively just a slight variation on the normal syntax for a certain special case of a select-expression.

Duplicate Elimination

The operations DISTINCT, GROUP BY, UNION, EXCEPT, and INTERSECT (without the ALL option, in the last three cases) are all defined to eliminate redundant duplicate rows.* However, the definition of "duplicate rows" requires some refinement in the presence of nulls. Let *Left* and *Right* be as defined for the subsection on "Comparison Conditions" in Section 16.3 above. Then *Left* and *Right* are defined to be *duplicates* of one another if and only if, for all i in the range 1 to n, either "$Li = Ri$" is *true,* or Li and Ri are both null.

Note, therefore, that "*Left* and *Right* are duplicates of one another" does not imply that "*Left = Right* is *true*"! Note too that if "UNIQUE (SELECT * FROM T)" evaluates to *true,* it does not imply that "SELECT * FROM T" and "SELECT DISTINCT * FROM T" have the same cardinality!

Ordering

Although not technically part of a table expression per se, the ORDER BY clause is used (within a cursor definition) to impose an ordering on the result of such an expression. The question that arises is: What is the relative ordering for scalar values A and B if A is null or B is null (or both)? The answer defined by the SQL standard is as follows:

- For ordering purposes, all nulls are considered to be equal to one another.

Furthermore:

- For ordering purposes, all nulls are considered *either* to be greater than all nonnull values *or* less than all nonnull values. Which of the two possibilities applies is implementation-defined.

Outer Join

We discussed join expressions in some detail in Chapter 11. However, we deferred discussion of the various "outer" joins to the present chapter, on the grounds that they all had to do with nulls. We now explain these operations.

The basic idea behind outer join is as follows. Suppose we are trying to construct the ordinary ("inner") join of two tables *T1* and *T2*. Then any

---

*For GROUP BY it is perhaps not so much a matter of *eliminating* duplicates as it is of deciding what things are duplicates of one another.

row in either *T1* or *T2* that matches no row in the other table (under the
relevant join condition) simply does not participate in the result. In an outer
join, by contrast, such a row does participate in the result—to be more
precise, it appears exactly once in the result—and the column positions that
would have been filled with values from some matching row in the other
table (if such a matching row had in fact existed) are filled with nulls instead. Thus, the outer join "preserves" nonmatching rows in the result,
where the inner join "loses" them. *Note:* A left outer join of *T1* with *T2*
preserves nonmatching rows from *T1*; a right outer join of *T1* with *T2* preserves nonmatching rows from *T2*; a full outer join of *T1* with *T2* preserves
nonmatching rows from both *T1* and *T2*.

The syntax for an outer join expression is:

```
table-reference [ NATURAL ] outer-join-type JOIN table-reference
    [ ON conditional-expression | USING ( column-commalist ) ]
```

"Outer join type" here is one of the following:

```
LEFT [ OUTER ]
RIGHT [ OUTER ]
FULL [ OUTER ]
```

If NATURAL is specified, neither an ON clause nor a USING clause can be
specified; otherwise, one of the two *must* be specified. *Note:* The optional
OUTER is a mere noiseword and has no effect on the overall meaning of
the expression.

To fix our ideas, let us concentrate on LEFT outer joins. Then there
are three cases to consider:

```
1. table-reference LEFT JOIN table-reference
                   ON conditional-expression

2. table-reference LEFT JOIN table-reference
                   USING ( column-commalist )

3. table-reference NATURAL LEFT JOIN table-reference
```

In each case, let *A* and *B* be the tables resulting from evaluation of the
two table references. Then *Case 1* ("*A* LEFT JOIN *B* ON *C*," where *C* is
a conditional expression) can perhaps most easily be explained by defining
it to be equivalent to the following pseudoSQL expression:*

```
SELECT A.*, B.*
FROM   A, B
WHERE  C

UNION   ALL
```

---

*It is only "pseudoSQL" for at least two reasons: (a) "NULL" is not a valid select-item; (b)
"A.*" is not a valid row constructor.

```
SELECT A.*, NULL, NULL, ..., NULL
FROM   A
WHERE  A.* NOT IN ( SELECT A.*
                    FROM   A, B
                    WHERE  C    )
```

In other words, the result consists of the "UNION ALL" of (a) the corresponding *inner* join and (b) the collection of all rows of *A* that do not participate in that inner join, each one concatenated with a row of all nulls (one null for each column of *B*; the pseudoSQL expression "NULL, NULL, . . . , NULL" is supposed to be understood as containing one NULL for each column of *B*). The column names of the result are identical to those of the corresponding inner join.

We remark that, in general, the result will include some rows that do not satisfy the conditional expression *C*.

In *Case 2,* let the commalist of columns in the USING clause be *C1, C2, . . . , Cn*. Each of *C1, C2, . . . Cn* must be *un*qualified and must identify both a column of *A* and a column of *B*. Then the left outer join expression is defined to be semantically identical to a Case 1 left outer join expression in which the ON clause is of the form—

```
ON A.C1 = B.C1 AND A.C2 = B.C2 AND ... AND A.Cn = B.Cn
```

—except that (a) each of the common columns *C1, C2, . . . , Cn* appears only once, not twice, in the final result; (b) for each such result column, *Ci* say, the value contained in any given row is defined to be COALESCE(*A.Ci,B.Ci*);* and (c) the result column ordering is different— the common columns appear first (i.e., at the left), then the other columns of *A,* then the other columns of *B*.

Finally, a *Case 3* left outer join expression is defined to be semantically identical to a Case 2 left outer join expression in which the commalist of columns specifies *all* of the columns that are common to *A* and *B*. *Note:* It is possible that there are no common columns at all, in which case *A* NATURAL LEFT JOIN *B* degenerates to *A* CROSS JOIN *B*.

Here are some examples (all based as usual on the suppliers-and-parts database):

```
S LEFT JOIN SP ON S.SNO = SP.SNO

S LEFT JOIN SP USING ( SNO )

S LEFT NATURAL JOIN SP
```

These three expressions are all equivalent, except that the first produces a table with two SNO columns and the second and third produce a table

---

*See Section 16.2 for an explanation of COALESCE.

with just one such column. For example, the result of the first expression looks like this (assuming, as always, data values as given in Fig. 2.1):

SNO	SNAME	STATUS	CITY	SNO	PNO	QTY
S1	Smith	20	London	S1	P1	300
S1	Smith	20	London	S1	P2	200
S1	Smith	20	London	S1	P3	400
S1	Smith	20	London	S1	P4	200
S1	Smith	20	London	S1	P5	100
S1	Smith	20	London	S1	P6	100
S2	Jones	10	Paris	S2	P1	300
S2	Jones	10	Paris	S2	P2	400
S3	Blake	30	Paris	S3	P2	200
S4	Clark	20	London	S4	P2	200
S4	Clark	20	London	S4	P4	300
S4	Clark	20	London	S4	P5	400
S5	Adams	30	Athens	---	---	---

We have represented nulls by a line of dashes ("---") in this result.
Here by contrast is the result of the second (or third) expression:

SNO	SNAME	STATUS	CITY	PNO	QTY
S1	Smith	20	London	P1	300
S1	Smith	20	London	P2	200
S1	Smith	20	London	P3	400
S1	Smith	20	London	P4	200
S1	Smith	20	London	P5	100
S1	Smith	20	London	P6	100
S2	Jones	10	Paris	P1	300
S2	Jones	10	Paris	P2	400
S3	Blake	30	Paris	P2	200
S4	Clark	20	London	P2	200
S4	Clark	20	London	P4	300
S4	Clark	20	London	P5	400
S5	Adams	30	Athens	---	---

Definitions of the RIGHT and FULL outer joins are left as an exercise for the reader.

Union Join

"Union join," like outer join, is represented by an additional version of the explicit join expressions introduced in Chapter 11.* The syntax is:

---

*We deliberately make no attempt here to explain the operation in intuitive terms. It seems to be an attempt (but an inaccurate attempt) to define what is more usually known as "outer union." Even if it were defined correctly, however, it is this writer's opinion that it would still not be worth trying to explain it intuitively, for reasons beyond the scope of this text. The interested reader is referred to Warden's paper "Into the Unknown" (included in C. J. Date, *Relational Database Writings 1985–1989,* Addison-Wesley, 1990), for a detailed—and critical—discussion of outer union.

```
table-reference UNION JOIN table-reference
```

Let A and B be the tables resulting from evaluation of the two table references. Then the union join expression can most easily be explained by defining it to be equivalent to the following pseudoSQL expression:

```
SELECT A.*, NULL, NULL, ..., NULL
FROM   A

UNION  ALL

SELECT NULL, NULL, ..., NULL, B.*
FROM   B
```

In other words, the result is constructed by (a) extending each operand table with all of the columns of the other operand; (b) filling those added columns with nulls; and finally (c) taking the "union all" of those two extended tables. The column names of the result are identical to those of the Cartesian product of A and B.

16.5 EFFECT OF NULLS ON INTEGRITY CONSTRAINTS

As explained in Chapter 14, an integrity constraint is basically a conditional expression that must not evaluate to *false*. Note, therefore, that the constraint is not considered to be violated if it evaluates to *unknown*. Technically, of course, we should say in such a case that it is *not known* whether the constraint is violated, but, just as SQL regards *unknown* as *false* for the purposes of a WHERE clause, so it regards *unknown* as *true* for the purposes of an integrity constraint (speaking a trifle loosely).

The foregoing remarks are directly applicable to domain constraints, general constraints ("assertions"), and check constraints, and effectively dispose of the issue for these three cases.* Candidate key definitions and foreign key definitions require additional consideration, however.

Candidate Keys

A candidate key definition takes the form[†]

---

*Perhaps we should point out, however, that since (a) as explained in Chapter 14, constraints typically begin (explicitly or implicitly) with "NOT EXISTS," and (b) as explained in Section 16.3, NOT EXISTS sometimes returns *true* when *unknown* would be more logically correct, therefore (c) updates will sometimes succeed when they really ought not to. For example, consider what the system will do, given the constraint "All red parts must be stored in London," with an attempt to INSERT a part row in which the COLOR is "Red" but the CITY is null. This row surely does violate the real-world constraint that the SQL constraint is attempting to enforce, but the INSERT will succeed.

[†]Ignoring the optional constraint name specification.

```
{ PRIMARY KEY | UNIQUE } ( column-commalist )
```

As explained in Chapter 14, the database will satisfy this candidate key constraint if and only if it satisfies the "check constraint"

```
CHECK ( UNIQUE ( SELECT column-commalist FROM T )
         [ AND column-commalist IS NOT NULL ] )
```

where T is the base table that contains the candidate key in question (and where the "AND column-commalist IS NOT NULL" portion of the constraint applies only for PRIMARY KEY, not for UNIQUE). In other words, SQL's definition of "uniqueness" for candidate keys is identical to its definition of "uniqueness" in the context of the UNIQUE condition. Note in particular, therefore, that if the candidate key consists of a single column—and is not in fact the *primary* key—then that column can contain *any number* of nulls (together with any number of nonnull values, all of which must be distinct).

More generally, let CK be some candidate key, possibly involving multiple columns, for some base table T, and let $ck2$ be a new value for CK that some user is attempting to introduce (via an INSERT or UPDATE operation) into table T. That INSERT or UPDATE will be rejected if $ck2$ is the same as some value for CK, $ck1$ say, that already exists within table T. What then does it mean for the two values $ck1$ and $ck2$ to be "the same"? It turns out that *no two* of the following three statements are equivalent:

1. $ck1$ and $ck2$ are the same for the purposes of a comparison condition
2. $ck1$ and $ck2$ are the same for the purposes of candidate key uniqueness
3. $ck1$ and $ck2$ are the same for the purposes of duplicate elimination

Number 1 is defined in accordance with the rules of three-valued logic, Number 2 is defined in accordance with the rules for the UNIQUE condition, and Number 3 is defined in accordance with the definition of duplicates in Section 16.3 above. Suppose, for example, that CK involves just one column. Then if $ck1$ and $ck2$ are both null, Number 1 gives *unknown,* Number 2 gives *false,* and Number 3 gives *true.* However, it is at least true that if Number 1 gives *true,* Numbers 2 and 3 must both necessarily give *true,* and if Number 2 gives *true,* then Number 3 must necessarily give *true.*

Note: While all of the foregoing is true (in SQL) for candidate keys in general, matters are considerably simpler for *primary* keys, because no component of a primary key value is allowed (in SQL) to be null. The three statements shown above *are* all equivalent (in SQL) for primary keys.

Foreign Keys

A foreign key definition takes the form*

```
FOREIGN KEY ( column-commalist )
   REFERENCES base-table [ ( column-commalist ) ]
[ MATCH { FULL | PARTIAL } ]
[ ON DELETE { NO ACTION | CASCADE | SET DEFAULT | SET NULL } ]
[ ON UPDATE { NO ACTION | CASCADE | SET DEFAULT | SET NULL } ]
```

We did not discuss the MATCH option in Chapter 14 because (once again) it had significance only in the presence of nulls; we now explain it, as follows.[†]

Let us agree for the moment to ignore the ON DELETE and ON UPDATE clauses. Then the database will satisfy the foreign key constraint shown above if and only if it satisfies the "check constraint"

```
CHECK ( fk MATCH [ PARTIAL | FULL ] ( SELECT ck FROM T ) )
```

where (a) *fk* is a row constructor corresponding to the column-commalist that represents the foreign key, (b) *ck* is a select-item-commalist corresponding to the column-commalist that represents the referenced candidate key, (c) *T* is the base table that contains that candidate key, and (d) PARTIAL is specified if and only if PARTIAL appears in the foreign key definition (and likewise for FULL). In other words, SQL's definition of "matching" for a foreign-key/candidate-key pair is identical to its definition of "matching" in the context of the MATCH condition.[‡] Specifically:

- If neither PARTIAL nor FULL is specified:

  The referential constraint is satisfied if and only if, for each row *r2* of the referencing table, either (a) at least one component of *r2.fk* is null, or (b) *T* contains exactly one row, *r1* say, such that the comparison condition "*r2.fk = r1.ck*" evaluates to *true*.

- If PARTIAL is specified:

  The referential constraint is satisfied if and only if, for each row *r2* of the referencing table, either (a) every component of *r2.fk* is null, or (b)

---

*Ignoring the optional constraint name specification.

[†]It is worth pointing out immediately that the MATCH option has no effect—and can thus be ignored—if either (a) the foreign key is noncomposite (i.e., consists of a single column), or (b) every component column of the foreign key has "nulls not allowed." Refer back to the explanation of the MATCH condition in Section 16.3.

[‡]Note that there is no need to state UNIQUE in the "equivalent" MATCH condition, because *ck* represents a candidate key and so is necessarily "unique."

T contains exactly one row, *r1* say, such that each nonnull component within *r2.fk* is equal to its counterpart in *r1.ck*.

- If FULL is specified:

The referential constraint is satisfied if and only if, for each row *r2* of the referencing table, either (a) every component of *r2.fk* is null, or (b) every component of *r2.fk* is nonnull and *T* contains exactly one row, *r1* say, such that the comparison condition "*r2.fk = r1.ck*" evaluates to *true*.

In all three cases, an INSERT on the referencing table, or an UPDATE on the foreign key in the referencing table, that would violate the referential constraint will fail.

Nulls also have implications for the "referential actions" specified in the ON DELETE and ON UPDATE clauses. In order to explain those implications, we must first define the concept of *referencing rows*.* Let *T2* and *T1* be a referencing table and the corresponding referenced table, and let *T2.FK* and *T1.CK* be the foreign key and corresponding candidate key, respectively. Then:

- For a given row *r1* of *T1*, the set of rows *r2* of *T2* for which "*r2.fk = r1.ck*" evaluates to *true*—or, if PARTIAL is specified, the set of rows *r2* of *T2* for which the nonnull components of *r2.fk* are equal to their counterparts in *r1.ck*—is said to be the set of *referencing rows* for *r1*.

- Furthermore, in the PARTIAL case, a referencing row for *r1* is said to reference *r1* *exclusively* if it is not a referencing row for any other row *r* of *T1*. (The point here is that *T1.CK* might involve multiple columns, at least one of which might permit nulls. Thus we might have, e.g., two distinct rows of *T1*, both including a *CK* value of (*x*,null), say. Any referencing row for either of these two distinct rows will necessarily be a referencing row for the other as well, and so will not reference either row *exclusively*.[†])

Now we can explain the effect of the ON DELETE clause. Recall that the possible specifications are NO ACTION, CASCADE, SET DEFAULT, and SET NULL. We assume that the user has attempted to delete row *r1* from table *T1*.

---

*The standard calls them *matching* rows, but this term is misleading because "matching" here does *not* mean "matching in accordance with the rules of the MATCH condition" as previously discussed.

[†]The standard term for referencing rows that reference some row exclusively is "unique matching rows," but this term is misleading because it is the *referenced* row that is supposed to be unique, not the *referencing* rows.

1. *NO ACTION:* The DELETE fails if it would cause the referential constraint to be no longer satisfied. See above for an explanation of what it means for the constraint to be satisfied in the various possible cases (FULL, PARTIAL, neither FULL nor PARTIAL).

2. *CASCADE:* Row *r1* is deleted and the DELETE cascades to delete all referencing rows for *r1* also—or, for PARTIAL, all rows that reference *r1* exclusively.

3. *SET DEFAULT:* Row *r1* is deleted and each component of the foreign key is set to the applicable default value in all referencing rows for *r1*— or, for PARTIAL, in all rows that reference *r1* exclusively.

4. *SET NULL:* Row *r1* is deleted and each component of the foreign key is set to null in all referencing rows for *r1*—or, for PARTIAL, in all rows that reference *r1* exclusively.

And here are the specifics of the ON UPDATE clause. Again, the possible specifications are NO ACTION, CASCADE, SET DEFAULT, and SET NULL. We assume that the user has attempted to update the candidate key within row *r1* of table *T1*.

1. *NO ACTION:* The UPDATE fails if it would cause the referential constraint to be no longer satisfied. See above for an explanation of what it means for the constraint to be satisfied in the various possible cases (FULL, PARTIAL, neither FULL nor PARTIAL).

2. *CASCADE:* Row *r1* is updated and the UPDATE "cascades" to update the foreign key in all referencing rows for *r1* also—or, for PARTIAL, in all rows that reference *r1* exclusively, and then only for components of the foreign key that were previously nonnull.

3. *SET DEFAULT:* Row *r1* is updated and each component of the foreign key that corresponds to a component that has been changed in row *r1* is set to the applicable default value in all referencing rows for *r1*—or, for PARTIAL, in all rows that reference *r1* exclusively, and then only for components of the foreign key that were previously nonnull.

4. *SET NULL:* Row *r1* is updated and each component of the foreign key that corresponds to a component that has been changed in row *r1* is set to null in all referencing rows for *r1*—or, for PARTIAL, in all rows that reference *r1* exclusively, and then only for components of the foreign key that were previously nonnull.

16.6 A RECOMMENDATION

Avoid nulls.

17

Dates and Times

17.1 INTRODUCTION

The standard includes an extensive set of features for support of dates and times. However, that support is unfortunately quite complex (please note that this remark is not intended as a criticism—the fact is, many aspects of dates and times are *inherently* complex, as is well known). Therefore, rather than discussing the features in question in detail in Chapter 7 ("Scalar Objects, Operators, and Expressions")—even though such a discussion would have most logically belonged in that chapter—it seemed better to relegate it to this later part of the book.

One preliminary note on terminology: We follow the standard in using the term "datetime" to mean "date or time or timestamp"; for example, we use the term "datetime data types" to mean the data types DATE and TIME and TIMESTAMP, considered collectively (with or without WITH TIME ZONE, in the last two cases). Note, however, that there is also an INTERVAL data type, which, though certainly part of the overall date and time support, is not classified as a "datetime" data type per se.

17.2 DATA TYPES

As indicated above, SQL supports an INTERVAL data type and several "datetime" data types. Interval and datetime values each include one or more of the following *datetime fields:*

```
YEAR
MONTH
DAY
HOUR
MINUTE
SECOND
```

The intuitive interpretation of these fields is obvious. The significance of their ordering as shown above is also obvious: YEAR is the most significant, then MONTH, and so on, down to SECOND (least significant). Not all fields need be present within a given interval or datetime value, but those that are must form a contiguous subset of the full ordered set as shown above (the specific rules vary with the specific data type—see below). Each field always has a decimal integer value, except possibly for SECOND, which can optionally include a decimal fraction also (again, the specific rules vary with the specific data type).

Intervals

An interval is a period of time, such as "3 years" or "90 days" or "5 minutes 30 seconds." For example, subtracting the time "9:00 AM" from the time "10:15 AM" yields the interval "1 hour 15 minutes" (*Note:* The expressions "3 years," "10:15 AM," etc., are not intended to represent valid SQL literal formats.) There are two kinds of intervals, *year-month* intervals and *day-time* intervals. A year-month interval consists of either or both of the fields YEAR and MONTH, in that order; a day-time interval consists of any contiguous subset of the fields DAY, HOUR, MINUTE, and SECOND, in that order.* Thus, the syntax of an INTERVAL data type definition is

```
INTERVAL start [ TO end ]
```

where each of "start" and "end" is one of the datetime fields (YEAR, MONTH, DAY, HOUR, MINUTE, SECOND), optionally followed in the

---

*The reason for not permitting MONTH and DAY within the same interval is, of course, that different months have different numbers of days. As a result, a value such as "2 months 10 days," if permitted, would be ambiguous. (Would it or would it not be the same interval as "70 days"? Or "71 days"? Or "72 days"? What about February?) Consider the effect of such complications on assignment, comparison, date arithmetic, etc.

case of "start" by an unsigned integer in parentheses giving a *precision* for the corresponding item. *Note:* The scale, of course, is zero, since the datetime field values are all integers, except possibly for SECOND; these remarks on precision need some refinement in the case of SECOND (see below).

Here are some examples of interval definitions:

```
INTERVAL YEAR
INTERVAL YEAR TO MONTH
INTERVAL MONTH
INTERVAL DAY (3)
INTERVAL HOUR TO MINUTE
INTERVAL SECOND (5,3)
INTERVAL DAY (3) TO SECOND (3)
```

Each of these could be the data type specification within a base table column definition (or within a domain definition). Points arising:

- If "TO end" is omitted, the interval contains just the datetime field specified as "start." If "TO end" is stated explicitly, the interval contains all datetime fields from "start" to "end" inclusive ("start" must be more significant than "end").

- If "start" specifies YEAR, "end" (if stated) must specify MONTH. If "start" specifies MONTH or SECOND, "TO end" must be omitted.

- A precision p ($p > 0$) can always be specified for "start." The maximum value is implementation-defined, but must be at least 2 (which is the default).

- If "start" is SECOND and if p is specified explicitly, then the number of significant digits q ($q \geq 0$) in the fractional part of the SECOND value can optionally be specified too. The syntax is SECOND(p,q).* The maximum value of q is implementation-defined, but must be at least 6 (which is the default).

- If and only if "end" is SECOND, a precision q (an unsigned integer in parentheses following the key word) can be specified for "end," giving the number of significant digits in the *fractional* part of the SECOND value. Here q is as defined above (but note that the syntax is just q, not $p.q$—p is always 2 in this context).

---

*Note the difference between these rules and the rules for numeric data types. For example, the specification NUMERIC(p,q) means p digits in total, with an assumed decimal point q digits from the right (i.e., the integer part is $p - q$ digits and the fraction is q digits). By contrast, the specification SECOND(p,q) means $p + q$ digits in total, with p digits in the integer part and q digits in the fraction.

- The value of the leading (most significant) field within an interval is unconstrained; thus, e.g., an interval might specify "45 hours," "90 minutes," "18 months," etc. The value of a field that is not in the leading position is constrained as indicated below:

```
MONTH  : 0 to 11
HOUR   : 0 to 23
MINUTE : 0 to 59
SECOND : 0.000... to 59.999...
```

- Values of type INTERVAL can be either positive or negative; e.g., "-5 years" is a legal interval.

Datetimes

A datetime represents an absolute position on the timeline (for DATE and TIMESTAMP) or an absolute time of day (TIME).* For example, a date or a timestamp might both represent "January 18th, 1941"; the date, however, would be accurate only to the day, while the timestamp might be accurate (e.g.) to the microsecond, or even further. A time might represent "7:30 AM." *Note:* The expressions "January 18th, 1941" and "7:30 AM" are not intended to represent valid SQL literal formats.

The datetime data types are DATE, TIME (optionally WITH TIME ZONE), and TIMESTAMP (again, optionally WITH TIME ZONE). Ignoring time zones for the moment, a DATE value consists of fields YEAR, MONTH, and DAY, in that order; a TIME value consists of fields HOUR, MINUTE, and SECOND, in that order; and a TIMESTAMP value consists of fields YEAR, MONTH, DAY, HOUR, MINUTE, and SECOND, in that order. Thus, the syntax of a datetime data type definition is one of the following—

```
DATE
TIME
TIMESTAMP
```

—optionally followed, in the case of TIME and TIMESTAMP, by an unsigned integer value q in parentheses giving a *fractional* precision for the SECOND field within the corresponding item (i.e., the number of significant digits in the fractional part of the SECOND value). The maximum value of q is implementation-defined (but must be at least 6); the default is

---

*Note that "absolute position on the timeline" really means a *relative* position with respect to a specific origin, namely midnight on the day preceding January 1st, 1 AD. Note too that dates and timestamps are always positive (no BC values). Also, times and timestamps are always in terms of a 24-hour clock (no AM or PM qualifiers).

0 for TIME and 6 for TIMESTAMP. Here are some examples of datetime definitions:

```
DATE
TIME
TIME (6)
TIMESTAMP
TIMESTAMP (10)
```

Each of these could be the data type specification within a domain definition or base table column definition. Note that the values of fields within a datetime are all integers (except possibly for the SECOND field) and are constrained as indicated below:

```
YEAR   : 0001 to 9999
MONTH  : 01 to 12
DAY    : 01 to 31
HOUR   : 00 to 23
MINUTE : 00 to 59
SECOND : 00.000... to 61.999...
```

Points arising:

- Observe that MONTH values range from 1 to 12 in a datetime but from 0 to 11 in an interval (assuming in the interval case that the YEAR field is present, for otherwise the MONTH field is unconstrained and can even have a value greater than 11).

- The curious upper limit on SECOND values in a datetime is explained by the following quote from the standard: "On occasion, UTC [see below for an explanation of UTC] is adjusted by the omission . . . or insertion of a *leap second* in order to maintain synchronization with sidereal time. [This possibility] implies that sometimes, but very rarely, a particular minute will contain 59, 61, or 62 seconds." *Note:* Datetime arithmetic (see Section 17.5) that involves leap seconds will produce implementation-defined results (as will datetime arithmetic that involves any discontinuities in the calendar, incidentally).

- All other fields have the same range for both datetimes and intervals, except that, as already mentioned, the leading field of an interval, whatever it happens to be, is unconstrained. If it is a YEAR field, it can even have a value greater than 9999 (although, to repeat, the YEAR component of a datetime cannot).

    Permitted datetime values are thus as follows:

- *DATE:* Legal dates in the range 0001–01–01 (January 1st, 1 AD) to 9999–12–31 (December 31st, 9999 AD) inclusive

- *TIME:* Legal times in the range 00:00:00 . . . to 23:59:61.999 . . . inclusive

- *TIMESTAMP:* Legal timestamps in the range 0001–01–01 00:00:00 . . . to 9999–12–31 23:59:61.999 . . . inclusive

DATE values are further constrained by the rules of the Gregorian calendar; thus, e.g., invalid dates such as 1999–04–31 ("April 31st, 1999") or 2000–02–29 ("February 29th, 2000") are not permitted. Similarly for TIMESTAMP values, of course.

Time Zones

Consider the following example. Suppose a user in San Francisco, California, enters a time value into the database of "10:00 AM." To a user in London, England, that time is equivalent to a local time of "6:00 PM." To another user in Helsinki, Finland, it is equivalent to "8:00 PM." Clearly, these three time values, even though their *external representation* is different in every case, do all have the same *denotation* (i.e., they do all represent the same absolute time).

Because of problems such as the foregoing, the standard specifies that all time values must be held inside the system in *Universal Coordinated Time,* UTC.* Thus, each of the three values in the example above will be held internally as "6:00 PM." In order that a given time value may be properly interpreted, an appropriate "time zone displacement" value must be added to the internal representation, to give the local time. In the case under consideration, the time zone displacement for San Francisco would be "−8 hours." For Helsinki, it would be "+2 hours."

If the definition of a column of data type TIME includes the optional specification WITH TIME ZONE,[†] the time value will include two additional (trailing) datetime fields, TIMEZONE_HOUR and TIMEZONE_MINUTE. When a value is placed into such a column through an INSERT or UPDATE operation, appropriate values for these two additional fields will also be specified, either explicitly by the user or implicitly by the system (see the discussion of SET TIME ZONE, later). Values in such a column are interpreted in terms of their specified TIMEZONE_HOUR and TIMEZONE_MINUTE. If the definition of a column of data type TIME does not include WITH TIME ZONE, values in that column are interpreted in terms of the time zone displacement for the SQL-session (again, see SET TIME ZONE below).

---

*Note that the abbreviation *is* UTC, not UCT. UTC corresponds to what used to be (and often still is) referred to as Greenwich Mean Time, GMT.

[†]WITH TIME ZONE, if stated, follows the parenthesized precision specification, if stated.

An example is in order. Suppose table *T* is defined as follows:

```
CREATE TABLE T
      ( ... ,
        STARTTIME TIME WITH TIME ZONE,
        ... )
```

A user in San Francisco then might execute the following INSERT operation:

```
INSERT INTO T ( ..., STARTTIME, ... )
        VALUES ( ..., TIME '10:00:00-08:00', ... )
```

Users in London and Helsinki retrieving this time value will see it as

```
TIME '18:00:00+00:00'
```

and

```
TIME '20:00:00+02:00'
```

respectively. *Note:* If the time zone displacement "−8:00" had been omitted from the original INSERT, the time zone displacement for the SQL-session would have been inserted by default.

Time zone displacement values are effectively defined as being of data type INTERVAL HOUR TO MINUTE; possible values range from −12:59 to +13:00.* Let *t* be a local time value; let *d* be the possibly negative time zone displacement associated with *t*; and let the absolute (unsigned) values of the HOUR and MINUTE components of *d* be *dh* and *dm,* respectively. Then if *d* is negative, the interpretation of *t* as a UTC value is (*t* + *dh* hours + *dm* minutes). If it is positive, the interpretation is (*t* − *dh* hours − *dm* minutes).

Note: The somewhat counterintuitive nature of the foregoing is worth pointing out explicitly. For instance, in the INSERT example shown above, the expression "10−8" (a simplified version of the San Francisco expression) evaluates to 18, not 2!—that is, the time zone displacement is added to the *UTC* time to obtain the *local* time, not the other way around. In other words, the arithmetic seems to go the wrong way.

As indicated above, each SQL-session has an associated time zone displacement, to be used when no explicit value is provided by the user. This value is initialized to an implementation-defined default when the SQL-session is initiated, but can subsequently be changed at any time by means of the SET TIME ZONE operation—syntax:

---

*The range *is* −12:59 to +13:00, not (as might have been expected) −11:59 to +12:00, because (as the standard puts it) it is "governed by political decisions . . . rather than by any natural law."

```
SET TIME ZONE { displacement | LOCAL }
```

The time zone displacement for the SQL-session is set to the specified value ("displacement" is an interval expression—see Section 17.5—of type INTERVAL HOUR TO MINUTE; LOCAL refers to the initial implementation-defined SQL-session default value).

One final remark: Everything in this subsection on time zones having to do with TIMEs applies to TIMESTAMPs also, mutatis mutandis.

17.3 LITERALS

Datetime literals are of three kinds, namely date literals, time literals, and timestamp literals. The syntax is given below.

date
: Written as the key word DATE, followed by a *date string* of the form *yyyy-mm-dd* enclosed in single quotes

    Examples:
    ```
    DATE '1941-01-18'
    DATE '1999-12-25'
    ```

time
: Written as the key word TIME, followed by a *time string* of the form *hh:mm:ss.nnnnnn* (with an optional time zone interval of the form $+hh{:}mm$ or $-hh{:}mm$) enclosed in single quotes

    Examples:
    ```
    TIME '09:30:00'
    TIME '17:45:45.75'
    TIME '10:00:00-08:00'
    ```

timestamp
: Written as the key word TIMESTAMP, followed by a *timestamp string* of the form *yyyy-mm-dd hh.mm.ss.nnn-nnn* (with an optional time zone interval of the form $+hh{:}mm$ or $-hh{:}mm$) enclosed in single quotes

    Examples:
    ```
    TIMESTAMP '1998-04-28 12:00:00.000000'
    TIMESTAMP '1944-10-17 18:30:45'
    ```

Points arising:

- The enclosing single quotes are considered to be part of the date, time, or timestamp string (as applicable).

- The YEAR, MONTH, DAY (etc., etc.) components are all unsigned decimal integers of exactly four digits (for the YEAR component) and exactly two digits (for everything else except the *nnnnnn*—i.e., fractional—portion of the SECOND component, which can include as many digits as necessary).

- The *nnnnnn* portion of the SECOND component can optionally be omitted, in which case that component has no fractional portion. If the *nnnnnn* portion is omitted, the preceding period can optionally be omitted also.

- A timestamp literal *must* include exactly one space between the date and time portions.

- The data type of a datetime literal is derived in an obvious manner from the way in which the literal is written.

Turning now to interval literals: Interval literals are of two kinds, namely year-month literals and day-time literals. The syntax is given below.

year-month   Written as the key word INTERVAL, followed by an optional sign, followed by an *interval string* consisting of either or both of *yyyy* and *mm* (with a minus sign separator if both are specified), enclosed in single quotes, and followed by YEAR, MONTH, or YEAR TO MONTH (as appropriate)

Examples: INTERVAL -'1' YEAR
             INTERVAL '2-6' YEAR TO MONTH

day-time   Written as the key word INTERVAL, followed by an optional sign, followed by an *interval string* consisting of a contiguous subset of *dd, hh, mm,* and *ss.nnnnnn* (with a space separator between *dd* and the rest, if *dd* is specified, and colon separators elsewhere), enclosed in single quotes, and followed by the appropriate "*start* [TO *end*]" specification

Examples: INTERVAL '1' MINUTE
             INTERVAL '2 12' DAY TO HOUR
             INTERVAL '2:12:35' HOUR TO SECOND
             INTERVAL -'4.50' SECOND

Points arising:

- The enclosing single quotes are considered to be part of the interval string.

- The YEAR, MONTH, DAY (etc., etc.) components are all unsigned decimal integers of not more than four digits (for the YEAR component) and not more than two digits (for everything else except the *nnnnnn*—i.e., fractional—portion of the SECOND component, which can include as many digits as necessary).

- The data type of an interval literal is derived in an obvious manner from the way in which the literal is written.

17.4   DATA CONVERSION

As we saw in Chapter 7, the CAST operator is used to perform explicit data type conversions of all kinds. Simplifying slightly, the general syntax is as follows:

```
CAST ( scalar-expression AS { data-type | domain } )
```

In particular, CAST provides a basis for dealing with datetimes and intervals within a host language that has no directly equivalent data types, because it can be used to convert other scalar values (e.g., character strings and numbers) to the various datetime and interval data types, and vice versa.

CAST also allows datetime values to be converted from one datetime data type to another. Specifically, a date or a time can be converted to a timestamp, and a timestamp can be converted to a date or a time (for the details of these conversions, especially with respect to the manner in which time zones are handled, we refer the reader to the official standard). Note in particular, however, that no conversions are supported between dates and times, nor between datetimes and intervals, nor between year-month intervals and day-time intervals.

In the remainder of this section, we concentrate on (a) conversions between non-datetime values and datetimes and (b) conversions between non-interval values and intervals.

Conversions Involving Datetimes

- A character string can be converted to a date, time, or timestamp so long as the value of that character string represents a literal of the appropriate type (except that it may optionally include leading or trailing spaces, which will be ignored). The result of the conversion is a date, time, or timestamp with the obvious value.

- A date, time, or timestamp can be converted to a fixed or varying length character string. The result of the conversion is a character string representing the value of the date, time, or timestamp as a literal of the appropriate type (padded at the right with spaces if necessary, in the fixed length case).

Conversions Involving Intervals

- A character string can be converted to an interval so long as the value of that character string represents a literal of the appropriate type (except that it may optionally include leading or trailing spaces, which will be ignored). The result of the conversion is an interval with the obvious value.

- An interval can be converted to a fixed or varying length character string. The result of the conversion is a character string representing the value of the interval as a literal of the appropriate type (padded at the right with spaces if necessary, in the fixed length case).

- An exact numeric value can be converted to an interval that contains just one datetime field. The result of the conversion is an interval with the obvious value.

- An interval can be converted to an exact numeric value, so long as the interval contains just one datetime field. The result of the conversion is a number with the obvious value.

Certain of the foregoing conversions can lead to overflow exceptions in fairly obvious ways. We omit the details.

17.5 SCALAR OPERATORS AND FUNCTIONS

The numeric operators "+", "−", "*", and "/" can be used to perform certain arithmetic operations on datetimes and intervals; for example, a date and an interval can be added to yield another date. The details are somewhat complicated, however; for that reason, we choose to discuss the other operators (actually functions) first. *Note:* We remind the reader that (as explained in Chapter 14) the niladic functions CURRENT_DATE, CURRENT_TIME, and CURRENT_TIMESTAMP are not permitted within integrity constraints.

- CURRENT_DATE

  Returns the current date, i.e., the date "today." *Note:* When any given SQL statement is executed, all references to CURRENT_DATE are (to quote the standard) "effectively evaluated simultaneously"; i.e., they are all based on a single reading of the local clock. Thus, e.g., the conditional expression "CURRENT_DATE = CURRENT_DATE" is guaranteed always to evaluate to *true.* An analogous remark applies to CURRENT_TIME and CURRENT_TIMESTAMP (see below); furthermore, all references to any of these three functions within a given SQL statement are always "in synch," in the sense that CURRENT_DATE and CURRENT_TIMESTAMP always designate the same day and CURRENT_TIME and CURRENT_TIMESTAMP always designate the same time.

- CURRENT_TIME

  Returns the current time, i.e., the local time "now," with time zone displacement equal to the time zone displacement for the SQL-session (e.g., invoking CURRENT_TIME at 10:00 AM local time in San Francisco will return TIME '10:00:00−08:00'—assuming, of course, that the SQL-session time zone displacement has been set appropriately). The function name can optionally be followed by an unsigned integer value q in parentheses specifying the fractional precision for the SECOND field within the value returned (see the discussion of the TIME data type in Section 17.2).

- CURRENT_TIMESTAMP

  Returns the current timestamp, i.e., the date "today" concatenated with the local time "now," with time zone displacement equal to the time zone displacement for the SQL-session. The function name can optionally be followed by an unsigned integer value q in parentheses specifying the fractional precision for the SECOND field within the value returned (see the discussion of the TIMESTAMP data type in Section 17.2).

- EXTRACT

  EXTRACT is used to extract the numeric value of an individual field of a specified datetime or interval. More precisely, the expression EXTRACT (*field* FROM *scalar-expression*), where *field* is YEAR, MONTH, DAY, HOUR, MINUTE, SECOND, TIMEZONE_HOUR, or TIMEZONE_MINUTE, and *scalar-expression* is either a datetime expression or an interval expression, is defined to return the value of *field* as a value with data type exact numeric, with implementation-defined precision and scale 0 (or, if SECOND is specified, implementation-defined precision and implementation-defined scale—though the scale must not be such as to lose digits).

  Note that EXTRACT returns a *numeric* value (it is an additional form of "numeric primary"—see Chapter 7, Section 7.4). Note too that EXTRACT applied to a negative interval returns a negative value.

  We close this discussion of functions with a brief remark on the *aggregate* functions, to wit: While all five of the aggregate functions (COUNT, MAX, MIN, SUM, and AVG) can be used with intervals, only the first three (COUNT, MAX, and MIN) can be used with datetimes.

  We turn now to the arithmetic operators. First, we should warn the reader that not all operations that might appear to make sense are in fact permitted; for example, it is not permitted to divide one interval by another (e.g., "10 days" divided by "2 days") to obtain a number. The table below summarizes those operations that *are* permitted.

1st operand	operator	2nd operand	result
datetime	–	datetime	interval
datetime	+	interval	datetime
datetime	–	interval	datetime
interval	+	datetime	datetime
interval	+	interval	interval
interval	–	interval	interval
interval	*	number	interval
interval	/	number	interval
number	*	interval	interval

Notes:

1. If two datetimes appear in the same datetime expression (basically possible only if one is being subtracted from the other), they must be both dates or both times or both timestamps.

2. If two intervals appear in the same interval expression (basically possible only if one is being added to or subtracted from the other), they must be both year-month intervals or both day-time intervals.

3. If a datetime and an interval appear in the same datetime expression (basically possible only if the interval is being added to or subtracted from the datetime), the interval must contain only datetime fields that are also contained within the datetime.

Here then is the syntax:

```
datetime-expression
    ::=   datetime-term
        | interval-expression + datetime-term
        | datetime-expression { + | - } interval-term

datetime-term
    ::=   datetime-primary
                    [ AT { LOCAL | TIME ZONE displacement } ]

interval-expression
    ::=   interval-term
        | interval-expression { + | - } interval-term
        | ( datetime expression - datetime-term ) start [ TO end ]

interval-term
    ::=   interval-factor
        | interval-term { * | / } numeric-factor
        | numeric-term * interval-factor

interval-factor
    ::=   [ + | - ] interval-primary
```

Points arising:

- A datetime expression evaluates to a datetime; an interval expression evaluates to an interval. More precisely, a datetime expression involving dates evaluates to a date, one involving times evaluates to a time, and one involving timestamps evaluates to a timestamp. Likewise, an interval expression involving year-month intervals evaluates to a year-month interval, and one involving day-time intervals evaluates to a day-time interval.

- For an explanation of "numeric term" and "numeric factor," see Chapter 7 (Section 7.4).

- A "datetime primary" is any of the following: (a) a possibly qualified column name; (b) a datetime literal; (c) a reference to a scalar function—possibly CASE or CAST—or aggregate function; (d) a table expression enclosed in parentheses; or (e) a datetime expression enclosed in parentheses. In each case, of course, the "datetime primary" must yield a value of one of the datetime data types.

- An "interval primary" is analogous, except of course that it involves interval literals or expressions instead of datetime literals or expressions, and it must yield a value of type INTERVAL.*

- AT LOCAL or AT TIME ZONE can be specified only if the datetime primary evaluates to a time or a timestamp ("displacement" is an interval expression of type INTERVAL HOUR TO MINUTE). The effect in both cases is to cause the value of the associated datetime primary to be adjusted in accordance with the specified time zone displacement. For example, TIME '18:00:00 + 00:00' will be converted to TIME '10:00:00 − 08:00' if AT TIME ZONE INTERVAL − '08:00' is specified. AT LOCAL (meaning the time zone displacement for the SQL-session) is assumed if nothing is specified.†

Here are some examples:

```
DATE '1972-08-17' - DATE '1969-10-28'
DATE '1972-08-17' - CAST ( ' DATE''1969-10-28'' ' AS DATE )

STARTTIME + INTERVAL '5' MINUTE
INTERVAL '5' MINUTE + STARTTIME
```

---

*If and only if the interval primary is represented by a question mark (i.e., it constitutes a "placeholder" in a dynamically prepared SQL statement—see Chapter 20), it must include a "start [TO end]" specification.

†We remark that the meaning of LOCAL is context-dependent. In SET TIME ZONE, it means the *initial* SQL-session default time zone displacement; in a datetime expression, it means the *current* SQL-session time zone displacement.

```
STARTTIME - INTERVAL '4:30' MINUTE TO SECOND
STARTTIME + ( 3 * INTERVAL '1:4:30' HOUR TO MINUTE )

CURRENT_TIMESTAMP + INTERVAL '1.500000' SECOND
```

Interval expressions are effectively evaluated by converting the operands to integers (e.g., the operand INTERVAL '2-6' YEAR TO MONTH might be converted to the integer 30, meaning 30 months), evaluating the resulting numeric expression, and then converting the result back to the required interval format (*start* TO *end*). We omit the details, since they are essentially straightforward. Datetime expressions are evaluated in accordance with the Gregorian calendar and permissible datetime values. Thus, for example, the expression

```
DATE '1998-07-31' + INTERVAL '1' MONTH
```

("July 31st, 1998 plus one month") correctly evaluates to

```
DATE '1998-08-31'
```

("August 31st, 1998"). Likewise, the expression

```
DATE '1998-12-31' + INTERVAL '1' MONTH
```

("December 31st, 1998 plus one month") correctly evaluates to

```
DATE '1999-01-31'
```

("January 31st, 1999"), and the expression

```
DATE '1999-01-31' + INTERVAL '30' DAY
```

("January 31st, 1999 plus 30 days") correctly evaluates to

```
DATE '1999-03-02'
```

("March 2nd, 1999"). In general, adding an interval to a datetime is performed by adding the least significant field values, then the next least, and so on; and, as the second and third examples above illustrate, any of these individual additions has the potential of causing a carry to the next more significant datetime field. Note, however, that the next *less* significant field will *not* be adjusted; thus, for example, the expression

```
DATE '1998-08-31' + INTERVAL '1' MONTH
```

("August 31st, 1998 plus one month") apparently evaluates to

```
DATE '1998-09-31'
```

("September 31st, 1998"), and thus fails (an "invalid date" exception is raised). It does *not* evaluate (as might perhaps have been expected) to

DATE '1998-10-01'

("October 1st, 1998"), because such a result would require an adjustment to the DAY field after the MONTH addition has been performed. In other words, if interval *i* is added to date *d,* and *i* is of type year-month, then the DAY value in the result is the same as the DAY value in *d* (i.e., the DAY value does not change).

Subtraction is performed analogously, except that carries, if any, are *from,* not to, the next more significant field.

Note: If the datetime expression involves TIMEs, arithmetic on the HOUR field is performed modulo 24 (e.g., "10 PM" plus 4 hours gives "2 AM"). The same is not true for TIMESTAMPs, of course, where HOURs carry to or from DAYs in the normal way.

17.6 ASSIGNMENTS AND COMPARISONS

Assignments

As always in an assignment, the data type of the source and the data type of the target must be *compatible.* For datetimes and intervals, compatibility is defined as follows:

1. All dates are compatible with one another.
2. All times are compatible with one another.
3. All timestamps are compatible with one another.
4. All year-month intervals are compatible with one another.
5. All day-time intervals are compatible with one another.
6. There are no other instances of compatibility.

Cases 4 and 5 require some elaboration, however. First we examine Case 4. Let *B* and *A* be two year-month intervals, and consider what is involved in assigning *B* to *A.*

▪   If *B* and *A* are both of type INTERVAL YEAR TO MONTH, or both of type INTERVAL YEAR, or both of type INTERVAL MONTH, the assignment is straightforward.

▪   If *B* is of type INTERVAL YEAR but *A* is of type INTERVAL YEAR TO MONTH, *B* is effectively extended at the least significant end by attaching a MONTH field with a value of 0. The assignment is then straightforward.

▪   If *B* is of type INTERVAL MONTH but *A* is of type INTERVAL YEAR TO MONTH, *B* is effectively extended at the most significant end by attaching a YEAR field with a value of 0. *B* might then have to be adjusted so that it conforms to the rules for valid intervals (e.g., the value "15 months" would be adjusted to "1 year 3 months"). The assignment is then straightforward.

- If *B* is of type INTERVAL YEAR or INTERVAL YEAR TO MONTH but *A* is of type INTERVAL MONTH, *B* is effectively converted to type INTERVAL MONTH before the assignment is performed (e.g., "2 years" would be converted to "24 months").

- If *B* is of type INTERVAL MONTH or INTERVAL YEAR TO MONTH but *A* is of type INTERVAL YEAR, *B* is effectively converted to type INTERVAL YEAR before the assignment is performed (e.g., "24 months" would be converted to "2 years"). If the conversion causes a loss of information, an exception is raised.

Analogous (but somewhat tedious) considerations apply to Case 5. We omit the details here.

Comparisons

The basic form of a comparison (as always) is

```
comparand  operator  comparand
```

where:

- The two comparands must be *compatible* (as that term is defined under "Assignments" above).

- The comparison operator is one of the usual set $(=, < >, <, < =, >, > =)$.

- Datetime comparisons are performed in accordance with chronologic ordering. Interval comparisons are performed in accordance with their sign and magnitude.

- When two intervals are to be compared, a process analogous to that described under "Assignments" may have to be carried out—i.e., either comparand (or both) may have to be extended, at either or both ends, by attaching new datetime fields with an initial value of zero; the comparand(s) may then have to be adjusted to conform to the rules for valid intervals. The comparison can then be performed in the normal manner. (The net effect is that, e.g., the intervals "1 hour" and "60 minutes" are considered to be equal.)

OVERLAPS Condition

SQL also provides a special comparison operator, OVERLAPS, to test whether two time periods overlap. The time periods in question are represented in each case either by their start and end points or by a start point and an interval (they do not both have to be represented in the same way). Thus, the syntax is

```
left OVERLAPS right
```

(an additional case of "simple condition"—see Chapter 12), where:

- "Left" and "right" are each row constructors of exactly two components.

- The first component in "left" and "right" must be of data type DATE in each case, TIME in each case, or TIMESTAMP in each case.

- The second component in "left" and "right" must *either* be of the same datetime data type as the corresponding first component *or* be of an INTERVAL data type that involves only datetime fields that are also contained within the corresponding first component.

Let the two components of "left" (in order) be *L1* and *L2* and the two components of "right" (in order) be *R1* and *R2,* respectively. *L1* and *L2* define a certain time period in an obvious way—either from *L1* to *L2,* if *L1* and *L2* are both datetimes, or from *L1* to *L1* + *L2,* if *L2* is an interval. Note that if the end point is earlier in time than the start point, or if the start point is null, the two are conceptually interchanged.* Let *Ls* and *Le* be that start point and end point, respectively (after any necessary interchanging). Define *Rs* and *Re* analogously. Then the original OVERLAPS condition is defined to be semantically equivalent to the conditional expression

```
( Ls > Rs AND ( Ls < Re OR Le < Re ) ) OR
( Rs > Ls AND ( Rs < Le OR Re < Le ) ) OR
( Ls = Rs AND Le IS NOT NULL AND Re IS NOT NULL )
```

For example, the OVERLAPS condition

```
( TIME '08:00:00', TIME '09:00:00' )
  OVERLAPS
( TIME '08:30:00', TIME '09:30:00' )
```

evaluates to *true. Note:* So too does the condition that is obtained from the one just shown by replacing the end point of the second time period by null.

By contrast, the OVERLAPS condition

---

*The purpose of the interchange in the case where the start point is null is simply to avoid dealing with time periods in which the end point is known but the start point is not (i.e., the start point can be unknown after the interchange only if the end point is too).

```
( TIME '08:00:00', TIME '09:00:00' )
  OVERLAPS
( TIME '09:00:00', TIME '09:30:00' )
```

evaluates to *false*. Note the asymmetry, incidentally; e.g., consider what happens if $Rs = Re$—i.e., *Right* is a time *point* rather than a time period—and it happens to coincide with (a) the start point of *Left*, (b) the end point of *Left*.

18

Temporary Tables

18.1 INTRODUCTION

So far in this book we have concerned ourselves solely with what might be called *permanent* base tables—where by "permanent" we mean that the tables in question, once created, persist in the database until such time as they are explicitly removed by means of an explicit DROP operation. Sometimes, however, applications have a need for tables that will be used only to pass intermediate results from one portion of the application to another, and hence will persist only for a comparatively short time (certainly not beyond the lifetime of the application in question). Furthermore, such tables are typically "private" to the application that uses them—there is no question of having to share the data they contain with other applications, concurrent or otherwise.

Now, it would of course be possible to use "permanent" tables for such purposes. However, the standard explicitly supports the concept of "temporary" tables (specifically, temporary *base* tables) that can be used to simplify the process slightly. In a nutshell, a temporary table is a base table that:

- Is explicitly stated to be TEMPORARY when it is defined;
- Is always empty at the start of the SQL-session;
- Can optionally be returned to an empty state at each COMMIT;

and

■   Will be dropped automatically (if it has not already been dropped explicitly) at the end of the SQL-session.

Also, transactions are allowed to update temporary tables even if they
(the transactions) have been specified to be READ ONLY.

Temporary tables in the standard fall into three types, which we might
as well refer to simply as Type 1, Type 2, and Type 3. (The standard uses
the terms *declared local* temporary tables, *created local* temporary tables,
and *global* temporary tables, respectively; however, these terms are cumber-
some, and in this writer's opinion do not serve to characterize the real differences among the three cases any better than the simple labels "Type 1,"
"Type 2," and "Type 3" do.) We discuss Type 1 in Section 18.2 immediately following and Types 2 and 3 in Section 18.3, later.

18.2   TYPE 1: "DECLARED" TEMPORARY TABLES

A Type 1 temporary table is *declared* (not "created," please note) by means
of an appropriate DECLARE statement. Such a table can be referenced
only by procedures in the module that contains the corresponding
DECLARE; observe that such DECLAREs must precede all cursor and
procedure definitions within the module in question. *Note:* We referred to
such DECLAREs as "temporary table definitions" in Chapter 6 (Section
6.2).

Here then is the syntax for a "temporary table definition":

```
DECLARE LOCAL TEMPORARY TABLE MODULE . base-table
      ( base-table-element-commalist )
      [ ON COMMIT { PRESERVE | DELETE } ROWS ]
```

Here "base table" is an *un*qualified table name; note that all references to
the table must be of the special form "MODULE.X," where X is the name
specified as "base table" in the DECLARE. The "base table elements" are
as for CREATE TABLE—in other words, each is either a column definition
or a base table constraint definition (see below). The "ON COMMIT"
clause specifies whether the table is to be automatically emptied (DELETE)
or left unchanged (PRESERVE) at each COMMIT; the default is
DELETE.

The current authID (i.e., the authID of the owner of the containing
module, if such an owner exists, or the SQL-session authID otherwise) is
automatically granted all privileges—but not "grant authority"—on the
new Type 1 table. The user granting these privileges is considered to be the
special authID _SYSTEM.

As indicated above, a Type 1 table is effectively private to the module in which it is declared; it cannot be referenced in any other module. If any base table integrity constraints are specified (within the DECLARE) for such a table, those constraints are not allowed to refer to any named tables that are not themselves temporary tables in turn (of any of the three types). Furthermore, *general* constraints (specified by CREATE ASSERTION) are not allowed to reference temporary tables at all; neither are domain constraints, nor base table constraints that are attached to permanent base tables.

View definitions are allowed to reference temporary tables of Types 2 and 3, but not Type 1. Note that such a view definition might be regarded as defining a kind of "temporary view" (but this term is not used in the standard).

All Type 1 tables are automatically dropped at the end of the SQL-session; in fact, explicit DROP TABLE operations are not even permitted, and nor are ALTER TABLE operations, though such operations *are* permitted for Types 2 and 3. Indeed, Type 1 tables are not even mentioned in "the Information Schema" (see Chapter 21), again unlike Types 2 and 3. Overall, it seems better to think of Type 1 tables as not belonging to the database at all, and hence not being described by any schema; instead, they should be regarded as purely private objects, kept in the application's private address space along with other local variables.*

18.3 TYPES 2 AND 3: "CREATED" TEMPORARY TABLES

Type 2 and 3 temporary tables are defined by means of a CREATE TABLE statement (not a DECLARE statement, please note) that specifies TEMPORARY. However, such a statement is really quite different in kind from a regular CREATE TABLE. It should certainly not be thought of as actually creating a new base table then and there, as a regular CREATE TABLE does (and so the syntax "CREATE TABLE" is really quite inappropriate). Instead, the table is actually created—the standard uses the term "materialized" or "instantiated"—*when it is first referenced,* either within a module (for Type 2) or within an SQL-session (for Type 3). In other words, each module activation effectively has its own private version of each Type 2 table, and each SQL-session effectively has its own private version of each Type 3 table; thus, Type 2 tables cannot be used to pass

---

*Actually, the standard does regard a Type 1 table as belonging to a kind of secret schema, whose "effective <schema name> ... may be thought of as [a combination of] the implementation-dependent SQL-session identifier associated with the SQL-session and a unique implementation-dependent name associated with the SQL-session and a unique implementation-dependent name associated with the <module> that contains the <temporary table declaration>."

information from one module activation to another, and Type 3 tables cannot be used to pass information from one SQL-session to another.

Note: In practice there will often be a one-to-one correspondence between module activations and SQL-sessions anyway, in which case the real distinction between Type 2 and Type 3 becomes very minor indeed. (And the real distinction between Type 1 and Type 2 is also fairly minor, in this writer's opinion—after all, both are "module-local"; the principal difference is merely that *any* module can reference a Type 2 table without bothering to declare it, whereas only the module that declares it can reference a Type 1 table.)

Here then is the syntax for creating Type 2 and 3 tables:

```
CREATE { LOCAL | GLOBAL } TEMPORARY TABLE base-table
    ( base-table-element-commalist )
    [ ON COMMIT { PRESERVE | DELETE } ROWS ]
```

LOCAL corresponds to our "Type 2" and GLOBAL to our "Type 3." "Base table" is as for the regular CREATE TABLE,* and "base table elements" and the "ON COMMIT" clause are as for Type 1 tables (see Section 18.2)—*except* that any named tables referenced within any integrity constraints within the CREATE TABLE must themselves be Type 2 or Type 3 tables (for LOCAL), or just Type 3 tables (for GLOBAL).

The current authID (i.e., the authID of the owner of the containing module, if there is such a containing module and it does have an owner, or the SQL-session authID otherwise) is automatically granted all privileges—*with* "grant authority"†—on the new Type 2 or Type 3 table. The user granting these privileges is considered to be the special authID _SYSTEM.

---

*Except that it must definitely be an *un*qualified name (furthermore, all references to the table must also be via that *un*qualified name). Type 2 and Type 3 tables are considered to belong to a schema, but that schema is *not* the one normally assumed by default. To quote the standard again: " . . . because global temporary table contents are distinct within SQL-sessions, and created local temporary tables are distinct within <module>s [i.e., module *activations*] within SQL-sessions, the *effective* <schema name> of the schema in which [the description of] the global temporary table or the created local temporary table is instantiated is an implementation-dependent <schema name> that may be thought of as having been effectively derived from the <schema name> of the schema in which the global temporary table or created local temporary table is defined and the implementation-dependent SQL-session identifier associated with the SQL-session. In addition, the *effective* <schema name> of the schema in which [the description of] the created local temporary table is instantiated may be thought of as being further qualified by a unique implementation-dependent name associated with the <module> [i.e., module *activation*] in which the created local temporary table is referenced." Well, that certainly seems clear enough.

†Any GRANT or subsequent REVOKE against the Type 2 or Type 3 table *must* specify ALL PRIVILEGES.

We remind the reader that, as stated in Section 18.2, general constraints and ''permanent'' base table constraints are not allowed to reference temporary tables at all, and nor are domain constraints. By contrast, view definitions are allowed to reference temporary tables of Types 2 and 3, but not Type 1. As with Type 1, all Type 2 and Type 3 tables are automatically dropped at the end of the SQL-session, unless they have already been explicitly dropped (explicit DROP TABLE—and ALTER TABLE—operations are allowed for Type 2 and Type 3 tables). Finally, Type 2 and Type 3 tables, unlike Type 1 tables, are described in the Information Schema (again, see Chapter 21).

19

Character Data

19.1 INTRODUCTION

Traditional programming languages have tended to treat as a "character" any value that can be stored in a single addressable location in computer memory. Typically, there are 256 such values, as a direct consequence of the typical 8-bit byte being the smallest unit of addressability. The fact that many of these values map to typical "atoms" of written language, such as letters, numerals, punctuation marks, and so on, has been the concern not of programming languages per se, but rather of I/O devices such as keyboards, visual display units, and printers. Well-known coding schemes such as ASCII and EBCDIC have been used to map 8-bit values to named symbols such as "upper-case A," "lower-case q," "space," "zero," "comma," and so on. Such named symbols are often referred to as *graphemes,* although this term is not used in the SQL standard.

Traditional programming languages have also provided special operators and notation for the treatment of *character strings* (often abbreviated in this chapter to just *strings*), and the reader will no doubt be very familiar with notations for:

- Representing a character string literal by enclosing a sequence of symbols in quotation marks

- Comparing two strings character by character, from the first character

271

to the last ("left to right"), to determine whether the first is less than, equal to, or greater than the second according to some *collating sequence**

- Joining two strings together to make a new string—*concatenation*
- Extracting some contiguous portion of a given string—*substring*
- Searching a given string from left to right to see at what *position,* if any, a given substring first occurs

In databases, character strings have many typical uses. They are the obvious choice for representing written text and names of people, places, and things. They are a common, if less obvious, choice for codes such as part numbers, supplier numbers, and personnel numbers, even when such things really are just numbers. They have also been used, where the database language offers nothing more suitable, for highly specialized and often quite complex data that requires special software, external to the DBMS, to encode, decode, and interpret it.

SQL's support for character data embraces all of the foregoing, and more besides. Additional complications arise from the increasingly compelling need to support databases with an international community of users, which in turn implies a need to cope with the ways in which computerized treatment of written text varies from one national language to another. For example:

- Different languages use different sets of graphemes.
- There is little or no correspondence between the graphemes of one language and those of another.
- Indeed, the number of distinct graphemes varies from a few dozen (in most European languages) to many thousands (notably in Chinese). In some languages there are far too many distinct symbols to be mappable to the 256 possible values of an 8-bit byte, so 16-bit coding schemes are used instead. However, there is understandable reluctance to use 16-bit coding schemes for languages where 8 bits are sufficient.
- Two languages that use approximately the same alphabet may vary in their use of diacritical marks such as accents, and accented letters are typically required to appear close to their unaccented counterparts in the collating sequence.

---

*Historically the collating sequence has typically been just the numerical order of the values of the 8-bit codes, treated as numbers in base 2. However, there is no intrinsic reason why the collating sequence should necessarily depend on the internal coding scheme, and the two concepts are distinguished in SQL (under the names *collation* and *form-of-use,* respectively), as we shall see in Section 19.2.

- Even internationally accepted coding schemes for languages based on the (so-called) Latin alphabet* reserve some codes for national variations.

The reader will probably begin to appreciate the point that SQL's support for character data is quite complex, owing in part to difficulties such as those outlined above. However, the standard does provide an elaborate system of *defaults* to keep matters relatively simple in the majority of cases, as we shall see.

19.2 PROPERTIES OF CHARACTER STRINGS

A character string is a sequence of zero or more characters, all of which are drawn from the same *character set,* which must always be specified, even for an empty string (though such specifications will very often be implicit). A character set is a named combination of a *character repertoire* in combination with a *form-of-use.*[†] A character repertoire (repertoire for short) is a named collection of characters. A form-of-use is a named one-to-one mapping between the characters of some repertoire and a set of internal codes (such as, but not necessarily, 8-bit values).

Note: It is probably worth mentioning that character repertoires and forms-of-use are provided in SQL primarily as building blocks for the construction of character sets. Character sets play a major role in the language, of course; character repertoires and forms-of-use per se, by contrast, do not.

Now, when we say that a character string is a "sequence" of (say) L characters, we mean that it consists of an ordered collection of L characters ($L \geq 0$), not necessarily all distinct. Within that ordered collection, there is exactly one, uniquely determined character at each ordinal position p ($1 \leq p \leq L$). The value L (the total number of ordinal positions within the collection) is the *character length* (or just *length*) of the string. Observe that the character length is not necessarily the same as the *octet length,* which is (informally) the amount of computer memory, in 8-bit bytes, minimally needed to accommodate the string.[‡]

---

*"So called" because it includes letters such as W and Y that were not originally part of Latin at all.

[†]A character set also has one or more associated *collations,* of which exactly one is the *default* collation for that character set (see later in this section).

[‡]Indeed, two strings might have the same character length but different octet lengths. More precisely, "same character length" implies "same octet length" only in the special (though common) case in which the form-of-use is a *fixed-length coding*—i.e., a form-of-use in which the same number of bits is used for every character.

A character string also has a pair of separate but interconnected properties that determine whether and how that string can be compared with others, a *coercibility* property (the "whether") and—unless the coercibility property specifies otherwise—a *collation* property (the "how").

- A *collation* (also, and more familiarly, known as a collating sequence) is a rule associated with a specified character set that governs the comparison of strings drawn from that set. Let C be a collation for character set S, and let a and b be any two characters (not necessarily distinct) of S. Then collation C must satisfy the condition that exactly one of the comparisons

  ```
  a < b     a = b     a > b
  ```

  evaluates to *true* and the other two to *false* (under C).

  Note that the comparison $a = b$ might evaluate to *true* under C even if a and b are distinct characters. For example, we might define a collation called CASE_INSENSITIVITY (for the character set in question) under which each lower-case letter is considered to "compare equal" to its upper-case counterpart.

- The *coercibility* property of a given string determines which collation, if any, applies to that string (speaking somewhat loosely). Coercibility is discussed in detail in Section 19.7.

In summary, every character string has:

- A character set, being the combination of some character repertoire R and some form-of-use F
- A length, L
- For every ordinal position $p \leq L$, a pth character drawn from R and represented by an internal code determined by F
- A coercibility property and (usually) an associated collation, being any of possibly several collations that apply to the string's character set

19.3 CHARACTER SETS AND COLLATIONS

As we just saw, every character string has an associated character set and—usually—an associated collation. In this section we explain how character sets and collations are defined and destroyed in SQL. As the reader might expect, the relevant statements are CREATE and DROP CHARACTER SET and CREATE and DROP COLLATION, respectively. However, there is one point we should probably make clear right away, and that is that, ultimately, (a) the specific characters contained within a given character set (i.e., the character repertoire), (b) the associated character coding scheme (i.e., the form-of-use), and (c) the specific character ordering represented by a given collation, are all defined outside the framework of SQL per se; in other words, all character sets and all collations are, ultimately, defined in terms of some "external" specification, as we shall see.*

Note: As mentioned in Chapter 4, character set definitions and collation definitions are both "schema elements"; in other words, CREATE CHARACTER SET and CREATE COLLATION (like CREATE TABLE and various other CREATE statements) can be executed as independent operations in their own right, or they can be included as components within a CREATE SCHEMA statement. DROP CHARACTER SET and DROP SCHEMA must be independent operations (like all other forms of DROP).

Character Sets

Here first is the syntax for a character set definition:

```
character-set-definition
    ::=  CREATE CHARACTER SET character-set [ AS ]
            GET existing-character-set
         [ COLLATE collation | COLLATION FROM collation-source ]
```

Here "character set" is the name of the new character set,[†] and "existing character set" is the name of some previously defined character set. This latter character set may have been defined via a CREATE CHARACTER SET operation in turn, or it may have been defined "externally," i.e., outside the scope of SQL per se (it might, for example, be defined in some national or international standard). *Note:* The implementation *must* support at least one "existing character set," called SQL_TEXT, whose character repertoire (also called SQL_TEXT) is required to contain (a) every character that is used in the SQL language itself (see Section 3.1), together with (b) every character that is included in any other character set supported by the implementation. AuthIDs, SQL-server names, and SQL-connection names are all SQL_TEXT character strings; in particular, the niladic builtin functions USER, CURRENT_USER, SESSION_USER, and SYSTEM_USER (see Chapter 15) all return character strings whose associated character set is SQL_TEXT.

---

*Those "external" objects are considered to belong to the Information Schema.

[†]If the name is qualified by a schema name and the CREATE CHARACTER SET appears within the context of a CREATE SCHEMA statement, then that schema name must identify the schema that would have been assumed by default anyway, viz. the schema being created (see Section 4.3). An analogous remark applies to CREATE COLLATION and CREATE TRANSLATION (see later).

"COLLATE . . . " and "COLLATION FROM . . . " are alternative ways of defining the *default collation* for the new character set. (See below for the syntax of the "collation source" operand of COLLATION FROM.) If neither COLLATE nor COLLATION FROM is specified, COLLATION FROM DEFAULT is assumed (see below); thus, every character set *always* has a default collation.*

A "collation source" is any of the following:

```
EXTERNAL ( 'external-collation' )
collation
DESC ( collation )
DEFAULT
translation-collation
```

We explain these possibilities as follows.

- *EXTERNAL:* "External collation" identifies some collation that is defined externally (e.g., in some national or international standard).

- *Collation:* "Collation" is the name of some existing collation (previously defined by some CREATE COLLATION operation).

- *DESC:* "Collation" is as in the previous case, and the character set being defined has a default collation that is the reverse of the one so identified.

- *DEFAULT:* The default collation is "the order of characters as they appear in the character repertoire." This concept is not further defined or clarified in the standard.

- *Translation collation:* The syntax for this case is

```
TRANSLATION translation [ THEN COLLATION collation ]
```

Here "collation" (once again) is the name of some existing collation. However, that existing collation does not necessarily have to be for the character set being defined, because "translation" identifies an existing *translation* (see Section 19.6) that maps strings of the character set being defined to strings of the character set to which "collation" *does* apply. If "THEN COLLATION collation" is omitted, the default collation for the target character set of "translation" is taken as the specified collation source.

---

*It is worth pointing out too that every collation always has a corresponding character set; that is, a collation cannot exist without a corresponding character set (see the definition of CREATE COLLATION, later).

Finally, we turn to DROP CHARACTER SET. The syntax is:

```
DROP CHARACTER SET character-set
```

Note that (in contrast to most other DROP statements) there is no explicit RESTRICT/CASCADE option. However, RESTRICT is effectively implied—that is, there must be no outstanding references (in other schema elements) to the specified character set, or the DROP will fail.

Collations

The syntax for "collation definition" is:

```
collation-definition
    ::=   CREATE COLLATION collation
            FOR   character-set
            FROM collation-source
          [ PAD SPACE | NO PAD ]
```

Here "collation" is the name of the new collation,* "character set" identifies the character set whose elements are ordered by this collation, and "collation source" defines that ordering. (We defer discussion of the optional PAD SPACE and NO PAD specifications to Section 19.7, except to note that the default is NO PAD if "collation source" specifies a collation to which NO PAD applies, and PAD SPACE otherwise.) The collation source can be any of the following:

```
EXTERNAL ( 'external-collation' )
collation
DESC ( collation )
DEFAULT
translation-collation
```

(just as in the COLLATION FROM clause in CREATE CHARACTER SET). The meanings of these various possibilities are analogous to those already explained under the discussion of CREATE CHARACTER SET above.

And here is the syntax for DROP COLLATION:

```
DROP COLLATION collation
```

As with DROP CHARACTER SET, neither CASCADE nor RESTRICT can be specified; however, this fact does not mean that the DROP will fail if there are any outstanding references to the specified collation. On the contrary, any such references (e.g., within a character set definition or base table column definition or view definition) will simply be deleted without warning! For

---

*See the second footnote on page 275.

example, if the example collation we mentioned earlier (in Section 19.2), CASE_INSENSITIVITY, is dropped, and there exists a character set CASE_INSENSITIVE for which COLLATE CASE_INSENSITIVITY was specified, CASE_INSENSITIVE will be internally redefined as if COLLATION FROM DEFAULT had been specified instead (and so the name originally chosen for this character set may become quite inappropriate).

19.4   DATA TYPES

In Chapter 7, we said that SQL supported the following character string data types:

CHARACTER(n)   Fixed length string of exactly n characters ($n > 0$)

CHARACTER   Varying length string of up to n characters ($n > 0$)
VARYING(n)

Now, of course, we can see that a certain amount of refinement is needed. In fact, since every character string has an associated character set and—usually—an associated collation also, we must extend the basic syntax for "character string data type" (within a column or domain definition) to include optional CHARACTER SET and COLLATE specifications, thus:*

```
CHARACTER [ VARYING ] [ ( length ) ]
        [ CHARACTER SET character-set ]
        [ COLLATE collation ]
```

If the CHARACTER SET clause is omitted, the default character set for the relevant schema is assumed by default† (see later in this section for an explanation of the schema default character set). If the COLLATE clause is omitted, then (a) in the context of a column definition, for column *C* say, where column *C* is defined on domain *D,* say, the collation that applies to domain *D* is assumed by default; (b) in the context of a domain definition, or the column definition for a column that is not defined on a domain, the default collation for the (explicit or implicit) CHARACTER SET character set is assumed by default.

In addition to the basic syntax explained above, SQL provides certain

---

*In the interest of accuracy we should make it clear that the COLLATE clause is not technically part of the data type specification per se.

†Assuming that the "character string data type" specification is indeed (as stated) part of a column or domain definition. "Character string data type" specifications can also appear within CAST expressions and parameter definitions, in which case the default character set is implementation-defined. The COLLATE clause is not allowed within CAST expressions and parameter definitions.

shorthands, some of which have already been described in Chapter 7 but are repeated here for completeness. *Note:* Of these shorthands, one seems to be truly useful, the others seem to be merely time-honored abbreviations.

- CHARACTER without a length specification means the same as CHARACTER(1)

- CHAR means the same as CHARACTER

- VARCHAR means the same as CHARACTER VARYING (or CHAR VARYING)

- NATIONAL CHARACTER (the useful one) means the same as CHARACTER . . . CHARACTER SET *ncs,* where *ncs* is the name of a particular character set that the implementation has designated as the "national" one

- NCHAR means the same as NATIONAL CHARACTER

The Schema Default Character Set

To repeat a remark made earlier in this section, if the CHARACTER SET specification is omitted from a character string data type specification, the default character set for the relevant schema is assumed by default. The default character set for a given schema is specified as part of the CREATE SCHEMA statement. The syntax of that statement, to repeat from Chapter 4, is as follows:

```
CREATE SCHEMA [ schema ] [ AUTHORIZATION user ]
               [ DEFAULT CHARACTER SET character-set ]
               [ schema-element-list ]
```

The default character set for the schema is specified by the DEFAULT CHARACTER SET clause. If that clause is omitted, an implementation-defined character set is assumed by default.

19.5 LITERALS

As explained in Chapter 7, SQL supports the familiar notation for a character string literal, viz. a sequence of symbols enclosed in quotation marks, where each character is represented by one symbol (except for the quotation mark itself, which is represented by two adjacent quotation marks). Examples are:

```
'This is a string!'
'Here''s another one.'
'SQL'
'p23'
```

and, often sadly overlooked,

     ' '

(the empty string). *Note:* We remind the reader that SQL also supports an extended format for writing string literals that span multiple text lines. Refer to Chapter 7 for the details.

The foregoing notation is clearly sufficient to represent both the actual sequence of characters constituting the value of a literal string* and, by implication, the length of such a string. However, it is not sufficient to represent the string's character set and collation properties. Thus, certain extensions to the basic syntax are necessary.

First, to specify the *character set* of a character string literal, the name of the character set, prefixed with an underscore, is written in front of the literal itself. For example:

    _FRANCAIS 'Comment ça va?'

The characters that appear between the delimiting quotation marks must all, of course, belong to the repertoire of the named character set, in this case FRANCAIS. Note, incidentally, that the character set name is intended in the example to be the same as the name of the language it is supporting, but has an ordinary C instead of Ç ("C-cedilla"). We shall return to this point in Section 19.8.

At this point SQL introduces another useful shorthand, as follows: The expression

    N'string'

where "string" is a sequence of characters (exactly as in a regular character string literal) is defined to be shorthand for the expression

    _national-character-set 'string'

where "national character set" is the name of the character set that the implementation has designated as the national one. *Note:* National (type N) character string literals can span multiple lines, just like other string literals; again, see Chapter 7 for the details.

If a character string literal is presented without an explicit accompanying character set specification, then *either* the characters of that literal must

---

*Well, perhaps we should point out one tiny possible problem. The term "character" is presumably intended to include what used to be called "nonprintable" characters (such as carriage return, backspace, etc.) as well as graphemes such as "A", "a", etc. However, the standard makes no special provisions for writing literal strings that include such characters.

all be SQL language characters (see Chapter 3) *or* the character set of the literal defaults to:

- The relevant module's default character set, if the literal appears within a module (see Section 19.8)
- The relevant schema's default character set, if the literal appears within a standalone CREATE SCHEMA (see Section 19.4)
- The default character set of the SQL-session, if the literal appears within a dynamically prepared SQL statement (see Chapter 20)

Second, to specify the *collation* of a character string literal, the expression "COLLATE collation" (where "collation" identifies the collation required) is written immediately following the literal itself. For example:

```
'How''s it going?' COLLATE CASE_INSENSITIVITY
```

If "COLLATE collation" is not explicitly specified, the literal inherits the default collation of its explicitly or implicitly specified character set.

Note: COLLATE is really a scalar builtin function (just like, e.g., SUBSTRING); the expression "literal COLLATE collation" is really just unorthodox syntax for a certain function reference. Since the COLLATE function is available for character string expressions in general, it is discussed further in Section 19.6 ("Scalar Operators and Functions"), which follows immediately.

19.6   SCALAR OPERATORS AND FUNCTIONS

Most of the scalar operators and functions (SUBSTRING, POSITION, etc.) that either operate on or yield character strings have already been discussed in Chapter 7 (Section 7.4), and the reader is referred to that chapter for details. Three rather specialized functions, TRANSLATE, CONVERT, and COLLATE (the last of which is very important), remain to be described.

TRANSLATE

TRANSLATE translates a specified character string, character by character, into another string of the same length, using a predefined *translation* that maps a *source* character set to a *target* character set. The source and target character sets can be the same, and the mapping can be many-to-one or one-to-one.

More precisely, the expression TRANSLATE (*string* USING *translation*), where *string* is any arbitrary character string expression, returns a string whose characters are determined from those of *string* according to *translation* and whose "coercibility" (see Section 19.7) is defined to be **implicit,** with collation *C,* where *C* is the default collation for the target character set. Here is an example: The expression

```
TRANSLATE ( 'A,B,C,D' USING PUNCTUATION_TO_SPACES )
```

will return the string

```
'A B C D'
```

(assuming that PUNCTUATION_TO_SPACES is a translation that translates commas and other punctuation marks into spaces and leaves other characters unchanged). The result string will have **implicit** coercibility, with collation the default collation for the target character set of the translation called PUNCTUATION_TO_SPACES. *Note:* The two character sets (source and target) are obviously the same, or at least very similar, in this particular example, but in general there is no reason why this need be so. Note too that the "fold" functions UPPER and LOWER discussed in Section 7.4 might well be regarded as special cases of TRANSLATE.

Translations are defined using CREATE TRANSLATION, which can be performed (like all other CREATE operations, except for CREATE SCHEMA itself) either standalone or as part of a CREATE SCHEMA operation. The syntax is:

```
translation-definition
    ::=  CREATE  TRANSLATION translation
             FOR   source-character-set
             TO    target-character-set
             FROM  translation-source
```

Here "translation" is the name of the new translation,* "source character set" and "target character set" are the names of existing character sets, and "translation source" specifies a many-to-one or one-to-one mapping of the source character set to the target character set. The "translation source" can be any of the following:

```
EXTERNAL ( 'external-translation' )
IDENTITY
translation
```

- *EXTERNAL:* "External translation" identifies some translation that is defined externally (e.g., in some national or international standard).

- *IDENTITY:* Every character in the repertoire of the source character set must occur in the repertoire of the target character set (i.e., the

---

*See the second footnote on page 275.

source repertoire must be a subset of the target repertoire). The translation maps each character in the source to its counterpart in the target.

- *Translation:* "Translation" is the name of some existing translation (previously defined by some CREATE TRANSLATION operation).

Observe that all translations (like all character sets and all collations) are, ultimately, defined in terms of some external specification.

Translations are destroyed via DROP TRANSLATION. The syntax is:

```
DROP TRANSLATION translation
```

As with DROP CHARACTER SET, there is an implicit RESTRICT option (neither CASCADE nor RESTRICT can be specified explicitly); that is, the DROP will fail if there are any outstanding references to the specified translation—*except* for references to the specified translation within a character set or collation definition, which will simply be deleted without warning.

CONVERT

CONVERT converts a specified character string, character by character, into another string of the same length, using a predefined *form-of-use conversion* that maps a *source* character set to a *target* character set. The source and target character sets must have the same character repertoire.

More precisely, the expression CONVERT (*string* USING *conversion*), where *string* is any arbitrary character string expression, returns a string whose characters are determined from those of *string* according to *conversion* and whose "coercibility" (see Section 19.7) is defined to be **implicit,** with collation *C,* where *C* is the default collation for the target character set.

Here is an example. Let EBCDIC_TO_ASCII be a conversion that converts from EBCDIC to ASCII. Then, for example, the expression

```
CONVERT ( TOUCHSTONE USING EBCDIC_TO_ASCII )
```

can be used to convert values (assumed to be EBCDIC strings) within the column called TOUCHSTONE to their ASCII equivalents.

Note: Actually this example is slightly fraudulent (despite the fact that essentially the same example is quoted within the standard itself!), because EBCDIC and ASCII do not have quite the same character repertoires and thus do not satisfy the prerequisites for CONVERT. Indeed, it seems to be quite difficult to find two genuinely distinct character sets that in fact do have exactly the same character repertoire. Furthermore, it is very unclear to this writer as to why CONVERT is provided anyway, since its functionality appears to be totally subsumed by that of TRANSLATE; i.e., there is nothing that can be done with CONVERT that cannot equally well be done with TRANSLATE.

Although a conversion name can include a schema name qualifier, the schema specified *must* be the Information Schema (see Chapter 21). The standard does not provide any "CREATE CONVERSION" or "DROP CONVERSION" operations, nor does it specify any privileges that might be needed to use conversions. Rather, all such matters are apparently implementation-defined.

COLLATE

The expression *"string* COLLATE *collation"* (where string is any arbitrary character string expression) returns a string that has the same value and character set as *string,* but with **explicit** coercibility (see Section 19.7) and with the specified collation. Here is an example (repeated from the end of the previous section):

```
'How''s it going?' COLLATE CASE_INSENSITIVITY
```

Note in particular that the COLLATE function can be used in a GROUP BY clause—provided the relevant grouping column is of type character string, of course—to specify a collation to be used for grouping purposes. It can also be used in an analogous manner in an ORDER BY clause to specify a collation to be used for ordering purposes.

19.7 ASSIGNMENTS AND COMPARISONS

In Chapter 7, we stated that assigning some *source* to some *target* was allowed if and only if *source* and *target* were "compatible" (i.e., had compatible data types). We further stated that "all character strings are compatible with one another." This latter statement now clearly requires some refinement. To be more specific, the definition of "compatibility" must be extended, for the purposes of assignment, to include the requirement that the source and target have *the same character set.* (Note, however, that the TRANSLATE function is available for translating strings from one character set to another. See Section 19.6 above.)

What about *comparisons?* In Chapter 7, we stated that any two character strings could be compared with one another; again, however, this statement now clearly requires some refinement. The general rule is as follows: Two character strings can be compared if and only if they have the same *collation* (or at least can be "coerced" to have the same collation)—which implies that they must have the same character set, since (as mentioned in Section 19.3) every collation is associated with precisely one character set, but has further implications besides.

The reason for the foregoing general rule is, of course, that character string comparisons must always be performed according to some specific collating sequence. Therefore, given a comparison of the form

```
comparand   operator   comparand
```

(where for the moment we assume "operator" to be any one of the usual dyadic comparison operators, and the two comparands are both character string expressions), we need a set of rules to determine the specific collation that will govern the comparison. In what follows, we explain the rules adopted in SQL for this purpose.

First we consider what it means to compare two strings under some given collation. Basically, such comparisons are performed character by character, pairwise, from left to right. If the strings are of equal length, then if every pairwise comparison yields "equal" under the specified collation, the character strings are equal; otherwise, the first pairwise comparison that does not yield "equal" determines the overall result. If the strings are of different lengths, then the rules depend on whether the collation was defined with PAD SPACE or NO PAD (refer back to Section 19.3 if you need to refresh your memory regarding these options):

- Under a PAD SPACE collation, the shorter is conceptually padded at the right with spaces to make it the same length as the longer before the comparison is done.

- Under a NO PAD collation, a string *s1* that is shorter than some other string *s2,* but "compares equal" to that leading substring of *s2* that is the same length as *s1,* is considered to be less than *s2* even if all remaining characters of *s2* are spaces.

Examples: Let X, Y, Z be strings (all having the same collation *C,* and therefore necessarily all drawn from the same character set) with values as indicated:

```
X    'ijk'      (length 3)
Y    'ijk  '    (length 5)
Z    'ij'       (length 2)
```

Furthermore, let collation *C* be such that the familiar "Latin" alphabetic ordering is preserved. Then the following table shows the results of the indicated comparisons under collation *C* (a) if PAD SPACE applies, (b) if NO PAD applies:

Comparison	PAD SPACE	NO PAD
X = Y	true	false
X < Y	false	true
X > Z	true	true

In the last example we have made the additional assumption that "space" precedes "k" under collation *C*.

Now we turn to the question of deciding what collation to use for a given comparison. That question, not surprisingly, turns on the question of what collations (if any) are associated with the two comparand strings; and *that* question leads us to the question of determining what collation (if any) is associated with the result of evaluating an arbitrary character string expression.

To this end, the standard introduces the notion of "coercibility." Every string has a *coercibility* property, the possible values of which are **explicit, implicit, coercible,** and **no collating sequence.** *Note:* It must be said immediately that the name "coercibility" offers little guidance to the property's intuitive meaning—especially since three of the four possible values of the "coercibility" property apparently mean that the string in question is *not* "coercible"! Furthermore, the connection between (a) the intuitive interpretation of the terms **explicit, implicit,** and so forth, on the one hand, and (b) their actual significance in the present context on the other, is tenuous at best. Accordingly, we will simply set the terms in **boldface** throughout in order to stress the fact that they are to be interpreted in a specialized and formal manner, and give only a *very* informal characterization of their intuitive meaning here. We will then follow that informal characterization with a more formal set of definitions.

First, then, the informal characterization. We remind the reader that for the comparison to be even feasible, the two comparands must at least have the same character set, and so we assume throughout the following discussion that such is indeed the case.

1. A string with **no collating sequence** can be a comparand only if the other comparand has an **explicit** collation (in which case the **explicit** collation governs the comparison). An example of a string with **no collating sequence** is the result produced by concatenating two strings, *s1* and *s2* say, where *s1* and *s2* are values from columns with different collating sequences. (Note, however, that a **no collating sequence** string can easily be given an **explicit** collation by means of the COLLATE function.) We ignore **no collating sequence** strings in paragraphs 2, 3, and 4 below.

2. A **coercible** string is always a legal comparand; its collation will be "coerced" to that of the other comparand, if necessary. (We will see below that if *both* comparands are **coercible,** they will necessarily have the same collation, so no "coercing" will be necessary.) An example of a **coercible** string would be a character string literal. We ignore **coercible** strings in paragraphs 3 and 4 below.

3. A string with an **implicit** collation can always be compared with one with an **explicit** collation (the **explicit** collation taking precedence); it can be compared with one with an **implicit** collation only if the two **implicit** collations are the same. Columns of base tables always have **implicit** collations. We ignore **implicit** strings in paragraph 4 below.

4. Finally, two strings both having an **explicit** collation can be compared only if the **explicit** collations are the same. The result of an invocation of the COLLATE function always has an **explicit** collation.

In all except the **no collating sequence** case, of course, we also need to specify what the associated collation *is*. Here then are the formal rules, specifying the character set, coercibility, and associated collation for the result of evaluating an arbitrary character string expression.

- The character set for a character string literal is determined as explained in Section 19.5 above. Such a string is **coercible,** with collation the default collation for its character set. *Note:* In fact, **coercible** *always* means that the corresponding collation is the default collation for the applicable character set.

- The character set for a character string parameter or host variable can be specified by means of an explicit CHARACTER SET specification on the parameter or host variable declaration (as in a column or domain definition). If that specification is omitted, then the default is implementation-defined. Such a string is **coercible,** with collation the default collation for its character set.

- The character set for a character string "placeholder" in dynamic SQL (denoted by a question mark—see Chapter 20) is the default character set for the SQL-session (again, see Chapter 20).* Such a string is **coercible,** with collation the default collation for its character set.

- Strings produced by CAST are **coercible,** with collation the default collation for their character set.

---

*The reader is warned that this statement is merely an educated guess on the part of the writers. The "placeholder" case is apparently overlooked in the standard.

- Strings in the same column of the same base table all have the same character set and collation, as explained in Section 19.4 above. The coercibility of such strings is **implicit,** with collation *C,* where *C* is the collation defined for the column in question.

- Strings derived from a single string (other than those returned by TRANSLATE, CONVERT, and COLLATE)—in particular, those returned by TRIM and SUBSTRING—inherit their character set, coercibility, and collation from that single string.

- Strings returned by TRANSLATE and CONVERT have the specified target character set, with **implicit** coercibility and with collation *C,* where *C* is the default collation for that character set.

- The coercibility of strings returned by COLLATE is **explicit,** with collation *C,* where *C* is the specified collation. The character set of such strings is inherited from the single string operand.

- The character set, coercibility, and collation of strings derived from two strings—which is to say, strings returned by *concatenation*—are determined as follows. Let *s1* and *s2* be the two operands, and let *sr* be the returned string. The operands must be drawn from the same character set, and *sr* inherits that character set. Furthermore:

  1. If *s1* and *s2* have the same coercibility and collation, *sr* inherits that coercibility and that collation.

  2. If one of *s1* and *s2* has an **implicit** collation *C* and the other is **coercible,** then *sr* has **implicit** collation *C*.

  3. If one of *s1* and *s2* has an **explicit** collation *C* and the other has an **implicit** collation, is **coercible,** or has **no collating sequence,** then *sr* has **explicit** collation *C*.

  4. If *s1* and *s2* have different **explicit** collations, the expression is illegal.

  5. In all other cases, the coercibility of *sr* is **no collating sequence.**

  Note: It follows from the foregoing rules that the only way in which a string that has **no collating sequence** can be generated from string(s) that do all have some collating sequence is by means of an expression of the form *s1||s2,* where *s1* and *s2* have the same character set (necessarily) but different collations, both of which are **implicit.** In all other cases, the result can have **no collating sequence** only if at least one of the operands has **no collating sequence.**

Now we can present the formal rules for dyadic comparisons. Let *s1* and *s2* be the two comparands (we remind the reader yet again that *s1* and *s2* must be drawn from the same character set).

- If either *s1* or *s2* has **no collating sequence,** the comparison is illegal unless the other has an **explicit** collation.

- Otherwise, if *s1* has an **explicit** collation and *s2* does not, or if *s1* and *s2* both have the same **explicit** collation, then the comparison is performed in accordance with that **explicit** collation. If *s1* and *s2* have different **explicit** collations, the comparison is illegal.

- Otherwise, if *s1* and *s2* both have the same **implicit** collation, then the comparison is performed in accordance with that **implicit** collation. If *s1* and *s2* have different **implicit** collations, the comparison is illegal.

- Otherwise, if *s1* has an **implicit** collation and *s2* is **coercible,** the comparison is performed in accordance with that **implicit** collation.

- Otherwise, *s1* and *s2* must both be **coercible,** and the comparison is performed in accordance with the default collation for the character set of *s1* and *s2*.

Finally, conditional expressions that are not just simple comparisons—expressions involving operators such as LIKE, MATCH, etc.—are defined in accordance with these same general principles. We omit the details here; they are tedious but straightforward, for the most part (but see the subsection entitled "Equal But Distinguishable" at the end of this section).

Some examples are in order. Let columns C1 and C2 contain strings from the same character set, and let CASE_INSENSITIVITY be the name of a collation that, among other things, equates lower-case letters from that character set to their upper-case counterparts. Then the expression

```
C1 = C2 COLLATE CASE_INSENSITIVITY
```

is interpreted to mean some "equals" comparison of the string returned by the (trivial) expression "C1" with that returned by the (less trivial) expression "C2 COLLATE CASE_INSENSITIVITY." This latter expression returns a string with **explicit** collation CASE_INSENSITIVITY; the other expression returns a string with some **implicit** collation. The comparison is therefore performed according to the **explicit** collation (which takes precedence).

Note, incidentally, that the comparisons

```
C1 COLLATE CASE_INSENSITIVITY = C2
```

and

```
C1 COLLATE CASE_INSENSITIVITY = C2 COLLATE CASE_INSENSITIVITY
```

are both equivalent to the first one above. By contrast, the comparison

```
C1 COLLATE CASE_INSENSITIVITY = C2 COLLATE CASE_SENSITIVITY

                        -- This is *** ILLEGAL *** !!!
```

is *** *ILLEGAL* ***, since the comparands have two different **explicit** collations. Similarly, the comparison

```
C1 = C2                 -- This is *** ILLEGAL *** !!!
```

is also *** *ILLEGAL* ***, unless the the two **implicit** collations for C1 and C2 happen to be the same.

Another example:

```
SP.PNO = 'P23'
```

Here the left-hand side is a column name, and has some **implicit** collation; the right-hand side is a literal, and so is **coercible.** The comparison is performed in accordance with the **implicit** collation (we are assuming that the character set for column SP.PNO is the same as the default character set that applies to the literal—see Section 19.5 above).

Finally, here is an example of the case in which both operands are **coercible:**

```
:THIS_VAR = 'P23'
```

Here the left-hand side is a host variable and the right-hand side is a literal (as in the previous example). The comparison is performed in accordance with the default collation for the character set of the comparands (we are assuming that the explicit or implicit character set for the host variable is the same as the default character set that applies to the literal—again, see Section 19.5 above).

In conclusion, we remark that the rules summarized above for determining coercibility, collation, how to evaluate comparisons, etc., are certainly quite complex, but they do mostly lead to what one would intuitively expect.

"Equal But Distinguishable"

We have seen that two characters from a given character set may be distinct and yet be treated as equal according to some collation. We have also seen that two strings may be distinct, inasmuch as they are of different lengths, and yet be treated as equal when they are compared (at least under PAD SPACE), because the shorter of the two is conceptually padded with spaces for the purposes of the comparison. Both of these facts imply that there exist pairs of character strings (*s1,s2*) such that *s1* is distinguishable from *s2* in some way, and yet the comparison "*s1 = s2*" evaluates to *true*. We will use the term "equal but distinguishable" to refer to such pairs of strings.

The kind of equality that is implied when operators such as MATCH, LIKE, UNIQUE, and NATURAL JOIN are used in connection with character strings is indeed "equal even if distinguishable." For example, suppose once again that CASE_INSENSITIVITY is a collation under which lower-case letters of the so-called Latin alphabet are treated as equal to their upper-case counterparts. Suppose also that PAD SPACE applies to this collation. Then, if the PNO columns of tables P and SP both use this collation, and if

```
'P23   '
```

and

```
'p23'
```

are PNO values in, respectively, some row of P and some row of SP, those two rows will be regarded as satisfying a referential constraint between the PNO columns of the two tables, despite the lower-case "p" and the missing trailing spaces in the foreign key value.

When operators such as UNION, INTERSECT, NATURAL JOIN, GROUP BY, and DISTINCT are used in table expressions, the system might have to decide which of two or more equal but distinguishable character string values is chosen for some column in some single result row. The standard does not lay down any rules to govern such arbitrary choices; rather, all such matters are stated to be implementation-dependent.

It follows from the foregoing that certain table expressions are *indeterminate* (the standard term is "possibly nondeterministic"), in the sense that the standard does not fully specify how they should be evaluated, and indeed they might give different results on different evaluations, even under the very same SQL-implementation against the very same SQL-data. For example, if table T has a character string column C with collation CASE_INSENSITIVITY, then the expression "SELECT MAX (C) FROM T" might return "ZZZ" on one evaluation and "zzz" on another, even if no change has occurred to table T in the interim.*

Here then are the rules.† A given table expression, *T* say, is considered by the standard to be *indeterminate* ("possibly nondeterministic") if and only if any of the following is true:

---

*One bizarre consequence of this lack of determinacy is that the result of (e.g.) a UNION might quite legally include a row that does not appear in either of the operands!

†These rules are essentially the ones given in the standard, but they do not seem to be either accurate or complete. See Appendix D.

- *T* is a *union* (without ALL), *intersection,* or *difference* (see Chapter 11, Section 11.4, for definitions of these terms), and the operand tables include a column of type character string.

- *T* is a *select-expression* (see Section 11.6), the select-list includes a select-item (*C* say) of type character string, and:

  (a) The select-list is preceded by the key word DISTINCT, *or*

  (b) *C* involves a MAX or MIN function reference, *or*

  (c) *T* directly includes a GROUP BY clause and *C* is one of the grouping columns.

- *T* is a *select-expression* that directly includes a HAVING clause and the conditional expression in that HAVING clause includes *either* a reference to a grouping column of type character string *or* a MAX or MIN function reference in which the argument is of type character string.

As mentioned in Chapter 14, the standard prohibits the appearance of such indeterminate expressions within integrity constraints, on the grounds that to permit them could cause certain updates to succeed or fail unpredictably.

19.8 CHARACTER SETS FOR IDENTIFIERS

We close this chapter with a brief discussion of the character sets used to write identifiers. *Note:* This discussion does not really belong in a chapter concerned with character *data,* but it does rely on some of the ideas introduced earlier in this chapter and would not have made much sense before.

First, we remind the reader that to specify the character set of a character string *literal,* we write the name of the character set, prefixed with an underscore, in front of the literal per se. For example:

```
_FRANCAIS 'Comment ça va?'
```

The same technique is used for identifiers—for example:

```
_FRANCAIS LIBERTÉ
```

or even

```
_FRANCAIS LIBERTÉ . _FRANCAIS ÉGALITÉ . _FRANCAIS FRATERNITÉ
```

(this latter might be the name of a base table, qualified by the name of the containing schema, qualified by the name of the containing catalog).

Now, we pointed out previously (in Section 19.5) that the name of the character set in our examples is FRANCAIS, not FRANÇAIS—i.e., it has a Latin C instead of Ç ("C-cedilla"). The reason is that, although (as we have just seen) identifiers in general can be written using any character set we please, an exception is made in the case of identifiers that represent character set names themselves; such identifiers are limited to the letters A–Z (or a–z), the digits 0–9, and underscores (see Section 3.4 for further discussion). And the reason for this limitation is the obvious problem of recursion that would otherwise arise. For example, if we wanted to name the character set in our example FRANÇAIS instead of FRANCAIS, then the "introducer" _FRANÇAIS would in principle have to be written an infinite number of times.*

> *Aside:* Note, however, that a character set name (and therefore an introducer) may be qualified by a schema name that may in turn be qualified by a catalog name, and schema names and catalog names are identifiers for which character sets *can* be specified. As a consequence, the standard, although it does avoid the need for an infinite *sequence* of "introducers," does not avoid the need for an infinite *nest* of them! *End of aside.*

If an identifier is written without an explicit character set name prefix (the normal case, of course), then *either* the characters in that identifier must all be SQL language characters (see Chapter 3) *or* the default character set for the relevant module is assumed by default.† The default character set for a given module is specified as part of the module definition. The syntax for a module definition, to repeat from Chapter 6, is:

```
module-definition
    ::=   MODULE [ module ] [ NAMES ARE character-set ]
          LANGUAGE { ADA | C | COBOL | FORTRAN | MUMPS
                   | PASCAL | PLI }
          [ SCHEMA schema ] [ AUTHORIZATION user ]
          [ temporary-table-definition-list ]
          module-element-list
```

The default character set for the module is specified by the NAMES ARE clause. If that clause is omitted, an implementation-defined character set that includes at least all characters used in the SQL language itself (see Section 3.1) is assumed by default. *Note:* An embedded SQL program can optionally include the analogous specification:

```
SQL NAMES ARE character-set
```

---

*In the interest of accuracy we should mention that the standard uses the term "introducer" to mean just the leading underscore. It does not seem to have a term for what we are calling an introducer, viz. the whole construct (underscore plus character set name).

†Unless the identifier appears within a standalone CREATE SCHEMA statement, in which case the default character set for the schema is assumed instead.

If this specification is omitted, an implementation-defined character set is assumed that (again) must include at least all characters used in the SQL language itself. *Note:* If an "SQL NAMES ARE . . ." specification is stated explicitly, then that specification must appear *within* an embedded SQL declare section, *before* any host variable declarations within that declare section, *without* an EXEC SQL prefix, and *without* a statement terminator.

20

Dynamic SQL

20.1 INTRODUCTION

It is customary when discussing the implementation of programming languages to distinguish between *compilers* and *interpreters*. A compiler requires each source program to be subjected to some kind of preparatory processing before it can be executed; the purpose of that preliminary *compilation step* is to produce an executable version of the program that can subsequently be run many times, thereby amortizing the cost of actually doing the compilation over many executions. An interpreter, on the other hand, requires no such preparatory step, but just executes the source program directly—in effect, by compiling each statement "on the fly" as it encounters it at run time.

Now, it is well known that, for performance reasons, compilation "ahead of time"—i.e., prior to run time—is the preferred approach in many situations (though by no means all). Certainly many current SQL products do use such an approach. Furthermore, the SQL standard does seem to assume that the implementation will indeed use such an approach, although to be fair it never states as much explicitly.*

---

*In fact it is at least arguable that the opposite is true, inasmuch as the standard does effectively provide for interpretive implementation through its "direct SQL" feature. However, direct SQL is very far from being computationally complete (i.e., it is quite inadequate for most applications), because it does not include anything in the way of traditional flow control constructs such as IF–THEN–ELSE or DO–WHILE.

The trouble is, however, there are some applications—typically "general-purpose" applications, such as ad hoc query utilities and database design tools—for which it is simply not possible to provide all of the information needed to do the compilation prior to run time. For example, consider a natural language query application that allows an end-user to enter queries expressed in (say) English and responds to those queries by retrieving data from an SQL database. It is obviously not feasible to "hard-code" every possible SQL statement that might ever be needed as part of the original application source code. Instead, therefore, the application must:

1. *Generate* the necessary SQL statements dynamically (i.e., at run time, on an "as needed" basis); then

2. *Compile* such statements dynamically, by invoking the SQL compiler at run time (again on an "as needed" basis); and finally

3. *Execute* the newly compiled statements as and when necessary.

We give a small PL/I example (accurate but unrealistically simple) in order to illustrate the foregoing process.

```
DCL SQLSOURCE CHAR VARYING (65000) ;

SQLSOURCE = 'DELETE FROM SP WHERE SP.QTY < 300' ;
EXEC SQL PREPARE SQLPREPPED FROM :SQLSOURCE ;
EXEC SQL EXECUTE SQLPREPPED ;
```

Explanation:

1. The name SQLSOURCE identifies a PL/I varying length character string variable in which the program will somehow construct the source form (i.e., character string representation) of some SQL statement—a DELETE statement, in our particular example.

2. The name SQLPREPPED, by contrast, identifies an *SQL* variable, not a PL/I variable, that will be used (conceptually) to hold the compiled form of the SQL statement whose source form is given in SQLSOURCE. *Note:* The names SQLSOURCE and SQLPREPPED are arbitrary, of course.

3. The assignment statement "SQLSOURCE = . . . ;" assigns to SQLSOURCE the source form of an SQL DELETE statement. In practice, of course, the process of constructing such a source statement is likely to be much more complex—perhaps involving the input and analysis of some request from the end-user, expressed in natural language or some other form more "user-friendly" than plain SQL, stark and unadorned.

4. The PREPARE statement then takes that source statement and "prepares" (i.e., compiles) it to produce an executable version, which it stores in SQLPREPPED.

5. Finally, the EXECUTE statement executes that SQLPREPPED version and thus causes the actual DELETE to occur. Feedback information from the DELETE (SQLSTATE value, etc.) is returned exactly as if the DELETE had been directly executed in the normal way.

Note, incidentally, that since it denotes an SQL variable, not a PL/I variable, the name SQLPREPPED does *not* have a colon prefix when it is referenced in the PREPARE and EXECUTE statements. Note too that such SQL variables are not explicitly declared.

Thus we see that the standard does provide a set of features—PREPARE, EXECUTE, etc.—to permit the writing of general-purpose applications. The features in question are referred to collectively as *dynamic SQL,* and are the subject of the present chapter. By contrast, all other aspects of the language are referred to as *static* SQL. *Note:* Actually, the term "static SQL" is neither defined nor used in the standard; nor need it be, though it is common parlance in SQL circles. It is sufficient to say just that there is SQL, and some part of SQL is a discrete "detachable" piece called dynamic SQL.*

There are a couple of further points that we might as well get out of the way before we start getting into too much detail:

- First, it goes without saying that the privileges needed to execute some "prepared" statement *S* are exactly the same as they would be if *S* were to be executed directly as part of static SQL.

- Second, as we shall see in Section 20.3, "prepared" statements come in two varieties, local and global. Local prepared statements are considered to belong to the module containing the relevant PREPARE statement. Global prepared statements, by contrast, are considered to belong to an implementation-defined "SQL-session module" that is distinct from all other modules currently existing in the same SQL-environment. (Actually, this remark concerning the SQL-session module seems to have little if any operational significance. Probably it was

---

*As we saw in Chapter 6, the standard includes a classification scheme for SQL statements, one category of which is *SQL dynamic statements*. The reader is warned, however, that this category does not include all of the statements that go to make up what most people would call dynamic SQL. Specifically, it does not include any cursor statements, not even those cursor statements that make use of the special facilities described in the present chapter. Instead, all cursor statements, static or dynamic, are classified simply as *SQL data statements*.

included in the standard purely so that there should be no exception to the general rule that SQL statements are *always,* at least conceptually, contained within some module,* as explained in Chapter 6.)

20.2   WHAT IS THE PROBLEM?

Dynamic SQL is remarkably complex, even by SQL standards. Before studying it in detail, therefore, it is as well to familiarize oneself with the special problems that are faced by general-purpose application developers, for otherwise the rationale for many of the facilities provided will not be at all obvious. In this section, therefore, we describe some of those problems briefly, and sketch the relevant facilities of dynamic SQL in each case.

- As we have already seen, a general-purpose application might need to generate SQL statements at run time. An example might be an interactive database creation utility that allows its end-user to enter SQL data definition statements (e.g., CREATE TABLE, CREATE VIEW) from a workstation or terminal. This utility cannot be written in static SQL, because the SQL statements to be executed are not known until run time.

  Dynamic SQL's EXECUTE IMMEDIATE statement[†] addresses this problem (see Section 20.3).

- Consider an ad hoc query utility that allows end-users to develop and submit queries (not necessarily in SQL per se) and to display the results of those queries as reports or charts. In order to display the result of a given query, the utility needs to find out at run time how many columns there are in that result; for each such column, it also needs to find out the name, the data type, and many other things.

  Dynamic SQL includes an elaborate *descriptor* mechanism to address this problem (see Section 20.4). *Note:* Please observe that the descriptors we are talking about here are nothing to do with the descriptors found in schemas, whose purpose is to describe objects such as base tables, views, domains, constraints, etc., as explained in Chapter 4. Please observe too that we will use the term "descriptor" throughout this chapter to refer to the dynamic SQL construct, not the schema construct.

---

*Except possibly for certain CREATE SCHEMA statements, as explained in Chapter 4.

[†]EXECUTE IMMEDIATE effectively combines the functions of PREPARE and EXECUTE into a single operation, loosely speaking.

■   Suppose the ad hoc query utility mentioned above also allows the user
to save queries for subsequent reuse. Suppose further that the user is
allowed to save a *generic form* of some common query, implying that
certain *arguments* or parameter values will have to be provided every
time the query is executed. For example, suppose we frequently need
to find out about the suppliers in some given city. When that city is
Paris, the SQL statement that must be executed—i.e., the *internal form*
of the query, inside the query utility—is:

```
SELECT  S.SNO, S.SNAME, S.STATUS
FROM    S
WHERE   S.CITY = 'Paris'
```

In static SQL, a generic form of this SQL statement might look
something like this:

```
SELECT  S.SNO, S.SNAME, S.STATUS
FROM    S
WHERE   S.CITY = :CITY_PARAM
```

Note: CITY_PARAM here is either a parameter or a host variable,
depending on whether we are using the module language or embedded
SQL. To fix our ideas, we assume the latter case.

Remember, however, that we are talking about *dynamic* SQL. A
moment's thought will reveal why host variables cannot be used in the
same way in dynamic SQL. For one thing, it is not known at compilation time how many such variables will be needed, nor what data type
they should be; for another, host variables are declared in the application program itself, and their names are not known to the end-user
(which would thus make it difficult for the application to prompt for
arguments at run time). We therefore need some other way in dynamic
SQL to mark places to be filled at run time and to supply such run-
time arguments.

We have already seen that dynamic SQL provides the **PREPARE**
statement for compiling SQL statements at run time. Furthermore,
those SQL statements can include *placeholders*—i.e., they can represent *generic* statements. When such generic statements are subsequently
executed, there are facilities for providing arguments to be substituted
for the placeholders. The same descriptor interface as that mentioned
above (for describing the columns of a query result to the application)
is used to describe such placeholders, or *parameters,* to the system.
Again, see Section 20.4 for detailed discussion. *Note:* "Parameters" is
the standard term. However, such parameters are nothing to do with
the parameters of the module language, discussed in Chapter 6. In the
hope of avoiding confusion, therefore, we will (throughout the remain-

der of this chapter) always use "placeholders" for the dynamic SQL construct, reserving "parameters" for the module language construct.

▪ In dynamic SQL, as in static SQL, multiple-row access is done by means of a cursor, using OPEN, FETCH, and CLOSE operations (possibly UPDATE and DELETE CURRENT operations too). In static SQL, the DECLARE CURSOR statement includes a *cursor specification* that, among other things, defines the table to be accessed. As a reminder, here is the syntax of "cursor specification," repeated from Chapter 10:

```
    table-expression
[ ORDER BY order-item-commalist ]
[ FOR { READ ONLY | UPDATE [ OF column-commalist ] } ]
```

There is a counterpart of DECLARE CURSOR in dynamic SQL; however, it involves a *level of indirection* between the cursor declaration per se and the cursor specification portion, so that this latter portion can be the subject of a separate PREPARE and can vary from one opening of the cursor to the next. See Section 20.5.

▪ But even a dynamic variant of DECLARE CURSOR is inadequate if the application does not know *how many* cursors it will be required to have open concurrently during any particular invocation. For example, the ad hoc query utility referred to above, with the aid of a modern windowing system, might want to support the concurrent display of an arbitrary number of query results, each in its own window.

Dynamic SQL therefore provides an ALLOCATE CURSOR statement, which effectively supports the generation of new cursors "on the fly." Again, see Section 20.5.

▪ In static SQL, there are rules for determining the missing high-level qualifiers (catalog name and schema name) for object references when no such qualifiers are specified explicitly. Similarly, there is a rule for determining the relevant character set for identifiers and character string literals when no such character set is specified explicitly. All of these rules take effect at compilation time. Partly for that reason, however, the rules are, typically, inappropriate for applications that use dynamic SQL, because such applications are, typically, meant for use with a multiplicity of different databases in a multiplicity of different environments. Therefore, dynamic SQL includes special statements to specify the default catalog name, schema name, and character set name for an SQL-session, and it is these *session* defaults that are used in the dynamic SQL context. The statements in question are SET CATALOG, SET SCHEMA, and SET NAMES. See Section 20.6.

This concludes our brief survey of dynamic SQL and the kinds of problems it is intended to solve. Without further ado, let us now begin our detailed examination of the various features and facilities that dynamic SQL provides.

20.3   STATEMENT PREPARATION AND EXECUTION

In this section we discuss the basic PREPARE and EXECUTE operations and various associated facilities. We begin with the "shorthand" form EXECUTE IMMEDIATE.

EXECUTE IMMEDIATE

A given SQL statement can be "executed immediately"—i.e., it can be the subject of an EXECUTE IMMEDIATE statement—provided that:

- It does not contain any placeholders.

- It is *preparable* (we will define this latter term precisely in a moment; here we merely note that, e.g., EXECUTE IMMEDIATE itself is *not* preparable).

- It does not retrieve any data; specifically, it is not a single-row SELECT statement, nor more generally a table expression of any kind (refer to Chapter 11 if you need to refresh your memory regarding table expressions). *Note:* Although table expressions in general are not normally regarded as statements per se, they are nevertheless preparable, as we shall see. But they cannot be the subject of an EXECUTE IMMEDIATE, for essentially the same reason that a multiple-row SELECT cannot be executed directly in embedded SQL or the module language.

Here then is the syntax of EXECUTE IMMEDIATE:

```
EXECUTE IMMEDIATE source-statement-container
```

"Source statement container" here is a parameter or host variable, of type character string, that contains the source form of the SQL statement to be executed. Note that the source statement in question must not include an EXEC SQL prefix or a statement terminator. However, the parameter or host variable does require a colon prefix (as always).

Here is an example. Suppose again (as in the first of the examples in Section 20.2) that we have an interactive database creation utility that allows its end-user to enter SQL data definition statements (CREATE TABLE, etc.) from the terminal. If that utility is written in embedded SQL, it might look something like this:

```
EXEC SQL BEGIN DECLARE SECTION ;

   /* variable to contain SQL statement (source form) */

   DCL SQLSOURCE CHAR VARYING (65000) ;

   /* SQL return code variable */

   DCL SQLSTATE CHAR (5) ;

EXEC SQL END DECLARE SECTION ;

/* code to execute SQL statements entered by end-user */

GET LIST ( SQLSOURCE ) ;
DO WHILE ( SQLSOURCE ¬= '' ) ;
   EXEC SQL EXECUTE IMMEDIATE :SQLSOURCE ;
   PUT SKIP LIST ( 'Return code:', SQLSTATE ) ;
   GET LIST ( SQLSOURCE ) ;
END ;
```

This code executes SQL statements submitted from the terminal until the
end-user enters an empty line.

Note: For definiteness, all examples in this chapter will be shown in
embedded SQL rather than the module language. Also, for brevity we will
henceforth omit the BEGIN and END DECLARE SECTION statements.
We will, however, *not* omit the EXEC SQL prefixes, because it is desirable
to distinguish clearly between statements of dynamic SQL per se and statements of the host language (PL/I in our examples).

PREPARE

As explained in Section 20.1, the basic purpose of PREPARE is to "prepare" some specified SQL statement for execution—i.e., to produce a
"prepared" (or *object* or *compiled* or *executable* or, very informally,
"prepped") form of that specified SQL statement. As indicated by the example in that section, there must be a *name* (an identifier) by which the
prepared form of the statement can be referenced—indirectly, please note—
in subsequent EXECUTE statements and elsewhere. This name, which
must be supplied by the user, can be specified either directly or indirectly.
Accordingly, there are two distinct PREPARE formats. The first is:

```
PREPARE prepped-statement-container
        FROM source-statement-container
```

Here "source statement container" is as for EXECUTE IMMEDIATE, and
"prepped statement container" is the name of an SQL variable.* The state-

---

*"SQL variable" is not an official standard term. Moreover, what we are here (accurately)
referring to as the name of that variable is referred to in the standard as the (user-supplied)
name of the *prepared statement* instead. But it seems to this writer that this latter nomenclature

ment in "source statement container" is compiled and the compiled form is placed in the SQL variable denoted by "prepped statement container." Here is an example (repeated from Section 20.1):

```
EXEC SQL PREPARE SQLPREPPED FROM :SQLSOURCE ;
```

Note that there is no explicit declaration of the SQL variable SQLPREPPED. Note too that if that same SQL variable has already been specified in some previous PREPARE, then the new PREPARE effectively overwrites the previous value of that variable (i.e., the result of the previous PREPARE is lost).

Now, in the foregoing example, the name SQLPREPPED is clearly "hard-coded" into the PREPARE statement. Requiring such names always to be hard-coded in this way would lead to an undesirable loss of flexibility and would make certain applications very awkward to write. This is the justification for the second format of PREPARE:

```
PREPARE prepped-statement-name-container
        FROM source-statement-container
```

Here "source statement container" is as before, and "prepped statement name container" is a parameter or host variable (with a colon prefix) of type character string, with octet length not greater than 128, whose *value* is an identifier. In other words, before executing the PREPARE, the user must have placed in "prepped statement name container" the (user-generated) *name* of an "SQL variable".* The PREPARE then causes the statement in "source statement container" to be compiled and the compiled form placed in that SQL variable. Again, if that SQL variable already contains the compiled form of some SQL statement, then the new PREPARE effectively overwrites the previous value of that variable (i.e., the previously compiled statement is lost).

Here is an example of the second PREPARE format:

```
SQLPREPPEDNAME = 'SQL_STMT' || N ;

EXEC SQL PREPARE :SQLPREPPEDNAME FROM :SQLSOURCE ;
```

---

is unnecessarily confusing, because it skips a significant level of indirection. It is desperately important to preserve conceptual clarity wherever possible, above all in a context that is as inherently complex as dynamic SQL is. In this chapter, therefore, we will usually mention the standard nomenclature in passing, but we will use our own.

*The standard nomenclature is again very bad in this area—it actually refers to the "prepped statement name container" parameter or host variable as a *statement* per se! That is, it actually uses the term "statement name" (more precisely, "*extended* statement name," which seems even less appropriate) to mean the name of the specified parameter or host variable, instead of the value of that parameter or host variable. In our opinion, this is not just confusing, it is *confused*. We will stay with our own terminology.

Aside: The "prepped statement name container" in the second format of PREPARE can optionally include a LOCAL or GLOBAL prefix— for example:

```
EXEC SQL PREPARE LOCAL :SQLPREPPEDNAME FROM :SQLSOURCE ;
```

LOCAL (which is the default) means the scope of the SQL variable name given in "prepped statement name container" is the containing module; GLOBAL means it is the current SQL-session. Every reference to "prepped statement name container" in subsequent EXECUTE statements and elsewhere must also specify LOCAL or GLOBAL, as appropriate. For simplicity, we ignore the GLOBAL possibility throughout the remainder of this chapter, thus effectively treating all SQL variable names (implicitly) as LOCAL. *End of aside.*

Preparable Statements

We turn now to the definition of what it means for a statement to be preparable. First, such a statement cannot include any comments, host variables, or parameters. Second, it must be one of the following:

- *SQL data statements* (also referred to in this book as *data manipulation statements*):

  ```
  single-row SELECT (without an INTO clause)
  INSERT, searched UPDATE, searched DELETE
  DECLARE CURSOR (cursor specification portion only)
  positioned UPDATE, positioned DELETE
  ```

  Note: The preparable forms of UPDATE and DELETE CURRENT differ slightly from their static SQL counterparts. See Section 20.5, later.

- *SQL schema statements* (also referred to in this book as *data definition statements*, except for CREATE and DROP ASSERTION and GRANT and REVOKE):

  ```
  CREATE SCHEMA, DROP SCHEMA
  CREATE DOMAIN, ALTER DOMAIN, DROP DOMAIN
  CREATE TABLE, ALTER TABLE, DROP TABLE
  CREATE VIEW, DROP VIEW
  CREATE CHARACTER SET, DROP CHARACTER SET
  CREATE COLLATION, DROP COLLATION
  CREATE TRANSLATION, DROP TRANSLATION
  CREATE ASSERTION, DROP ASSERTION
  GRANT, REVOKE
  ```

- *SQL transaction statements*:

  ```
  SET TRANSACTION
  SET CONSTRAINTS
  COMMIT, ROLLBACK
  ```

- *SQL session statements*:

```
SET SESSION AUTHORIZATION
SET CATALOG
SET SCHEMA
SET TIME ZONE
SET NAMES
```

- *Other statements* (as defined by the implementation)

Placeholders

A preparable statement is permitted to include any number of *placeholders,* each denoted in the source form of the statement by a question mark ("?"). The placeholders must be replaced by actual argument values when the prepared version is later executed. Here is an example:

```
SQLSOURCE = 'DELETE FROM SP WHERE SP.QTY > ? AND SP.QTY < ?' ;

EXEC SQL PREPARE SQLPREPPED FROM :SQLSOURCE ;

LOW = 100 ;
HIGH = 300 ;

EXEC SQL EXECUTE SQLPREPPED USING :LOW, :HIGH ;
```

The effect of this example is to delete all shipments with a quantity in the indicated range. *Note:* We will have a lot more to say about the EXECUTE . . . USING statement later in this section—also in Section 20.4, later.

Placeholders (i.e., question marks) are permitted only where *literals* are permitted. Note in particular, therefore, that they cannot be used to represent *names* (of tables, columns, etc.). Furthermore, they are subject to the following dazzling array of additional prohibitions:*

- They cannot be "select items," i.e., elements of a select-list. Thus, e.g., the following is illegal:

```
SELECT ?, ?, ?                     -- This is *** ILLEGAL *** !!!
FROM    ...
```

The following, by contrast, is legal:

```
SELECT 0 + ?, 0 + ?, 0 + ?
FROM    ...
```

The reason is, of course, that the prefix "0 +" ensures that the placeholder (question mark) must be of type numeric. Concatenation with

---

*The general intent of these prohibitions is to ensure that placeholders can appear only in positions where the data type of the corresponding argument can be determined at PREPARE time. Note, however, that "CAST (? AS data-type)" is *always* legal, and can effectively be used to specify a placeholder of any desired data type. For example, "SELECT ? AS X" is not legal, but "SELECT CAST (? AS REAL) AS X" is legal.

an empty bit or character string could be used in a like manner to ensure that a given placeholder is of type BIT or CHARACTER.

- They cannot appear as the operand of a monadic operator. Thus, e.g., the scalar expression "+ ?" is illegal. (The expression "0 + ?", by contrast, is legal.)

- They cannot appear as both operands of a dyadic operator. Thus, e.g., the scalar expressions "? + ?" and "?||?" are both illegal.

- They cannot appear as both operands of a comparison operator. Thus, e.g., the following is illegal:

```
SELECT *
FROM    ...
WHERE   ? = ?                        -- This is *** ILLEGAL *** !!!
```

(but if we replaced either question mark by "0 + ?" the comparison would then be legal).

This rule extends to corresponding components of rows, so that a comparison such as "(X,?) > (?,Y)" is legal, but "(X,?) > (Y,?)" is not. Furthermore, "((1,?),(2,?))" is not a valid table constructor,* because it has placeholders in the second column position in both rows.

- They cannot appear as both operands in POSITION.

- They cannot appear as the sole operand in UPPER or LOWER.

- They cannot appear as the first operand in SUBSTRING.

- They cannot appear as both second and third operand in TRIM.

- They cannot appear as the FROM operand in EXTRACT.

- They cannot appear as the first operand in TRANSLATE, CONVERT, or COLLATE.

- They cannot appear as the argument to an aggregate function such as MAX.

- They cannot appear as the left-hand operand (or any component of the left-hand operand) of IS [NOT] NULL.

- Neither operand of OVERLAPS can have a placeholder as its second component.

---

*Except in the special case where it represents the source table expression in an INSERT statement.

- The first operand of COALESCE cannot be a placeholder; neither can the first WHEN operand of a CASE expression, nor can either operand of NULLIF.

DEALLOCATE PREPARE

The purpose of DEALLOCATE PREPARE is to "DROP" a previously prepared statement. There are two formats, corresponding to the two formats of PREPARE:

```
DEALLOCATE PREPARE { prepped-statement-container |
                     prepped-statement-name-container }
```

"Prepped statement container" and "prepped statement name container" are as for PREPARE. Note that, as already suggested under the discussion of PREPARE above, an appropriate DEALLOCATE PREPARE is executed automatically if PREPARE specifies an SQL variable (either directly or indirectly) that already contains a previously prepared statement.

It is worth mentioning that the standard explicitly permits—but does not require—the implementation to "DROP" existing prepared statements automatically at COMMIT (and ROLLBACK). As the standard puts it, not very elegantly: "The validity of [a prepared statement] in an SQL-transaction different from the one in which the statement was prepared is implementation-dependent."

EXECUTE

The general form of the EXECUTE statement is:

```
EXECUTE { prepped-statement-container |
          prepped-statement-name-container }
                    [ INTO places ] [ USING arguments ]
```

As the syntax suggests, the first operand is either an SQL variable that contains a prepared statement, or a parameter or host variable that contains the name of an SQL variable that in turn contains such a prepared statement. The prepared statement thus specified (either directly or indirectly) is executed. Furthermore:

- If the statement to be executed is a single-row SELECT statement, an INTO clause must be specified; "places" (see below) indicates where the retrieved data is to be placed.

- If the statement to be executed includes any placeholders, a USING clause must be specified; "arguments" (see below) provides the necessary argument values to fill the gaps corresponding to those placeholders.

Note: Although (as previously indicated) cursor specifications are preparable, they cannot be the object of an EXECUTE statement. Instead, FETCH and other cursor operations have to be used, more or less as in static SQL, in order to access the data corresponding to a prepared cursor specification. See Section 20.5, later.

The "places" operand takes one of the following two forms:

```
target-commalist | SQL DESCRIPTOR descriptor
```

In the first format, each "target" is a parameter or host variable, optionally accompanied by an indicator parameter or host variable, exactly as described in Chapter 16; there must be exactly one target for each item in the select-list of the single-row SELECT, and the target identified by the ith entry in the target-commalist corresponds to the ith select-item. The second format is intended for use when (e.g.) the number of select-items is not known at compilation time. We defer further discussion of this case to Section 20.4 below.

The "arguments" operand also has two possible formats:

```
argument-commalist | SQL DESCRIPTOR descriptor
```

In the first format, each "argument" is a parameter or host variable, optionally accompanied by an indicator parameter or host variable, again as described in Chapter 16; there must be exactly one argument for each placeholder in the source form of the prepared statement, and the argument identified by the ith entry in the argument-commalist corresponds to the ith placeholder in that statement as written. The second format is intended for use when (e.g.) the number of arguments is not known at compilation time; again, we defer further discussion of this case to Section 20.4 below.

Let us revise our example from the subsection "Placeholders" above. First, we repeat from that subsection the source form of the statement to be prepared and the corresponding PREPARE:

```
SQLSOURCE = 'DELETE FROM SP WHERE SP.QTY > ? AND SP.QTY < ?' ;
EXEC SQL PREPARE SQLPREPPED FROM :SQLSOURCE ;
```

Here now is a possible execution sequence, a little more complete and more realistic than the one we showed previously:

```
DCL LOW  FIXED DECIMAL (5) ;
DCL HIGH FIXED DECIMAL (5) ;

/* obtain values for the arguments */

GET LIST ( LOW, HIGH ) ;

/* now perform the DELETE */

EXEC SQL EXECUTE SQLPREPPED USING :LOW, :HIGH ;
```

As already mentioned, the commalist form, whether it be for "places" or for "arguments," is inappropriate in cases where the number of result columns or placeholders (or their data types) cannot be determined at compilation time. It is for this reason that the alternative "SQL DESCRIPTOR" formats are provided. The "descriptor" operand of those formats identifies something called an *SQL descriptor area,* and that brings us to a complex subject, which we discuss in the next section.

20.4 SQL DESCRIPTOR AREAS

Overview

We begin by considering a simple example. Suppose we have an application that needs to prepare and execute a single-row SELECT statement, the details of which will not be known until run time. The dynamic facilities discussed so far are inadequate to handle this case; the reason is, of course, that SELECT is different from other SQL statements, in that it returns data to the application (other statements return feedback information only).

Clearly, the application needs to know something about the data values to be retrieved in order to be able to process those values properly. To be more specific, it needs to know at least how many scalar values there will be in the result row, and also what the data types, lengths, precisions, etc. (as applicable) of those values will be. If the SELECT is generated dynamically, it will usually not be possible for the application to know this information in advance; therefore, it must obtain the information dynamically. SQL descriptor areas are provided to address such requirements. In outline, the procedure the application must go through is as follows.

1. First, it creates an SQL descriptor area, *xyz* say, using ALLOCATE DESCRIPTOR. This area can be thought of as consisting of a list or one-dimensional array of individual *item* descriptors—one for each of the values in the result row that will be produced when the single-row SELECT is actually executed—together with a count of the number of entries (i.e., individual item descriptors) in that array. *Note:* ALLOCATE DESCRIPTOR does not *populate* the descriptor area, it merely allocates storage for it. However, it is necessary to assume that the application does at least know an upper bound for the number of values to be expected in the result row, in order to be able to allocate a descriptor area of adequate capacity.

2. Next, it builds and prepares the single-row SELECT. Remember from Section 20.3 that this SELECT will *not* include an INTO clause.

3. It then executes a DESCRIBE OUTPUT . . . USING SQL

DESCRIPTOR *xyz* against the prepared single-row SELECT. The effect of this statement is to populate the descriptor area *xyz*; i.e., it places a count of the number of values in the result row into *xyz*, and a description of the *i*th value in the result row (data type, etc.) into the *i*th item descriptor within *xyz*.

4. It then executes the prepared single-row SELECT by means of an EXECUTE statement of the form EXECUTE . . . INTO SQL DESCRIPTOR *xyz*. The *i*th value in the SELECTed row is retrieved into the *i*th item descriptor within *xyz*.

5. It uses GET DESCRIPTOR operations repeatedly against *xyz* to discover the data type, length, etc., of the retrieved values and to transfer such values, one at a time, from *xyz* to other chosen locations as desired.

So much for our introductory example. To complete this brief overview, here is a summary list of the SQL statements having to do with SQL descriptor areas:

```
ALLOCATE DESCRIPTOR, DEALLOCATE DESCRIPTOR
GET DESCRIPTOR, SET DESCRIPTOR
DESCRIBE
```

In addition, the EXECUTE, dynamic OPEN, and dynamic FETCH statements can all include clauses of the form "INTO (or USING) SQL DESCRIPTOR . . . " (see Section 20.5 for a description of the dynamic OPEN and FETCH statements). We remark that the apparently redundant qualifier "SQL" in "SQL DESCRIPTOR" is *required* in the context of an INTO or USING clause, and is *prohibited* in all other contexts (such as, e.g., ALLOCATE DESCRIPTOR). We remark also that the key word DESCRIPTOR refers to the entire SQL descriptor area in some contexts (e.g., ALLOCATE DESCRIPTOR), but to an individual item descriptor in others (e.g., GET DESCRIPTOR).

SQLDAs

As already indicated, an SQL descriptor area—SQLDA for short—can be thought of as consisting of a *count,* together with a list or one-dimensional *array* of individual item descriptors, all item descriptors having the same (composite) structure. Each item descriptor describes either

- A column of the table that results from executing some prepared statement (in the case of "places"), or

- An argument to replace some placeholder in some prepared statement (in the case of "arguments").

Aside: "SQLDA" is a useful abbreviation, but it is not an official standard term. Note clearly, moreover, that several SQL products do already support some kind of SQLDA, and even refer to it by that name, but those SQLDAs are quite definitely not the same as the "SQLDA" defined in the standard. In particular, the standard SQLDA is "encapsulated," whereas the SQLDAs in today's products are typically not. This encapsulation provides several advantages:

1. It conceals the differences among different products.

2. It provides explicit facilities for allocating and deallocating the necessary SQLDA storage.

3. It also provides explicit facilities for fetching and storing data values.

Points 2 and 3 taken together imply (among other things) that the facilities of dynamic SQL can be used with host languages such as COBOL and FORTRAN that do not support dynamic storage allocation or pointers. *End of aside.*

To return to the main thread of our discussion: Now, although it is helpful to think in terms of the aforementioned array of item descriptors, it is important to understand that the user is not concerned with the actual structure of an SQLDA, because all SQLDA access is by means of special SQL statements (e.g., GET and SET DESCRIPTOR) that are deliberately designed to conceal such details from the user. In other words—as indicated in the previous paragraph—SQLDAs are *encapsulated:* Their internal structure is not visible to the user, and is not explicitly specified in the standard.

Each item descriptor within an SQLDA consists of a number of named elements, each of which represents some particular aspect of the "place" or "argument" described by the item descriptor in question. We list below some of the more important of these elements (together with their data type in each case); for a complete list, the reader is referred to the official standard. Note that not all elements have meaning in all contexts.

```
NAME                    character string
UNNAMED                 exact numeric with scale 0
TYPE                    exact numeric with scale 0
LENGTH                  exact numeric with scale 0
RETURNED_LENGTH         exact numeric with scale 0
RETURNED_OCTET_LENGTH   exact numeric with scale 0
PRECISION               exact numeric with scale 0
SCALE                   exact numeric with scale 0
DATA                    (depends on TYPE, LENGTH, etc.)
INDICATOR               exact numeric with scale 0
```

Note the DATA element, which is used to contain an actual scalar value (e.g., a retrieved value, if the item descriptor is part of a "places" SQLDA).

If the INDICATOR value is negative, the DATA value is undefined ("null"). Note also the UNNAMED element, which is set to 1 if the NAME value is implementation-dependent (loosely, if the corresponding column is unnamed).

ALLOCATE DESCRIPTOR

The syntax of ALLOCATE DESCRIPTOR is:

```
ALLOCATE DESCRIPTOR descriptor [ WITH MAX occurrences ]
```

Here (a) "descriptor" is a literal, parameter, or host variable—*not* an identifier, please note!*—of type character string, with octet length not greater than 128, whose *value* is an identifier; (b) "occurrences" is a literal, parameter, or host variable of type exact numeric with scale 0, whose value is a positive integer. An SQLDA is created with the value of "descriptor" as its name, of sufficient size to accommodate at least M item descriptors, where M is the value of "occurrences." If "WITH MAX occurrences" is omitted, an implementation-defined value (at least 1) is assumed for M.

Here is an example:

```
EXEC SQL ALLOCATE DESCRIPTOR 'SPIDA' WITH MAX 1000
```

If an SQLDA with the name SPIDA ("suppliers-and-parts information descriptor area") already exists, an exception is raised. Contrast the situation with PREPARE: If an SQL variable is reused (either directly or indirectly) in PREPARE, a DEALLOCATE PREPARE is performed implicitly to destroy the prepared statement contained in that variable.

> *Aside:* The "descriptor" specification in ALLOCATE DESCRIPTOR (like the "prepped statement name container" specification in the second format of PREPARE) can optionally include a LOCAL or GLOBAL prefix—for example:

```
EXEC SQL ALLOCATE DESCRIPTOR LOCAL 'SPIDA' WITH MAX 1000
```

> The significance is analogous: LOCAL (the default) means the scope of the SQLDA name is the containing module, GLOBAL means it is

---

*The reason it is not an identifier is, of course, the added flexibility that accrues from the possibility of using a parameter or host variable. Note, however, that the fact that it is not an identifier means that we are flouting our own syntax conventions here. In Chapter 3 we said that if *xyz* is an SQL object type, then in syntax rules the syntactic category *xyz* would stand for the *name* of an object of that type, thus writing, e.g., "CREATE TABLE *table*," where *table* stands for the name of some base table. But "descriptor" above does not stand for the name of a descriptor, it stands for a literal or the name of a parameter or the name of a host variable, whose *value* is that descriptor name.

the current SQL-session, and all subsequent references to "descriptor" in (e.g.) DESCRIBE statements must also specify LOCAL or GLOBAL, whichever is appropriate. For simplicity, we ignore the GLOBAL possibility throughout the remainder of this chapter. *End of aside.*

Of course, ALLOCATE DESCRIPTOR does not *populate* the newly created SQLDA; on the contrary, every element of every individual item descriptor is initially undefined. There are several different ways of populating a given SQLDA, for example the SQLDA called SPIDA in our example:

1. We can specify

   ```
   INTO SQL DESCRIPTOR 'SPIDA'
   ```

   in an EXECUTE statement (in which case the prepared statement that is being executed must be a single-row SELECT). This case has already been discussed briefly in the "Overview" subsection above.

2. We can specify

   ```
   INTO SQL DESCRIPTOR 'SPIDA'
   ```

   in a dynamic FETCH statement. See Section 20.5 for further discussion of this case.

3. We can specify

   ```
   USING SQL DESCRIPTOR 'SPIDA'
   ```

   in a DESCRIBE INPUT or DESCRIBE OUTPUT statement. This is the recommended method for the most highly generalized type of application. We describe DESCRIBE in the subsection "DESCRIBE" below.

4. We can execute one or more statements of the form

   ```
   SET DESCRIPTOR 'SPIDA' ...
   ```

   Each such statement will assign values to elements within *a single item descriptor* within SQLDA. Note, therefore, that one difference between SET DESCRIPTOR and DESCRIBE is that DESCRIBE populates the entire SQLDA en bloc, whereas SET DESCRIPTOR populates only a single item descriptor (and very likely only portions of that descriptor, at that). We describe SET DESCRIPTOR in the subsection "SET DESCRIPTOR" at the end of the present section.

Before we go on to explain any of these methods in detail, however, let us first dispose of DEALLOCATE DESCRIPTOR.

DEALLOCATE DESCRIPTOR

If ALLOCATE DESCRIPTOR is thought of as "CREATE SQLDA"—which is effectively what it is—then DEALLOCATE DESCRIPTOR is the corresponding DROP. The syntax is:

```
DEALLOCATE DESCRIPTOR descriptor
```

"Descriptor" here is exactly as for ALLOCATE DESCRIPTOR.

DESCRIBE

DESCRIBE causes the system to "describe" some specified prepared statement—i.e., to place descriptor information for that prepared statement into some specified SQL descriptor area. There are two formats, DESCRIBE INPUT and DESCRIBE OUTPUT; DESCRIBE INPUT is for an "arguments" area, DESCRIBE OUTPUT is for a "places" area (and thus the terms INPUT and OUTPUT are to be interpreted from the system's point of view—"arguments" are input *to* the system, and "places" are where output *from* the system is to go).

Here first is the syntax of DESCRIBE INPUT:

```
DESCRIBE INPUT { prepped-statement-container |
                 prepped-statement-name-container }
                    USING SQL DESCRIPTOR descriptor
```

"Prepped statement container" and "prepped statement name container" are as for PREPARE (as usual); whichever is specified, it must identify a prepared statement, either directly or indirectly, that involves N placeholders ($N \geq 0$). The value N is placed within the SQLDA identified by "descriptor" (where "descriptor" is as for ALLOCATE DESCRIPTOR), and a description of the ith placeholder—and hence of the ith argument needed at execution time—is placed in the ith item descriptor within that SQLDA. *Note:* If N is greater than the maximum number of item descriptors that the SQLDA can accommodate, then a warning condition is raised, and no item descriptors are set (though the count is set to N).

And here is the syntax of DESCRIBE OUTPUT:

```
DESCRIBE [ OUTPUT ] { prepped-statement-container |
                      prepped-statement-name-container }
                       USING SQL DESCRIPTOR descriptor
```

Note that the key word OUTPUT is optional. Again, "prepped statement container" and "prepped statement name container" are as for PREPARE; whichever is specified, it must identify (directly or indirectly) either a prepared single-row SELECT statement or a prepared cursor specification, both of which will produce a result table of N columns ($N > 0$)

at execution time (in the case of a single-row SELECT, of course, that table should have at most one row). The value N is placed within the SQLDA identified by "descriptor" (which is again as for ALLOCATE DESCRIPTOR), and a description of the ith column is placed in the ith item descriptor within that SQLDA. *Note:* Again, if N is greater than the maximum number of item descriptors that the SQLDA can accommodate, then a warning condition is raised, and no item descriptors are set (though the count is set to N).

GET DESCRIPTOR

GET DESCRIPTOR is for retrieving specified information from a specified SQLDA (usually from a *specified item descriptor* within a specified SQLDA). There are two formats. The first simply retrieves a count of the number of populated item descriptors in the specified SQLDA:

```
GET DESCRIPTOR descriptor target = COUNT
```

"Descriptor" specifies an SQLDA in the usual way; "target" is a parameter or host variable of type exact numeric with scale 0. The count of the number of populated item descriptors in the specified SQLDA is placed in the specified target.

The second GET DESCRIPTOR format is:

```
GET DESCRIPTOR descriptor VALUE subscript assignment-commalist
```

Once again "descriptor" specifies an SQLDA in the usual way; "subscript" is a literal, parameter, or host variable of type exact numeric with scale 0, whose value i identifies the ith item descriptor in that SQLDA. The assignments in the "assignment commalist" retrieve values from that ith item descriptor. Each such assignment is of the form

```
target = source
```

where "target" is a parameter or host variable, and "source" is the name of one of the elements (TYPE, LENGTH, DATA, etc.) within the item descriptor. Of course, each target must have a data type compatible with that of its source; in the special case where the source is DATA, the target must be of a data type that is consistent with the values for TYPE, LENGTH, PRECISION, SCALE, etc., in the same item descriptor.

An Example

The following somewhat lengthy example shows how the ideas discussed so far might fit together in practice. The assumption is that we need to prepare and execute a single-row SELECT statement, and we do not know at the time we write the program how many values (or columns) are involved in the result row, nor how many placeholders are involved in the request. For simplicity, we give the text of the SELECT as an explicit character string literal below (and hence the number of columns and number of placeholders clearly *are* known), but the reader should understand that in practice the exact format of the SELECT will not usually be known so readily.

```
/* variable to hold source form of SELECT statement */

DCL SQLSOURCE CHAR VARYING (65000) ;

/* construct source form of SELECT statement */

SQLSOURCE = 'SELECT  P.CITY, P.WEIGHT, P.COLOR
             FROM    P
             WHERE   P.PNO = ?' ;

/* construct prepped form of SELECT statement */

EXEC SQL PREPARE SQLPREPPED FROM :SQLSOURCE ;

/* create SQLDAs for SELECT columns and arguments */

EXEC SQL ALLOCATE DESCRIPTOR 'SELCOLS' WITH MAX 256 ;
EXEC SQL ALLOCATE DESCRIPTOR 'SELARGS' WITH MAX 40 ;

/* populate the SQLDAs */

EXEC SQL DESCRIBE INPUT SQLPREPPED USING SQL DESCRIPTOR 'SELARGS' ;
EXEC SQL DESCRIBE OUTPUT SQLPREPPED USING SQL DESCRIPTOR 'SELCOLS' ;

/* code needed here to place SELECT arguments into SELARGS */
/* SQLDA (because for the sake of the example we will say  */
/* EXECUTE ... USING SQLDA, though EXECUTE ... USING arg-  */
/* commalist would be simpler); we omit this code from the */
/* example, for brevity, but it would bear some similarity */
/* to the code shown below for retrieving results from the */
/* SELCOLS SQLDA                                           */

/* perform the SELECT */

EXEC SQL EXECUTE SQLPREPPED INTO SQL DESCRIPTOR 'SELCOLS'
                            USING SQL DESCRIPTOR 'SELARGS' ;

/* variable to hold column count */

DCL DEGREE FIXED BINARY (15) ;

/* how many columns are there in the result? */

EXEC SQL GET DESCRIPTOR 'SELCOLS'
                        :DEGREE = COUNT ;

/* variables to receive column information from SELCOLS */

DCL DATA_TYPE FIXED BINARY (15) ;
DCL DATA_LEN  FIXED BINARY (15) ;
```

```
/* loop control variable */

DCL I FIXED BINARY (15) ;

DO I = 1 TO DEGREE ;

    /* get data type and length of Ith result column */

    EXEC SQL GET DESCRIPTOR 'SELCOLS' VALUE :I
                 :DATA_TYPE = TYPE,
                 :DATA_LEN = LENGTH ;

    /* can now allocate a suitable variable, say DATA_VAL, */
    /* into which Ith column data value can be retrieved    */

    /* get data value from Ith result column */

    EXEC SQL GET DESCRIPTOR 'SELCOLS' VALUE :I
                 :DATA_VAL = DATA ;

END ;

/* and so on, and so on, and so on */
```

SET DESCRIPTOR

As already indicated, SET DESCRIPTOR is for populating or updating the contents of an SQLDA, or rather of an individual item descriptor within an SQLDA, in piecemeal fashion. Now, it is very unlikely that anyone would want to populate an entire SQLDA using SET DESCRIPTOR; a more likely thing to do would be to populate the area using DESCRIBE, and then change certain parts of it using SET DESCRIPTOR.

Why might it be desirable to overwrite the descriptor information produced by DESCRIBE? One important reason is as follows. Suppose that DESCRIBE OUTPUT reports a certain result column to be of some data type, say DECIMAL, that is not supported by the host language. In such a case, SET DESCRIPTOR could be used to change the data type to REAL, to inform the system that decimal-to-real conversion is to take place when a value is retrieved from that column. *Note:* When we say "change the data type" here, what we mean, of course, is that we are changing the *descriptor* of the column in the SQLDA in a certain way. The system will now know that we want to see values of that column as REAL, even though it knows those values are actually DECIMAL (it knows this from its own "private" descriptor, which is of course not accessible to—and certainly not changeable by—the user). The system will therefore perform an appropriate data type conversion (CAST operation) on the decimal values when they are retrieved.*

---

*The legal conversions are not necessarily identical to (nor are they limited to) those supported by CAST. Rather, the rules are implementation-defined.

Like GET DESCRIPTOR, SET DESCRIPTOR comes in two formats. The first is used to establish the count of the number of item descriptors in the specified SQLDA that are to be populated:

```
SET DESCRIPTOR descriptor COUNT = source
```

"Descriptor" specifies an SQLDA in the usual way; "source" is a literal, parameter, or host variable of type exact numeric with scale 0. The count of the number of item descriptors to be populated in the specified SQLDA is set to the specified value.*

The second SET DESCRIPTOR format is:

```
SET DESCRIPTOR descriptor VALUE subscript assignment-commalist
```

Once again "descriptor" specifies an SQLDA in the usual way; "subscript" is a literal, parameter, or host variable of type exact numeric with scale 0, whose value i identifies the ith item descriptor in that SQLDA. The assignments in the "assignment commalist" update values in that ith item descriptor. Each such assignment is of the form

```
target = source
```

where "source" is a literal, parameter, or host variable, and "target" is the name of one of the elements (TYPE, LENGTH, DATA, etc.) within the item descriptor. Of course, each source must have a data type compatible with that of its target. Here is an example of the second format:

```
EXEC SQL SET DESCRIPTOR 'SELARGS' VALUE :I
                       TYPE = 12,
                       LENGTH = 100 ;
```

Let the current value of the variable I be i. Then the effect of this SET DESCRIPTOR is update the ith item descriptor in the SQLDA called SELARGS. The assignments to TYPE and LENGTH indicate that the data type CHARACTER VARYING (100) will be used for values of the ith argument (we assume that SELARGS is an "arguments" SQLDA; 12 is the TYPE code for CHARACTER VARYING). Once again, the reader is referred to the official standard document for details of the elements included within item descriptors, for details of the values those elements are permitted to have, and for an explanation of the meanings of those permitted values.

---

*One possible use for this first SET DESCRIPTOR format might be to initialize the COUNT to zero immediately after ALLOCATE DESCRIPTOR, in order to reduce the risk of a program "running wild" if it inadvertently accesses an SQLDA that has not yet been the target of a DESCRIBE.

20.5 CURSOR OPERATIONS

We begin by repeating a few points previously made in Section 20.2:

- First, multiple-row access in dynamic SQL, like multiple-row access in static SQL, is done by means of a cursor, using OPEN, FETCH, and CLOSE operations (possibly UPDATE and DELETE CURRENT operations too).

- Second, the dynamic version of DECLARE CURSOR is more flexible than the static version, in that it introduces a level of indirection between the cursor declaration per se and the cursor specification portion, so that this latter portion can be the subject of a separate PREPARE and can vary from cursor opening to cursor opening.

- Third, there is one additional cursor operation available in dynamic SQL, viz. ALLOCATE CURSOR, which effectively supports the generation of new cursors "on the fly." Note, however, that there is no corresponding DEALLOCATE CURSOR, at least not explicitly.

We now proceed to examine these ideas in detail.

DECLARE CURSOR

Cursors defined by the dynamic version of DECLARE CURSOR (or generated by ALLOCATE CURSOR) are said to be *dynamic cursors*. If the application can manage with a "hard-coded" dynamic cursor name, the dynamic variety of DECLARE CURSOR will suit. The syntax is:*

```
DECLARE cursor [ INSENSITIVE ] [ SCROLL ] CURSOR
        FOR prepped-statement-container
```

"Cursor" here is the name of the dynamic cursor; "prepped statement container" is the name of an SQL variable that—by the time the cursor is opened—will contain the prepared form of a cursor specification. Note that the operand *is* "prepped statement container," not "prepped statement *name* container" ("prepped statement name container" is the operand for ALLOCATE CURSOR, q.v.). Here is an example:

```
EXEC SQL DECLARE X CURSOR FOR SQLPREPPED ;
```

---

*The only difference vis-à-vis the static variety is that "prepped statement container" appears in place of a cursor specification. Refer to Chapter 10 if you need to refresh your memory regarding INSENSITIVE and SCROLL.

Before cursor X can be opened, a PREPARE must be done to place the prepared form of a cursor specification into SQLPREPPED. Our "cursor X" example might thus continue as follows:

```
DCL SQLSOURCE CHAR VARYING (65000) ;

SQLSOURCE = 'SELECT SP.PNO, SP.QTY
             FROM   SP
             WHERE  SP.SNO = ''S2''
             ORDER  BY PNO' ;

EXEC SQL PREPARE SQLPREPPED FROM :SQLSOURCE ;
```

Now the cursor can be opened:

```
EXEC SQL OPEN X ;
```

See the subsection "OPEN and CLOSE" below for further discussion of OPEN.

ALLOCATE CURSOR

When DECLARE CURSOR is not appropriate because of its insistence on a hard-coded cursor name, ALLOCATE CURSOR must be used instead. The syntax is:

```
ALLOCATE cursor-name-container [ INSENSITIVE ] [ SCROLL ]
         CURSOR FOR prepped-statement-name-container
```

Here "cursor name container" and "prepped statement name container" are both parameters or both host variables (of type character string with octet length not greater than 128 in each case). "Cursor name container" must contain a user-generated identifier that will be used to refer to the cursor that is dynamically created by the ALLOCATE CURSOR operation.* "Prepped statement name container" must contain the user-generated identifier of an SQL variable that *already contains* the prepared form of a cursor specification.

> *Aside:* "Cursor name containers," like "prepped statement name containers" and "descriptors," can optionally include a LOCAL or GLOBAL prefix. Once again, we ignore the GLOBAL possibility for simplicity, treating all cursor names as LOCAL by default. *End of aside.*

---

*The standard uses the term "cursor name" (more precisely, "*extended* cursor name," which seems even less appropriate) to refer, very confusingly, to the name of the specified parameter or host variable, instead of to the value of that parameter or host variable. Once again it has to be said that the official terminology is not very good, and we will avoid it.

Here is an ALLOCATE CURSOR version of our DECLARE CURSOR example above:

```
DCL SQLSOURCE        CHAR VARYING (65000) ;
DCL SQLPREPPEDNAME CHAR VARYING (128) ;
DCL XNAME            CHAR VARYING (128) ;

SQLSOURCE = 'SELECT SP.PNO, SP.QTY
             FROM   SP
             WHERE  SP.SNO = ''S2''
             ORDER  BY PNO' ;

SQLPREPPEDNAME = 'SELECT_STMT_1' ;

EXEC SQL PREPARE :SQLPREPPEDNAME FROM :SQLSOURCE ;

XNAME = 'CURSOR_1' ;

EXEC SQL ALLOCATE :XNAME CURSOR FOR :SQLPREPPEDNAME ;

EXEC SQL OPEN :XNAME ;
```

We close this discussion by repeating the point that there is no "DEALLOCATE CURSOR." However, if a prepared cursor specification *C* is dropped via DEALLOCATE PREPARE, and *D* is an "allocated" dynamic cursor that is currently associated with *C* (i.e., an ALLOCATE CURSOR has been executed associating *C* with *D*), then *D* is destroyed automatically.

OPEN and CLOSE

The dynamic version of OPEN looks like this:

```
OPEN { cursor | cursor-name-container } [ USING arguments ]
```

"Cursor" and "cursor name container" are as for DECLARE CURSOR and ALLOCATE CURSOR, respectively. The "arguments" option has the same two possible formats as it does in EXECUTE:

```
argument-commalist | SQL DESCRIPTOR descriptor
```

The USING clause must be provided if the cursor specification associated with the cursor to be opened contains any placeholders. Here is a modified version of our ALLOCATE CURSOR example to illustrate the point:

```
DCL SQLSOURCE        CHAR VARYING (65000) ;
DCL SQLPREPPEDNAME CHAR VARYING (128) ;
DCL XNAME            CHAR VARYING (128) ;
DCL SNO              CHAR (5) ;

SQLSOURCE = 'SELECT SP.PNO, SP.QTY
             FROM   SP
             WHERE  SP.SNO = ?
             ORDER  BY PNO' ;
```

```
SQLPREPPEDNAME = 'SELECT_STMT_1' ;

EXEC SQL PREPARE :SQLPREPPEDNAME FROM :SQLSOURCE ;

XNAME = 'CURSOR_1' ;

EXEC SQL ALLOCATE :XNAME CURSOR FOR :SQLPREPPEDNAME ;

GET LIST ( SNO ) ;

EXEC SQL OPEN :XNAME USING :SNO ;
```

And, of course, the dynamic version of CLOSE looks like this:

```
CLOSE { cursor | cursor-name-container }
```

For example:

```
EXEC SQL CLOSE :XNAME ;
```

FETCH

The dynamic version of FETCH takes the form:

```
FETCH [ [ row-selector ] FROM ]
        { cursor | cursor-name-container } INTO places
```

Cursor" and "cursor name container" are as for OPEN, "row selector" is as explained in Chapter 10, and "places" is as for EXECUTE—i.e., it takes one of the following forms:

```
target-commalist | SQL DESCRIPTOR descriptor
```

To continue with our running example:

```
EXEC SQL OPEN :XNAME USING :SNO ;

EXEC SQL ALLOCATE DESCRIPTOR 'SELCOLS' WITH MAX 256 ;

EXEC SQL DESCRIBE OUTPUT :SQLPREPPEDNAME
            USING SQL DESCRIPTOR 'SELCOLS' ;

EXEC SQL FETCH ABSOLUTE :I FROM :XNAME
            INTO SQL DESCRIPTOR 'SELCOLS' ;
```

If the host variable I has the value 42 (say), this FETCH will retrieve values from the 42nd row of the ordered collection of rows associated with the current opening of the dynamic cursor whose name is given in the host variable XNAME.* Those values will be retrieved into the SQLDA called SELCOLS. The application will then have to use GET DESCRIPTOR

---

*The "ALLOCATE :XNAME CURSOR . . ." statement would have had to have specified SCROLL for this FETCH ABSOLUTE to succeed.

statements to copy those values into variables of its own. Assuming for the sake of simplicity that all columns are of type SMALLINT, and nulls are not permitted for any of them, the following code could be used to display the row just fetched:

```
DCL DEGREE        FIXED BINARY (15) ;
DCL COLUMN_NAME   CHAR VARYING (128) ;
DCL COLUMN_VALUE  FIXED BINARY (15) ;
DCL COLUMN_NUMBER FIXED BINARY (15) ;

EXEC SQL GET DESCRIPTOR 'SELCOLS' :DEGREE = COUNT ;

DO COLUMN_NUMBER = 1 TO DEGREE ;

    EXEC SQL GET DESCRIPTOR 'SELCOLS' VALUE :COLUMN_NUMBER
                                      :COLUMN_NAME = NAME,
                                      :COLUMN_VALUE = DATA ;

    PUT SKIP LIST ( COLUMN_NAME || ':', COLUMN_VALUE ) ;

END ;
```

Positioned UPDATE and DELETE

The dynamic SQL versions of UPDATE CURRENT and DELETE CURRENT differ from their static counterparts in certain important respects. In particular, each comes in two varieties, a preparable form and a nonpreparable form, as we shall see.

1. The nonpreparable form is identical to the static SQL counterpart except that the "WHERE CURRENT OF" clause can specify *either* a cursor in the usual way, as in static SQL, *or* a cursor name container (as is only to be expected).

2. By contrast, the preparable form:

   - *Cannot* be executed except via PREPARE and EXECUTE (or EXECUTE IMMEDIATE);
   - *Must* specify a cursor in the usual way, not a cursor name container;
   - *Need not* name the table in which a row is to be updated or from which a row is to be deleted, because that table is implied by the cursor specification anyway.* (Since the cursor specification is constructed at run time, the table name would typically not be known at compilation time. In order to include that table name in a positioned UPDATE or DELETE, therefore, the application would have

---

*Note that the same is true in static SQL! In this writer's strong opinion, it should not be necessary to name the table in the static versions of the statements either.

to parse the cursor specification at run time—clearly an undesirable state of affairs.)

DELETE is simpler, and we therefore treat it first. The syntax is:

```
DELETE [ FROM table ]
WHERE   CURRENT OF { cursor | cursor-name-container }
```

For example:

```
DELETE WHERE CURRENT OF X
```

(a preparable positioned DELETE).

And here is the syntax for UPDATE:

```
UPDATE [ table ]
SET    assignment-commalist
WHERE   CURRENT OF { cursor | cursor-name-container }
```

Since the column names of "table" (which are needed for the assignments) are almost certainly not known at compilation time, in practice the UPDATE statement is likely to be built at run time and then explicitly prepared. Let us imagine a simple-minded application that displays the row most recently fetched in a window where the user can, if desired, overtype the displayed values (all of which are small integers, remember). Then a suitable UPDATE statement might be built and prepared as follows:

```
DCL DEGREE         FIXED BINARY (15) ;
DCL COLUMN_NAME    CHAR VARYING (128) ;
DCL COLUMN_VALUE   FIXED BINARY (15) ;
DCL COLUMN_NUMBER  FIXED BINARY (15) ;

DCL SQLUPD         CHAR VARYING (65000) ;

DCL COMMA          CHAR (1) ;

EXEC SQL GET DESCRIPTOR 'SELCOLS' :DEGREE = COUNT ;
SQLUPD = 'UPDATE SET' ;
COMMA  = ' ' ;

DO COLUMN_NUMBER = 1 TO DEGREE ;

    EXEC SQL GET DESCRIPTOR 'SELCOLS' VALUE :COLUMN_NUMBER
                                 :COLUMN_NAME = NAME ;
    SQLUPD = SQLUPD || COMMA || COLUMN_NAME || ' = ?' ;
    COMMA = ',' ;

END ;

/* assume an appropriate ALLOCATE :XNAME CURSOR ... has */
/* already been done                                    */

SQLUPD = SQLUPD || ' WHERE CURRENT OF ' || XNAME ;

EXEC SQL PREPARE SQLUPDPREPPED FROM :SQLUPD ;
```

In order to execute the UPDATE, we go through the following steps:

```
EXEC SQL ALLOCATE DESCRIPTOR 'UPD_VALUES' WITH MAX 50 ;
EXEC SQL DESCRIBE INPUT SQLUPDPREPPED
               USING SQL DESCRIPTOR 'UPD_VALUES' ;
```

Suppose that a row has been fetched, displayed, and overtyped by the user, and suppose that the new column values have been read into an array of small integers called NEW_VALUE. The prepared and described UPDATE statement can now be executed to update the current row, as follows:

```
DO COLUMN_NUMBER = 1 TO DEGREE ;
   COLUMN_VALUE = NEW_VALUE ( COLUMN_NUMBER ) ;
   EXEC SQL SET DESCRIPTOR 'UPD_VALUES' VALUE :COLUMN_NUMBER
                                        DATA = :COLUMN_VALUE ;
END ;

EXEC SQL EXECUTE SQLUPDPREPPED USING SQL DESCRIPTOR 'UPD_VALUES' ;
```

How to handle tables whose columns are not all of the same data type is, of course, an added complication, but we have shown how all the information needed by the writer of such a program is available in the SQL descriptor area, and we leave the solution, as they say, as an exercise for the *writer!*

20.6 SESSION DEFAULTS

Consider the case of a generalized "off the shelf" software package that uses dynamic SQL. With such a package, the very same code might be executed by different users, against different databases, on different computer installations, in different organizations, maybe even using different DBMSs.

For such an application, the static SQL rules that determine the default catalog and schema names for the resolution of unqualified table names, domain names, etc., are not at all suitable. Quite apart from anything else, they would require all users always to work with the same defaults! And, of course, analogous remarks apply to the default character set that is used for character string literals and SQL identifiers. Thus, a mechanism is clearly needed to allow programs that use dynamic SQL to specify their defaults at run time. This is the purpose of the operations SET CATALOG, SET SCHEMA, and SET NAMES.*

---

*Obviously SET CATALOG and SET SCHEMA are the operations that set the default catalog and schema names; why the operation that sets the default character set should be SET *NAMES* is (to this writer, at least) not so obvious.

Each of these operations establishes a default (for the specified item) for the *SQL-session*. The syntax is:

```
SET { CATALOG | SCHEMA | NAMES } { string | user-function }
```

Here *string* is a literal, parameter, or host variable, of type character string in each case, and "user function" is USER, CURRENT_USER, SESSION_USER, or SYSTEM_USER (see Chapter 15). The value specified by *string* is established as the session default for the specified item. *Note:* Each of the three items is set to an implementation-defined "default default" when the SQL-session is initiated, as explained in Chapter 5.

It must be made very clear that the defaults established by these special SET operations apply only to SQL statements that are prepared and/or executed dynamically.* A program that uses a mixture of static and dynamic SQL would have to beware of the possibility that the defaults used for its static statements are not the same as those used for its dynamic statements.

Note, incidentally, that if a *qualified* schema name is specified as the default in SET SCHEMA, as in (e.g.) the following example—

```
FULL_NAME = CAT_NAME || '.' || SCHEMA_NAME ;
EXEC SQL SET SCHEMA :FULL_NAME ;
```

—then the default catalog name and default schema name for the session are effectively both established, just as if the following pair of statements had been executed:

```
EXEC SQL SET CATALOG :CAT_NAME ;
EXEC SQL SET SCHEMA   :SCHEMA_NAME ;
```

---

*And to statements of "direct" (i.e., interactive) SQL.

21

The Information Schema

21.1 INTRODUCTION

Recall from Chapters 2 and 4 that the SQL-environment includes a set of *catalogs*, each of which includes a set of *schemas*. Each schema in turn has a single *owner*, represented of course by an authID (note, however, that the same authID can own any number of schemas, in any number of catalogs). The purpose of each schema is to describe a certain collection of base tables, views, etc., that are all owned by the owner of that schema and thus somehow—in some implementation-defined way—constitute some operational unit within the SQL-environment.

Now, the standard does not specify the detailed structure and content of schemas in general. However, it does require each catalog to include exactly one schema called "the Information Schema" (INFORMATION_SCHEMA), which effectively repeats all of the descriptions contained in all of the other schemas in all of the catalogs in the same cluster as the catalog in question (see Chapter 2), but does so in a prescribed manner.* More precisely, the Information Schema is defined to contain a set of *views* of a hypothetical "Definition Schema." The SQL-implementation is not required to support the Definition Schema per se, but it is required (a) to support *some* kind

---

*It also describes itself, i.e., the Information Schema is *self-describing*.

of "Definition Schema," and (b) to support views of that "Definition Schema" that do look like those of the Information Schema.

Note: The Information Schema is considered to have been created by means of a CREATE SCHEMA operation of the form:

```
CREATE SCHEMA INFORMATION_SCHEMA
               AUTHORIZATION INFORMATION_SCHEMA
```

Despite the AUTHORIZATION clause, however, the Information Schema is "globally accessible," at least for retrieval purposes, thanks to a set of "GRANTs to PUBLIC" (see Section 21.2 below).

Now, given the indisputable facts that (a) existing SQL-implementations most certainly do support something akin to the "Definition Schema," but (b) those "Definition Schemas" do vary widely from SQL-implementation to SQL-implementation (even when the SQL-implementations in question come from the same vendor), the idea of requiring only that the SQL-implementation support certain predefined views of its "Definition Schema" clearly makes sense. However, that idea does lead immediately to certain anomalies. For example, consider our running example (the suppliers-and-parts database). To define that database, we start with an appropriate CREATE SCHEMA—for example:

```
CREATE SCHEMA S_P_SCHEMA ...
```

And we go on to create all of the necessary base tables, views, etc., that we want to be described by this particular schema. The descriptors for all of those objects will be included within the schema called S_P_SCHEMA.

Note, however, that even though this schema is "our" schema ("we" created it), *we cannot access it*. For example, to find out what named tables are described by this schema, we *cannot* say (e.g.)

```
SELECT TABLE_NAME
FROM   S_P_SCHEMA.TABLES           -- This is *** ILLEGAL *** !!!
```

(even though such a formulation might seem very natural). Instead, we have to say something like

```
SELECT TABLE_NAME
FROM   INFORMATION_SCHEMA.TABLES
WHERE  INFORMATION_SCHEMA.TABLES.TABLE_SCHEMA = 'S_P_SCHEMA'
AND    INFORMATION_SCHEMA.TABLES.TABLE_CATALOG = ...
```

There is another point to be made here also. Most of the views in the Information Schema are defined in terms of the niladic builtin function CURRENT_USER, which returns the current authID (see Chapter 15). In other words, the Information Schema effectively describes only those objects that can be accessed by the current user (loosely speaking). Now, this limitation is probably reasonable, so long as the current authID is the same as the authID of the user that owns the objects in question, which in practice it often will be. However, note that the standard thus provides no direct means for a given user *A* to see definitions ("descriptors") for objects that belong to some distinct user *B,* nor—more generally—for some user with higher authorization (e.g., the "database administrator") to see definitions of "all" objects, regardless of owner.

21.2 INFORMATION SCHEMA TABLES

In this section, we list all of the tables (actually views) that are required by the standard to be included in the Information Schema. For each one, we give a single-sentence summary of its content (we leave the details to the official standard document). The standard states that the SELECT privilege on each of these views is granted to PUBLIC "with the grant option," but that no further privileges are granted at all—implying, among other things, that the views cannot be the target of an SQL INSERT, UPDATE, or DELETE operation. (Refer to Chapter 15 for an explanation of PUBLIC.)

Note: The Information Schema is expressly permitted to include additional tables, over and above the views required by the standard. Likewise, the views required by the standard are expressly permitted to include additional columns.

For emphasis, we repeat the point that each of the views listed below provides information for *one authID* (unless otherwise noted). The authID in question is represented by the niladic builtin function CURRENT_USER.

- INFORMATION_SCHEMA_CATALOG_NAME

  A single-column, single-row table containing the name of the catalog in which this particular Information Schema resides. *Note:* This table, unlike all the others in the Information Schema, is actually a base table, not a view.

- SCHEMATA

  Lists all schemas created by CURRENT_USER.

- DOMAINS

  Lists all domains accessible to CURRENT_USER or PUBLIC.

- TABLES

  Lists all named tables (base tables and views) accessible to CURRENT_USER or PUBLIC. *Note:* The standard says that TABLES identifies only "persistent" tables, but the intent seems to be to include Type 2 and 3 temporary tables also. An analogous remark applies to COLUMNS (see below).

- VIEWS

    Lists all views accessible to CURRENT_USER or PUBLIC.

- COLUMNS

    Lists all columns of all named tables accessible to CURRENT_USER or PUBLIC.

- TABLE_PRIVILEGES

    Lists all privileges on all named tables either granted by CURRENT_USER or granted to CURRENT_USER or PUBLIC.

- COLUMN_PRIVILEGES

    Lists all privileges on all columns of all named tables either granted by CURRENT_USER or granted to CURRENT_USER or PUBLIC.

- USAGE_PRIVILEGES

    Lists all privileges on all domains, character sets, collations, and translations granted by CURRENT_USER or granted to CURRENT_USER or PUBLIC.

- DOMAIN_CONSTRAINTS

    Lists all domain constraints for all domains created by CURRENT_USER. *Note:* There is another slight oddity here, viz.: Apparently, user *U* is not allowed to see the constraints that apply to domain *D,* even if *U* is allowed to update some column defined on *D,* unless *U* actually *owns D.* A similar comment applies to TABLE_CONSTRAINTS, REFERENTIAL_CONSTRAINTS, CHECK_CONSTRAINTS, KEY_COLUMN_USAGE, and ASSERTIONS (see below).

- TABLE_CONSTRAINTS

    Lists all base table constraints for all base tables created by CURRENT_USER.

- REFERENTIAL_CONSTRAINTS

    Lists all referential constraints for all base tables created by CURRENT_USER.

- CHECK_CONSTRAINTS

  Lists all check constraints for all base tables created by CURRENT_USER.

- KEY_COLUMN_USAGE

  Lists all columns participating in candidate keys or foreign keys within base tables created by CURRENT_USER.

- ASSERTIONS

  Lists all general constraints created by CURRENT_USER.

- CHARACTER_SETS

  Lists all character sets available to CURRENT_USER or PUBLIC.

- COLLATIONS

  Lists all collations available to CURRENT_USER or PUBLIC.

- TRANSLATIONS

  Lists all translations available to CURRENT_USER or PUBLIC.

- VIEW_TABLE_USAGE

  For all views owned by CURRENT_USER, shows which named tables the definitions of those views depend on.

- VIEW_COLUMN_USAGE

  For all views owned by CURRENT_USER, shows which columns of which named tables the definitions of those views depend on.

- CONSTRAINT_TABLE_USAGE

  For all constraints owned by CURRENT_USER, shows which named tables the definitions of those constraints depend on.

- CONSTRAINT_COLUMN_USAGE

  For all constraints owned by CURRENT_USER, shows which columns of which named tables the definitions of those constraints depend on.

- COLUMN_DOMAIN_USAGE

  For all columns of all named tables accessible to CURRENT_USER or PUBLIC, shows which columns are defined on which domains.

- SQL_LANGUAGES

  Shows which SQL dialects (e.g., SQL/86, SQL/89, SQL/92) the SQL-implementation supports.

  For completeness, we should mention that in addition to the tables just listed, the Information Schema is also considered to contain:

- Certain *domains,* viz. SQL_IDENTIFIER, CHARACTER_DATA, and CARDINAL_NUMBER, consisting of all possible SQL identifiers, all possible character strings, and all possible nonnegative integers, respectively

- A general *integrity constraint* called INFORMATION_SCHEMA_CATALOG_NAME_CARDINALITY, to the effect that the table INFORMATION_SCHEMA_CATALOG_NAME contains exactly one row

- The *character set* SQL_TEXT (see Chapter 3), and all other standard- or implementation-defined character sets*

- All other *character sets* not explicitly assigned (via an appropriate CREATE statement) to some other schema

- All *collations* not explicitly assigned (via an appropriate CREATE statement) to some other schema

- All *translations* not explicitly assigned (via an appropriate CREATE statement) to some other schema

- All *form-of-use conversions*

---

*It is difficult to believe that the standard really intends the character sets per se (as opposed to a set of *descriptors* for those character sets) to be components within the Information Schema (especially considering that there is a distinct Information Schema in every catalog), but that is what it says.

22

Exception Handling

22.1 STATUS CODES

We remind the reader that (as explained in Chapter 6) after the execution of a given SQL statement, certain "status codes" reflecting the outcome of that execution are placed in either or both of two special parameters called SQLCODE and SQLSTATE (every procedure is required to include at least one of these). The SQLCODE value is an integer, the SQLSTATE value is a character string of length 5; the exact data types depend on the applicable host language—see the official standard for details. *Note:* As mentioned in Chapter 6, SQLSTATE is the preferred status parameter; SQLCODE is now a "deprecated feature"—meaning that it is a feature of the standard that is retained only for compatibility with SQL/89 and is likely to be dropped at some time in the future.

To be a little more specific regarding status code values:

- *SQLCODE:* A SQLCODE value of 0 means that the SQL statement executed successfully and no errors occurred; a value of $+100$ means that no rows were found to satisfy the request; all other values are implementation-defined, except that values representing errors must be negative.

- *SQLSTATE:* SQLSTATE values consist of a two-character "class code" followed by a three-character "subclass code." Each of the five characters is a digit (0–9) or an upper case letter (A–Z). Class code 00 means that the statement executed successfully (the subclass code will be 000 in this case). Class code 01 means that the statement did execute, but some warning condition exists (e.g., class code 00 with subclass code 003 means that nulls were ignored in the evaluation of an aggregate function). Class code 02 means that no data was found (again, the subclass code will be 000 in this case). For details of other possible values, see the subsection "SQLSTATE Values" below.

Note: An extensive set of additional status information is also placed in the *diagnostics area* (see Section 22.2).

It follows from the foregoing that, in principle at least, every SQL statement should be followed by a test of the returned SQLCODE or SQLSTATE value. In embedded SQL (but not in the module language), the WHENEVER statement can be used to simplify this process. Refer to Chapter 6 (Section 6.3) for a description of the WHENEVER statement.

One final point to close this introduction: The standard distinguishes between *exception* conditions and *completion* conditions. A statement that raises an exception condition is defined to have no effect apart from placing the appropriate feedback information into SQLCODE, SQLSTATE, and the diagnostics area (loosely speaking, therefore, the statement fails—i.e., the requested function is not performed). A statement that raises a completion condition is permitted to have additional effects—e.g., to return data to the invoking procedure, or to change the state of the database, or to initiate an SQL-transaction, etc.* In other words, "exception conditions" in the standard correspond to what are usually called *error* conditions, and "exception conditions" and "completion conditions" taken together correspond to what are usually called *exception* conditions! The standard does not seem to have a single term that corresponds to "exceptions" in this broader and more usual sense (the sense, indeed, that is implied by the title of the present chapter).

SQLSTATE Values

As indicated above, SQLSTATE values consist of a two-character *class* value followed by a three-character *subclass* value. Class values that begin with a digit in the range 0–4 or a letter in the range A–H are reserved for conditions explicitly defined in the standard; other classes are reserved for implementation-defined conditions and are called *implementation-defined*

---

*The completion conditions are the ones corresponding to the SQLSTATE classes "successful completion" (class 00), "warning" (class 01), and "data not found" (class 02).

classes. Likewise, subclass values that begin 0–4 or A–H within classes that also begin 0–4 or A–H are reserved for conditions explicitly defined in the standard; other subclasses within such classes, and all subclasses within implementation-defined classes,* are reserved for implementation-defined conditions and are called *implementation-defined subclasses.*

This is not the place to describe all of the possible SQLSTATE values in detail; we content ourselves with merely listing the standard *class* values, with their generic interpretation in each case (see the table below). For more information, refer to the official standard.

class	condition
00	successful completion
01	warning
02	data not found
07	dynamic SQL error
08	connection error
0A	feature not supported
21	cardinality violation
22	data exception
23	constraint violation
24	invalid cursor state
25	invalid transaction state
26	invalid statement name
27	triggered data change violation
28	invalid authID specification
2A	direct SQL syntax or access error
2B	dependent privileges exist
2C	invalid character set name
2D	invalid transaction termination
33	invalid SQLDA name
34	invalid cursor name
35	invalid condition number
37	dynamic SQL syntax or access error
3C	ambiguous cursor name
3D	invalid catalog name
3F	invalid schema name
40	rollback
42	syntax or access error
44	check option violation
HZ	Remote Database Access condition

22.2 THE DIAGNOSTICS AREA

Each SQL-agent has an associated diagnostics area, which is used to hold "conditions" (i.e., feedback information relating to the most recently executed SQL statement). The area is automatically emptied before each SQL statement starts execution (except for the SQL statement GET DIAGNOSTICS, q.v.). The size of the diagnostics area in "conditions"

---

*Except for subclass 000, which always means "no subclass."

(i.e., its maximum capacity at any time) is established by the SET TRANSACTION statement (see Chapter 5); for example, the statement

```
SET TRANSACTION DIAGNOSTICS SIZE 5
```

will establish a diagnostics area that is large enough to hold five conditions. The default size is implementation-defined (but must be at least one).

The detailed layout of the diagnostics area is not specified in the standard. Instead, a statement called GET DIAGNOSTICS is provided for the purpose of retrieving information from the diagnostics area in a flexible, disciplined, and precisely defined manner; in other words, SQL diagnostics areas, like SQL descriptor areas (see Chapter 20), are *encapsulated*.

There are basically two formats of the GET DIAGNOSTICS statement. Format 1 retrieves information relating to *the overall execution* of the immediately preceding SQL statement.* The syntax is:

```
GET DIAGNOSTICS assignment-commalist
```

Each assignment is of the form

```
target = source
```

where "target" is a parameter or host variable, and "source" is one of the following:

```
NUMBER
MORE
COMMAND_FUNCTION
DYNAMIC_FUNCTION
ROW_COUNT
```

NUMBER returns an integer representing the number of conditions raised by the original SQL statement. MORE returns "Y" or "N"; "Y" means that not all conditions raised were stored in the diagnostics area, "N" means the opposite. COMMAND_FUNCTION returns a character string identifying the original SQL statement (e.g., "UPDATE WHERE" for a searched UPDATE). DYNAMIC_FUNCTION returns a similar character string identifying the statement executed if the original SQL statement was an EXECUTE or EXECUTE IMMEDIATE. ROW_COUNT returns an integer representing the number of rows directly affected by the original SQL statement (for INSERT, searched UPDATE, and searched DELETE only).

Based on information gleaned from executing one or more Format 1

---

*Not counting GET DIAGNOSTICS statements—i.e., any given SQL statement can be followed by multiple GET DIAGNOSTICS statements, each one focusing in on some particular aspect of the execution of the original SQL statement.

GET DIAGNOSTICS statements, the user might wish to go on to retrieve more specific information regarding some particular exception(s). This is the purpose of Format 2 of the statement—syntax:

```
GET DIAGNOSTICS EXCEPTION exception assignment-commalist
```

Here "exception" is a literal, parameter, or host variable of type exact numeric (with scale zero) whose value identifies one of the conditions in the diagnostics area. *Note:* Condition number 1 is required to be the condition that corresponds to the values returned in SQLCODE and SQLSTATE. Other conditions, if any, appear in an implementation-dependent sequence.

Each assignment is of the form

```
target = source
```

where "target" is a parameter or host variable, and "source" is one of the following:

```
CONDITION_NUMBER
RETURNED_SQLSTATE
CLASS_ORIGIN
SUBCLASS_ORIGIN
SERVER_NAME
CONNECTION_NAME
CONSTRAINT_CATALOG
CONSTRAINT_SCHEMA
CONSTRAINT_NAME
CATALOG_NAME
SCHEMA_NAME
TABLE_NAME
COLUMN_NAME
CURSOR_NAME
MESSAGE_TEXT
MESSAGE_LENGTH
MESSAGE_OCTET_LENGTH
```

Most of these items seem fairly self-explanatory; we elaborate below only on those that seem to require such elaboration.

- RETURNED_SQLSTATE is the SQLSTATE value that would have been returned if this condition had been the only one raised.

- CLASS_ORIGIN is "ISO 9075" if the class value of RETURNED_ SQLSTATE is one of the SQLSTATE values defined within the standard, and some (different) implementation-defined value otherwise. SUBCLASS_ORIGIN is analogous.

- MESSAGE_TEXT is an implementation-defined character string with length as given by MESSAGE_LENGTH (in characters) and MESSAGE_OCTET_LENGTH (in octets). The intent is, of course, to permit the implementation to provide additional specific information regarding the exception that occurred, perhaps in a form suitable for textual display to an end user.

APPENDIXES

The appendixes that follow cover a somewhat mixed bag of topics. Appendix A presents an SQL BNF grammar. Appendix B discusses the question of compliance with the standard. Appendix C discusses ways in which the new standard differs from the previous version. Appendix D is the list (promised in the preface of this book) of issues that are not satisfactorily described in the standard at the present time. Finally, Appendix E presents an overview of the proposed extensions to the standard known informally as "SQL3," and Appendix F offers a list of references and suggested further reading.

An SQL Grammar

A.1 INTRODUCTION

Any formal language definition, standard or otherwise, necessarily involves at least two parts, a syntactic part and a semantic part—where, loosely speaking, *syntax* is how you say it and *semantics* is what it means. In the SQL standard (and in this book), the syntactic part of the language is defined by means of a BNF grammar, together with certain additional "syntax rules" expressed in English prose; the semantic part is defined purely by a set of "general rules" expressed (again) in English prose.* We remark in passing that other, more formal, definitional techniques do exist; however, such matters are beyond the scope of this book.

A language is thus certainly not just syntax. Nevertheless, it is always convenient to have a summary of the syntax of a language—i.e., a complete BNF grammar—for ease of reference. Despite this fact, the official standard document does not include any such summary. We therefore present one (or at least an approximation to one) in this appendix.

The grammar that follows deliberately does not try to use the same terminology as the official standard, for reasons explained in Section 3.6; in fact, it does not always use the same terminology as the body of the

---

*Actually, the distinction between syntax and general rules in the standard is not nearly as clearcut as this simple characterization would suggest.

book, because of certain naming conflicts that would arise if it did. It does use the "-list" and "-commalist" constructs (again, see Section 3.6 for details). It also uses a few simplifying abbreviations, as follows:

```
exp    --    expression
cond   --    condition, conditional
ref    --    reference
def    --    definition
```

The following are all defined to be *identifiers* in this grammar:

```
catalog
column
cursor
host-variable (except that a colon prefix is required)
module
parameter (except that a colon prefix is required)
prepped-statement-container
procedure
range-variable
user
```

The following are terminal categories (i.e., are undefined) with respect to this grammar:

```
data-type
identifier
integer
literal
scalar-function-ref
```

(though it is perhaps worth mentioning explicitly that "scalar function ref" is intended to include both CASE and CAST expressions, and that "identifier" is intended—sometimes!—to include an associated null indicator). We present the grammar top-down (more or less).

Note: In the interests of clarity and brevity, our grammar is indeed (as suggested above) only an approximation to a true grammar for the SQL language. It differs from a fully accurate SQL grammar in at least the following three respects.

1. First, it does not attempt to reflect all of the syntactic limitations of SQL but is instead quite permissive, in the sense that it allows the generation of many constructs that are not legal in genuine SQL. For example, it permits the argument to an aggregate function such as AVG to consist of a reference to another such function, which SQL does not in fact allow.

2. It also does not bother to show all possible syntactic permutations in cases where such permutations do not affect the meaning. For example, the various options in SET TRANSACTION can actually appear in any order, but our grammar does not show this.

3. Finally, it simply omits some of the more esoteric features of the language. For example, a grouping column (in a GROUP BY clause) can

optionally have an associated COLLATE clause if and only if that grouping column is of type character string, but our grammar does not show this possibility.

Our reason for making all of these simplifications is that SQL is a very context-sensitive language, and attempts to reflect context sensitivity in BNF tend to lead to a rather unwieldy set of production rules.

Despite all of the foregoing inaccuracies, we still believe that a syntax summary such as the one that follows is a useful thing to have, but the reader is cautioned against taking it as gospel. Where there is a discrepancy between our grammar and the body of the text, the body of the text should be taken as correct.

A.2 SESSIONS, CONNECTIONS, AND TRANSACTIONS

```
connect
   ::=    CONNECT TO { DEFAULT
                    | lit-param-or-var [ AS lit-param-or-var ]
                                       [ USER lit-param-or-var ] }

set-connection
   ::=    SET CONNECTION { DEFAULT | lit-param-or-var }

disconnect
   ::=    DISCONNECT { DEFAULT | CURRENT | ALL | lit-param-or-var }

set-catalog
   ::=    SET CATALOG { lit-param-or-var | user-function-ref }

set-schema
   ::=    SET SCHEMA { lit-param-or-var | user-function-ref }

set-names
   ::=    SET NAMES { lit-param-or-var | user-function-ref }

set-authorization
   ::=    SET SESSION AUTHORIZATION
                    { lit-param-or-var | user-function-ref }

set-time-zone
   ::=    SET TIME ZONE { interval-exp | LOCAL }

commit
   ::=    COMMIT [ WORK ]

rollback
   ::=    ROLLBACK [ WORK ]

set-transaction
   ::=    SET TRANSACTION
             [ READ ONLY | READ WRITE ]
             [ DIAGNOSTICS SIZE integer ]
             [ ISOLATION LEVEL { READ UNCOMMITTED
                               | READ COMMITTED
                               | REPEATABLE READ
                               | SERIALIZABLE } ]
```

A.3 DATA DEFINITION

```
schema-def
   ::=   CREATE SCHEMA [ schema ] [ AUTHORIZATION user ]
             [ DEFAULT CHARACTER SET character-set ]
             [ schema-element-list ]

schema-element
   ::=   domain-def
       | base-table-def
       | view-def
       | authorization-def
       | general-constraint-def
       | character-set-def
       | collation-def
       | translation-def

domain-def
   ::=   CREATE DOMAIN domain [ AS ] data-type
             [ default-def ]
             [ domain-constraint-def ]

default-def
   ::=   DEFAULT { literal | niladic-function-ref | NULL }

base-table-def
   ::=   CREATE [ [ GLOBAL | LOCAL ] TEMPORARY ] TABLE base-table
             ( base-table-element-commalist )
             [ ON COMMIT { DELETE | PRESERVE } ROWS ]

base-table-element
   ::=   column-def | base-table-constraint-def

column-def
   ::=   column { data-type | domain }
             [ default-def ]
             [ column-constraint-def-list ]

view-def
   ::=   CREATE VIEW view [ ( column-commalist ) ]
             AS table-exp
                   [ WITH [ CASCADED | LOCAL ] CHECK OPTION ]

authorization-def
   ::=   GRANT { privilege-commalist | ALL PRIVILEGES }
                ON accessible-object TO grantee-commalist
                               [ WITH GRANT OPTION ]

general-constraint-def
   ::=   CREATE ASSERTION constraint CHECK ( cond-exp )
                               [ deferrability ]

deferrability
   ::=   INITIALLY { DEFERRED | IMMEDIATE }
         [ NOT ] DEFERRABLE

privilege
   ::=   SELECT
       | INSERT [ ( column-commalist ) ]
       | UPDATE [ ( column-commalist ) ]
       | DELETE
       | REFERENCES [ ( column-commalist ) ]
       | USAGE
```

```
accessible-object
    ::=    DOMAIN domain
        |  [ TABLE ] table
        |  CHARACTER SET character-set
        |  COLLATION collation
        |  TRANSLATION translation

grantee
    ::=    user | PUBLIC

character-set-def
    ::=  CREATE CHARACTER SET character-set [ AS ]
             GET character-set
             [ COLLATE collation | COLLATION FROM collation-source ]

collation-source
    ::=    EXTERNAL ( 'collation' )
        |  collation
        |  DESC ( collation )
        |  DEFAULT
        |  TRANSLATION translation [ THEN COLLATION collation ]

collation-def
    ::=  CREATE COLLATION collation
             FOR   character-set
             FROM collation-source

translation-def
    ::=  CREATE TRANSLATION translation
             FOR   character-set
             TO    character-set
             FROM translation-source

translation-source
    ::=    EXTERNAL ( 'translation' )
        |  IDENTITY
        |  translation

domain-alteration
    ::=    ALTER DOMAIN domain domain-alteration-action

domain-alteration-action
    ::=    domain-default-alteration-action
        |  domain-constraint-alteration-action

domain-default-alteration-action
    ::=    SET default-def
        |  DROP DEFAULT

domain-constraint-alteration-action
    ::=    ADD domain-constraint-def
        |  DROP CONSTRAINT constraint

base-table-alteration
    ::=    ALTER TABLE base-table base-table-alteration-action

base-table-alteration-action
    ::=    column-alteration-action
        |  base-table-constraint-alteration-action
```

```
column-alteration-action
  ::=    ADD [ COLUMN ] column-def
      | ALTER [ COLUMN ] column
                { SET default-def | DROP DEFAULT }
      | DROP [ COLUMN ] column { RESTRICT | CASCADE }

base-table-constraint-alteration-action
  ::=    ADD base-table-constraint-def
      | DROP CONSTRAINT constraint { RESTRICT | CASCADE }

schema-drop
  ::=    DROP SCHEMA schema { RESTRICT | CASCADE }

domain-drop
  ::=    DROP DOMAIN domain { RESTRICT | CASCADE }

base-table-drop
  ::=    DROP TABLE base-table { RESTRICT | CASCADE }

view-drop
  ::=    DROP VIEW view { RESTRICT | CASCADE }

authorization-drop
  ::=    REVOKE [ GRANT OPTION FOR ] privilege-commalist
                ON accessible-object FROM grantee-commalist
                                      { RESTRICT | CASCADE }

general-constraint-drop
  ::=    DROP ASSERTION constraint

character-set-drop
  ::=    DROP CHARACTER SET character-set

collation-drop
  ::=    DROP COLLATION collation

translation-drop
  ::=    DROP TRANSLATION translation
```

A.4 MODULES

```
module-def
  ::=    MODULE [ module ] [ NAMES ARE character-set ]
         LANGUAGE { ADA | C | COBOL | FORTRAN | MUMPS
                  | PASCAL | PLI }
       [ SCHEMA schema ] [ AUTHORIZATION user ]
       [ temporary-table-def-list ]
         module-element-list

temporary-table-def
  ::=    DECLARE LOCAL TEMPORARY TABLE MODULE . base-table
              ( base-table-element-commalist )
              [ ON COMMIT { PRESERVE | DELETE } ROWS ]

module-element
  ::=    cursor-def
       | dynamic-cursor-def
       | procedure-def
```

```
procedure-def
    ::=     PROCEDURE procedure
            { parameter-def-list | ( parameter-def-commalist ) } ;
            SQL-statement ;
```

Note: "SQL-statement" is defined in Chapter 6, Section 6.2.

```
parameter-def
    ::=     parameter data-type
          | SQLCODE
          | SQLSTATE
```

A.5   DATA MANIPULATION

```
single-row-select
    ::=     SELECT [ ALL | DISTINCT ] select-item-commalist
            INTO    target-commalist
            FROM    table-ref-commalist
          [ WHERE   cond-exp ]
          [ GROUP   BY column-ref-commalist ]
          [ HAVING  cond-exp ]

insert
    ::=     INSERT INTO table
            { [ ( column-commalist ) ] table-exp | DEFAULT VALUES }

searched-update
    ::=     UPDATE table
            SET     update-assignment-commalist
          [ WHERE   cond-exp ]

update-assignment
    ::=     column = { scalar-exp | DEFAULT | NULL }

searched-delete
    ::=     DELETE
            FROM    table
          [ WHERE   cond-exp ]

cursor-def
    ::=     DECLARE cursor [ INSENSITIVE ] [ SCROLL ] CURSOR FOR
                    table-exp
                  [ ORDER BY order-item-commalist ]
            [ FOR { READ ONLY | UPDATE [ OF column-commalist ] } ]

order-item
    ::=     { column | integer } [ ASC | DESC ]

open
    ::=     OPEN cursor

fetch
    ::=     FETCH [ [ row-selector ] FROM ] cursor
                                     INTO target-commalist

row-selector
    ::=     NEXT | PRIOR | FIRST | LAST
                 | ABSOLUTE number | RELATIVE number
```

```
positioned-update
   ::=    UPDATE table
          SET    update-assignment-commalist
          WHERE  CURRENT OF cursor

positioned-delete
   ::=    DELETE
          FROM   table
          WHERE  CURRENT OF cursor

close
   ::=    CLOSE cursor
```

A.6   TABLE EXPRESSIONS

```
table-exp
   ::=    join-table-exp | nonjoin-table-exp

join-table-exp
   ::=    table-ref [ NATURAL ] [ join-type ] JOIN table-ref
                     [ ON cond-exp | USING ( column-commalist ) ]
        | table-ref CROSS JOIN table-ref
        | ( join-table-exp )

table-ref
   ::=    table [ [ AS ] range-variable
                     [ ( column-commalist ) ] ]
        | ( table-exp ) [ AS ] range-variable
                     [ ( column-commalist ) ]
        | join-table-exp

join-type
   ::=    INNER
        | LEFT [ OUTER ]
        | RIGHT [ OUTER ]
        | FULL [ OUTER ]
        | UNION

nonjoin-table-exp
   ::=    nonjoin-table-term
        | table-exp { UNION | EXCEPT } [ ALL ]
              [ CORRESPONDING [ BY ( column-commalist ) ] ]
                     table-term

nonjoin-table-term
   ::=    nonjoin-table-primary
        | table-term INTERSECT [ ALL ]
              [ CORRESPONDING [ BY ( column-commalist ) ] ]
                     table-primary

table-term
   ::=    nonjoin-table-term
        | join-table-exp

table-primary
   ::=    nonjoin-table-primary
        | join-table-exp
```

```
nonjoin-table-primary
    ::=    TABLE table
         | table-constructor
         | select-exp
         | ( nonjoin-table-exp )

table-constructor
    ::=    VALUES row-constructor-commalist

row-constructor
    ::=    scalar-exp | ( scalar-exp-commalist ) | ( table-exp )

select-exp
    ::=    SELECT [ ALL | DISTINCT ] select-item-commalist
              FROM table-ref-commalist
                [ WHERE cond-exp ]
                  [ GROUP BY column-ref-commalist ]
                    [ HAVING cond-exp ]

select-item
    ::=    scalar-exp [ [ AS ] column ]
         | [ range-variable . ] *
```

A.7 CONDITIONAL EXPRESSIONS

```
cond-exp
    ::=    cond-term
         | cond-exp OR cond-term

cond-term
    ::=    cond-factor
         | cond-term AND cond-factor

cond-factor
    ::=    [ NOT ] cond-test

cond-test
    ::=    cond-primary
              [ IS [ NOT ] { TRUE | FALSE | UNKNOWN } ]

cond-primary
    ::=    simple-cond | ( cond-exp )

simple-cond
    ::=    comparison-cond
         | between-cond
         | like-cond
         | in-cond
         | match-cond
         | all-or-any-cond
         | exists-cond
         | unique-cond
         | overlaps-cond
         | test-for-null

comparison-cond
    ::=    row-constructor comparison-operator row-constructor
```

```
comparison-operator
  ::=   = | < | <= | > | >= | <>

between-cond
  ::=   row-constructor [ NOT ] BETWEEN row-constructor
                                  AND row-constructor

like-cond
  ::=   character-string-exp
        [ NOT ] LIKE character-string-exp
             [ ESCAPE character-string-exp ]

in-cond
  ::=   row-constructor [ NOT ] IN ( table-exp )
      | scalar-exp [ NOT ] IN ( scalar-exp-commalist )

match-cond
  ::=   row-constructor MATCH [ UNIQUE ]
                         [ PARTIAL | FULL ] ( table-exp )

all-or-any-cond
  ::=   row-constructor
            comparison-operator { ALL | ANY | SOME }
                                      ( table-exp )

exists-cond
  ::=   EXISTS ( table-exp )

unique-cond
  ::=   UNIQUE ( table-exp )

overlaps-cond
  ::=   ( scalar-exp, scalar-exp )
            OVERLAPS ( scalar-exp, scalar-exp )

test-for-null
  ::=   row-constructor IS [ NOT ] NULL
```

A.8 CONSTRAINTS

```
domain-constraint-def
  ::=   [ CONSTRAINT constraint ] CHECK ( cond-exp )
                                      [ deferrability ]

base-table-constraint-def
  ::=   [ CONSTRAINT constraint ]
          candidate-key-def [ deferrability ]
      | [ CONSTRAINT constraint ]
          foreign-key-def [ deferrability ]
      | [ CONSTRAINT constraint ]
          check-constraint-def [ deferrability ]

candidate-key-def
  ::=   { PRIMARY KEY | UNIQUE } ( column-commalist )

foreign-key-def
  ::=   FOREIGN KEY ( column-commalist ) references-def
```

```
references-def
   ::=    REFERENCES base-table [ ( column-commalist ) ]
             [ MATCH { FULL | PARTIAL } ]
             [ ON DELETE referential-action ]
             [ ON UPDATE referential-action ]

referential-action
   ::=    NO ACTION | CASCADE | SET DEFAULT | SET NULL

check-constraint-def
   ::=    CHECK ( cond-exp )

column-constraint-def
   ::=    [ CONSTRAINT constraint ]
             NOT NULL [ deferrability ]
        | [ CONSTRAINT constraint ]
             { PRIMARY KEY | UNIQUE } [ deferrability ]
        | [ CONSTRAINT constraint ]
             references-def [ deferrability ]
        | [ CONSTRAINT constraint ]
             CHECK ( cond-exp ) [ deferrability ]

set-constraints
   ::=    SET CONSTRAINTS { constraint-commalist | ALL }
                                    { DEFERRED | IMMEDIATE }
```

A.9 DYNAMIC SQL

```
execute-immediate
   ::=    EXECUTE IMMEDIATE param-or-var

prepare
   ::=    PREPARE prepared FROM param-or-var

prepared
   ::=    prepped-statement-container | param-or-var

deallocate-prepare
   ::=    DEALLOCATE PREPARE prepared

execute
   ::=    EXECUTE prepared [ INTO places ] [ USING arguments ]

places
   ::=    target-commalist | SQL DESCRIPTOR descriptor

arguments
   ::=    target-commalist | SQL DESCRIPTOR descriptor

descriptor
   ::=    lit-param-or-var

allocate-descriptor
   ::=    ALLOCATE DESCRIPTOR descriptor
                  [ WITH MAX lit-param-or-var ]

deallocate-descriptor
   ::=    DEALLOCATE DESCRIPTOR descriptor
```

```
describe-input
   ::=   DESCRIBE INPUT prepared
                 USING SQL DESCRIPTOR descriptor

describe-output
   ::=   DESCRIBE [ OUTPUT ] prepared
                 USING SQL DESCRIPTOR descriptor

get-descriptor-1
   ::=   GET DESCRIPTOR descriptor target = COUNT

get-descriptor-2
   ::=   GET DESCRIPTOR descriptor
             VALUE number get-assignment-commalist

get-assignment
   ::=   target = item-descriptor-element
```

Note: "Item-descriptor-element" is explained in Chapter 20, Section 20.4.

```
set-descriptor-1
   ::=   SET DESCRIPTOR descriptor COUNT = lit-param-or-var

set-descriptor-2
   ::=   SET DESCRIPTOR descriptor
             VALUE number set-assignment-commalist

set-assignment
   ::=   item-descriptor-element = lit-param-or-var
```

Note: "Item-descriptor-element" is explained in Chapter 20, Section 20.4.

```
dynamic-cursor-def
   ::=   DECLARE cursor [ INSENSITIVE ] [ SCROLL ] CURSOR
         FOR prepared

allocate-cursor
   ::=   ALLOCATE param-or-var [ INSENSITIVE ] [ SCROLL ] CURSOR
         FOR prepared

dynamic-open
   ::=   OPEN dynamic-cursor [ USING arguments ]

dynamic-cursor
   ::=   cursor | param-or-var

dynamic-close
   ::=   CLOSE dynamic-cursor

dynamic-fetch
   ::=   FETCH [ [ row-selector ] FROM ] dynamic-cursor
             INTO places

dynamic-positioned-delete
   ::=   DELETE [ FROM table ]
         WHERE CURRENT OF dynamic-cursor
```

```
dynamic-positioned-update
    ::=    UPDATE [ table ] SET assignment-commalist
           WHERE CURRENT OF dynamic-cursor
```

A.10 SCALAR EXPRESSIONS

```
scalar-exp
    ::=    numeric-exp
         | character-string-exp
         | bit-string-exp
         | datetime-exp
         | interval-exp

numeric-exp
    ::=    numeric-term
         | numeric-exp { + | - } numeric-term

numeric-term
    ::=    numeric-factor
         | numeric-term { * | / } numeric-factor

numeric-factor
    ::=    [ + | - ] numeric-primary

numeric-primary
    ::=    column-ref
         | lit-param-or-var
         | scalar-function-ref
         | aggregate-function-ref
         | ( table-exp )
         | ( numeric-exp )

aggregate-function-ref
    ::=    COUNT(*)
         | { AVG | MAX | MIN | SUM | COUNT }
             ( [ ALL | DISTINCT ] scalar-exp )

character-string-exp
    ::=    character-string-concatenation
         | character-string-primary

character-string-concatenation
    ::=    character-string-exp || character-string-primary
```

Note: The symbol "||" here represents the concatenation operator—it should not be confused with the vertical bar "|" that is used to separate alternatives in the grammar.

```
character-string-primary
    ::=    column-ref
         | lit-param-or-var
         | user-function-ref
         | scalar-function-ref
         | aggregate-function-ref
         | ( table-exp )
         | ( character-string-exp )
```

```
bit-string-exp
    ::=    bit-string-concatenation
        | bit-string-primary

bit-string-concatenation
    ::=    bit-string-exp || bit-string-primary
```

Note: The symbol "||" here represents the concatenation operator—it should not be confused with the vertical bar "|" that is used to separate alternatives in the grammar.

```
bit-string-primary
    ::=    column-ref
        | lit-param-or-var
        | scalar-function-ref
        | aggregate-function-ref
        | ( table-exp )
        | ( bit-string-exp )

datetime-exp
    ::=    datetime-term
        | interval-exp + datetime-term
        | datetime-exp { + | - } interval-term

datetime-term
    ::=    datetime-primary
                   [ AT { LOCAL | TIME ZONE interval-exp } ]

datetime-primary
    ::=    column-ref
        | lit-param-or-var
        | datetime-function-ref
        | scalar-function-ref
        | aggregate-function-ref
        | ( table-exp )
        | ( datetime-exp )

interval-exp
    ::=    interval-term
        | interval-exp { + | - } interval-term
        | ( datetime exp - datetime-term ) start [ TO end ]
```

Note: The values "start" and "end" here are datetime fields. See Chapter 17.

```
interval-term
    ::=    interval-factor
        | interval-term { * | / } numeric-factor
        | numeric-term * interval-factor

interval-factor
    ::=    [ + | - ] interval-primary [ start [ TO end ] ]
```

Note: The values "start" and "end" here are datetime fields, and appear only in a certain dynamic SQL context. See Chapters 17 and 20.

```
interval-primary
    ::=    column-ref
         | lit-param-or-var
         | scalar-function-ref
         | aggregate-function-ref
         | ( table-exp )
         | ( interval-exp )
```

A.11 MISCELLANEOUS

```
schema
    ::=    [ catalog . ] identifier

domain
    ::=    [ schema . ] identifier

table
    ::=    base-table | view

base-table
    ::=    [ schema . ] identifier

view
    ::=    [ schema . ] identifier

constraint
    ::=    [ schema . ] identifier

character-set
    ::=    [ schema . ] identifier

collation
    ::=    [ schema . ] identifier

translation
    ::=    [ schema . ] identifier

conversion
    ::=    [ schema . ] identifier

column-ref
    ::=    [ column-qualifier . ] column

column-qualifier
    ::=    table | range-variable

param-or-var
    ::=    parameter [ [ INDICATOR ] parameter ]
         | host-variable [ [ INDICATOR ] host-variable ]

lit-param-or-var
    ::=    literal | param-or-var

target
    ::=    param-or-var

number
    ::=    lit-param-or-var
```

```
niladic-function-ref
    ::=    user-function-ref
         | datetime-function-ref

user-function-ref
    ::=    USER
         | CURRENT_USER
         | SESSION_USER
         | SYSTEM_USER

datetime-function-ref
    ::=    CURRENT_DATE
         | CURRENT_TIME [ ( integer ) ]
         | CURRENT_TIMESTAMP [ ( integer ) ]
```

Language Levels
and Conformance

B.1 INTRODUCTION

The official SQL standard document defines three language *levels*: Full SQL, Intermediate SQL, and Entry SQL. The general idea is that Full SQL is the entire standard, Intermediate SQL is a proper subset of Full SQL, and Entry SQL is a proper subset of Intermediate SQL. The intent is to permit implementation to be "staged," so that over time support can progress from Entry to Intermediate to Full SQL support (see below). Section B.2 summarizes the major features of Full SQL that are omitted from Intermediate SQL, and Section B.3 summarizes the major features that are additionally omitted from Entry SQL.

The SQL language defined by the standard is said to be "conforming SQL language." An implementation is said to be a "conforming SQL implementation" if it processes conforming SQL language according to the specifications of the standard. Thus, a conforming SQL implementation must support conforming SQL language to at least Entry level. Such an implementation must also support at least one "binding style" (module, embedded SQL, or direct), and, in the module and embedded SQL cases, at least one of the official host languages (Ada, C, COBOL, FORTRAN,

MUMPS, Pascal, or PL/I). Furthermore, such an implementation must also provide documented definitions for all features of conforming SQL language that are stated by the standard to be implementation-defined.

Note, however, that a conforming implementation is explicitly permitted:

- To provide support for additional facilities or options not specified in the standard
- To provide options to process conforming SQL language in a nonconforming manner
- To provide options to process nonconforming SQL language

On the other hand, an implementation that claims conformance to the standard at any level—except possibly Entry level—is also required to provide an *SQL Flagger* option to flag items that do not conform to the specified level. See Section B.4.

Then again, many aspects of the standard are explicitly stated to be "implementation-dependent," i.e., undefined; in fact, certain aspects seem—presumably unintentionally—to be *im*plicitly undefined also (see Appendix D). Even if two implementations can both legitimately claim to be conforming, therefore, there can be no absolute guarantee of application portability.

The standard specifically does not define the method by which an embedded SQL application program is compiled or otherwise processed.

B.2   INTERMEDIATE SQL

In this section we list some of the major differences between Full SQL and Intermediate SQL. Please note that we are *not* aiming at completeness in what follows; the intent is merely to give the reader a general idea of how Full SQL and Intermediate SQL differ. For the specifics, the reader is referred to the standard document per se.

First, here is a list of Full SQL constructs that are omitted entirely from Intermediate SQL:

- Identifiers in which the final character is an underscore
- Explicit catalog names
- SET CATALOG, SET SCHEMA, SET NAMES
- CONNECT, SET CONNECTION, DISCONNECT
- Everything to do with bit strings
- Everything to do with translations, conversions, and (explicit) collations

- Explicit precision specification for TIMEs and TIMESTAMPs
- Datetime or interval SECOND values with more than microsecond accuracy
- POSITION, UPPER, LOWER
- UNION JOIN
- CORRESPONDING on UNION, EXCEPT, and INTERSECT
- IS [NOT] TRUE, IS [NOT] FALSE, IS [NOT] UNKNOWN
- MATCH conditions and MATCH in foreign key definitions
- General constraints (CREATE and DROP ASSERTION)
- Base table check constraints that reference other tables
- ON UPDATE in foreign key definitions
- Deferrable constraints and SET CONSTRAINTS
- "Global" and "declared local" temporary tables
- Column-specific INSERT privileges
- LOCAL or CASCADED in check options (though CASCADED must be supported implicitly)
- ALTER DOMAIN
- INSENSITIVE cursors
- The specification "TABLE table" within a table expression
- Parameters or host variables as SQL descriptor area names
- Everything to do with user-generated statement names
- Everything to do with user-generated cursor names
- DEALLOCATE PREPARE, DESCRIBE INPUT, and (in EXECUTE) INTO "places"

And here is a list of additional restrictions:

- A table reference cannot be a table expression in parentheses.
- The operator DISTINCT is permitted within a table expression at most once at each level of nesting.
- The list of comparands on the right-hand side of an IN condition must not include any item more complex than a literal, a column reference, or a niladic builtin function.
- If an aggregate function reference specifies DISTINCT, the argument must consist of a simple column reference.
- The REFERENCES privilege is not required for columns referenced in a check constraint. *Note*: This is actually the *opposite* of a restriction.

It implies that Intermediate SQL is not quite a "proper subset" of Full SQL after all.

- If a cursor definition includes ORDER BY, FOR READ ONLY is implied.

- An INSERT, UPDATE, or DELETE statement cannot include a WHERE clause (either directly in the case of a searched operation, or via the cursor definition in the case of a positioned operation) that references the table that is the target of that INSERT, UPDATE, or DELETE statement.

- Certain Information Schema tables (e.g., TRANSLATIONS) must not be referenced.

B.3 ENTRY SQL

In this section we list some of the additional features of Full SQL that are omitted from Entry SQL, over and above those already omitted from Intermediate SQL. Please note once again, however, that we are *not* aiming at completeness here; the intent again is just to give the general idea.

- Identifiers of more than 18 characters
- Lower case letters in identifiers
- SET SESSION AUTHORIZATION
- Varying length strings
- Implementation-defined character sets, including national character strings
- Everything to do with datetimes and intervals
- Domains
- Explicit constraint names
- CURRENT_USER, SESSION_USER, and SYSTEM_USER (USER is supported, however)
- CHARACTER_LENGTH, OCTET_LENGTH
- SUBSTRING, TRIM, EXTRACT
- Concatenation
- CASE
- CAST
- DEFAULT in INSERT and UPDATE

- JOIN
- EXCEPT and INTERSECT
- Select-items of the form "R.*"
- UNIQUE conditions
- DROP SCHEMA
- DROP TABLE
- ON DELETE in foreign key definitions
- ALTER TABLE
- DROP VIEW
- REVOKE
- SET TRANSACTION
- Dynamic SQL
- SCROLL cursors
- FOR UPDATE on a cursor definition
- Conversion between exact and approximate numeric on assignment
- The Information Schema
- GET DIAGNOSTICS

And here is a list of additional restrictions:

- A row constructor must include exactly one component, *except* for the special case in which the row constructor is a component within a table constructor (in which case it must be the *only* such component) *and* that table constructor is being used to define the source for an INSERT operation.
- A table expression in parentheses is not allowed to include UNION.
- If the FROM clause in a select-expression references a view whose definition involves a GROUP BY or HAVING clause, then (a) that FROM clause must not mention any other tables, (b) that select-expression cannot include a WHERE, GROUP BY, or HAVING clause, and (c) the SELECT clause in that select-expression must not include any aggregate function references.
- A single-row SELECT statement cannot include a GROUP BY or HAVING clause and cannot reference a view whose definition involves a GROUP BY or HAVING clause.
- If either comparand of a comparison condition is a select-expression in parentheses, that select-expression must not contain a GROUP BY or

HAVING clause and must not reference a view whose definition contains a GROUP BY or HAVING clause.

- For UNION, the data types of corresponding columns must be *exactly* the same (and NOT NULL must apply either to both or to neither).

- In a LIKE condition, the first operand must be a column reference and "pattern" and "escape" must each be a literal, parameter, or host variable.

- In a test for null, the operand must be a column reference.

- CREATE SCHEMA must include an AUTHORIZATION clause and must not include a schema name.

- A module definition must include an AUTHORIZATION clause and must not include a SCHEMA clause.

- Every column mentioned in a candidate key definition must be explicitly defined to be NOT NULL.

- The key word TABLE must not appear in GRANT.

- COMMIT and ROLLBACK must include the noiseword WORK.

B.4   SQL FLAGGER

As mentioned in Section B.1, an implementation that claims conformance to the standard at any level is required to provide an *SQL Flagger*. The purpose of the Flagger is to flag any implementation-specific SQL constructs—i.e., SQL constructs that are recognized and supported by the implementation but do not conform to the level of the standard to which conformance is claimed. The intent is to identify SQL features that might produce different results in different environments, i.e., features that might require attention if applications or SQL requests are moved from one environment to another. Such considerations might be relevant, for example, if an application is developed on a workstation but executed on a mainframe.

An implementation that claims *Full SQL* conformance must provide an SQL Flagger that supports the following options:

- *Entry SQL flagging* (i.e., an option to flag SQL constructs that do not conform to Entry SQL)

- *Intermediate SQL flagging* (i.e., an option to flag SQL constructs that do not conform to Intermediate SQL)

- *Full SQL flagging* (i.e., an option to flag SQL constructs that do not conform to Full SQL)

It must also support both "syntax only" and "catalog lookup" checking options. "Syntax only" checking means that the implementation is required only to perform those checks that are possible without access to the Definition Schema. "Catalog lookup" checking means that the implementation is additionally required to perform those checks (except privilege checks) that are possible if the Definition Schema is available. *Note*: In both cases, the intent is that the checking be "static" (i.e., "compilation time") checking only; there is no requirement to check for items that cannot be determined until execution time.

An implementation that claims *Intermediate SQL* conformance must provide an SQL Flagger that supports Entry SQL and Intermediate SQL flagging, and must support at least "syntax only" checking.

An implementation that claims *Entry SQL* conformance may optionally provide an SQL Flagger that supports at least "syntax only" Entry SQL flagging.

SQL/92 vs. SQL/89

C.1 INTRODUCTION

For the benefit of the reader who may be familiar with the previous version of the standard, viz. "SQL/89," we present in this appendix a brief summary of the major differences between that version and the new standard, viz. "SQL/92." Section C.2 lists the major extensions—i.e., features of SQL/92 that had no counterpart in SQL/89. Section C.3 describes all known incompatibilities between the two versions. Finally, Section C.4 gives a list of "deprecated features" (officially so designated) of the new standard.

C.2 EXTENSIONS

In this section we summarize the major new features introduced in SQL/92.

- Everything to do with embedded SQL. *Note*: Embedded SQL was the subject of a separate ANSI standard, "Database Language Embedded SQL," but was never part of SQL/89 per se, nor was it an ISO standard. Furthermore, that separate ANSI standard did not include MUMPS support, and SQL/89 did not include Ada or C support either.

- Everything to do with catalogs, and almost everything to do with schemas. SQL/89 did have a statement called CREATE SCHEMA—but no DROP SCHEMA!—and all CREATE TABLEs, CREATE VIEWs, and GRANTs had to be specified as "schema elements" within such a CREATE SCHEMA statement (i.e., there was no concept of executing such statements independently, as there is in SQL/92). However, the schema concept per se was essentially undefined. Note too that CREATE TABLE, CREATE VIEW, and GRANT were the *only* data definition operations in SQL/89; DROP TABLE, ALTER TABLE, etc., did not exist.

- The ability to include all kinds of SQL statements within a module. As already mentioned, CREATE TABLE, CREATE VIEW, and GRANT had to be executed as components of a CREATE SCHEMA operation in SQL/89; in fact, CREATE SCHEMA, CREATE TABLE, CREATE VIEW, and GRANT together constituted a separate "schema language" that was quite distinct from the "module language." The undesirable and unnecessary distinction between schema language and module language has been almost eliminated in SQL/92.

- The ability to include all kinds of SQL operations—in particular, the ability to mix data definition and data manipulation operations—in a single transaction. Because of the separation between schema and module languages mentioned in the previous paragraph, SQL/89 did not have this capability.

- Everything to do with SQL-connections and SQL-sessions.

- The SET TRANSACTION statement, including in particular the ability to specify an isolation level (SQL/89 supported SERIALIZABLE only, and that only implicitly).

- Everything to do with domains, including CREATE, ALTER, and DROP DOMAIN.

- ALTER and DROP TABLE.

- Everything to do with temporary tables.

- CASCADED and LOCAL variants of the check option on CREATE VIEW.

- DROP VIEW.

- Almost everything to do with integrity constraints, except for candidate key and foreign key definitions and one simple form of base table check constraint. SQL/89 did have candidate keys and foreign keys, and it did have single-row check constraints (i.e., constraints that could be tested for a given row by examining just that row in isolation). However, it did not have general (multiple-row) constraints, it did not have FULL vs. PARTIAL matching on foreign keys, it did not have any explicit referential actions, and it did not have any deferred checking (DEFERRABLE, INITIALLY DEFERRED, SET CONSTRAINTS, etc.).

- REVOKE.

- Varying length character strings.

- Bit strings, both fixed and varying length.

- Everything to do with dates and times.

- Almost everything to do with character sets, collations, translations, and conversions (including national character set support and character sets for identifiers). SQL/89 did support a fixed-length character string data type, together with an associated set of assignment and comparison operators, but that was about all (in particular, the character set and collating sequence were essentially implementation-defined).

- All scalar operators and functions (except +, −, *, /, and USER), including in particular the CASE operator, and CAST for controlling data type conversions.

- Greatly improved orthogonality in scalar expressions, including in particular the ability to use scalar values from the database as operands within such an expression. *Note*: See the subsection "A Note on Orthogonality" at the end of this section for a brief explanation of the concept of orthogonality.

- The FOR UPDATE, SCROLL, and INSENSITIVE specifications on DECLARE CURSOR.

- Greatly improved orthogonality in table expressions, including (a) the ability to introduce result column names and table names, (b) a set of column name inheritance rules, and (c) the ability to nest table expressions.

- Explicit support for INTERSECT, EXCEPT, and JOIN (including natural join and outer join).

- Row constructors, including in particular the ability to use such constructors in conditional expressions as well as scalars.

- New MATCH and UNIQUE conditions.

- New IS [NOT] TRUE, IS [NOT] FALSE, and IS [NOT] UNKNOWN conditions.

- Everything to do with dynamic SQL.

- The Information Schema.

- SQLSTATE and everything to do with the Diagnostics Area.
- A more comprehensive treatment of direct SQL (though many of the specifics are still implementation-defined).

A Note on Orthogonality

Orthogonality means *independence*. A language is orthogonal if independent concepts are kept independent and are not mixed together in confusing ways. An example of *lack* of orthogonality in SQL/89 was provided by the rule that a scalar value in an INSERT statement had to be represented by a simple variable or literal, not by an arbitrary scalar expression. Orthogonality is desirable because the less orthogonal a language is, the more complicated it is and—paradoxically but simultaneously—the less powerful it is. "Orthogonal design maximizes expressive power while avoiding deleterious superfluities" (from A. van Wijngaarden et al., eds., *Revised Report on the Algorithmic Language Algol 68*, Springer-Verlag, 1976).

C.3 INCOMPATIBILITIES

The SQL/92 document includes an "annex" (i.e., appendix) identifying a number of incompatibilities between SQL/92 and SQL/89. We list those incompatibilities below. *Note*: It is not always clear exactly what it is that constitutes an incompatibility; in some respects the concept is rather elusive. For example, consider the specification PRIMARY KEY, which implies NOT NULL in SQL/92 but not in SQL/89. There is clearly an incompatibility here of a kind. However, SQL/89 had an additional rule to the effect that every column mentioned in a PRIMARY KEY specification must be *explicitly declared* to be NOT NULL; hence a program that did not produce an error in this area in SQL/89 will also not produce an error in this area in SQL/92, and so the incompatibility is presumably unimportant. On the other hand, of course, a program that was deliberately intended to produce some specific error in SQL/89 might fail to do so in SQL/92.

Here anyway are the incompatibilities identified in the SQL/92 document:

- First, SQL/92 has well over 100 additional reserved words. For specifics, the reader is referred to the standard document.
- In SQL/89, the implied module for embedded SQL had an implementation-defined authID; in SQL/92, it has no authID at all.
- Parameter names did not have a colon prefix in SQL/89. Such a prefix is required in SQL/92.

- SQL/89 allowed two distinct candidate key definitions for the same base table to specify the same set of columns. SQL/92 does not.

- SQL/89 did not preclude the possibility of defining a view recursively, i.e., in terms of itself. SQL/92 does preclude such a possibility.

- The semantics of WITH CHECK OPTION were ambiguous in SQL/ 89 but have been clarified in SQL/92. (At least, this is what the SQL/ 92 document claims. It would be more accurate to say that the check option was not inheritable in SQL/89 but (by default) is so in SQL/ 92—i.e., this change is truly an incompatibility, not just a "clarification." See the discussion of LOCAL and CASCADED in Chapter 13.)

- Let cursor *C* be declared without an ORDER BY clause, and let cursor *C* be opened multiple times within the same SQL-transaction. In SQL/ 89, the rows accessed by cursor *C* must be returned in the same order on each opening. In SQL/92, the order is implementation-dependent on each opening, and thus can differ from one opening to the next.

  Note: A similar remark presumably applies if ORDER BY *is* specified but does not define a total ordering for the rows (see Chapter 10), but the SQL/92 document does not explicitly say as much.

- In SQL/89, if a cursor is on or before some row and that row is deleted, the cursor is positioned before the next row or (if there is no next row) after the last row. In SQL/92, this cursor state change is defined only if the DELETE is done via the cursor in question; otherwise the effect on the cursor is implementation-dependent.

- In SQL/89, the SELECT privilege was required only for tables accessed via FETCH or single-row SELECT statements. In SQL/92, it is additionally required for tables mentioned in certain table expressions, conditional expressions, and scalar expressions.

- Finally, the SQL/92 document identifies one additional known incompatibility, which (as with a couple of other aspects of the standard— see, e.g., the explanation of CREATE . . . TEMPORARY TABLE in Chapter 18) we cannot do better than describe in a slight paraphrase of the standard's own words:*

  "[SQL/89] did not preclude the possibility of using outer references in < set function specification > s in < subquery > s contained in the < search condition > of a < having clause > , but did not define the semantics of such a construction. [SQL/92] adds a Syntax Rule in [the definition of] < set function specification > and a Syntax Rule in [the definition of] < where clause > to preclude that possibility."

---

*Though we did make an attempt at a better description in Section 7.5. See paragraph number 5 following the definition of the syntax of "aggregate function reference."

Note: The term ''<set function specification>'' corresponds to what we have been calling an aggregate function reference in this book.

The Syntax Rules referred to are as follows. First, in the definition of <set function specification> we find the following:

''If the [argument] contains a <column reference> that is an outer reference, then that outer reference shall be the only <column reference> contained in the [argument] . . . [and] . . . the <set function specification> shall be contained in either:

''(a) a <select list>, or

''(b) a <subquery> of a <having clause>, in which case the scope of the explicit or implicit <qualifier> of the <column reference> shall be a <table reference> that is directly contained in the [select-expression] that directly contains the <having clause>.''

And in the definition of <where clause> we find:

''If a [scalar-expression] directly contained in the <search condition> is a <set function specification>, then the <where clause> shall be contained in a <having clause> or <select list> and the <column reference> in the <set function specification> shall be an outer reference . . . No <column reference> contained in a <subquery> in the <search condition> that references a column of *T* shall be specified in a <set function specification>.''

The foregoing is intended to be an exhaustive list; to quote the SQL/92 document, ''unless specified in this Annex, features and capabilities of [SQL/92] are compatible with [those of SQL/89].'' However, there seem to be a few additional areas where SQL/92 and SQL/89 are in some disagreement:

- As mentioned in Section C.2, SQL/89 consisted of two distinct languages, a module language and a schema language (more precisely, a schema *definition* language). CREATE TABLE, CREATE VIEW, and GRANT statements could appear only as elements within a CREATE SCHEMA statement, and that statement in turn was a schema definition language statement; thus, CREATE SCHEMA (and hence CREATE TABLE, CREATE VIEW, and GRANT, a fortiori) could *not* appear within a module. In an apparent attempt to remain compatible with this rather curious state of affairs, SQL/92 does refer repeatedly to the idea that a CREATE SCHEMA statement might be ''stand-alone,'' i.e., not included within a module; however, there does not seem to be any way that such a possibility can occur (as explained in Chapter 6, there is *always* a module, at least implicitly).

- In SQL/89, the REFERENCES privilege was required only for candidate keys that were referenced by some foreign key. In SQL/92, it is required for every column that is mentioned in some integrity constraint.

- SQL/89 permitted qualified column names in the ORDER BY clause. SQL/92 does not. *Note*: This change is perhaps better regarded as a correction rather than an incompatibility. Qualified column names in ORDER BY were a mistake in SQL/89, since the scope of the relevant range variable did not include (or, at least, should not have included) the ORDER BY clause.

- In SQL/92 USER returns the current authID, not a schema or module authID. In SQL/89 it returned the module authID.

   Note: This is certainly a definitional change, but perhaps it should not be regarded as an incompatibility per se (i.e., it should not cause an SQL/89 program to fail under SQL/92, thanks to SQL/92's system of defaults).

- In SQL/89, the high-level qualifier for (e.g.) base table names was an authID. In SQL/92 it is a schema name, which in turn includes a possibly implicit catalog name as another (next higher level) qualifier.

   Note: Like the previous point, this is certainly a definitional change, but perhaps it should not be regarded as an incompatibility per se.

C.4   DEPRECATED FEATURES

The SQL/92 document also includes an annex identifying "deprecated features"—i.e., features that are retained in SQL/92 only for compatibility with SQL/89 and are likely to be dropped in some future version of the standard. We list those features below.

- SQLCODE (SQLSTATE is preferred). Consequently, a COBOL integer variable defined as USAGE IS COMPUTATIONAL is also deprecated, since this USAGE is supported only for SQLCODE.

- Unsigned integers as order-items within an ORDER BY clause (the use of column names, perhaps introduced via an AS clause on the relevant select-items, is preferred).

- Unparenthesized lists of parameter definitions in procedures (parenthesized commalists are preferred).

Some Outstanding Issues

If you're not confused by all this,
it just proves you're not thinking clearly (anon).

D.1 INTRODUCTION

As mentioned in the preface to this book, there are many aspects of the standard that appear to be inadequately defined, or even incorrectly defined, at this time. Despite the fact that the standard per se has been formally ratified, therefore, it is likely that a number of formal follow-up documents will be needed to clarify and elaborate on various specific aspects of the standard over the next few years. In this appendix we identify and comment on a number of features that seemed to the present authors, during the writing of this book, to be insufficiently or incorrectly specified—in other words, features that constitute outstanding or unresolved issues. In doing this, we have two broad purposes in mind:

- For *implementers*, the appendix serves to pinpoint aspects of the standard that (at the very least) deserve further study, and perhaps omission from a first product release in some cases.

- For *users*, the appendix serves to provide a checklist of features that should be used with some circumspection, or perhaps even avoided for the time being.

A couple of additional preliminary remarks:

1. In the interests of brevity, we concentrate on issues over which there may genuinely be some confusion, ignoring items that are wrong only

in some trivially obvious way. For example, the standard states that "[A scalar] value is primitive in that it has no logical subdivision within this [standard]." Now, this statement is clearly incorrect in the case of datetime and interval values, and arguably in the case of other scalar values also, such as strings; however, the error is not very significant, and is thus scarcely worth discussing further. The standard contains literally dozens of such "trivially" incorrect statements, and there is simply no point in trying to deal with them all here.

2. Since it looks as if the standard is necessarily going to be the subject of a continual revision and clarification process for some time to come, it is entirely possible that some of the remarks in this appendix may no longer be valid by the time this book appears in print, or by the time it reaches the reader's hands. Also, of course, it is entirely possible that the authors may have misconstrued the standard in the first place and that some of our remarks may be incorrect. If so, we apologize.

Hugh Darwen adds a personal statement:

In endorsing this list of criticisms, which I have carefully reviewed, I find myself in a rather strange and possibly embarrassing position, for I have been, since 1988, an active and contributing member of the ISO committee responsible for the SQL standard. Personally, I lay most of the blame for the following problems (if problems they be) firmly on SQL itself. If the world needs a better database standard, it should prepare itself to move to a better database *language*.

D.2 THE ISSUES

In this section we present the list of issues, in a sequence that approximates the sequence in which the relevant topics were first discussed in the body of the text (although the assignment of issues to categories is sometimes a little arbitrary). Some of the points, and some of the commentary thereon, are essentially just a repetition of material from the main part of the book; other items are new.

Basic Terminology

- In Chapter 1 we introduced the important terms "implementation-defined" and "implementation-dependent." Here are the standard's definitions of these terms:

Implementation-defined: Possibly differing between SQL-implementations, but specified . . . for each particular SQL-implementation.

Implementation-dependent: Possibly differing between SQL-implementations, but not specified by this International Standard and not required to be specified . . . for any particular SQL-implementation.

The trouble with these definitions is that they effectively confuse the notions of an *implementation* and an implementation *instance* (or DBMS and DBMS instance, to make matters more concrete). For example, the maximum length of a character string and the default SQL-server are both stated by the standard to be implementation-defined. However, the former will be the same for all instances of a given implementation, while the latter will vary from one instance of a given implementation to another. National character sets and default time zones are other important examples of "implementation-defined" constructs that will clearly vary from instance to instance, in general.

Basic Language Elements

- According to the standard, "&" (ampersand) is an SQL special character, while "[" and "]" (left and right bracket) are SQL embedded language characters. This slight discrepancy is a trifle mysterious, given that the only use for all three characters is in embedded SQL programs (ampersand in MUMPS, and left and right bracket in Pascal and C).

- The rule by which it is determined within the standard that one key word is reserved while another is not is not clear.

- We pointed out in Chapter 19 (Section 19.8) that, although the standard does avoid the need for an infinite *sequence* of identifier "introducers" (i.e., character set name prefixes, such as _FRANCAIS), it does not avoid the need for an infinite *nest* of them.

Catalogs and Schemas

- As mentioned in Appendix C, the standard refers repeatedly to the idea that a CREATE SCHEMA statement might be "standalone," i.e., not included within a module, yet there does not seem to be any way that such a possibility can occur (there is *always* supposed to be a module, at least implicitly).

- Note that, since individual SQL statements are supposed to be "atomic," the elements within a single CREATE SCHEMA must somehow be thought of as all being executed simultaneously. In particular, therefore, it must be possible for (e.g.) two CREATE TABLE operations within a single CREATE SCHEMA each to include a foreign key definition that references the other. The full implications of such circular references and such simultaneity of execution are not clear.

- A specific instance of the foregoing arises in connection with CREATE CHARACTER SET and CREATE COLLATION. Consider the following:

```
CREATE CHARACTER SET CHARSET1 AS
       GET ...
       COLLATE COLL1

CREATE COLLATION COLL1
       FOR CHARSET1
       FROM ...
```

Since every character set has one default collation and every collation has one associated character set, some circularity of reference is unavoidable. Thus, it appears that the two CREATEs above cannot be executed independently but *must* be included within a CREATE SCHEMA operation.

Connections, Sessions, and Transactions

- There seems to be a certain amount of confusion over the "SQL-environment" and "SQL-implementation" concepts. First, an SQL-environment is defined to include an SQL-implementation (and the indefinite article "an" here strongly suggests the interpretation "exactly one"). An SQL-implementation, in turn, is defined to be just a database management system (DBMS) that conforms to the standard. So far, therefore, we would seem to be justified in thinking of the SQL-environment concept as essentially just an abstraction of the notion of an operational DBMS installation at a single computer site.

  Following on from the foregoing, it would seem reasonable to regard a system that supports some form of multisite or distributed processing as one that involves multiple SQL-environments, and multiple SQL-implementations, that are somehow capable of communication with one another.

  However, the standard goes on to state categorically that "within an SQL-environment, an SQL-implementation may be considered to effectively contain an SQL-client component and one or more SQL-server components"—implying that if the SQL-client and SQL-servers are at different sites, then all sites involved are considered to be part of the same SQL-environment. Yet each of those SQL-servers surely corresponds to what is usually thought of as a single DBMS. So now it looks as if a single SQL-environment, and a single SQL-implementation, can include multiple DBMSs and can span multiple sites, in general.

Note that the distinction between these two interpretations (one site vs. multiple sites per environment and implementation) is certainly significant, given that catalog names, authIDs, and module names are all required to be "unique within the SQL-environment." This requirement might be quite difficult to satisfy if the "multiple sites per environment" interpretation is indeed the correct one.

Of course, it is easy to speculate as to the source of the foregoing confusion. It seems to this writer extremely likely that the historical development of the concept went somewhat as follows:

1. Originally the "environment" idea was indeed supposed to be an abstraction of a single-site system.

2. However, somebody pointed out that, increasingly, real systems were beginning to support various kinds of distributed processing (especially client/server processing).

3. The standard committee therefore extended the environment notion to include the client and server concepts; i.e., the environment notion was redefined to include a *client*, together with one or more *servers* that were at least conceptually distinct from the client and from one another.

4. In order to support this change, the definition of the CONNECT operation was revised to say that a connection was established to a *server*, instead of to an *environment*. (An analogous revision was made to SET CONNECTION also.) *Note*: These particular revisions certainly did occur, as the historical record shows.

5. At the time of the foregoing revisions, the point was overlooked that (as stated above) authIDs, catalog names, and module names are defined to be unique within the *environment*, not (e.g.) within the *server*.

- (This point follows on from the previous one.) If a single SQL-implementation can truly span multiple servers, the possibility arises that those servers might come from multiple distinct implementers. If such is the case, the concepts "implementation-dependent" and (more importantly) "implementation-defined" become somewhat suspect.

- The standard allows the implementation to support transactions that span multiple SQL-servers, and hence span multiple *sessions* also (see Chapter 5). Such a possibility does not accord well with the usual intuitive interpretation of the terms "transaction" and "session"; surely there should be just one *session*, involving possibly multiple *connections*. But the standard states quite explicitly that "an SQL-session is associated with an SQL-connection" and that "an SQL-session involves an SQL-agent, an SQL-client, and an SQL-server." Both of these statements clearly imply that *one* session has *one* corresponding connection.

- Following on from the previous point: It seems that the optional support for multisession transactions was added at a late stage in the development of the standard, and certain implications of such support were not fully thought through. For example, the standard states that the effects of SET CONSTRAINTS are session-local (i.e., apply only to the current session). But what about the SET CONSTRAINTS ALL IMMEDIATE that is implicitly executed during COMMIT? Surely this particular SET CONSTRAINTS must apply to *all* sessions, dormant as well as current? Perhaps the standard should say something along the lines of "during COMMIT processessing, the pair of statements (SET CONNECTION, SET CONSTRAINTS ALL IMMEDIATE) is implicitly executed for every session."

    Likewise, the implicit CLOSE that is performed during COMMIT for all open cursors must apply to all open cursors *in all sessions*. And the implicit DELETE FROM T that is performed during COMMIT for certain temporary tables T must also apply *to all sessions*.

- Yet another confusion arises over the fundamental concepts discussed under the previous bullet item. As we saw, an SQL-implementation is defined to contain an SQL-client component, and again the indefinite article "an" strongly suggests the interpretation "exactly one." This interpretation in turn implies that if two different users at two different workstations connect simultaneously to the same mainframe DBMS (or server), then we are talking about two different environments!—which again raises questions about the scope of names (for authIDs, catalog names, and module names) and the meaning of "implementation-defined."

- Is it an error for a client C to CONNECT to server S if there is already an existing connection from C to S? If not, are there now two connections (and two sessions) between *C* and *S*? What are the implications for multisession transactions and the semantics of SET CONSTRAINTS ALL . . . (etc.)?

- The specification READ ONLY on SET TRANSACTION prohibits updates (except to temporary tables). The standard does not say whether it prohibits "SQL schema statements," which imply updates to *schemas* (and catalogs).

- The standard tends to suggest, but never quite states explicitly, that isolation level READ UNCOMMITTED guarantees that no concurrent transaction will be permitted to UPDATE or DELETE a row to which the READ UNCOMMITTED transaction has addressability (i.e., a row the READ UNCOMMITTED transaction has a cursor positioned on). To put it another way, it is not clear exactly what READ UNCOMMITTED does guarantee.

- In the "Concepts" section explaining transactions, the standard refers to the SQL-environment as a "resource manager." Surely it is the *SQL-implementation* (or perhaps the *SQL-server*), not the SQL-environment, that is a resource manager?

- The standard provides a variety of "SET" statements—SET CONNECTION, SET CONSTRAINTS, SET TRANSACTION, SET CATALOG, SET SCHEMA, SET NAMES, SET SESSION AUTHORIZATION, and SET TIME ZONE—each of which can be regarded as assigning a value to some hidden "system variable" (e.g., the name of the default catalog for the SQL-session, in the case of SET CATALOG). With one exception, however, the standard does not provide any way of discovering the current value of that system variable (the exception is SESSION AUTHORIZATION, whose value is returned by the niladic builtin function SESSION_USER). Note in particular that there is no CURRENT_TIMEZONE function (although the value of the "current time zone" system variable can be referenced implicitly via the AT TIME ZONE option in a datetime expression).

Modules, Embedded SQL, and Direct SQL

- We stated in the body of the text that there is *always* a module, at least conceptually, but the standard does not seem to say as much explicitly in the case of direct SQL. Presumably the module *ought* to be the "SQL-session module" in this case, but, to repeat, the standard does not say (although it does say that the current authID for direct SQL is the session authID).

Scalar Objects, Operators, and Expressions

- The standard states that "a numeric data type descriptor contains . . . the name of the specific numeric data type (NUMERIC, DECIMAL, INTEGER, SMALLINT, FLOAT, REAL, or DOUBLE PRECISION)"—implying that it is not quite accurate to say that REAL and DOUBLE PRECISION are just shorthands for FLOAT with a specific precision. The implications of this point are unclear.

- It is not clear why POSITION applies only to character strings, not to bit strings. Possibly this is just an oversight.

Domains and Base Tables

- The reader is cautioned that the behavior of the different varieties of DROP is very inconsistent. In particular, DROP DOMAIN, DROP TABLE, DROP COLLATION, and DROP TRANSLATION all behave differently with respect to their CASCADE effects (or lack of same). Refer to the body of the book for the specifics.

Noncursor Operations

- It is not clear why a single-row SELECT statement is not allowed to involve any UNION, INTERSECT, or EXCEPT operators (i.e., at the outermost level). The rule is particularly strange, given that "SELECT . . . FROM *T*," where *T* in turn is an arbitrarily complex table expression (possibly involving UNION, etc.) enclosed in parentheses, *is* legal.

Cursor Operations

- The standard requires the *n* in "ABSOLUTE *n*" or "RELATIVE *n*" (within a FETCH statement) to be a literal, parameter, or host variable, not a general numeric expression. It is not clear why this should be so.

- The standard says that UPDATE CURRENT cannot be used on column *C* if column *C* was mentioned in the ORDER BY clause for the relevant cursor. Why is there not a syntax rule for DECLARE CURSOR that says that no column mentioned in the ORDER BY clause can be explicitly mentioned in the FOR UPDATE clause, and why is not FOR UPDATE without a column-commalist defined to be shorthand for a FOR UPDATE clause with a column-commalist that specifies all and only those columns not mentioned in the ORDER BY clause?

- Consider the following example, which is based (as usual) on the suppliers-and-parts database.

```
DECLARE X CURSOR
    FOR SELECT SP.SNO, SP.QTY
        FROM   SP
```

Note that (a) cursor X is "updatable"; (b) the table that is visible through cursor X permits duplicate rows; (c) the underlying table (table SP) does *not* permit duplicate rows. Now suppose that a positioned UPDATE or DELETE operation is executed on cursor X (UPDATE or DELETE . . . WHERE CURRENT OF X). Then there is no way, in general, to define precisely which row of table SP is being updated or deleted by that operation.

Table Expressions

- Part of the standard's explanation of the FROM clause reads as follows: "The . . . Cartesian product, *CP*, is the multiset of all rows *R* such that *R* is the concatenation of a row from each of the identified tables. . . ." Note carefully, therefore, that *CP* is not well-defined!— despite the fact that the standard goes on to say that "The cardinality of *CP* is the product of the cardinalities of the identified tables." Consider the tables T1 and T2 shown below:

T1	C1		T2	C2
	0			1
	0			2

Either of the following fits the above definition for "the" Cartesian product *CP* of T1 and T2 (i.e., either one could be "the" multiset referred to):

CP1	C1	C2		CP2	C1	C2
	0	1			0	1
	0	1			0	2
	0	2			0	2
	0	2			0	2

Note, moreover, that the only way to resolve the ambiguity is by effectively defining a mapping from each of the (multiset) argument tables to a proper *set*, and likewise defining a mapping of the (multiset) result table—i.e., the desired Cartesian product—to a proper *set*. In other words, this whole area serves to emphasize the point once again that one of the most fundamental concepts in the entire SQL language (namely, the concept that tables should permit duplicate rows) is *fundamentally flawed*—and cannot be repaired without, in effect, dispensing with the concept altogether.

- It is still the case in SQL/92 (as it was in SQL/89, though it was never clear why) that in a SELECT clause of the form "SELECT *" (where the "*" is unqualified), the commalist of items following the key word "SELECT" must consist of just that "*" and nothing else. Why? *Note*: Not only does this rule seem to have no good justification, it is actively annoying. For example, it means that the following perfectly reasonable and useful query is *** *ILLEGAL* ***:

```
SELECT *, QTY/10 AS TENTH        -- This is *** ILLEGAL *** !!!
FROM    S, SP
WHERE   S.SNO = SP.SNO
```

- The standard gives rules defining the data type of each column of the result of evaluating a given table expression, but those rules overlook the fact that such a column might correspond to the NULL or DEFAULT specification in an expression of the form

```
VALUES ( ..., NULL, ... )
```

or

```
VALUES ( ..., DEFAULT, ... )
```

What are the result column data types in these cases? *Note*: This is not a burning issue, since DEFAULT and NULL can be specified only in the context of an INSERT operation, implying that, no matter what the result column data type is, it will be converted to that of the corresponding column of the INSERT target anyway.

- (With acknowledgments to Phil Shaw.) The following discussion is concerned not with an "unresolved issue," but rather with a matter that seemed a little too complex to discuss at the point where it logically belonged in Chapter 11. It has to do with the scope of range variable names in the context of a join expression. Consider the example

```
T1 JOIN T2 ON ( cond-1 )
   JOIN
       T3 JOIN T4 ON ( cond-2 )
ON ( cond-3 )
```

Here "cond-1" is the join condition for the join of *T1* and *T2*, "cond-2" is the join condition for the join of *T3* and *T4*, and "cond-3" is the join condition for the join of the results of the other two joins. Then:

- "cond-1" can reference *T1* and *T2* but not *T3* or *T4*

- "cond-2" can reference *T3* and *T4* but not *T1* or *T2*

- "cond-3" can reference all four of *T1*, *T2*, *T3,* and *T4*

And if the overall expression appears as the operand of a FROM clause, then the associated SELECT clause, WHERE clause, etc., can also reference all four of *T1*, *T2*, *T3*, and *T4*.

Now let us modify the example slightly to introduce explicit range variables *TA* and *TB* for the two intermediate joins:

```
T1 JOIN T2 ON ( cond-1 ) AS TA
   JOIN
       T3 JOIN T4 ON ( cond-2 ) AS TB
ON ( cond-3 )
```

The rules are now as follows:

- "cond-1" can reference *T1* and *T2* but not *T3*, *T4*, *TA*, or *TB*

- "cond-2" can reference *T3* and *T4* but not *T1*, *T2*, *TA*, or *TB*

- "cond-3" can reference *TA* and *TB* but not *T1*, *T2*, *T3,* or *T4*

And (again) if the overall expression appears as the operand of a FROM clause, then the associated SELECT clause, WHERE clause, etc., can also reference *TA* and *TB* but not *T1*, *T2*, *T3*, or *T4*.

Now let us modify the example again to introduce an explicit range variable *TC* for the overall result:

```
T1 JOIN T2 ON ( cond-1 ) AS TA
   JOIN
       T3 JOIN T4 ON ( cond-2 ) AS TB
ON ( cond-3 ) AS TC
```

The rules are now as follows:

- "cond-1" can reference *T1* and *T2* but not *T3*, *T4*, *TA*, *TB*, or *TC*

- "cond-2" can reference *T3* and *T4* but not *T1*, *T2*, *TA*, *TB*, or *TC*

- "cond-3" can reference *TA* and *TB* but not *T1*, *T2*, *T3,* *T4*, or *TC*

And (once again) if the overall expression appears as the operand of a FROM clause, then the associated SELECT clause, WHERE clause, etc., can reference *TC* but not *T1*, *T2*, *T3*, *T4*, *TA*, or *TB*.

- In Chapter 19, we gave the standard's rules for deciding whether a given table expression is indeterminate (the standard term is "possibly nondeterministic"). For reference, we repeat those rules here. A given table expression, T say, is considered to be *indeterminate* ("possibly nondeterministic") if and only if any of the following is true:

  - T is a union (without ALL), intersection, or difference, and the operand tables include a column of type character string.

  - T is a select-expression, the select-list includes a select-item (C say) of type character string, and:

    (a) The select-list is preceded by the key word DISTINCT, *or*

    (b) C involves a MAX or MIN function reference, *or*

    (c) T directly includes a GROUP BY clause and C is one of the grouping columns.

  - T is a select-expression that directly includes a HAVING clause and the conditional expression in that HAVING clause includes *either* a reference to a grouping column of type character string *or* a MAX or MIN function reference in which the argument is of type character string.

  However, these rules seem to be neither accurate nor complete. For example:

  - A union *with* ALL is surely still indeterminate if one of its operands is a "possibly nondeterministic" select-expression.

  - An explicit NATURAL JOIN or JOIN USING has exactly the same potential for indeterminacy as (e.g.) an intersection.

  - A difference with ALL cannot possibly be indeterminate if its first operand is not.

  Furthermore, the rules are certainly stronger than they need to be in some cases; for example, suppose NO PAD applies, and the collation in effect is one in which there are no characters that are "equal but distinguishable."

Integrity

- There are various subtle differences between stating a constraint "in line" in (e.g.) a base table definition and stating that very same constraint "out of line" in CREATE ASSERTION. For example, an attempt to drop column C (specifying RESTRICT) will succeed if (a) C

is referenced in exactly one integrity constraint and (b) that integrity constraint is specified as part of the relevant CREATE TABLE and (c) that integrity constraint does not reference any other columns, and yet (d) will fail if that very same integrity constraint is specified in CREATE ASSERTION instead. The full extent of such differences is not clear.

- It is strange that a column check constraint can reference only the column in whose definition the constraint appears, whereas a domain constraint is allowed (almost) unrestricted access to any part of the database. (Certainly there are those who would argue that it should be the other way around.) This difference between the two kinds of constraint explains the remark we made in Chapter 14, to the effect that it is not possible, in general, to derive a column check constraint from a domain constraint by simply replacing each occurrence of VALUE by the relevant column name.

Security

- The standard states that the mapping of authIDs to operating system users is implementation-dependent. Should not that be implementation-*defined*?

- The standard's definition of the GRANT and REVOKE statements is very complicated and appears to suffer from numerous problems. Moreover, those problems are too complex, and too much interwoven with one another, to admit of succinct explanation here. The interested reader is referred to the standard itself for the specifics.

- The standard's discussion of security makes use of a concept called "applicable privileges." Here is the text from the standard that explains this term:

  "The phrase *applicable privileges* refers to the privileges defined by the privilege descriptors that define privileges granted to the current < authorization identifier >.

  "The set of applicable privileges for the current < authorization identifier > consists of the privileges defined by the privilege descriptors associated with that < authorization identifier > and the privileges defined by the privilege descriptors associated with PUBLIC."

  Points arising: First, note that we have two consecutive paragraphs giving (slightly) conflicting definitions of the same thing. Second, the phrase "privileges defined by the privilege descriptors that define privileges" could surely be abbreviated to just "privileges" without significant loss. Third, what does "associated with" mean? Fourth, why is the term "authorization identifier" repeatedly enclosed in angle brackets?

Missing Information and Nulls

In principle, the number of anomalies that can arise in connection with SQL-style nulls is quite literally infinite. Most readers will already be familiar with many such anomalies, however. In what follows, therefore, we merely present a short, select list of nulls-related peculiarities—in particular, peculiarities introduced with SQL/92—that might perhaps be less familiar than others.

- The BETWEEN condition "x BETWEEN $+1$ AND -1" ought always to evaluate to *false**—yet, if x happens to be null, it evaluates not to *false* but to *unknown*.

  The reason we mention this particular anomaly is that the standard goes out of its way to avoid certain similar anomalies in connection with OVERLAPS, and OVERLAPS is analogous to BETWEEN in certain respects (though more complex). For example, an OVERLAPS condition of the form

  ```
  ( TIME '08:00:00', TIME '09:00:00' )
     OVERLAPS
  ( TIME '08:30:00',          NULL      )
  ```

  (not intended to be valid SQL syntax) is defined to evaluate to *true*, not *unknown*. (This is one reason why the definition of OVERLAPS is so complex. See the subsection entitled "Dates and Times" below.)

- There is definitely an inconsistency of approach here. If the foregoing treatment of OVERLAPS is regarded as reasonable, then surely the (much simpler) expression "A LIKE '%'" should by analogy be defined to return *true* for any A, even if A is null. And "$A - A$" should return zero even if A is null. And "$A = A$" should return *true* even if A is null. And "$A / 0$" should be a "zero divide" error even if A is null. And so on.

- If column C is defined to be of data type CHAR(5), say, then the expression CHAR_LENGTH (C) should surely always return 5, even if C happens to be null. And then, if $C1$ and $C2$ are both of data type character string, and if CHAR_LENGTH($C1$) $<>$ CHAR_LENGTH($C2$), and if NO PAD applies, then "$A = B$" should

---

*Note that BETWEEN is asymmetric; thus, the expressions "x BETWEEN $+1$ AND -1" and "x BETWEEN -1 AND $+1$" are not equivalent (another trap for the unwary).

always return *false*, and "*A* $<>$ *B*" should always return *true*, even if *A* or *B* is null. And so on.

Dates and Times

- One of the standard's rules for "interval qualifiers" requires "start" to be more significant than "end," while another permits "start" and "end" to be identical. *Note*: "Interval qualifier" is the official standard term for an expression of the form "start [TO end]" (see Chapter 17).

- We remark on an ugly asymmetry in the definition of OVERLAPS. Let the two time periods be *Left* and *Right*, with start points *Ls* and *Rs* and end points *Le* and *Re*, respectively. Then a symmetric definition would say that the OVERLAPS condition is equivalent to

```
Re > Ls AND Rs < Le
```

The standard, however, says it is equivalent to

```
( Ls > Rs AND ( Ls < Re OR Le < Re ) ) OR
( Rs > Ls AND ( Rs < Le OR Re < Le ) ) OR
( Ls = Rs AND Le IS NOT NULL AND Re IS NOT NULL )
```

One implication is that if *Right* is a time period of zero length that happens to coincide with either *Le* or *Ls*, the symmetric definition yields *false* (no overlap); the standard's definition yields *false* (no overlap) if *Right* coincides with the end point of *Left*, but *true* (overlap) if it coincides with the start point.

Temporary Tables

- Why must a GRANT against a "created" temporary table specify ALL PRIVILEGES?

- Temporary tables can have associated base table constraints but cannot be referenced in "general" constraints (specified via CREATE ASSERTION). This is a rather strange restriction, given that *any* base table constraint can in principle be rewritten as a general constraint and vice versa. It is true that "temporary" base table constraints are not allowed to reference permanent base tables (whether this rule is reasonable is another matter); however, a precisely analogous rule could be specified for general constraints, if desired.

- We remind the reader that CREATE TABLE does *not* create a table at all, if the table in question is TEMPORARY; it "primes the pump" for the actual creation, which is done at some later (and conceptually quite distinct) time. See Chapter 18 for further discussion.

Character Data

- The standard states that a character string value, *B* say, can be assigned to a character string target (e.g., a character string column), *A* say, "if and only if [*A* and *B* have] the same [character] repertoire." Should not "character repertoire" here be "character *set*" (as stated in Chapter 19)? For otherwise there is an implication that if *A* and *B* have different forms-of-use, the assignment will cause an implicit form-of-use conversion to be performed, which is a little hard to believe (especially as the system might not even have knowledge of how to perform such a conversion).

- To follow on from the previous point: Actually, it is not even clear what the phrase "the same character set" means. Are character sets *C1* and *C2* "the same" if they have the same character repertoire and the same form-of-use, but different names? Are they "the same" if they have repertoires *R1* and *R2* respectively, but *R1* and *R2* each involve exactly the same collection of characters? Etc.

- Another related point: The standard states (indirectly) that if two character strings are concatenated, they must be drawn from the same character repertoire. Surely (again) it should be "from the same character *set*"?—for otherwise, what form-of-use applies to the result?

- And another: The standard says that two character strings can be compared if and only if they are "mutually assignable" and can be coerced to have the same collation. But if they [can be coerced to] have the same collation, they must have the same *character set* (not just the same character repertoire), because every collation has just one associated character set. And if they have the same character set, they are certainly "mutually assignable." So it is redundant, and arguably much too weak, to say that they must be "mutually assignable."

- For CONVERT, the two character repertoires are required to be identical. Is this ever the case? Note in particular that it is not the case for EBCDIC and ASCII (despite the fact that converting from EBCDIC to ASCII or vice versa is the very example quoted in the standard itself).

- Why is CONVERT provided anyway? Its functionality appears to be totally subsumed by that of TRANSLATE (i.e., there does not seem to be anything that can be done with CONVERT that cannot equally well be done with TRANSLATE).

- The default collation for a given character set is specified either by the COLLATE option or by the COLLATION FROM option in the CREATE CHARACTER SET statement. It is not clear why two distinct options (COLLATE and COLLATION FROM) are provided. Perhaps the intent was that the COLLATE option *must* specify a user-defined collation (i.e., a collation explicitly created via CREATE COLLATION), and the COLLATION FROM clause *must* specify one defined "externally" (i.e., a collation defined outside the framework of SQL per se). Indeed, having two distinct options would seem to make sense only if the possible COLLATE specifications and the possible COLLATION FROM specifications formed two disjoint sets. Yet such does not seem to be the case.

- A parameter definition, a host variable definition, and the target data type specification in a CAST expression can all include the specification "CHARACTER SET character-set"; if that specification is omitted, an implementation-defined character set is assumed by default. It would be more consistent, and more user-friendly, to assume the default character set for the module instead (or possibly the default character set for the schema, in the case of CAST, if the CAST expression appears within a CREATE SCHEMA statement).

Dynamic SQL

- In Chapter 20, we stated that a preparable statement cannot include any parameters or host variables. This statement is surely correct; however, the only hint of a mention of the matter in the standard is in the definition of two constructs called "<value specification>" and "<target specification>," where we find the following (part of a syntax rule):

  "Each <parameter name> shall be contained in a <module>. Each <embedded variable name> shall be contained in an <embedded SQL statement>."

  If these two sentences are indeed intended to imply that parameters and host variables cannot appear in preparable statements, then there surely must be a clearer way of stating this important fact. Furthermore, it would surely have been better to state it as part of the definition of the construct called "<preparable statement>."

- We also stated in Chapter 20 that the character set for a character string placeholder (denoted by a question mark) in dynamic SQL was the default character set for the SQL-session. Actually the standard does not seem to address this question at all.

- Following on from the previous point: Why cannot a character string placeholder have an "introducer" to override the default character set, whatever it may be?

The Information Schema

- Despite its name, the Definition Schema is not a true SQL-schema and is not contained in a catalog (in fact it spans multiple catalogs, in general). It is still the case, however, that no SQL-schema can have an unqualified name of DEFINITION_SCHEMA.

- The Information Schema provides no direct way for a given user V to see definitions for objects that belong to some distinct user U, nor—more generally—for some user with higher authorization (e.g., the "database administrator") to see definitions of "all" objects, regardless of owner.

- (A particular, and peculiar, illustration of the previous point.) Let user U be the owner of a base table B, and suppose U has created an integrity constraint C on B. Suppose also that U has granted UPDATE on B to some other user V. Then V is constrained by C, and yet V is not allowed to see the definition of C in the Information Schema.

Language Levels and Conformance

- (This point was noted by Ed Dee.) In Entry SQL, the USER function returns a character string whose associated character set is implementation-defined. In Intermediate and Full SQL, it returns a character string whose associated character set is SQL_TEXT.

An Overview of SQL3

E.1 INTRODUCTION

As explained in the Preface, the dialect of SQL discussed in this book has been known for several years, informally, as *SQL2*, but is likely to be known henceforth—albeit still informally—as *SQL/92*. The scope and functional content of SQL/92 were "frozen" (not entirely successfully) in 1989. Prior to that time, the ISO SQL committee, and the national standardization bodies participating in that ISO committee, had been considering a number of additional features that were also felt—to a greater or lesser extent—to be desirable extensions to the existing standard. However, the features in question were also felt to be longer-term, in the sense that it would be a long time before they would be firm enough for standardization, and a long time before they would find their way into actual implementations. In order to avoid further delay in the appearance of SQL/92, therefore, those features were excised and transferred to the working draft of the definition of a new language known informally as *SQL3*. In this appendix, we present a brief overview of those additional features.*

---

*Of course, SQL3 is intended to be an upward compatible extension of SQL2 (= SQL/92), just as SQL/92 is intended to be an upward compatible extension of SQL/89.

While the main task of the various SQL committees between 1989 and 1992 was to complete the definition of SQL/92 and iron out its wrinkles, the SQL2-SQL3 segregation did permit those people looking to the more distant future to proceed in a comparatively uninhibited fashion. As a result, the mid 1992 draft of the SQL3 document (on which this appendix is based) includes much that is only tentative, and some of its specifications are known to be incomplete. In presenting a brief summary of the salient new features of that draft, therefore, we do not risk any predictions about the relative probabilities of appearance of this or that feature in any future version of the standard.

At over 900 pages, the SQL3 document is already more than a third bigger again than the SQL/92 specification. The new features addressed in the extra 300+ pages can be categorized as follows:

1. Data definition and manipulation
   - New builtin data types
   - User-defined "NULL classes"
   - User-defined data types
   - Subtables and supertables
   - CREATE TABLE LIKE
   - Temporary views
   - SENSITIVE cursors

2. Functions and operators
   - User-defined functions
   - New JOIN types
   - Recursive UNION queries
   - New quantifiers
   - SIMILAR condition
   - DISTINCT condition

3. Updating and integrity
   - New features of foreign keys
   - Triggered actions
   - Enhanced updatability of table expressions (and therefore of views), including "updatable joins"

4. Security and authorization
   - User-defined "roles"
   - Column-specific SELECT privileges

5. Sessions and transactions
   - Asynchronous statement execution
   - Transaction savepoints

E.2 DATA DEFINITION AND MANIPULATION

New Builtin Data Types

Two new builtin data types are supported, BOOLEAN and ENUMERATED. First, BOOLEAN. With the advent (at long last, many will say) of this data type, truth-valued or conditional expressions (see Chapter 12) will finally be generating values of a data type that is known to the SQL language. Thus, columns in base tables can be defined to be of this data type, and columns in derived tables (final or intermediate results) can get their values from arbitrary truth-valued expressions.

A word of warning is appropriate here, however: Although (as explained in Chapter 16) SQL is based on three-valued logic, BOOLEAN comprises only two values, *true* and *false*; the third truth value, *unknown*, is represented (quite incorrectly!) by NULL.* To understand the seriousness of this flaw, the reader might care to meditate on the analogy of a "numeric" data type that used null instead of zero to represent zero.

The ENUMERATED data type supports the specification of a set of explicit undefined terms, represented by an ordered commalist of identifiers, as in, e.g.:

```
( "Sun", "Mon", "Tue", "Wed", "Thur", "Fri", "Sat" )
```

The ordinal positions of the identifiers are exploited in CAST, which recognizes the one-to-one correspondence between the n identifiers as specified and the first n positive integers. There is also what appears to be shorthand for casting from integer to enumerated term, using domain names. For example, if WEEKDAY is an ENUMERATED domain defined as above, the expression WEEKDAY(2) would return "Mon". However, there are as yet no "successor" or "predecessor" functions; thus, given a TODAY function, the function TOMORROW would have to be implemented as:

```
WEEKDAY ( 1 + CAST ( TODAY AS INTEGER ) )
```

(which wouldn't work on Saturdays, of course).

---

*See the paper entitled "NOT Is Not "Not"! (Notes on Three-Valued Logic and Related Matters)," in C. J. Date, *Relational Database Writings 1985-1989* (Addison-Wesley, 1990).

User-Defined Null Classes

The existing SQL nulls concept is extended to support multiple different *kinds* of null—the intent being, presumably, to handle "value unknown" nulls, "value does not apply" nulls, and so on. First, a new statement, CREATE NULL CLASS, is provided—syntax:

```
CREATE NULL CLASS class AS ( identifier-commalist )
```

Each identifier is considered to be the name of a "null state" in the specified null class. Definitions of columns and domains that are to permit nulls can now do so by naming a null class, in which case any of the null states defined for that class are permitted. For example:

```
CREATE NULL CLASS FISHY AS ( A_MARK, I_MARK )

CREATE DOMAIN INTEGER_OR_NULL AS INTEGER NULL IS FISHY
```

Now, if (e.g.) the QTY column in the shipments table SP is defined on the domain INTEGER_OR_NULL, the following possibilities arise:

- The DEFAULT clause for that column can specify a particular null state from the FISHY null class—for example, "DEFAULT NULL (A_MARK)"

- Particular null states can be explicitly tested for, as in "SP.QTY IS NULL (I_MARK)" or "SP.QTY IS NOT NULL (A_MARK)"

We remark that the amount of confusion that can arise from attempting to "take advantage" of SQL nulls is now to be multiplied by the cardinality of the union of all the null classes you define (plus one, as you can't avoid the confusion that already exists before you define any null classes at all).

User-Defined Data Types

It would be more fashionable to have the word "object" somewhere in the heading of this subsection, but the extent to which SQL3 will actually embrace the object paradigm is still a subject of hot debate. Any or all of the following may eventually have a place in SQL3:

- The ability to define "object" types, such that instances are identified by an *object identifier* (OID) and are "mutable" (i.e., the object value changes over time)

- The ability to define "value" types, where instances are defined by value and are *not* mutable (the builtin scalar data types are immutable in this sense)

- The ability to define "abstract" types with arbitrarily complex internal structure, using traditional aggregating operators and structures such as LIST, ARRAY, SET, MULTISET, and TUPLE*
- The ability to define functions and operators (including comparison and cast operators) and package them with type definitions in the object-oriented style, with specifiable "encapsulation levels" such as PUBLIC, PRIVATE, and PROTECTED

And much more.

Subtables and Supertables

Given a base table named SUPER, for instance, it is possible to create another base table, called SUB perhaps, that is defined to be a "subtable" of SUPER (and, yes, SUPER is said to be a "supertable" of SUB). SUB inherits all the columns of SUPER, plus its primary key (SUPER must *have* a primary key); however, the inherited columns can be renamed in SUB, and any number of additional columns and constraints can be defined for SUB. Every row in SUB has exactly one corresponding row in SUPER (identified by the inherited primary key value), from which it inherits values for all its inherited columns.

A supertable can have any number of subtables. In addition, of course, a subtable can be another subtable's supertable, and so on, to any depth.

Needless to say, there is a great deal more that could be said on this topic, but this is not the place to go into too much detail.

CREATE TABLE LIKE

In common with some current SQL implementations, SQL3 supports a LIKE operator on CREATE TABLE, permitting some or all of the column definitions of a new base table to be inherited from some existing named table (note the "named"—it is not possible to specify an arbitrary table expression).

Temporary Views

The basic idea of temporary tables—i.e., the ability to create a new base table that will be implicitly destroyed at the end of the SQL-session, as described in Chapter 18—is extended to views.

---

*Only the last of these has yet made any progress into the working draft. The obvious TABLE has not yet achieved any prominence, unfortunately, owing to a tendency to look only at traditional programming languages for ideas.

Sensitive Cursors

In SQL/92 a cursor can be declared to be INSENSITIVE, in which case (as explained in Chapter 10) OPEN will effectively cause the cursor to access a private copy of the data, implying that updates made through other cursors, or made without cursors at all, will not be visible through this opening of this cursor. In SQL3 a cursor can alternatively be declared to be SENSITIVE, in which case the user is asking that the cursor access "the real data," and hence that updates made through other cursors, or made without cursors at all, should be visible (if appropriate) through the cursor. *Note*: The default is neither SENSITIVE nor INSENSITIVE but "don't care."

Implementations are not required to support the semantics of SENSITIVE, but they are required at least to permit SENSITIVE as an option on a cursor declaration, and to generate a special exception on OPEN if the declared sensitivity cannot be provided.

E.3 FUNCTIONS AND OPERATORS

User-Defined Functions

The new facilities in this area, which are extensive, include the following:

- An SQL procedure may contain more than one SQL statement.

- Several new statements, supporting conditional and iterative execution of statements in SQL procedures in traditional programming style, are provided (principally CALL, RETURN, IF, CASE, LOOP WHILE, LEAVE, local variable declaration, and assignment).

- *Compound* SQL statements are supported (essentially consisting of a sequence of SQL statements bracketed by BEGIN and END).

- *SQL functions* can be defined for use in SQL expressions. An SQL function consists of zero or more parameter declarations, a single SQL statement (which may be compound, of course), and a specification of the data type of the returned value (which must be a scalar; there is apparently still no such thing in SQL3 as a function that returns a table).*

- *External* functions can be named for use in SQL expressions. From the user's point of view, an external function is very much like an SQL

---

*A *view* might be regarded as a function that returns a table, but views do not have parameters.

function; the point is, however, that it is written in some language other than SQL.

The effect of all of the above is, of course, to make SQL3 computationally complete—i.e., to convert it into a general-purpose programming language. This development is all to the good, in this writer's opinion, but it does serve to lend weight to the argument that the original approach of separating out the database access function into some kind of distinct "data sublanguage" (as SQL was at first intended to be) was a mistake. Surely it would have been preferable to incorporate the necessary database capabilities directly into the existing general-purpose languages (COBOL, PL/I, etc.).

New JOIN Types

The SQL/92 JOIN operator is extended in SQL3 with some new qualifiers, enabling joins to be specified by reference to table constraints. The new forms are "JOIN USING FOREIGN KEY," "JOIN USING PRIMARY KEY," and "JOIN USING CONSTRAINT constraint." They are all (inner) natural joins; however, the joining columns are specified indirectly by reference to certain integrity constraints, instead of as explained in Chapter 11 (note too that in every case both operands must be, specifically, base tables, not derived tables).

- If FOREIGN KEY is specified, then there must be exactly one foreign key in the left-hand operand table that references the right-hand operand table. The join is performed over that foreign key and the matching candidate key.

- If PRIMARY KEY is specified, then both operands must have a primary key; furthermore, the two primary keys must contain the same number of columns, and the data types of corresponding columns must be compatible. The join is performed over the primary keys (and, incidentally, the result of the join has the same primary key).

- JOIN USING CONSTRAINT is effectively the same as JOIN USING FOREIGN KEY (the specified constraint must be a referential one); it is for use when JOIN USING FOREIGN KEY would be ambiguous.

The results of these special joins are all updatable (with some interesting updating semantics, in keeping with the semantics of referential constraints and primary keys). However, it is obvious that the definitions of these operators are somewhat problematical, and it will be interesting to see in what form, if any, they finally emerge.

Recursive UNION Queries

There is a new dyadic table operator, RECURSIVE UNION, whose function is defined in the working draft as "to invoke a limited amount of recursion" (linear or nonlinear). This operator is intended to support, inter alia, the proverbial "bill of materials" application that has for so long been a *bête noire* of relational systems.

New Quantifiers

The new quantifiers FOR SOME and FOR ALL are supported, with syntax as follows:

```
FOR { SOME | ALL } table-expression-commalist
                        ( conditional-expression )
```

They are both three-valued, unlike the EXISTS of existing SQL.* The commalist of table expressions defines the same table as it would if it were specified in a FROM clause, viz. the Cartesian product of the tables that result from evaluating the individual table expressions. Let that table be *T*, and let the specified conditional expression be *C*. Then:

- FOR SOME returns *true* if *C* evaluates to *true* for at least one row of *T*, *false* if *C* evaluates to *false* for every row of *T*, and *unknown* otherwise

- FOR ALL returns *true* if *C* evaluates to *true* for every row of *T*, *false* if *C* evaluates to *false* for at least one row of *T*, and *unknown* otherwise

    Here is an example: The expression

```
FOR SOME ( SELECT * FROM S SX ) ( SX.CITY = 'London' )
```

will return *true* if at least one supplier is located in London.
    In addition, there is THERE IS:

```
( THERE IS table-expression-commalist
        WHERE conditional-expression )
```

The table expression commalist is as for FOR SOME and FOR ALL. As before, let *T* be the corresponding table, and let *C* be the specified conditional expression. Then the overall expression returns *true* if *C* evaluates to *true* for at least one row of *T*, *false* if *C* evaluates to *false* for every row of *T*, and *unknown* otherwise. *Note*: The distinction between THERE IS and FOR SOME—if any—is not clear to this writer.

---

*Indeed, FOR SOME was probably introduced precisely because EXISTS "does not work right" (as explained in Chapter 16). FOR ALL is useful, representing as it does direct support for the *universal* quantifier of (three-valued) logic.

SIMILAR Condition

SIMILAR, like LIKE, is intended for pattern matching—i.e., for testing a given character string to see whether it conforms to some prescribed pattern. The difference is that SIMILAR supports a more extensive range of possibilities ("wild cards," etc.) than LIKE does. The syntax is:

```
character-string-expression [ NOT ] SIMILAR TO pattern
                                      [ ESCAPE escape ]
```

The "pattern" and "escape" specifications are essentially as for LIKE, except that "pattern" can involve additional special characters—not just "%" (percent) and "_" (underscore) as in LIKE, but "*" (asterisk), "+" (plus), "−" (minus), and many others. The general intent seems to be to support the parsing of syntax strings in some formal language. *Note*: It is perhaps worth mentioning that the rules for SIMILAR were copied from the analogous function in POSIX.

DISTINCT Condition

SQL3 also provides a new DISTINCT condition (not to be confused with the existing UNIQUE condition, of course) for testing whether two rows are "distinct." Let the two rows in question be *Left* and *Right*; *Left* and *Right* must contain the same number, n say, of scalar components each. Let i range from 1 to n, and let the ith components of *Left* and *Right* be Li and Ri, respectively. The data type of Li must be compatible with the data type of Ri. Then the expression

```
Left IS DISTINCT FROM Right
```

returns *false* if and only if, for all i, either (a) "$Li = Ri$" is *true*, or (b) Li and Ri are the same null state; otherwise it returns *true*. (In other words, *Left* and *Right* are "distinct" if and only if they are not "duplicates" of one another. See Chapter 16.) Note that a DISTINCT condition never evaluates to *unknown*.

E.4   UPDATING AND INTEGRITY

New Features of Foreign Keys

In addition to the referential actions specified for SQL/92 (CASCADE, SET NULL, SET DEFAULT, and NO ACTION), SQL3 supports a new one called RESTRICT. RESTRICT is very similar—but not quite identical—to NO ACTION. The subtle difference between them is as follows. *Note*: To fix our ideas, we concentrate here on the delete rule; consideration of the update rule is essentially similar, mutatis mutandis.

- Let *T1* and *T2* be the referenced table and the referencing table, respectively; let *t1* be a row of *T1*, and let *t2* be a row of *T2* that corresponds to row *t1* under the referential constraint in question. What happens if an attempt is made to delete row *t1*?

- Under NO ACTION (as explained in Chapter 14), the system—conceptually, at least—actually performs the requested DELETE, then discovers that row *t2* now violates the constraint, and so undoes the DELETE again.

- Under RESTRICT, by contrast, the system realizes "ahead of time" that row *t2* exists and will violate the constraint if *t1* is deleted, and so rejects the DELETE out of hand.

And (as suggested in Chapter 14) there are indeed situations in which the slight difference between these two behaviors can have a significant effect on the overall result. The following example will serve to illustrate the point. Consider the referential structure shown below:

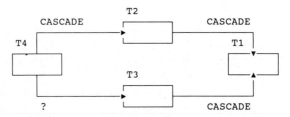

In this example, table *T4* references both tables *T2* and *T3*, each of which in turn references table *T1*. There are thus two paths from *T4* to *T1*; let us refer to the path via *T2* as the upper path and the path via *T3* as the lower path. Suppose for simplicity that each table contains just one column, which is the primary key for each table and also the necessary foreign key for tables *T2*, *T3*, and *T4*; suppose also that each table contains just one row, containing the single value *v* (say) in every case; suppose the delete rules are as indicated in the figure ("?" = either NO ACTION or RESTRICT); and suppose finally that we try to delete the single row from table *T1*. What happens?

Case 1: The "?" rule is RESTRICT.

- If the system applies the delete rules in the upper path first, the single row in *T2* and the single row in *T4* will both be deleted, because the rules are both CASCADE. When the system then applies the delete rules in the lower path, an attempt will be made to delete the single row from *T3*; this attempt will succeed, even though the "?" rule is RESTRICT, because there is now no matching row in *T4*, and hence no row to "restrict" the delete. The net effect is that all four rows will be deleted.

- If, on the other hand, the system applies the delete rules in the lower path first, the net effect is that the database will remain unchanged. For the row in *T4* will cause the attempt to delete the row from *T3* to fail (because of the RESTRICT rule), and hence the overall operation will fail.

Thus we see that (under RESTRICT) different execution sequences can produce different overall results.

Case 2: The "?" rule is NO ACTION.

- If the system applies the delete rules in the upper path first, the single row in *T2* and the single row in *T4* will both be deleted, because the rules are both CASCADE. When the system then applies the delete rules in the lower path, it will delete the single row from *T3*; this attempt will succeed without further checking, because of the NO ACTION rule. The system will then observe that no referential constraints are violated, and the final result (that all four rows are deleted) will be allowed to stand.

- If, on the other hand, the system applies the delete rules in the lower path first, it will delete the single row from *T3* without further checking; it will then apply the delete rules in the upper path, and delete the rows from *T2* and *T4*. It will then (as before) observe that no referential constraints are now violated, and the final result (that all four rows are deleted) will again be allowed to stand.

Thus we see that (under NO ACTION) different execution sequences have produced the *same* overall result.

In addition to the RESTRICT referential action discussed above, SQL3 also provides a kind of upward CASCADE, called (for some reason) PENDANT. PENDANT is intended to support the occasionally expressed requirement for a rule that deletes a target row when the last row referencing it is deleted (sometimes characterized as "Will the last one to leave please turn out the lights?"). It could be used, e.g., to trigger the automatic deletion of a department when the last employee is removed from that department (of course, such a rule would not prevent the insertion of a new department with no employees). *Note*: PENDANT is not considered as a referential action—indeed, the PENDANT option is quite distinct from the "referential action" option.

Triggered Actions

PENDANT (just discussed) is one of several new integrity features in SQL3 where actions can be specified for execution when "triggered" by some specified event. Others are as follows:

- The ability to specify on CREATE ASSERTION that a given constraint is to be checked only AFTER or BEFORE certain specified events occur. In this context, an "event" is an INSERT, UPDATE (optionally of specified columns), or DELETE against a specified named table.

- The new CREATE TRIGGER statement, which defines a *trigger*—i.e., a combination of an *event* specification and an *action* specification. The event specification is as for CREATE ASSERTION (see above), including optional AFTER or BEFORE specifications. The action specification defines an action (in effect, a procedure) that is to be performed every time the specified event occurs. More precisely, the action consists of an optional conditional expression (defaulting to *true*), and a list of SQL statements that will be executed if and only if the condition is *true* when the event occurs. The user can specify whether the action is to take place just once per occurrence of the event, or once FOR EACH ROW of the table with which the event is associated.

    Unlike ordinary constraints, triggers are permitted to refer (in the action specification) to "before" and "after" values in the table associated with the specified event, thus providing a kind of support for *transition constraints*.

Enhanced Updatability of Table Expressions

The fact that tables resulting from the new types of JOIN (USING FOREIGN KEY, etc.) are updatable in SQL3 has already been mentioned. In addition, SQL3 has some rules by which candidate keys of derived tables are determined, and these rules lead to major improvements in the system's understanding of updatability in general. As a consequence, many tables are considered to be updatable in SQL3 that are *not* so considered in SQL/92. In particular, all many-to-one joins of two updatable tables are considered to be updatable, no matter what syntactic style is used to express those joins. For example, the expression

```
SELECT *
FROM    S, SP
WHERE   S.SNO = SP.SNO
```

(which might, for example, constitute the body of a view definition) yields an updatable table.

It is also possible that SQL3 will include support for user-defined view updatability, such that a user can specify what actions are to take place in response to an INSERT, UPDATE, or DELETE against a particular named table.

E.5 SECURITY AND AUTHORIZATION

User-Defined Roles

The new CREATE ROLE statement supports the creation of named *roles*. An example might be "DBADM" ("database administration"). Role names must be unique, not only with respect to the set of role names, but also with respect to the set of authorization identifiers in the environment. Once created, a role can be granted privileges, just as if it were an authID. Furthermore, roles can be granted, like privileges, and, like all privileges, they can be granted either to an authID or to another role.

Column-Specific SELECT Privileges

The new "SELECT(x)" privilege allows the holder to access a specific column x of a specific named table, e.g., in a select-list.

E.6 SESSIONS AND TRANSACTIONS

Asynchronous Statement Execution

In SQL3, any SQL statement may be prefixed by an expression of the form

```
ASYNC ( identifier )
```

meaning that the statement can be executed when the system pleases, and control can be returned to the user before execution has completed. The identifier can subsequently be used in the new TEST and WAIT statements: TEST asks whether one or more specified statements have completed, WAIT waits for the completion of one or more specified statements.

Transaction Savepoints

The SQL3 savepoint mechanism allows transactions to be *partially* rolled back (on user request). The SAVEPOINT statement allows the user to establish a named "savepoint" within a transaction. Subsequently, a special form of the ROLLBACK statement—"ROLLBACK TO savepoint"— allows the user to undo all updates performed since the specified savepoint, while at the same time preserving updates performed prior to that point. Note that "ROLLBACK TO savepoint" (unlike the ordinary ROLLBACK statement) does not terminate the transaction.

The foregoing facility might be useful in certain kinds of "what if" processing.

References
and Bibliography

1. International Organization for Standardization (ISO): *Database Language SQL*. Document ISO/IEC 9075:1992. Also available as American National Standards Institute (ANSI) Document ANSI X3.135-1992.

    Defines the current standard, i.e., the subject of this book ("SQL/92").

2. International Organization for Standardization: *Database Language SQL*. Document ISO/IEC 9075:1987. Also available as American National Standards Institute (ANSI) Document ANSI X3.135-1986.

    Defines the original standard (i.e., "SQL/86").

3. International Organization for Standardization: *Database Language SQL*. Document ISO/IEC 9075:1989. Also available as American National Standards Institute (ANSI) Document ANSI X3.135-1989.

    Defines the original standard as extended to include the Integrity Enhancement Feature IEF (i.e., "SQL/89").

4. American National Standards Institute: *Database Language Embedded SQL*. Document ANSI X3.168-1989.

    Defines the ANSI embedded SQL standard.

5. International Organization for Standardization: (*ISO working draft*) *Database Language SQL3*. Document ISO/IEC JTC1/SC21/WG3 DBL OTT-003 (May

1992). Also available as American National Standards Institute (ANSI) Document ANSI X3H2 1992-109 (May 1992).

The current ISO/ANSI working draft of "SQL3." Note that this document is subject to rapid change, with new versions appearing frequently. Appendix E of the present book is based on the version identified above.

6. X/OPEN: *Relational Database Language (SQL) Portability Guide* (January 1987).

Defines the X/OPEN SQL standard.

7. U.S. Department of Commerce, National Institute of Standards and Technology: *Database Language SQL*. FIPS PUB 127-1 (2nd February 1990).

Defines the Federal Information Processing SQL standard. *Note:* A draft version of FIPS PUB 127-2, defining the proposed "SQL/92" version of this standard, is also available.

8. IBM Corp.: *Systems Application Architecture Common Programming Interface: Database Reference*. IBM Document No. SC26-4348.

Defines the IBM SAA SQL standard.

9. E. F. Codd: "A Relational Model of Data for Large Shared Data Banks." *Communications of the ACM*, Vol. 13, No. 6 (June 1970); reprinted in *Communications of the ACM*, Vol. 26, No. 1 (January 1983).

The paper that (apart from some early internal IBM papers, also by Codd) first proposed the ideas of the relational model.

10. C. J. Date: *An Introduction to Database Systems: Volume I* (5th edition, Addison-Wesley, 1990); *Volume II* (1st edition, Addison-Wesley, 1983).

These two volumes between them provide a basis for a comprehensive education in most aspects of database technology. In particular, they include a very detailed treatment of the relational approach.

11. D. D. Chamberlin and R. F. Boyce: "SEQUEL: A Structured English Query Language." Proc. ACM SIGMOD Workshop on Data Description, Access, and Control, Ann Arbor, Mich. (May 1974).

The paper that first introduced the SQL language (or SEQUEL, as it was originally called).

12. M. M. Astrahan and R. A. Lorie: "SEQUEL-XRM: A Relational System." Proc. ACM Pacific Regional Conference, San Francisco, Calif. (April 1975).

Describes the first prototype implementation of SEQUEL.

13. D. D. Chamberlin et al.: "SEQUEL/2: A Unified Approach to Data Definition, Manipulation, and Control." *IBM J. R&D*, Vol. 20, No. 6 (November 1976). See also errata in January 1977 issue.

Describes the revised version of SEQUEL called SEQUEL/2.

14. M. M. Astrahan et al.: "System R: Relational Approach to Database Management." *ACM Transactions on Database Systems*, Vol. 1, No. 2 (June 1976).

System R was intended as a major prototype implementation of the SEQUEL/2 (later SQL) language. This paper describes the architecture of System R as originally planned.

15. D. D. Chamberlin: "A Summary of User Experience with the SQL Data Sublanguage." Proc. International Conference on Databases, Aberdeen, Scotland (July 1980).

Includes details of several enhancements and revisions to SQL (previously SEQUEL/2) that were made during the lifetime of the System R project.

16. D. D. Chamberlin et al.: "A History and Evaluation of System R." *Communications of the ACM*, Vol. 24, No. 10 (October 1981).

Describes the pioneering work on relational implementation technology (specifically, on optimization technology) done as part of the System R project.

17. C. J. Date: *Relational Database: Selected Writings* (Addison-Wesley, 1986); *Relational Database Writings 1985–1989* (Addison-Wesley, 1990); (with Hugh Darwen) *Relational Database Writings 1989–1991* (Addison-Wesley, 1992).

These three books contain a collection of papers on various aspects of relational database management, including several (mostly somewhat critical) that discuss the SQL language. See in particular the papers "A Critique of the SQL Database Language" in the first volume, "What's Wrong with SQL?" and "EXISTS Is Not Exists!" in the second, and "Oh No Not Nulls Again" and "Without Check Option" in the third.

18. C. J. Date: *A Guide to INGRES* (Addison-Wesley, 1987); (with Colin J. White) *A Guide to SQL/DS* (Addison-Wesley, 1988); (with Colin J. White) *A Guide to DB2* (4th edition, Addison-Wesley, 1992). David McGoveran (with C. J. Date): *A Guide to SYBASE and SQL Server* (Addison-Wesley, 1992).

Detailed descriptions of some commercially significant SQL implementations.

Index